Everything you wanted to know about yourself, but were afraid to ask.

Too big a claim? With Gloria Star's new book *Astrology Woman to Woman*, this may not be too strong a claim. Even seasoned astrologers have said it is the best material they have ever seen for the female audience. Gloria is writing for today's women, young and old.

Perhaps one of the most useful sections is the one dealing with power issues. This is an area women have traditionally had some problems with, and Gloria presents an astrological picture that makes power not only seem possible, but even a good thing. She states,

> Personal power is an individual expression, and has different meanings for each person. As a woman in the world today, your opportunity to experience and express your personal power is largely dependent upon the manner in which you develop it. Particularly in the Western world, as times have changed and the power base has gradually evolved beyond the patriarchal control of the past, women are seeking to define their place in the world, collectively and individually. Gaining influence in the world through career and financial development, you begin to understand the different levels of power.

After an introductory section about the astrological chart, Gloria gets right down to cases with the multitude of factors that astrologers consider when they are doing a reading. She addresses just about everything you want to know about yourself and your place in the world, and she provides everything you need to get a good feel for your birth chart.

Gloria considers the planets, signs and houses throughout her book, and provides enough information for you to understand the nuts and bolts of astrology, even if you have never read any astrology books. For astrology students, this volume provides an in-depth examination of chart factors, and will become a valuable reference tool for you as you develop your interpretive skills.

∾

About the Author

An internationally renowned astrologer, author, and teacher, Gloria Star has been a professional astrologer for more than twenty years. She has written the *Sun Sign Book* for Llewellyn since 1990, and has been a contributing author of the *Moon Sign Book* since 1995. She edited and co-authored *Astrology for Women: Roles and Relationships* (Llewellyn, 1997), is the author of *Optimum Child: Developing Your Child's Fullest Potential through Astrology* (Llewellyn, 1987), and she has contributed to two anthologies: *Houses: Power Places in the Horoscope* (Llewellyn, 1990) and *How to Manage the Astrology of Crisis* (Llewellyn, 1993). Her astrological computer software, *Woman to Woman*, was released by Matrix software in 1997.

She has served on the faculty of the United Astrology Congress (UAC) since its inception in 1986, and lectures for groups and conferences throughout the United States and abroad. She is a member of the Advisory Board for the National Council for Geocosmic Research (NCGR), has served on the Steering Committee for the Association for Astrological Networking (AFAN), and is now on the Advisory Board. She writes a regular feature column for *The Mountain Astrologer* magazine, and her daily horoscopes appear online for *Astronet*.

Gloria Star lives in Connecticut with her husband and teenage son. She also has an adult daughter.

To Write to the Author

If you wish to contact the author or would like more information about this book, please write to the author in care of Llewellyn Worldwide and we will forward your request. Both the author and publisher appreciate hearing from you and learning of your enjoyment of this book. Llewellyn Worldwide cannot guarantee that every letter written to the author will be answered, but all will be forwarded. Please write to:

Gloria Star
℅ Llewellyn Worldwide
P.O. Box 64383, Dept. K686-6
St. Paul, MN 55164-0383, U.S.A.

Please include a self-addressed, stamped envelope with your letter.
If outside the U.S.A., enclose international postal coupons.

ASTROLOGY:
Woman to Woman

GLORIA STAR

1999
Llewellyn Publications
St. Paul, Minnesota U.S.A. 55164-0383

FIRST EDITION
First Printing, 1999

Cover design by Lisa Novak
Cover photo by Tim Gannon Photography
Astrological glyphs and illustrations by Richard H. Roess
Editing and layout by Deb Gruebele
Interior design by Connie Hill

Library of Congress Cataloging-in-Publication Data
Star, Gloria
    Astrology : woman to woman / Gloria Star — 1st ed.
p.   cm. --
    Includes bibliographical references and index.
    ISBN 1–56718–686–6 (pbk)
    1. Astrology. 2. Women—Miscellanea. I. Title.
BF1729.W64S73 1999
133.5'082—dc21   98-50802
                                                             CIP

Llewellyn Worldwide does not participate in, endorse, or have any authority or responsibility concerning private business transactions between our authors and the public.
 All mail addressed to the author is forwarded but the publisher cannot, unless specifically instructed by the author, give out an address or phone number.

The text for this book was adapted from the text of the author's astrological computer software program, *Woman to Woman*. The software was created by Matrix Software, and is an astrological report writer. It is available for purchase directly from Matrix. If you are interested in finding out more about the *Woman to Woman* software, call 1-800-PLANETS, or write to Matrix Software, 315 Marion Avenue, Big Rapids, MI 49307.

Llewellyn Publications
A Division of Llewellyn Worldwide, Ltd.
P.O. Box 64383, Dept. K686–6
St. Paul, Minnesota 55164-0383, U.S.A.

Printed in the United States of America

Contents

INTRODUCTION

*M*ost of the material in this book is the by-product of my work in creating the text for an astrological computer report writer for women. During my twenty-plus years as a professional astrologer, the majority of my clients have been women. Coming into my own maturity as a woman while counseling and advising other women about their lives through utilizing astrology, I began to develop an understanding of the astrological symbols as they apply specifically to the lives of my individual clients. Although I counsel both men and women, I'd not seen much in the astrological literature that addressed the differences between men and women. My personal study of history, sociology, and human development has included in-depth explorations of women's studies, particularly the history of ancient cultures and the evolution of myths in culture as they relate to the different roles women and men play in society. As a result of what I saw as a distinct need for clarification of the differences between male-centered and female-centered astrology, I began this work.

In the process of writing the material for the report, I realized that there was a sufficient amount of information that women and men alike might appreciate in book form. The text of the report-writer (which has received wonderful acclaim) has now been transformed into this book. I must admit that I really was not aware of the scope of the project I had undertaken when I first proposed the concept. As with all creative endeavors, as I immersed myself further into the work I discovered all sorts of trails in consciousness that lead to another series of self-transformations! I hope that by reading this material you, too, will share in this transformational experience. Please realize that I am addressing this information to my sisters in spirit. Men, too, will read this material and in the process have a chance to be privy to woman-centered conversations they might never have heard, but ladies, this work is for you, my friends, sisters, mothers, aunts, and grandmothers—the feminine core of the circle of life.

Your astrological chart provides an amazing guidepost to the most important aspect of your life: an understanding of yourself. As a woman today, you face the challenge of discovering yourself within the context of many life experiences. You wear a variety of faces and play many roles, experiences that can both enhance and complicate your feeling of satisfaction with yourself and your life. Your astrological chart provides indicators that help to define who you are, strengthening an understanding of your needs on every level. Each chart is different in its make-up, and the myriad combinations of influences help to underscore the importance of each person as an individual. Because of these differences, each chart reflects the uniqueness of the person. One thing you must remember when working with astrology: it is through your free will that you make choices. Your "chart" does not make you do anything!

We are finally acknowledging and realizing in today's world that men and women are definitely different. The workings of your psyche, symbolized by your astrological chart, are likely to be experienced quite differently through your filter as a woman than they would be if you were born male. This material is written for you, a woman in a world of change, a woman seeking to become whole. It is to the soul of the feminine essence that this work is dedicated—and you are a significant part of that essence.

CHAPTER ONE

AN OVERALL GLIMPSE OF YOUR ASTROLOGICAL CHART

*Y*our natal, or birth, chart is made up of several factors. Drawn upon a circular wheel, your natal chart shows the positions of the planets relative to your place, date, and time of birth. It is important that you have an accurate computation of your astrological chart completed by a competent professional astrologer or chart service. Some public libraries also have computers equipped with programs that will calculate your chart for you. It's much easier in today's world to obtain an accurate astrological chart than at any time in history! You may use the coupon in the back of this book to order your natal chart computation if you like.

Everything is indicated symbolically on your personal natal chart, with each symbol having specific meanings. The planets, Sun, and Moon are placed around the circle, and each is placed within a particular degree of a sign of the zodiac. The planets, Sun, and Moon are energy bodies, and the astrological signs indicate how these energies work. Just as you are a complex of feelings, needs, drives, and desires—your natal chart maps these qualities. *Table 1* lists the planets and their basic meanings, summarizing these expressions.

You will also notice that the planetary symbols fall within particular segments of the circle. These segments, called "houses," indicate the specific environments and relationships that are part of your life. *Illustration 1* on page 3 shows the astrological houses and their basic concept). Additionally, some of the houses are placed at positions that define the angles of your chart. The chart itself is calculated from the viewpoint of your place of birth, and the circle represents the heavens around you. If you draw a line from left to right intersecting the circle, that line will represent the horizon. The point at which that line intersects the circle on the left is called the ascendant. The astrological sign on your ascendant is called your rising sign. The point opposite your ascendant is your descendant. The lines that define the intersection of your chart from top to bottom are also angular lines, and the point at the top of your chart is called the midheaven and that point at the bottom of the chart is called the nadir.

THE PLANETS		
SYMBOL	**PLANET**	**MEANING**
☉	Sun	Ego Self
☽	Moon	Subconscious Self
☿	Mercury	Communication
♀	Venus	Expressiveness
♂	Mars	Drive
♃	Jupiter	Expansion
♄	Saturn	Focus
⚷	Chiron	Purpose
♅	Uranus	Individuality
♆	Neptune	Imagination
♇	Pluto	Regeneration

Table 1

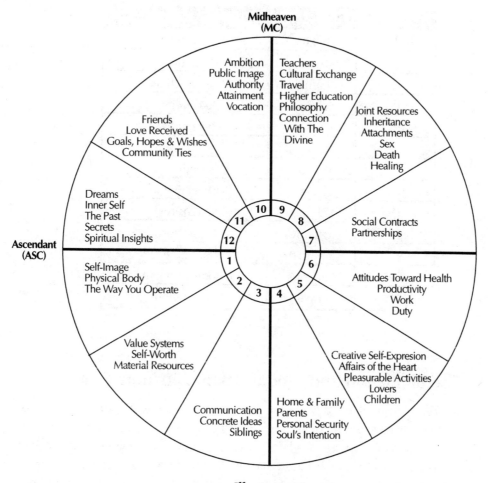

Illustration 1

There are twelve astrological signs. These signs operate like the adjectives and adverbs in a sentence. When I teach, I tell my students to think of the Sun, Moon, and planets as the actors in the personal drama of life, and to consider the signs as the equivalent roles the actors play, the costumes they wear, and the props they need for their full expression. *Table 2* on page 4 lists the astrological signs and their basic meanings.

THE SIGNS AND THEIR MEANINGS		
Symbol	**Sign**	**Key Concept**
♈	Aries	Initiative
♉	Taurus	Conservation
♊	Gemini	Versatility
♋	Cancer	Receptivity
♌	Leo	Magnetism
♍	Virgo	Discrimination
♎	Libra	Objectivity
♏	Scorpio	Intensity
♐	Sagittarius	Expansion
♑	Capricorn	Structure
♒	Aquarius	Unconventionality
♓	Pisces	Imagination

Table 2

The Elemental and Modal Balance in Your Chart

The astrological signs are defined by one of four elements: fire, earth, air, or water. The fire and air elements have a yang (masculine polarity) quality, and tend to be more outgoing and assertive in their nature, whereas the earth and water elements have a yin (feminine polarity) quality, and are more receptive by nature. *Illustration 2 on page 5* shows the element associated with each of the astrological signs. The elemental balance in your chart is determined by the amount of energy within each elemental sign. The factors added together to find this balance of energy include the Sun, Moon, planets, and the angles (your ascendant and midheaven). Although some people might qualify some of these factors as being stronger than others, for now just consider that each factor noted above has the same power. Make a list of all these factors by element. A strong preponderance or lack of any element adds a special weight to your chart. Think of the elemental balance as the background color of a painting. The interpretation of these factors is noted below.

THE FOUR ELEMENTS				
	FIRE	**EARTH**	**AIR**	**WATER**
CARDINAL	Aries ♈	Capricorn ♑	Libra ♎	Cancer ♋
FIXED	Leo ♌	Taurus ♉	Aquarius ♒	Scorpio ♏
MUTABLE	Sagittarius ♐	Virgo ♍	Gemini ♊	Pisces ♓

Table 3

Balanced Elements (Equal Balance of Each of the Elements)

An equal balance of each of the four elements shows that you can be quite comfortable in a wide variety of circumstances and with different types of people. You may also feel equally at ease with both men and women, particularly in situations where working together cooperatively is important. Your ability to maintain harmony within the context of the different demands of your life is strong, and you innately understand the importance of paying attention to all aspects of your life—physical, mental, emotional, and spiritual.

Fire Predominant

A strong predominance of fiery energy adds a special intensity to your personality and a strong level of vitality. You may be more action-oriented than some of your friends, and your adventurous enthusiasm may make you the topic of conversation among your friends. Your intuition and instincts are effective allies. Watch a tendency to push yourself too hard, since it's easy to burn out once you've gone beyond your limits. In relationships with others, you prefer to be around those who love the adventure of life and who appreciate your active inspirational nature.

Earth Predominant

A strong predominance of earth energy indicates that you are a "show me" kind of person. A practical, common sense approach to life feels most comfortable, and you'll most enjoy life when you have your feet on the ground. You're the earth mother type—with a natural inclination toward sensuality, practicality, and conservation. In any situation, you prefer to build strength and stability and you may be oriented toward producing. At the end of the day, you're much happier if you have something to show for your efforts, but be very careful of a tendency to narrow your vision to the dimension of the physical plane. There are multiple levels of reality!

Air Predominant

A strong predominance of air energy shows that you function very easily on the mental plane. Living in the world of ideas, you may also gain strength when you are connected to others—at least mentally. Your social calendar is important, not because it's frivolous, but because you need to make contact. Most comfortable with others who are intelligent or interesting, you may be a natural in public relations. It's easy for you to stay in your head, which can be wonderful if you're involved in a mental project or study. But if you're stuck worrying, you may find it difficult to break the habit.

Water Predominant

If water is your strongest element, you're a "feeling" type of woman. Your sensibilities can range from psychic to moody, but one thing is certain: you are definitely impressionable. Your artistic endeavors and creative expression may elicit a strong response from others, since you have a deep sense of passion. Your insightful nature can be especially keen, and your compassion for others can extend strong support. You may find it difficult to separate your feelings from those of everyone around you, and building some emotional boundaries can strengthen judgment of personal relationships. However, your concern for others can be a positive thing if you have a healthy way of channeling it.

When Two Elements are Strongest

You may note that more than one element is strong in your chart. If so, the additive factor of these elemental bonds is significant. This is particularly important if the two elements make up seventy-five percent or more of your chart balance (for example, four air and four fire, or six earth and five fire, and so on).

Fire and Earth Strongest

With fire and earth both very strong, you may be especially creative, and are focused on achieving high levels of productivity. You definitely make an impact on the people in your life, and can leave a lasting impression. Instead of waiting for life to happen to you, you prefer to create life on your terms, and may need to be more attentive to the responses of people who are in your path on the way to achieving the realization of your dreams. This combination of elements has been described as a steamroller type of personality, so keep that in mind before you take off on your next major project!

Fire and Air Strongest

With the elements of fire and air both very powerful, you may be both highly verbal and intuitive, in addition to being idealistic and focused on the future. Your ability to focus on an idea and to put it into action can be extraordinary, making you the perfect candidate to employ creative visualization in the creation of your life circumstances, but you may lack the ability to focus and ground your energy, and can easily exhaust your energy by getting carried away. Pacing yourself is not your strong suit! You may relate more easily to men than to women, and may resent the parts of yourself that are identified as "feminine," such as emotions. The fact that emotions are not logical can be rather bothersome to you, but if you can get it into your logical head that emotions are not logical, then perhaps you can accept the way you feel some of the time!

Fire and Water Strongest

With the powerful combination of fire and water as predominant elements, you can be rather intense. This steamy combination adds an intense, dramatic quality to your personality. You may also be quite sultry in your overall projection of yourself, and relate most easily on an emotional level. You may love the passion of romance or creative intensity, but may be frustrated when that passion cannot be sustained every moment of the day. People in relationship with you may feel like they're living in a pressure cooker, and your life can certainly reach that level of intensity. You are quite capable of emotional self-expression, and your enthusiasm and warmth, coupled with your protective nature, can be quite inviting.

Earth and Air Strongest

With a powerful combination of predominant earth and air energy, you may be able to support your ideas with a practical foundation. Your earthy nature helps to bring a grounded quality to your energy, which can be quite helpful when you're in the middle of deadlines or faced with developing an important idea. You may be a natural in the business world, where objectivity needs to be grounded, and your ability to work with others is usually quite good, although you may have more patience with those who are practical and intelligent.

Earth and Water Strongest

With a powerful emphasis on both earth and water elements in your chart, you may be very focused on achieving stability in the material world. Your needs for security are quite strong, and you may be especially capable of carrying on traditions. These elements here on the physical plane work together to form mud, and your life can become a quagmire of family, children, money, and responsibilities—leaving you feeling stuck. You may be seen as the woman who will always be there for everybody, but may wonder if you will ever receive the same level of support from them. If you find yourself feeling stuck in behaviors that are greedy or manipulative, take a look at the areas in which you feel threatened or unsupported. Maybe you need to get out of your rut and try something different—but first you have to remind yourself that change is safe.

Air and Water Strongest

The predominance of both air and water in your chart can indicate high levels of sensitivity that operate on many levels, but evidence of that sensitivity may be seen most powerfully through your endless creativity and fertile imagination. Your perceptive abilities are quite keen, since you can be both detached and involved in decision-making processes. You may be an excellent healer and counselor, since you can sense and objectify emotions for those who seek your advice. Although you can be comfortable with highly intellectual types, you also love the company of the creative, artistic, and musical who may share many of your own interests. You need relationships that give you plenty of freedom, but that allow you to express the full range of your emotions and needs.

Weak Elements

Those elemental factors that are weaker (two or less of a particular element) provide clues to areas in your chart that can be especially significant. The weak elements may show two or fewer (or even none!).

Fire Weak

If the elemental balance in your astrological chart shows fire as a weak factor, this may inhibit your ability to take action at times. Challenges, or even the thought of them, can exhaust you, but avoiding challenges may also take some of the spirit out of your life! If you're feeling uninspired or lacking in motivation at times, and want to change, expose yourself to situations that stimulate your sense of hope and optimism. Use fiery colors, candlelight, or even the glow of a fireplace on a winter evening to help re-focus your energy. Take time to exercise, since increasing your physical activity can also stimulate your mind and spirit. You may feel overwhelmed by others who are constantly on the go, even though your attraction to them can be immense.

Earth Weak

If the elemental balance in your astrological chart indicates that earth is a weak factor, then you may sometimes feel a need for greater stability. Practical matters may not always be a primary consideration when making major decisions. The problem with little earth is usually related to not being in touch with the physical plane, which can cause you to lose your focus or to ignore physical reality. During the times in your life when you feel out of touch or uncertain, get back to nature. Take a walk in the park or woods, hug a tree, garden, work with clay, or get a massage to remind yourself that you are part physical, too!

Air Weak

If the elemental balance in your astrological chart indicates that air is a weak factor, you may have little use for the purely abstract. Your preference for things you can touch, taste, or feel extends even to your choices in relationships and career, and long distance relationships can be difficult. Sometimes it can be difficult for you to adjust to new ideas or new people, and you may have trouble with objectivity. Even though you may be comfortable staying inside yourself for periods of time, you do need to connect and let others know what you think and feel. In fact, once a connection is made, you may even feel enlivened by sharing and opening up; but idle chatter can get on your nerves.

Water Weak

If the elemental balance in your astrological chart shows that water is a weak factor, emotional situations can be rather uncomfortable for you, although you may be somewhat fascinated by others who display their feelings readily. The world of your inner self, your emotional self, can seem tremendously difficult for you at times, and if you're overwhelmed by emotion, you may find yourself shutting down to keep your feelings under control in order to avoid pain. Your best therapy is to deal with your feelings, and to acknowledge them. You may also need to be more attentive to the feelings of others, or you could be accused of being cold or uncaring. Self-sufficiency is one thing, but total distance can be quite lonely. Stimulate your emotional nature in a positive sense by getting into the water element and enjoying it. Swim, take long soaking baths, or let yourself walk outside in the rain on a warm day. If you're really feeling brave, rent a tear-jerker movie, make a cup of tea, grab your hankies, and close the door.

The Modes

Another aspect of your basic nature and personality is determined by the balance of the modes in your chart. The modes (or qualities) are also defined by sign, which are grouped together as either Cardinal, Fixed, or Mutable. *Illustration 2* on page 5 also shows the signs according to mode or quality. Make a listing of the energies and angles in your chart by mode. The significance of the modal balance in your chart is explained below.

Balanced Modes

If your chart indicates a balance between the Cardinal, Fixed, and Mutable modes, you may have a strong ability to get things going, maintain your inspiration, carry through with your commitments, and complete projects. Your ability to deal with different styles and human diversity enhances your spirit of cooperation and makes you a good choice for leadership positions.

Cardinal Strongest

If your strongest mode is Cardinal, your basic approach to life is one of getting things started. You're an initiator and are happiest when you're beginning something new. This factor sometimes indicates an enhanced sense of courage and enthusiasm.

Fixed Strongest

If your Fixed energy is strongest, this factor helps to account for your ability to stay with a project, relationship, or idea until you are satisfied, or until your responsibility is fulfilled. The downfall of this strength is not knowing when to let go, and you can be quite stubborn when facing the possibility of change or challenge.

Mutable Strongest

If your strongest mode of energy is Mutable, you possess a powerful sense of adaptability in your personality. Your flexibility is your strength, but your distractible nature is your weakness. Sometimes you may feel like a circus juggler with too many objects in the air at one time, and you may need to constantly remind yourself to focus on the task at hand instead of leaving something midstream.

Look also at the mode that is second in weight, since that quality can support or complement the quality of greatest strength. If Cardinal is second in weight, your motivational spirit and your ability to initiate new situations or relationships will come into play. If Fixed signs are second in weight, you can maintain your focus and stability in the midst of change and complete your obligations. If Mutable signs are second in weight, your ability to remain flexible when necessary can be helpful.

The mode (or modes) that is (are) weakest can be significant, so pay attention to these potential deficiencies. If Cardinal is a weak link, you may sometimes feel reluctant to get started, especially in new situations. If Fixed is your weakest link, it can be an indicator that you sometimes fail to stay with a person, project, or situation until you've completed your obligation or task. And if Mutability is your weak point, you sometimes have trouble adapting to change or are somewhat inflexible in your attitudes.

Blending the Concepts of Element and Mode

If you make a small grid showing the number of Cardinal, Fixed, and Mutable signs in your chart, and another showing the elements fire, earth, air, and water, you will discover that you can distill a basic concept of your chart in another way. For example, if your chart shows that you have the fire element and Fixed mode as the top-ranking element and mode, then you could say you are "fixed fire." The Fixed fire sign of the zodiac is Leo, and regardless of your planetary make-up, the characteristics of Leo are recognizable in your personality projection. If the elemental balance shows the strongest element as earth and the strongest mode as Mutable, then the characteristics of the "mutable earth" sign of the zodiac, Virgo, would be recognizable in your personality.

Hemispheres in Your Chart

Your chart can also be viewed as a whole picture. Take a look at the circle for a moment. Are there areas that seem to be more strongly inhabited by planets? Are there areas that seem to be more heavily involved? These areas are the basic hemispheres of your chart and indicate specific information about your personality as a whole.

Left Hemisphere Emphasis

If there are more than six planets on the left side of your chart, the focus of your energy is concentrated here. This hemisphere strength indicates that you are driven by a need for independence and autonomy, and that you feel most validated when you know that you're living life on your own terms. You may find it difficult to allow others to support or help you, even when you want them to lend a hand, and can certainly have trouble asking for assistance (especially if you feel it diminishes your sense of self to do so!). Relationships can be difficult for you unless you are in a situation that allows equanimity and equality, but be careful of your tendency to want to take the lead all of the time. True equality means that both partners are powerful.

Right Hemisphere Emphasis

If you have more than six planets on the right side of your chart, your energies are concentrated strongly on relationships. This hemisphere strength indicates that you are driven by a need for connection to others, and you may seek validation from others as a means of confirming your sense of identity. It can be tempting to define your sense of self through your relationships, which can be a dangerous precedent if you have not yet determined what you really need and want from your life on your own terms. However, you also have a strength through this emphasis, and that is an ability to honor and understand the needs and demands of others. Just watch your tendency to put your needs at the bottom of the heap!

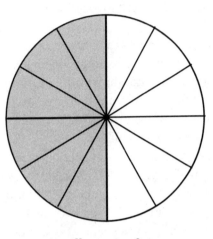

Illustration 3:

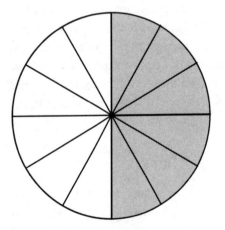

Illustration 4:
Right Hemisphere Emphasis

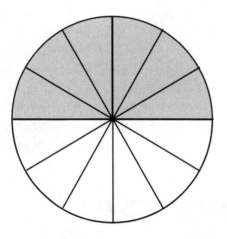

Illustration 5:
Top Hemisphere Emphasis

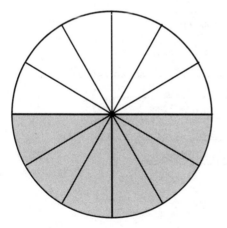

Illustration 6:
Bottom Hemisphere Emphasis

Top Hemisphere Emphasis

A concentration of six or more planets above the horizon indicates that you are driven by a need for recognition, and that you can be quite comfortable in the public eye. Career may have a high priority for you, and if you are not employed outside the home, you may be quite busy in community or civic affairs. You are drawn by the world, and your need for validation is most easily satisfied when your achievements are acknowledged and respected in some way. You may be quite influential in the lives of others, and have strong potential as a leader, teacher, or mentor. However, you also need to remember that you must allow some "down" time, and that your home and family may provide an important security base.

Bottom Hemisphere Emphasis

If more than six planetary energies are concentrated below the horizon, the significant thrust of your energy indicates that you are most comfortable away from the glare of the public, and that you safeguard your privacy. Building stability and security are a strong focus in your life, and your career may be a means to an end in that regard. You can be uncomfortable in situations where you feel that you are put on display, and may need to cultivate your ability to speak or appear in front of groups, since this may not come easily for you.

Empty Houses

You may also be concerned with the areas in your chart that appear to be empty. Never fear, these houses are not really vacant! You are just not placing as much emphasis on these relationships or environments, or you may be satisfying these needs through other dimensions of your life. Every house has a sign on the cusp, and that sign influences the qualities associated with the house. Each sign also corresponds to a particular planet, and that planet or energy associated with the sign on the cusp plays a significant role in the way you satisfy the needs indicated by the house. A table of sign and planetary correspondences is noted in *Table 4* below. Throughout your reading you may be directed to study the planet associated with a particular sign.

THE SIGNS AND THEIR RULERS	
Sign	**Planetary Ruler**
Aries ♈	Mars ♂
Taurus ♉	Venus ♀
Gemini ♊	Mercury ☿
Cancer ♋	Moon ☽
Leo ♌	Sun ☉
Virgo ♍	Mercury ☿
Libra ♎	Venus ♀
Scorpio ♏	Pluto ♇
Sagittarius ♐	Jupiter ♃
Capricorn ♑	Saturn ♄
Aquarius ♒	Uranus ♅
Pisces ♓	Neptune ♆

Table 4

Planetary Aspects

Since in Western astrology we draw the astrological chart on a circular wheel, it's easy to view the relationships between the planets through geometric associations. The angle formed when two planets connect to one another is called an aspect. There are many ways to determine aspects, but in this material we will utilize those noted in the following aspect table. Aspects are measured by the number of degrees that separate two planets or points on a chart.

Each aspect has a particular quality or nature, and that quality influences both of the energies or points involved in the aspect. These qualities are generally harmonious or discordant, and will add flow or friction to the energies or points involved. It is rare for the aspects to be perfect (e.g., exactly sixty degrees or exactly ninety degrees), and to allow those connections that are close, but not exact, there are allowable orbs. These orbs vary according to different schools of thought, and my perceptions are noted in the text that follows. The closer the orb, the more intense the aspect. Accordingly, wider orbs signify less powerful aspects.

THE ASPECTS			
Symbol	Aspect	Angle	Meaning
☌	Conjunction	0°	Focus
⌄	SemiSextile	30°	Opening
∠	SemiSquare	45°	Growth
✳	Sextile	60°	Flow
☐	Square	90°	Tension
△	Trine	120°	Opportunity
⊼	Quincunx	150°	Frustration
☍	Opposition	180°	Awareness

Table 5

When an Energy Has No Aspects

If the Sun, Moon, or a planet in your chart has no major aspects, it is said to be *peregrine*. To a large extent, this indicates that this energy is empowered, because it operates without undue influence from other energies in your chart. The qualities of this energy may be an outstanding force in your life, and this is the energy that people frequently associate with your identity.

If you find a peregrine energy, spend extra time focusing on the energy's sign and house placement. Each peregrine energy takes on a special quality. These concepts are defined below.

Sun: Your ego self can be very strongly developed, and you may feel more comfortable creating life on your own terms. It may be easier for you to own the masculine qualities of your psyche and to feel more comfortable expressing your individuality. You can be who you want to be!

Moon: Your emotional responses are easier to keep in check when you need to remain objective. However, you may sometimes find it difficult to express your emotions to others. Developing close friendships with other women can be positively self-confirming for you and may play a powerful role in your sense of feminine strength.

Mercury: Logical processes are very important, and your mind may never seem to stop whirring in your endless pursuit to rationalize everything. You could probably benefit from learning meditation techniques that allow you to move beyond your mind into a state of inner quiet.

Venus: You may find it easier to develop a strong sense of self worth, but only if you are clear about your true values. Expressing your sense of beauty and artistry may also be especially important to you, but you may not always feel comfortable in new situations or new relationships. Feeling loved is very important; the way you go about it centers in your ability to confirm that you deserve the love you need!

Mars: You're constantly doing, taking action, and may feel uncomfortable unless there's some kind of activity going on in your life. You may sometimes seem too assertive "for a woman," so try to be aware of the way others interpret your actions and attitudes.

Jupiter: Your personal philosophies, ideals, and beliefs form a major cornerstone of your identity. Defining these ideals and utilizing them to shape your ethical and moral values may set you aside as an outstanding and inspiring individual. This quality also adds to your independence.

Saturn: You're very critical of yourself with Saturn peregrine, and need to learn to take life less seriously if you want to enjoy the rewards of all your hard work. Taking the time to enjoy relaxing, entertaining, or even sometimes frivolous activities may actually lead to higher levels of productivity. Try it.

Uranus: As you develop your sense of personal identity, you'll discover that standing apart from the crowd is important to you, although that can sometimes be a lonely position. Nobody has to explain uniqueness to you! Additionally, you'll benefit from paying attention to your flashes of insight, since your intuitive "hunches" are usually right on the mark.

Neptune: Through turning inward and developing a relationship with your inner self, you discover a realm of imagination and spirituality that can be expressed through creative artistry. Your intuitive and psychic abilities may be very strong.

Pluto: Your personal power may not emerge until you are over thirty, but when you do accept and acknowledge your strengths, you can be a major force for healing and transformational change. Trusting your ability that tells you when to probe further and when to relax your intensity will go a long way toward helping you develop your ability to be an agent for regeneration.

What About Inconsistencies in the Chart?

You may find upon reading about your chart that there are a few contradictions. For example, one factor may indicate independence, while another shows strong dependency. It is not unusual to experience contradictions within yourself, and that is just what your chart illustrates about you! When you reflect upon these qualities within the context in which they are explained, you may discover some self-illuminating facts about yourself. Self-understanding has a marvelous way of emphasizing your complexity, talents, and your personal power!

CHAPTER TWO

PROJECTION OF YOUR REAL SELF

$\mathcal{S}$ ometimes showing the world who you really are is not easy, and sometimes the world may not respond as you had hoped! It's helpful to take a look at the differences and similarities between the attitudes, impressions, and images you project and the person who resides at the core of your being. The primary qualities that determine how others see you—what you project—can be understood by examining the Sun, Ascendant, and Moon in the context of your personality projection. There are many layers to each of the energies, and this layer frequently underscores the basic sense of self you embrace.

Your Sun and Your Personality

Your Sun is more than your ego self, and when other people encounter the energy of your Sun, it is the qualities that radiate through this energy that will leave a deep impression. Let's look at the different projections of the Sun in each of the signs.

Your Projection Through Your Sun in Aries

With the Sun in Aries, your independent way of thinking and doing things may be quite powerful. Your ego self is driven by a need for autonomy. You need plenty of room to move, and the idea of being penned in makes you feel unsettled. You simply do not like waiting, and prefer spontaneity to planned situations. You may also be more comfortable taking the lead, which can be daunting for some of the men in your life. Since your Sun indicates "who you think you are," you may realize that if you see yourself as autonomous, then situations in your life are more likely to develop that allow you to express yourself in a more self-determined manner.

Your Projection Through Your Sun in Taurus

With your Sun in Taurus, your steadfast, easygoing energy helps to keep you focused on your priorities. You're interested in a life that provides ample opportunities to grow, and your ego self is driven by a need to experience consistency. The beautiful things in life are most valuable to you, and your capacity for love is immense. Learning the difference between stability and stubbornness can be one of your biggest lessons. Since your Sun shows "who you think you are," you can grow to realize that loving thoughts produce amazing results.

Your Projection Through Your Sun in Gemini

With your Sun in Gemini, your inquisitive manner and quick wit may be your trademarks. You need variety, and whether in relationships, career opportunities, or creative endeavors will prefer to create a life that gives you plenty of options. You may radiate an air of intelligence, and most enjoy people and situations that stimulate your mind. The old truth, "you are what you think," is especially clear to you, and you have the ability to shift your consciousness and create a whole new realm of life experience by first altering your mental focus.

Your Projection Through Your Sun in Cancer

With your Sun in Cancer, you can radiate a kind of comfort and care that comes from the core of your being. You thrive most when you're taking part in nourishing—whether you're tending your garden, teaching others, safeguarding children, or fostering growth in a company. You may express strong sentimentality due to your attachment to the past, and can be especially tenacious with situations, people, and goals. Emotional sensitivity is simply a part of your essence, although your protective shell can fool people.

Your Projection Through Your Sun in Leo

With your Sun in Leo, you're likely to radiate a sense of regality and power, even if you're just sitting at home in your old jeans. Although you may not demand to be the center of attention, you can certainly carry it off when the spotlight is on you. You're driven by a need to create and express yourself, and enjoy playful people and situations. When challenged, your pride can get in your way unless you develop some objectivity about yourself, which can be a tough job if you're too self-absorbed. It's okay to think of yourself as royalty some of the time, but just remember that others may not see you that way!

Your Projection Through Your Sun in Virgo

With your Sun in Virgo, your ego is driven by a powerful need to do things well. Although you may not ask for recognition, and may act uncomfortable when it comes your way, you crave the confirmation it brings. Yes, you are a perfectionist, and you definitely have opinions. Yet you can be flexible when necessary. Just be sure that flexibility doesn't turn you into a doormat when you run into those people who are the controllers. It's okay to have things your way some of the time, too.

Your Projection Through Your Sun in Libra

With your Sun in Libra, your ego is driven by a need to relate. Now that doesn't mean that you must be married or in a love relationship. It is through connecting to others that you gain the feedback that allows you to maintain a balance in your life. This can be accomplished through friendships, work relationships, and social situations. You may also crave the best of everything (it's your good taste that can be your downfall if you're on a budget!), and you definitely love the most refined elements of life. At heart, you're artistic, but you can be tough to satisfy.

Your Projection Through Your Sun in Scorpio

With your Sun in Scorpio, your ego is driven by a need to be almost enigmatic. You're more comfortable when at least a little mystery surrounds you, and you can exude a strong level of sensual charm. You're rarely halfway about anything, and your intensity can be daunting to those who are uncomfortable with confrontation. Since your Sun speaks of "who you think you are," you may think that you're more mysterious than you are in actuality! No bother—you're still a mystery to most, so you're safe!

✓Your Projection Through Your Sun in Sagittarius

With your Sun in Sagittarius, you are a woman who thrives on the grand adventure of life. You may feed this urge through travel or education, but you also fulfill it through your spiritual quests. Your enthusiasm is difficult to miss, and you can inspire others to reach beyond their limitations through the example of your own life, but you can also be difficult to follow, and may head into a new territory before you've even warmed your chair.

Your Projection Through Your Sun in Capricorn

With your Sun in Capricorn, you are a woman who needs to be in control of your own life. You've probably taken on responsibilities from a very early age, and may be strongly determined to achieve your goals and realize your aspirations. Your practical approach to life may assure that you're equally at home in the workplace or making necessary repairs on your blender. It's easier for you when you can make the rules, or at the very least, enforce them!

Your Projection Through Your Sun in Aquarius

With your Sun in Aquarius, you are a woman whose spirit strikes forth into the realm of the unusual. As an individual you are unique, and you may pride yourself on the things that make you different from everyone else. You also have a strong desire to connect to those who are like minded, and may count your friends as your most significant blessings. Since your Sun speaks of "who you think you are," you need to realize that your powerful mind, which can be strongly focused, is your link to your future, and that you are the creator of that future.

Your Projection Through Your Sun in Pisces

With your Sun in Pisces, your ego dances most freely in the realm of imagination. Your compassion and sensitivity can stimulate your desire to give of yourself for the betterment of life. You may be quite responsive to the energy of your surroundings, and can be tempted, chameleon-like, to adapt to the needs and demands around you instead of determining what you really want, and the manner in which you want to project who you really are.

Your Ascendant and Rising Sign

The astrological sign at the cusp of the horizon on the left side of your chart is called your Rising Sign. This point usually corresponds to a point called the Ascendant. Your Ascendant is the face you present to the world, and shows how others see you. It's understandable that your Rising Sign would play an important part in the way you project yourself. This sign also filters your basic attitudes and indicates the qualities you most readily allow others to see.

The planet or energy associated with the sign on your Ascendant adds even more qualities to the way others see you. By including the elements of this association in your understanding of how your image is developed and projected, you can understand even more about the basic attitudes and qualities that filter through the image you project.

Aries Ascendant

You may give the appearance of assertive independence, and can be quite competitive when necessary. Your attitude toward life is generally adventurous, and you may love to take on challenges. Although you may not realize it sometimes, you can be abrasive, even though you have simply been blazing the trail along the path toward reaching your destination. Mars is the energy associated with Aries, and the sign of Mars in your chart will influence the way others see you.

Ascendant and Mars in Aries: Your personality exudes a high level of energy, and you may be quite athletic in your appearance and demeanor. You're always on the move and may enjoy an active lifestyle.

Mars in Taurus: Your easy, but deliberate, pace can project a strong sense of self-assurance, but if your energy is low, you can definitely project a sense of inertia or lethargy. You prefer to take the time to enjoy the fruits of life, and your attitudes and demeanor reflect that feeling.

Mars in Gemini: Your tendency to scatter your energy can make it difficult for others to keep up with you. You rarely stop, much like your mind, which is continually pursuing new pathways.

Mars in Cancer: Even when in hot pursuit, your approach is indirect. This leaves room for others to misread your intentions, so try to be clear about your desires.

Mars in Leo: You rarely do anything in a small way, and your way of moving may be bold and self-assured. Your confidence radiates through your personality, and you may have no difficulty at all dealing with the men in your life.

Mars in Virgo: Your methodical approach to doing things can even be seen in the way you carry yourself. Although you may be assertive, you usually are so in a logical manner.

Mars in Libra: You are competitive (despite your best efforts), but you may not want to own that part of your personality. Take advantage of your natural ability to assert yourself, and remember that it's okay to win!

Mars in Scorpio: Your intensity radiates through your personality, and you may exude an undercurrent of sexuality that is highly alluring.

Mars in Sagittarius: You may have a high level of athleticism and are likely to feel better if you adopt an active lifestyle. Your sometimes sassy attitude can be quite fascinating.

Mars in Capricorn: You may project a very controlling demeanor, and can be quite effective in positions of authority. A tailored appearance suits you.

Mars in Aquarius: You project an air of intellectual prowess, but you may also be quite adept in sports. You're a bit of a rebel, and that spirit is likely to shine through your attitude and self-projection.

Mars in Pisces: You can be assertive, although your strength of character is amplified because of your high levels of flexibility. You do not have to openly challenge others in order to prove yourself, but can easily rise to a challenge when necessary. Just be sure you're not always caving in to avoid confrontation.

Taurus Ascendant

Generally, Taurus rising appears to be quite calm, and you might even feel most confident in situations that are under control. Your appearance is also important, but usually not to the point of vanity. Others may see you as the one who is serene in the midst of a storm, but a few will complain that you can be too stubborn when it comes to change. You may notice that your attitudes can become too rigid unless you strive to nourish open-mindedness. The ruler of Taurus is Venus, and Venus' sign in your chart will influence your self-projection in a powerful way.

Venus in Aries: Your sense of beauty and independence shows in the way you present yourself to the world. Your manner of dress is likely to reflect a quality of fun and freedom, and you can project an image of independence and vitality.

Ascendant and Venus in Taurus: You're likely to love wearing beautiful, comfortable clothing, and may prefer natural fibers and earth tones. Your earthy sensuality is strongly projected through your personality.

Venus in Gemini: Your image may change from time to time, although your youthful quality is always easy to spot. You may have especially noticeable hands.

Venus in Cancer: Your voice and mannerisms are likely to project a lovely quality, and you look great in flowing skirts—which you probably adore. Your femininity shows through your personality quite clearly.

Venus in Leo: You may easily command attention when you enter a room, and may be quite comfortable in elegant dress. Your hair is a matter of pride for you, and you can change your entire personality by altering your hair style and color.

Venus in Virgo: You may prefer simple, practical styling in your manner of dress, although you rarely opt for anything of shoddy quality. You appreciate natural beauty, and may look and feel your best when you enhance your best natural qualities.

Venus in Libra: Others may see you as beautiful, and your affinity for the true nature of beauty can be developed into a powerful sense of refinement and ease. Your smile is one of your most inviting features.

Venus in Scorpio: You may possess an alluring presence, and can be exceptionally charismatic. A sultry quality radiates through your personality.

Venus in Sagittarius: Your love of adventure, travel, and knowledge radiates through your personality as an enthusiasm for life, which, in itself, is extremely attractive. Your laugh can be contagious.

Venus in Capricorn: A businesslike attitude is added to your demeanor. You can easily look the part of the executive, although when you're at home, you may opt for more practical attire.

Venus in Aquarius: You're a trend setter, and may be so far ahead of your time that others don't know what to make of your personal style, but you're most powerful when you allow your uniqueness to shine through, and when you are fully expressive. Your eyes may be your most outstanding feature.

Venus in Pisces: You may move with a gracefulness akin to dancing, and you can project a mystical beauty in your appearance. Flowing clothing is perfect for you.

Gemini Ascendant

You may always appear young, and are certainly likely to be young in your attitudes, regardless of your age. Others may see you as intelligent and witty, and your interest in a wide variety of ideas and people can certainly help you develop a cosmopolitan air. Whether or not you talk a lot, you are a communicator. Pay attention to your hands and facial movements. You have a lot to say! Gemini is ruled by the planet Mercury, and Mercury's placement by sign will also add a special flair to your personality projection.

Mercury in Aries: You show a strong-minded independence to the world. Others are likely to see you as mentally active and somewhat outspoken.

Mercury in Taurus: You may project a soft-spoken quality, and can appear to be quiet and observant.

Ascendant and Mercury in Gemini: You are likely to be quite animated and talkative, and most people will see you as highly communicative. Your manner can be quite breezy.

Mercury in Cancer: You may appear to be a good listener, and when you do speak your mind, the feeling behind what you say is difficult to ignore.

Mercury in Leo: Your voice and words can be powerful and commanding. Others are likely to take notice when you have something to say.

Mercury in Virgo: You are likely to present an image of a studious, intelligent woman. You project efficiency, and may be known for your discriminating taste.

Mercury in Libra: Your speech and mannerisms can be graceful and charming. It's difficult for you to be seen as offensive, since that would be out of character for you.

Mercury in Scorpio: You may not be especially outspoken, but you definitely have your opinions. You can project an image of intrigue.

Mercury in Sagittarius: You may be rather outspoken and direct in your manner. Your philosophical outlook definitely colors your personality, and you can be a great conversationalist.

Mercury in Capricorn: Your personality is influenced by your organized approach to thinking. Others are likely to see you as serious-minded, but you can also be quite witty when you're in comfortable surroundings.

Mercury in Aquarius: Your personality takes on an air of independence and futuristic thinking. You may actually invent a way to wear your computer and cell phone as jewelry.

Mercury in Pisces: Your quiet mannerisms can allow you to disappear when you do not want to be seen, but you can also be dramatic when necessary.

Cancer Ascendant

Through this influence, you may project a motherly quality—whether or not you have children. You may draw others to you who need support and care; even in the work place you take on the role of protector. You can also initiate emotional responses from others, and can use this quality to your advantage in many situations. Watch for your tendency to hide behind your shell. Sometimes those protective barriers can be quite cumbersome. The sign Cancer is ruled by the Moon, and the placement of your Moon by sign will add yet another dimension to your personality projection.

Moon in Aries: Your moods are generally upbeat. Your need for spontaneity adds a sense of independence to your personality projection.

Moon in Taurus: There's a powerful sense of steadfast, loving energy projected through your personality. You may be rather conservative in your demeanor.

Moon in Gemini: A delightful youthful quality emerges through your personality, and your versatility may be quite noticeable to others.

Ascendant and Moon in Cancer: Your personality is definitely influenced by your nurturing qualities, and you may draw others to you because they feel safe and comfortable with you.

Moon in Leo: A dramatic quality and regal manner emerge through your personality projection, and you enjoy the spotlight from time to time.

Moon in Virgo: A discriminating and analytical quality is added to your personality. You may prefer to dress in a practical manner, and are likely to be quite attentive to your health.

Moon in Libra: Your flair for color, harmony, beauty, and design extends to your personal appearance, and you prefer stylish dress and refined mannerisms.

Moon in Scorpio: A special emotional intensity emanates through your personality projection, and you may even have a sultry aura that draws others to you.

Moon in Sagittarius: An optimistic nature is projected through your personality expression, and you're most comfortable in the presence of open-minded individuals who have a good sense of humor.

Moon in Capricorn: A serious quality emanates through your personality projection, and you can also be quite conservative in your mannerisms and dress.

Moon in Aquarius: You radiate a quality of individuality and intellectuality, and you may even show an aloofness in some situations. But when you're with friends, you are much more responsive.

Moon in Pisces: A mystical quality exudes from your personality projection. You can be excessively sensitive to the emotions of others, and need to establish reasonable emotional boundaries.

Leo Ascendant

This signifies that you project a definite presence, a factor you can use to your advantage when you want to make a spectacular entrance. It's easy to command the attention of others (who may talk about you even when you're not around!). You can be quite comfortable in situations that call for direction or leadership, and can engender loyalty from those under your influence. You may take extra care with your hair style, hats, or other head adornments, since you know that they say a lot about who you are. The ruler of Leo is the Sun, and your Sun's sign will play an important part in the way you shine and project your sense of personal presence.

Sun in Aries: Your fiery independence will be hard to miss, and you may perform at your peak levels when you're dealing with challenges. Leadership looks great on you.

Sun in Taurus: Your personal magnetism takes on an earthy quality. Your conservative approach to life can create an energy of quiet elegance.

Sun in Gemini: Your wit adds a special sparkle to your personality projection. Your confident intelligence can help you in any situation.

Sun in Cancer: You may exude a warm comfort to those around you. Your personality may be quite inviting.

Ascendant and Sun in Leo: You are definitely difficult to miss. Your ability to influence and take charge of situations is rarely questioned once you go into action.

Sun in Virgo: Your discriminating attitude coupled with your magnetic personality can be an extremely powerful duo. Stop questioning whether or not you deserve to be the center of attention, and do something positive with your power!

Sun in Libra: You should have no trouble creating an image that will be both powerfully dramatic and elegant. You look marvelous when you feel good about yourself.

Sun in Scorpio: You may have a little internal conflict between the part of you that likes to be noticed and the part of yourself that prefers to keep a low profile. You can be highly charismatic, so enjoy the results from time to time.

√**Sun in Sagittarius:** You can exude a magnetic enthusiasm that inspires everyone around you. The only problem you may have is knowing when to pull back or when to stop tooting your own horn when you're overly excited.

Sun in Capricorn: You probably prefer understated elegance. Showing off is definitely not your style, but you still might enjoy wearing your favorite jewelry with your jeans.

Sun in Aquarius: You definitely prefer to create your own sense of style. You can operate very nicely in a setting that allows you to dramatize your individuality.

Sun in Pisces: You can be extremely dramatic when you want to be, but you also feel good about projecting serenity and peace, which in itself can be a dramatic contrast to many situations!

Virgo Ascendant

Through this influence, you may be somewhat the perfectionist in your appearance and may be most comfortable when you feel healthy and well-groomed. Others may view you as detail-oriented, which has its advantages if you know what you want. You may be extremely aware of your physical body, to the extent that you know when anything is not working properly. You'd better keep a nail file in your pocketbook, since you'll fiddle with that ragged nail all day if you don't have a chance to fix it! Virgo is ruled by the energy of Mercury, and this planetary energy will add its own influence to your personality expression.

Mercury in Aries: You show a strong-minded independence to the world. Others are likely to see you as mentally active and somewhat outspoken.

Mercury in Taurus: You may project a soft-spoken quality, and can appear to be quiet and observant.

Mercury in Gemini: You are likely to be quite animated and talkative, and most people will see you as highly communicative. Your manner is quite breezy.

Mercury in Cancer: You may appear to be a good listener, and when you do speak your mind, the feeling behind what you say is difficult to ignore.

Mercury in Leo: Your voice and words can be powerful and commanding. Others are likely to take notice when you have something to say.

Ascendant and Mercury in Virgo: You are likely to present an image of a studious, intelligent woman. You project efficiency and may be known for your discriminating taste.

Mercury in Libra: Your speech and mannerisms can be graceful and charming. It's difficult for you to be seen as offensive, since that would be out of character for you.

Mercury in Scorpio: You may not be especially outspoken, but you definitely have your opinions. You can project an image of intrigue.

Mercury in Sagittarius: You may be rather outspoken and direct in your manner. Your philosophical outlook definitely colors your personality, and you can be a great conversationalist.

Mercury in Capricorn: Your personality is influenced by your organized approach to thinking. Others are likely to see you as serious-minded, but you can also be quite witty when you're in comfortable surroundings.

Mercury in Aquarius: Your personality takes on an air of independence and futuristic thinking. You may actually invent a way to wear your computer and cell phone as jewelry.

Mercury in Pisces: Your quiet mannerisms can allow you to disappear when you do not want to be seen, but you can also be dramatic when necessary.

Libra Ascendant

You project an air of refinement and grace with Libra rising, and you may take special care with your wardrobe, hair, and appearance. Others may see you as beautiful. Your sense of color and style may be exceptional, and you can definitely pull off a class act when you want. You're most comfortable in a serene environment, and prefer to maintain a sense of social grace and charm whenever possible. If there is difficulty, you may be the one called upon to help achieve harmony. The energy of Venus is associated with the sign of Libra, and Venus' sign in your chart will definitely influence the manner in which you present yourself to the world.

Venus in Aries: Your sense of beauty and independence shows in the way you present yourself to the world. Your manner of dress is likely to reflect a quality of fun and freedom, and can you project an image of independence and vitality.

Venus in Taurus: You're likely to love wearing beautiful, comfortable clothing, and may prefer natural fibers and earth tones. Your earthy sensuality is strongly projected through your personality.

Venus in Gemini: Your image may change from time to time, although your youthful quality is always easy to spot. You may have especially noticeable hands.

Venus in Cancer: Your voice and mannerisms are likely to project a lovely quality, and you can look great in flowing skirts—which you probably adore. Your femininity shows through your personality quite clearly.

Venus in Leo: You may easily command attention when you enter a room, and may be quite comfortable in elegant dress. Your hair is a matter of pride for you, and you can change your entire personality by altering your hair style and color.

Venus in Virgo: You may prefer simple, practical styling in your manner of dress, although you rarely opt for anything of shoddy quality. You appreciate natural beauty, and may look and feel your best when you enhance your best natural qualities.

Ascendant and Venus in Libra: You may present a well-defined beauty. Others may see you as beautiful, and your affinity for the true nature of beauty can be developed into a powerful sense of refinement and ease. Your smile is one of your most inviting features, and is a definite asset.

Venus in Scorpio: You may possess an alluring presence, and can be exceptionally charismatic. A sultry quality radiates through your personality.

Venus in Sagittarius: Your love of adventure, travel, and knowledge radiates through your personality as an enthusiasm for life, which, in itself, is extremely attractive. Your laugh can be contagious.

Venus in Capricorn: A businesslike attitude is added to your demeanor. You can easily look the part of the executive, although when you're at home, you may opt for more practical attire.

Venus in Aquarius: You're a trend setter, and may be so far ahead of your time that others don't know what to make of your personal style, but you're most powerful when you allow your uniqueness to shine through, and when you are fully expressive. Your eyes may be your most outstanding feature.

Venus in Pisces: You may move with a gracefulness akin to dancing, and you can project a mystical beauty in your appearance. Flowing clothing is perfect for you.

Scorpio Ascendant

Through this quality you project an aura of intrigue and may not like to be the center of attention all the time. Even if you are comfortable with attention, you are not comfortable with a loss of privacy, and may have secrets from even your closest friends and companions. Your gaze may be intense, as though you are looking through someone—which you just might be, since you are likely to be quite perceptive. Scorpio is ruled by the energy of Pluto, and the sign Pluto was in at your birth will underscore your self-projection and influence the way others see you.

Pluto in Gemini: A penetrating and keen wit is added to your intense persona, and you may be known for your outspoken ideas. The sparkle in your eyes conveys a lot!

Pluto in Cancer: Part of your magnetism may stem from your awareness of the true power that resides in your being a woman. By embracing the full nature of this power, you project an aura of strength, courage, and intensity that few can ignore.

Pluto in Leo: Your personality projection may be strongly tied to your role as a career woman, or to your influence within your family or community. You can also be quite domineering, and need a positive outlet for your need to be in control.

Pluto in Virgo: A keen sensitivity is added to your physical body, and taking care of your health is a natural part of your life. Your concern for quality shows in the way you dress and live, and you may be most at ease when you're in control of your environment.

Pluto in Libra: Even though you may not want to admit it, the way other people feel about you is important to you. You're not comfortable in situations where you feel undermined, and are likely to ultimately turn the tables on anyone who tries to work against you. Becoming aware of the way you project yourself can help you, because you may be sending signals you had not intended to transmit. Just remember that your powerful charisma can be intimidating to those who are unsure of themselves.

Pluto and Ascendant in Scorpio: Your intensity can be much more powerful than you realize. Your awareness of underlying energy can be amazing. Others may be drawn to you because they sense your psychic energy. Your sense of what is happening beneath the surface penetrates the facade so many people project, although your responses from this level operate mostly on a subconscious level.

Sagittarius Ascendant

You're likely to project the image of an adventurer, and may be most comfortable when you're dressed for play or sports, but you can also have an air of classical elegance or wealth about you. Your manner can be quite direct, and others may sometimes see you as loud, boisterous, or messy if you've gotten out of control! You prefer to show an attitude of optimism, and may be known for your sense of humor. Others may never know when you're feeling low. Jupiter is the energy associated with your Rising Sign, and the placement of Jupiter by sign in your chart will influence the way others see you.

Jupiter in Aries: You're quite likely to speak your mind, and may be known for your outspoken opinions and ideas. Developing some athleticism can add a positive dimension to your presence.

Jupiter in Taurus: You may not care a great deal for physical exercise, although you probably love mental gymnastics and may be known for your conservative ideas and common sense approach to life.

Jupiter in Gemini: Your wide-ranging philosophical ideas can give you a definite cosmopolitan air. You're likely to attract intellectual types.

Jupiter in Cancer: You may be most at home with people you know well, like family and home-town friends. This quality quiets your Sagittarius Ascendant a little, and you might prefer to hold your adventures near the home front (and may also curb your opinions a little, unless you feel really passionate about them!).

Jupiter in Leo: You definitely know how to have a good time, and may attract a circle of friends who enjoy play as much as you do. Dressing up in your most elegant attire to attend gala events can be a lot of fun, and you can look absolutely fabulous when you turn on that smile.

Jupiter in Virgo: Your matter-of-fact attitude and common sense approach to doing things is a plus in situations where you are called on to teach or train others. But your expectations need to be geared toward what is realistically possible.

Jupiter in Libra: You can sometimes adopt a cavalier attitude that alienates others, but this stems from your high standards. You may expect even more from yourself than you do from others!

Jupiter in Scorpio: You tend to hold rather stubbornly to your ideals and attitudes. You may give the impression that you have a hidden agenda, even when you're trying to be straightforward.

Jupiter and Ascendant in Sagittarius: You make an unmistakable impression. Your outgoing personality and high-minded sense of humor can be excellent traits for working with others, public speaking, or leadership positions. You may focus more on tomorrow than today, but that's just part of your optimism.

Jupiter in Capricorn: You definitely operate from a set of rules and expectations, despite your open-minded appearances. You can be quite judgmental, and need to occasionally review your opinions and concepts to avoid getting stuck in prejudicial thinking and to avoid leaving the impression that your ideas are the only ones that count.

Jupiter in Aquarius: Your ability to see things from a universal perspective makes you a good candidate for public relations situations. Others may be inspired by your ground-breaking ideas, actions, and behavior.

Jupiter in Pisces: Your focus on spiritual matters is quite sincere, and you may be especially devoted to a set of ideals that form the guidelines for your behavior and life choices. Your helpful attitude toward others can stem from a strong sense of compassion.

Capricorn Ascendant

Your image may be one of seriousness, and you may appear quite sedate and controlled in your behavior and attitudes. Your need for respect dictates that you follow the rules, and even though you might like to go to work in jeans and a t-shirt, you're more likely to show up in an impeccably tailored suit, which looks quite nice on you, by the way. Additionally, your dry humor and solid reliability are always welcome. Since Saturn rules Capricorn, the placement of Saturn in your chart will have an effect on the way people see you.

Saturn in Aries: You may be very headstrong, and your need to take charge or maintain control is best expressed in situations that allow you to take a position of leadership.

Saturn in Taurus: Your attitudes toward change are likely to be quite conservative, and you can be excessively stubborn. Getting out of outworn situations can be difficult for you.

Saturn in Gemini: You may appear somewhat conservative, although you do have some flexibility since you're usually willing to look into a subject or situation before passing final judgment, but you may also try too hard to "prove" things through pure logic, which does have its limitations!

Saturn in Cancer: You let your conservative ideas show in the way you present yourself. These probably stem from your attachment to the traditions you've grown to respect over the course of your lifetime. Just be careful that your attachment to the past does not inhibit your opportunity to grow. Your love of old things can be an asset when you use it well, but you may have to guard against looking like you're out of place.

Saturn in Leo: You present a no-nonsense approach to life, and you can be quite demonstrative when stating your opinions or ideas. It may be difficult to keep an open mind, especially if something different threatens your sense of stability.

Saturn in Virgo: Your precise manner of doing things adds an air of perfection to your personality. It's easy to become overly critical, especially if you feel that the outcome of a situation will reflect on you. Your mind/body connection is exceptionally powerful.

Saturn in Libra: Your very definite opinions about the way you prefer to present yourself are easy to spot, although you may cave in to pressure to act or behave in certain ways in order to gain acceptance from others. As a child, this was a survival mechanism, but as a woman, you can develop a broader range of choices.

Saturn in Scorpio: Your honesty with yourself about feelings concerning personal power is absolutely crucial, since you can project a mistrust of your own power, and others may misread your intentions. Instead of striving for control, focus on developing clarity about your intention and directions.

Saturn in Sagittarius: Your attitudes about what is right reflect very strongly in the way you present yourself to the world. Any prejudicial thinking on your part is likely to be strongly radiated in your presentation of yourself.

Saturn and Ascendant in Capricorn: The set of standards you hold for yourself can be exceptionally high, and you may not be happy unless you feel you are producing something. This can be quite helpful in some situations, but others may see you as excessively controlling if you carry things too far.

Saturn in Aquarius: When your genius shines through, you may be happy until the realities of the world set in. It's okay to be involved in "mundane" activities. The world does not have to shake every moment, but you do enjoy it when others see your special talents and abilities.

Saturn in Pisces: It is crucial that your devotion to your ideals is pure and in harmony with your highest needs. Others will find it difficult to separate who you are from what you believe.

Aquarius Ascendant

You may be quite avant-garde, and can be a trend setter. It's possible that your disdain for the traditional and affinity for the unusual can leave an impression of eccentricity. You can carry it off, however, because you're not meant to follow cookie-cutter patterns: you're creating one of your own! Freedom is highly important to you, and your need for spontaneity enhances your ability to find the truly unique elements life has to offer. The placement of Uranus, which rules the sign on your Ascendant, will indicate particular qualities that will be seen in your self-projection.

Uranus in Aries: An exceptional level of independence is added to your personality, and you may find it easy to venture into new levels of personal exploration. You can be extremely rebellious, especially if you're challenged by too much restraint.

Uranus in Taurus: You may feel a need to break away from traditional roles, although you're more likely to alter the way you do things in order to make your life easier. You may be seen as artistically talented.

Uranus in Gemini: Your freethinking approach to life allows you to embrace change readily. You may be especially drawn to things that will keep you looking and feeling youthful, and others may value your forward-thinking ideas and fresh way of doing things, but you will have to safeguard against being seen as too "far-out."

Uranus in Cancer: You prefer to be seen as unique, although you may struggle with the idea of being totally alone. Your ideas about what you need in a family may go against the traditional roles, and you may prefer to avoid being tagged with the role of housewife or anything else deemed too traditional or inhibiting.

Uranus in Leo: Your strong projection of individuality may be expressed through creative or artistic means, and you may have an especially dramatic flair for being noticed. Relationships can be complicated with this combination of influences.

Uranus in Virgo: Your physical health may be particularly important to you, and you may lean toward alternative ideas and methods to keep yourself in top shape. You can also be a bit eccentric in your manner of dress, but usually opt for choices that are primarily comfortable.

Uranus in Libra: You may have a special flair in the way you dress, and can even be a trend setter. Your ideas about the social graces are not likely to be what you learned from your grandmother.

Uranus in Scorpio: You're likely to seek unusual ways to experience and express your sensual qualities. You may have an aura of intrigue about you and can be highly charismatic.

Uranus in Sagittarius: A quality of wisdom is added to your personality, and you may be revered for your perception and interest in new ideas. Your ability to relate to people from different backgrounds adds a true sense of diversity to your persona.

Uranus in Capricorn: You want to be seen as an individual, but you may approach the creation of your image through more traditional means. You value your freedom, and may not be willing to risk doing absurd things that might compromise your ability to maintain your independence.

Uranus and Ascendant in Aquarius: You definitely demonstrate a powerful level of individuality, and may not mind if others think you are a little eccentric. After all, your eccentricities may be some of your favorite qualities!

Uranus in Pisces: You may prefer to be considered as an individual on your own terms, although you also have a strong concern for others, and may not be willing to put yourself first if you feel that someone else has greater needs. The changes in your values over the years have significantly altered the manner in which you show yourself to the world.

Pisces Ascendant

Your dreamy-eyed expression may be a dead giveaway, and others may see you as more angelic than you are in actuality. It's easy for others to project whatever they wish onto you, and if you want to change that, you may have to drop down from your pedestal and insist that they see you as you are. You can create whatever image you like, especially if you take the time to determine what you want to project—and that's the hard part! The energy of Neptune is associated with your Rising Sign, and the placement of Neptune by sign in your chart is likely to influence the way others see you.

Neptune in Gemini: Your fascination with unusual ideas may have lead you through an interesting series of explorations throughout your life. Your intuitive abilities may be quite powerful and others may think of you as insightful and multifaceted.

Neptune in Cancer: You may be highly impressionable, and may find it somewhat difficult to deal with situations in which otheres are taking unnecessary advantage of you. Learning to avoid situations in which you are victimized can be especially empowering.

Neptune in Leo: Your love of dramatic, fairy-tale endings colors many of the choices you make about the way you present yourself to the world. You prefer to project love and compassion, and may find that doing so is extremely empowering.

Neptune in Virgo: Your physical body may be especially sensitive, and you may find that paying special attention to your diet and health regimen can have a positive effect on your health. You may feel most comfortable and look best in natural fiber clothing that is practical and in which you feel at ease. It's important to enhance your natural beauty.

Neptune in Libra: Your fascination with the nature and essence of beauty can be seen in the way you dress and present yourself to the world. You may love to wear fine fabrics like silk and are most at ease when you feel good about the way you look.

Neptune in Scorpio: An intensity is added to the way you project yourself, and your intuitive or psychic abilities may be closely tied to your identity. You can be especially sensual, and may be most at ease in flowing, comfortable dress that allows freedom of movement.

Neptune in Sagittarius: Your ideals play a powerful role in the way you present yourself to the world, and you may find it almost impossible to separate what you believe from the way you live your life. Others may see you as self-righteous, especially if you are condescending toward those who do not share your beliefs.

√**Neptune in Capricorn:** You may be known more for your friends and interests, and your role within your community can be more influential than you may realize. Your interest in doing things according to the rules can lead to a series of choices that reflect strong moral values and judgments.

Aspects to the Ascendant (ASC)

In addition to the sign and ruler of your Ascendant, the planets aspecting your Ascendant will also add special qualities to your self-projection. Just like adding ingredients to a recipe, the aspects to your Ascendant provide spice, subtlety, or innuendo to the person you project into the world.

Aspects from the Sun

Sun conjunct ASC: You project a powerful presence. You may love personal attention and enjoy being noticed most of the time. Even wearing a disguise may not work if you're trying to avoid attention, since your "sunny" disposition can be hard to miss. You need to give yourself ample opportunities for self-expression, and will be more satisfied with your life when you've created a sense of personal style. The primary downfall of this aspect is a tendency to become too self-absorbed, but if you're striving for reasonable objectivity, you (and everyone else) can cope more easily.

Sun semisquare ASC: Your desire to be noticed drives you toward your goals. You may feel somewhat frustrated because it's difficult to know when to move with will and power, and when to pull back. Learning to gauge the reactions of others will help you determine the best ways to assert yourself. If you're feeling alienated, retrace your actions and recall their impact. Then, you can get moving again with greater confidence.

Sun sextile ASC: You can be quite effective in meeting life on your own terms. Positions of respect and authority feel natural to you, and you can be an excellent leader. Applying your natural talents and abilities is easy for you; so easy, in fact, that you may not take full advantage of your personal resources.

Sun square ASC: You may sometimes feel that everyone is always on the defensive with you. You may even have learned to avoid asserting yourself just to avoid the pain of confrontation, but there are times when you do need to take a stand, or when you need things to go your way. Learning to ask for assistance is quite different from demanding it, and you'll gain greater support from others if everyone feels empowered.

Sun trine ASC: You may easily win respect and cooperation from others. This can be quite helpful when you need to accomplish important tasks. Your sense of confidence may be very strong, and you have high hopes for yourself and your life. Although you may have to learn to take advantage of your personal strengths, ultimately you discover that you can accomplish the goals you set for yourself, both in a personal and professional sense.

Sun quincunx ASC: You may be strongly driven toward achieving your aims, and may not know when to pull back. It's easy to exhaust your vitality by burning the candle at both ends, and learning to pace yourself when you have your eye on your goals can be your ultimate challenge. You may also find that it's not always easy to work cooperatively with others, particularly if their pace or style of doing things is different from your own. This can be especially trying in relationships. Ultimately, however, you are capable of making the necessary adjustments to keep things working smoothly.

Sun opposition ASC: You may feel a need for more attention, especially if you are in a relationship with someone who demands a lot of attention. You may also find that it can be easy to become too self-involved, particularly if you're feeling ignored. Others may resent it if you turn the conversation or attention toward yourself, especially if someone else actually needs the spotlight, and watch for your tendency to reluctantly step aside, and then resent it later! Honesty about your real desires in relationships is absolutely crucial, or you will feel that you are living on a battlefield.

Aspects from the Moon

Moon conjunct ASC: A special emotional sensibility is added to your personality. Even your friends may call you "Mom," because they feel your support and care.

Others are definitely likely to know how you feel, since you may wear your feelings in your expression and demeanor. In many situations, this can be a plus, particularly in creative self-expression. This emphasis can indicate increased moodiness and emotional sensitivity. You are especially sensitive of the cyclical nature of life on the physical plane, including your own physical cycles that manifest through your menstrual phases. By watching yourself and becoming more attentive to your natural cyclical rhythms, you can actually enhance your personal awareness and creativity. These cycles are, of course, much more than physical, and have dimensions that connect to your emotional, mental, and spiritual sensibilities. You may also be seen by others as a nurturing type, and in your relationships you may take on the role of nurturer. Just be sure you remember that you need some tender loving care, too.

Moon semisquare ASC: You may feel a little out of balance emotionally, and can have trouble separating your feelings from your thoughts and actions some of the time. There's absolutely nothing wrong with emotional sensitivity, but when emotional issues get in the way of your self-expression or clear thinking, then you can end up feeling rather frustrated. You may also be too sensitive to criticism from others. The key to working with this energy is learning to pull in your emotional boundaries: don't leave yourself open, and remind yourself that you are safe.

Moon sextile ASC: You have the capability of becoming well-rounded by integrating your feelings about things with the way they actually are. You've probably learned that if you're not comfortable with something, you should probably look into it further or avoid it altogether. You may also be quite adept in relationship matters, since you can be aware of the way others are feeling or reacting in addition to staying in touch with your own feelings about what's going on.

Moon square ASC: There is friction between the way you feel and who you are. The conflict arises when you feel one way about something or someone and do something else because you're concerned about the way that person is likely to respond. This can keep you in a ridiculous trap, since your only option seems to be to ignore your feelings and concentrate on everyone else. Consequently, you may have relationships in which nobody feels trusting or safe. You can turn it all around by becoming more honest with yourself about what you need and want, and realizing that you do not have to take care of everyone else's feelings in order to be happy. Learning not to resent yourself and your needs is an excellent beginning.

Moon trine ASC: You can have good feelings about yourself and your needs. This translates into a projection of confidence, and others may trust you more readily.

Your awareness of your own needs makes it easier to create a sense of safety and security in the world, and your guidance and support of others can help them accomplish similar goals. You may also find it easier to embrace your womanliness—the power of being a woman looks great on you!

Moon quincunx ASC: You may feel that you are always a little out of step, but you eventually catch up if you're concentrating! Your feelings can also catch you off-guard, particularly if you've tried to repress or ignore them. This discomfort with yourself can radiate an undercurrent of anxiety, unless you make an attempt to stay more personally connected with your inner nature.

Moon opposition ASC : You have conflicts between what you need for yourself and what others demand or need from you. You may also place too much emphasis on living your life based on taking care of others, and may feel emotionally drained as a result. Part of the undercurrent of this energy comes from wanting to be connected or needing a partner. This is perfectly okay as long as you create relationships in which your needs and desires count, too, but watch for a tendency for things to get one-sided, and remember to give yourself ample opportunities to fulfill your own needs.

Aspects from Mercury

Mercury conjunct ASC: Others will always see you as a communicator. You could be in the grocery store minding your own business and someone is likely to ask you a question—and generally, you know the answers! Your personality is outgoing, and may even be somewhat mischievous. Sharing your ideas is natural and easy, and you may be quite talkative. To enhance your communication abilities, concentrate on becoming an exceptional listener, too.

Mercury semisquare ASC: You may not display full confidence or trust in your own intellectual abilities. One of the best ways to deal with this dilemma is to develop your communication skills more fully and effectively. You may even find it helpful to take a few risks by entering into conversations with people you may not know very well. Challenge your mind by reading and studying material that is outside your everyday interests in order to expand your thinking. Most of all, make an effort to listen carefully or think things through before you automatically react to them.

Mercury sextile ASC: Your intellectual or communicative abilities may shine through in a positive manner. You may feel quite at ease in social situations, and have the ability to make others feel comfortable, too. This can be developed as a positive skill that is useful in every dimension of your life—from boardroom to bedroom.

Mercury square ASC: You may need to work harder to develop an easy presentation of yourself that others understand. You may mistrust your own abilities, and that mistrust can be projected as arrogance, but it can also be seen as incompetence if you're undermining yourself in some way. Certainly your interest and curiosity are strong, but you may have experienced frustrating situations when you were younger that tested your intellectual abilities in a harsh way and still undermine your self-confidence. By concentrating on your strengths and developing the areas of your communication that you feel are weak you can gain greater self-confidence and poise.

Mercury trine ASC: You may find it easy to express yourself and your ideas. This quality can be seen in social situations. You're a natural at breaking the ice in a conversation, and may also be highly diplomatic. You enjoy contact with others, and may be the quintessential networker.

Mercury quincunx ASC: You may have the embarrassing tendency to put your foot in your mouth! Speaking before you think can get you into hot water, but you are just as adept at dealing with these uncomfortable situations as you are at getting into them! You can benefit from learning to work effectively with others, regardless of their status on the totem pole of life.

Mercury opposition ASC: You may love a good debate. Now that does not mean that you necessarily disagree with everyone—just that you enjoy playing devil's advocate some of the time. You may be an especially good counselor, and can objectify things quite nicely for others. The trouble is that you cannot be quite as objective with yourself. Your tendency to compare yourself with others can be your downfall. Learn to appreciate yourself for who you are and for what you know.

Aspects from Venus

Venus conjunct ASC: A sense of style and grace is added to your personality and self-projection. Others may find you attractive, especially if you've learned to enhance your best attributes. You may be physically attractive, but are also capable of allowing your inner beauty to shine through, which compliments you in a very positive way. Your love of beauty and desire for harmony are high priorities, but you must be careful to avoid becoming too self-serving, expecting that just because you find something valuable, you must necessarily have it.

Venus semisquare ASC: You may feel some frustration between having what you want and dealing with the cost. Cost, of course, can be in the form of time, energy, or money. When you take a good look at your discontent, it may be that you are simply dissatisfied because you've been judging yourself according to values that really do not fit who you are. Learning to accept and fully embrace yourself is the key to softening those rough edges.

Venus sextile ASC: You may feel a greater sense of ease and self-acceptance. Your easy grace and charm are directly related to your sense of self-worth. Your energy and vitality radiate an inner beauty that has a direct effect upon the way others see you, and you may love the experience of creating your self-image. You have a good sense of color and style, and may enjoy wearing beautiful clothes and jewelry. You can be a bit self-indulgent and need to set reasonable limits—especially in the realm of sweets, which can be your downfall.

Venus square ASC: You may continually underestimate your worth or value as a person. You may have fallen victim to the idea that your appearance is the only key to your beauty, and whether or not you think you are physically attractive, you may never be quite satisfied with the way you look. On a deeper level, you may be dealing with a sense of inadequacy that stems from a feeling that you are not lovable. Being lovable begins with the way you feel about yourself, and by becoming more accepting and loving toward yourself, you nurture the true essence of love, which resides at the core of your inner self. You may also struggle with the experience of putting yourself at risk or putting forth effort in order to achieve the realization of your desires. You may find that you actually appreciate something more if you attain it through your own efforts than if it were simply given to you.

Venus trine ASC: You have a strong base of inner strength that is the result of a positive self-image. You may also find it easy and natural to support and compliment others, since your own self-worth may not be in jeopardy from such demons as jealousy. Although you may not like highly competitive situations, you're usually capable of rising to the occasion when you do need to prove yourself. Your sense of artistry and eye for refinement are always noticeable, and you may choose to develop your talents as part of your life path, but you may also need to be on the alert for tendencies toward laziness and self-indulgence. Just loving the best things in life is sometimes not enough to have them all the time!

Venus quincunx ASC: You have a tendency to overcompensate in order to gain acceptance. You may try too hard to please, and may even alienate those who would be supportive if you carry this behavior to the extreme. Gaining a sense of positive self-esteem is not always easy, but it does have an easy beginning. Ask yourself whether or not you would value or accept certain behaviors or attitudes unless they were "important" to achieve recognition by someone you deem valuable or important. Your real value lies not in what others think of you, but in how you feel about yourself. The adjustments you need to make may be as simple as determining what you need and want from your life, but when you start to think about it, you realize that this is not as easy as it sounds—after all, what would somebody else think? Oops . . . there's that trap!

Venus opposition ASC: You may be blessed with many social graces. You're quite comfortable around people, and may enjoy time spent with companions. Your determination to gain acceptance and improve your status in life is strong, and you may use your social contacts to reach those positions. Of course, that's how it's done in life, but you do need to watch a tendency to use people just because of their status. Developing relationships from a purely honest perspective is quite possible for you, since you appreciate what others have to offer, but you must also learn to appreciate what you bring to any situation, as well.

Aspects from Mars

Mars conjunct ASC: You are driven to accomplish what you set out to do. You're likely to be seen as active and energetic, and you are also unlikely to back down from a challenge. In order to achieve greater harmony with others in the world, you may need to pay more attention to the way others respond to you, your actions, and attitudes. You can be abrasive, or others may think you're pushy, even though that may not be your intent. Assertiveness is different from aggression, and you may be much happier when you feel confident in your assertive abilities. Driving yourself to the point of exhaustion is a temptation with this placement, since you may not know when and where to stop.

Mars semisquare ASC: You may rarely seem to stop, and can feel restless when you do. This restless quality can be filtered through different attitudes, and when you're unhappy with something, your agitation or frustration are easily noticed. You may say or do things that prove to be irritating to others, and you may draw others to you who are angry or frustrated themselves. To dissipate the potential hostility that can be present with this influence, it is crucial that you deal with your anger when it arises, and that you have ample opportunities to release any tension you feel.

Mars sextile ASC: You may be a hard worker, and are likely to be in continual motion. You're happiest when you are in active pursuit of something, and your energetic attitudes can frustrate those who always want to keep things quiet. Channeling some of this energy into fitness is a good option, since you may become emotionally agitated and restless if you fall into a sedentary lifestyle.

Mars square ASC: You have a strong tendency to do or say things that put others on the defensive. In a debate or an athletic event, this can be useful, but in relationship with others the same energy can be devastating unless you are aware of it. You may project anger more readily than you show tenderness, although other factors in your chart may offset this somewhat. Asserting yourself in a positive manner is quite different from boisterous or crude behavior, and you've probably seen the evidence of these differences in various circumstances. Your need to be seen as a powerful woman drives many of your actions, and finding positive ways to achieve this aim can help you redirect your desires.

Mars trine ASC: You can develop positive ways to assert yourself and achieve the realization of your desires. You may feel quite comfortable in competitive situations, and are likely to have a good ability to relate to men. Your physical vitality may be strong, and you may feel that you have a good energy reserve that can be further enhanced by staying physically fit and active. In positions of leadership, you're likely to take an equally active part with those who follow your direction.

Mars quincunx ASC: You may approach life somewhat unevenly. At times, you may be able to drive with great determination toward achieving your goals. At other times, you may lose interest or energy before you get there. These bursts of energy can frustrate you, but can also be difficult for others to understand. Instead of getting into a situation without thinking, try to take the time to assess it before you leap (this is especially true of relationships!). Also become clear of what you expect from yourself, since you can both overrate and underestimate your abilities. You love challenges, but need to choose those that will produce gratifying results.

Mars opposition ASC: A competitive edge is added to your personality. You're not likely to walk away from a challenge, although learning when to stand and fight, when to assert yourself, and when to let the other person take their shots is one of your more critical lessons in life. To avoid being seen as abrasive, remain alert to the way others are responding, and think before you act or simply react! If you are not aware of your own need for power, you may attract others who are power-hungry.

You're likely to resent them, or to feel hurt by their attitudes, until you learn healthy ways to take charge of your own life.

Aspects from Jupiter

Jupiter conjunct ASC: You are a natural promoter. When you believe in something, you're likely to let everyone know, and your enthusiasm can inspire others to follow your lead. Others cannot help but see your optimism and faith in the future. You can also be somewhat self-indulgent, and need to watch a tendency to think that you should have absolutely everything you want. This can be especially problematic in the weight-gain department, since knowing when to say "no" is not always easy for you. Physiologically, your body may expand much easier than it contracts!

Jupiter semisquare ASC: You are possessed with a powerful sense of optimism, but have a tendency to expect too much from yourself and others some of the time. Since you may prefer to think of life as a series of opportunities to grow, you may be more interested in pursuing new directions than continuing to develop an existing situation. Others can be frustrated if you've promised too much, or if you fail to follow through on your obligations. Explore your underlying motivations before you agree to take on another task.

Jupiter sextile ASC: Your positive attitudes can be contagious. You're a natural in situations that call for vision and insight into possibility, and may have great faith in the natural order of things. As a teacher, you can inspire others to pursue their dreams. As a partner or friend, your support and understanding can be the difference between success and failure. Your self-confidence can get you through circumstances that others would find daunting.

Jupiter square ASC: Your eternal optimism can get you into trouble. Certainly a positive attitude can be a magical elixir in creating what you want from life, but your expectations can definitely surge out of proportion with possibility some of the time. If you are unsure of yourself, you may overstate a situation just so you feel better, and then realize that you're caught in a rather prickly circumstance. In order to create the most honest and positive relationships, you need to learn to accept yourself first, and then to strive toward achieving those aims that are so delicious. Otherwise, you will run into problems with trust, which can be another very convoluted tale.

Jupiter trine ASC: Your jovial attitude can win a lot of friends. You prefer to laugh, and can be counted on to see the optimism in most situations. By developing your sense of humor, you'll go further toward achieving your personal aims. You may also enjoy circumstances that give you a chance to inspire others, and you can be an excellent promoter.

Jupiter quincunx ASC: Your optimism and generosity shine through in your personality. But you may be somewhat reckless with your promises, and attract others who are much the same. Taking responsibility for yourself can be a bit of a problem, especially when you're in over your head and just barely treading water. Before you leap into that ocean of frustration, consider changing the manner in which you offer yourself or your services.

Jupiter opposition ASC: You may have difficulty setting limits, and can be entirely too scattered. The positive quality of this placement involves your ability to attract situations that allow you to reach beyond your limitations, but in order to succeed, you may have to limit the number of options you're pursuing at one time! Relationships with others can be a double-edged sword as well, because you may gain great benefits through your association with a partner, but may not develop personal confidence in your abilities as an individual. Try to give yourself the same kind of enthusiastic support you offer to others, and notice the difference!

Aspects from Saturn

Saturn conjunct ASC: This aspect can be especially powerful. You may project a conservative, stable energy, and can be practical in your approach to life. Taking responsibility for yourself seems reasonable and natural, although you may sometimes get tired of feeling that you are the only grown-up among a crowd of perpetual children. Yet the power of self-control has been evident to you throughout your life, and you would much prefer to have control than to have others control you! Sometimes you may take yourself a bit too seriously, so remember to keep your sense of humor on call to avoid getting stuck in an attitude of depression or defeat when times are difficult.

Saturn semisquare ASC: Your pressing need to keep yourself (and everything else) in line can become a little frustrating. You may find it difficult to get away from the feeling that you are always being judged or criticized, and may even choose situations, like relationships, that constantly test you. You can alienate others if you're trying to be too much in control, or if you look for a scapegoat when you need to take responsibility.

Saturn sextile ASC: You can project a strong no-nonsense attitude, and may be the first person who comes to mind when someone is searching for a responsible manager or leader. Your practicality may even be expressed in the way you dress, although you're probably most comfortable in conservative attire. You appreciate order and consistency, and function best when you have your priorities clearly outlined and when your time is reasonably structured. Expecting everyone else to adhere to your standards or schedule may be asking a lot, so try to apply your sense of realism to your assessment of other people, too.

Saturn square ASC: You can be somewhat overbearing with your attitudes toward life. It's easier for you to see what is wrong than to see what is right, and you can be especially negative when you're facing a difficult challenge. When you step back and look at yourself, you may realize that a part of you actually likes challenges. It's the scrutiny and criticism from those who seem to deride your worth that hurts. By learning to accept both your strengths and limitations, you can make choices that will allow you to be involved with challenges that lead to growth and stability, instead of challenges that undermine your sense of self. You may cultivate more effective ways to separate your responsibilities for yourself from your responsibilities for others. Then, you can more easily step away from the guilt that arises when you are not carrying burdens that actually do not belong to you!

Saturn trine ASC: This aspect gives you a quality of positive responsibility and allows you to develop a positive sense of priorities. Although you may be alone in carrying some burdens, you can also be an effective manager, teacher, and guide. Your sense of self-respect engenders an attitude of respect from others. You can also be positively realistic, accepting situations that require you to take action or responsibility without becoming excessively depressed. Aging may not be a difficult prospect for you, and you may be able to grow stronger as you grow older. The status, respect, and self-reliability that come with maturity are valuable commodities to you.

Saturn quincunx ASC: You may struggle with the unnecessary burdens of guilt and depression, especially when you feel overwhelmed by a difficult challenge or situation. You may feel old before your time, and can be fearful of the process of growing older. Dealing with time and age can actually provide an awakening for you because these processes help you maintain a realistic assessment of what is happening. The workings of time do not have to be a mystery, but can instead become your ally. The answer is quite simple: learn to be in the moment of *now*. Hanging on to the burdens of the past, or fearing prospects of the future, can cripple your ability to live joyfully.

Saturn opposition ASC: Your standards are quite high. You may judge yourself by the opinions of others, or by your association with particular people, instead of accepting yourself for your personal strengths and limitations. Certainly you can rise above your limitations, but not by expecting someone else to carry you there! If you try to live your life through someone else, your unhappiness can become immeasurable because you have failed to be responsible to your own needs. You may also feel that your only choices in life result from answering the demands of others, and if you are in circumstances that require you to support or care for others, can grow to resent their dependence on you. Listening to your inner self and learning to accept positive ways to take responsibility for yourself will be personally empowering for you.

Aspects from Uranus

Uranus conjunct ASC: A definite sparkle exudes from your personality. Your unique sense of style can be seen in your manner of dress, which reflects your independence and autonomy. You're not interested in being a cookie-cutter image of anyone, and may also resent stepping into roles that require you to act or behave in a particular manner. In relationships, you need plenty of room to be yourself, and will appreciate a partner who gives you plenty of room to exercise your autonomy. You may attract irresponsible people into your life, but you can accept their individuality, even though they might not always be good for you. Other people may rely on your intuitive insights, and as you mature, you may realize that this is the quality that provides the circuitry for your personality.

Uranus semisquare ASC: You can be rebellious and inconsistent, but no one will ever accuse you of being boring! Sometimes, you may do certain things, dress in a particular manner, or take action just because you want to see the effect it can have. However, this can become destructive, especially if your rebellious attitudes negatively affect the lives or circumstances of others. Although your intention may not be destructive, you do not like restraint and are not comfortable in situations that dictate your every thought and action. Responsible rebellion is sometimes difficult to gauge, but you have the capability of developing a sense of timing that can allow you to escape repression without destroying the foundation of your life.

Uranus sextile ASC: A flair of independence and autonomy is added to your personality. You can feel quite comfortable letting your uniqueness shine through in your mannerisms, dress, and attitudes, and have a knack for doing things that can amaze and intrigue others. It's almost as though your sense of rhythm with the natural flow is finely tuned. Although you may not always be easy to accept, particularly by those who want everything to be predictable and traditional, you can take an alternative path and may be able to make it work quite nicely.

Uranus square ASC: You can be quite rebellious, and certainly have little interest in trying to be like everybody else. Granted, there are times you may feel rather alone, but you'll take freedom any day before you'll join the herd. You may not like playing the traditional roles that have been set forth for women, and may have some conflict about this since you may like the idea of home and family, but do not want to be tied to being the only caretaker. Other people can be a bit uncomfortable with some of your eccentricities (or what they perceive as different), simply because you challenge them to break out of their ruts. In order to satisfy your own internal conflict, you may need to develop an unusual occupation, or may be well-suited to working in fields that give you great amounts of freedom. You may also be more comfortable living away from your roots.

Uranus trine ASC: You can integrate your individuality and autonomy into your life in such a way that allows you to fit into society in a comfortable manner. Your uniqueness may be your trademark, and your ability to step into new situations is enhanced with this aspect. Your independent spirit is definitely present through your personality expression, but instead of trying to overturn the status quo, you may be able to inspire or initiate changes that will definitely alter it. You may be quite comfortable playing several roles, although you are likely to prefer freedom of expression in each of them.

Uranus quincunx ASC: You may find it difficult to stay the same. Your life can be filled with a series of changes, and you're likely to reflect these changes in your manner of dress, hair styles (including color), and self-image. In most instances, you're seeking to show your individuality, and some of your choices will definitely fare better than others! (This aspect does not necessarily confer good taste!) Your restlessness can make it difficult to focus for long periods of time, and you may prefer to keep your options open in your relationships and in your career. Physically, your nervous system can be highly charged, and you may need to adopt positive habits that help to calm your nervous system in order to function at your highest capacity. Your attitudes or eccentricities can sometimes be difficult for others to handle, particularly if they fly in the face of convention. Yet you do have choices about the way you create the space to be yourself. It's not necessary to cause a revolution in order to have things the way you want them.

Uranus opposition ASC: A powerful element of surprise is added to your self-projection. Others may never know what to expect from you, except that change is always a possibility. Even if you are married and playing the role of mother, you are not likely to do things in a traditional manner. You're the woman who can adopt a lifestyle that is definitely an alternative to the norm. But you may also resist making commitments, and can attract others who are just as stubbornly independent as yourself. If you wonder why the man (or woman) you love is not available, ask yourself if you really want to be strongly committed or emotionally available. You need ample room to experiment with your identity, to be free to express yourself. A partnership that supports your personal growth will work beautifully, but a situation that stifles your growth and independence will only spawn your rebellion.

Aspects from Neptune

Neptune conjunct ASC: You may be especially sensitive to your environment and the people within it. Your psychic abilities are intensified through this energy, and your impressions about things may be exceptionally clear. This is a particularly excellent connection if you work in the arts or theater, and can be quite helpful in any healing or counseling work. Your ability to adapt to your surroundings, including adapting to the mood of other people, adds a chameleon-like quality to your personality. The primary problem with this placement involves your ability to be seen, or to be seen as you wish to be. Others can project their feelings on you quite readily, and you may respond in such a way as to amplify their projection. Sometimes too, you may feel like the invisible woman. Your vigilance in maintaining your personal boundaries must always be strong, or you may fall into the role of the victim or martyr.

Neptune semisquare ASC: Increased sensitivity and impressionability are added to your personality. You may feel uncertain about your appearance or the way others see you, and can present an image that seems insecure or that reflects your uncertainty about yourself. It's easy to give too much credence to what others think instead of becoming more adept in your connection to yourself and trusting the way you feel about yourself. If your tendency is to try to cover up your identity by using clothes, hair color, or make-up to define who you are, you may glance in the mirror one day and wonder who that is staring back at you. Defining your image can be fun, and there's no reason not to enjoy it, but shaping your self image according to ideals that do not relate to your true sense of self can be emotionally devastating.

Neptune sextile ASC: You may have a very powerful mystical quality, and most people will find you quite charming. Your sensitivity toward others may be marked, and you may be quite adept in your perceptive abilities. This is an excellent energy connection if you are involved in the arts in any way, and you may be especially well-suited to the performing arts. You can be mesmerizing, and may be quite capable of changing your image to suit a variety of circumstances.

Neptune square ASC: A high level of impressionability is added to your personality. Although you can be rather charming, and may have strong psychic tendencies, you may not always be quite clear about your perceptions or your projection of yourself. You may have learned coping mechanisms as a young girl that taught you to bend your will to that of others, or you may have been victimized by others who were abusive or who ignored your needs to be yourself. Now that you are a woman, you may find that you get into situations in which you feel uncomfortable unless you're scrambling to adapt to someone else's needs. This can lead to a high level of co-dependency unless you learn to create positive emotional boundaries between yourself and others. Or, if you cannot deal with the realities of life, you may even find that you live to escape, and can fall into addictive behaviors. Your salvation resides in locating the power and solace of your inner self—embracing the Goddess within. This divine quality has its spark within you, and is the key to unleashing your powerful creativity, imagination, and spirituality.

Neptune trine ASC: An imaginative and mystical quality is added to your personality. Your artistic nature can be expressed in many ways, and you may become quite adept at developing your talents and sensibilities. Psychic abilities often accompany this aspect, and you may have a special sensitivity to your environment. You'll also find that you're more comfortable in surroundings that are serene, and may enjoy being surrounded by beautiful music.

Neptune quincunx ASC: You need to pay special attention to your responses to the people and the world around you. You may find it difficult to maintain your personal boundaries and can be too sensitive to the energies of others. Your inclination to reach out with compassion can be positive, but you can also be gullible, and unscrupulous individuals can take advantage of your need to be helpful. Learning to use your psychic sensitivities in tandem with your rational thoughts, and finding ways to stay reasonably grounded, you can become more adept at avoiding getting into abusive, addictive, or co-dependent situations. Pay particular attention to your physical health, since you may be overly sensitive to environmental pollution, medications, or toxic circumstances.

Neptune opposition ASC: You are especially sensitive to other people and their energy. You may even find that becoming involved in fulfilling the needs of others is easier than acknowledging your own needs. Psychologically, this aspect represents a strong tendency toward co-dependency, and also indicates the potential for developing addictive patterns in relationships. Your perceptions of others can be somewhat confusing, since you can look inside a person and see their potential, but you may not be able to see their human weaknesses or deceptive tendencies! It's easy to over-idealize, and then, when reality sets in, you tend to distrust yourself and can become disillusioned with your own judgment. Your compassion and desire to help are good things; you simply need to discover the person residing deep within yourself, and must learn to distinguish between your feelings and the needs and emotions of others. You may be so sensitive that another's emotions and needs feel like your own, but as you develop a powerful attunement to your inner self, you will easily distinguish your own melody from the song of another.

Aspects from Pluto

Pluto conjunct ASC: A powerful intensity is added to your personality. You can be both enigmatic and intimidating, and can project powerful charisma. Your perceptions about people can be quite keen, and you may have a sharp eye for details in behavior, manner, and attitude that others easily miss. The healing quality of your energy can have a powerful transformational effect in the lives of others, and you may be walking the path of the medicine woman. You're not likely to allow others to take advantage of you, but you can be intimidated by guilt, so anyone who knows your "guilt buttons" may have a bit of power over you. Your best protection is to discover those hidden issues and deal with them so that you are free of them, once and for all.

Pluto semisquare ASC: A quality of mystery and intrigue is added to your personality. You may wonder sometimes why trust is an issue in relationships, and it could be easily tied to the fact that you are struggling with the idea of giving up your power. When you realize that you do not have to relinquish your personal power in order to be close in a relationship, it might be easier for you to let down your shields a bit. Until then, you're likely to project a barrier between yourself and the world. You may carry old shame or resentments from past trauma as part of this barrier, and these feelings can also keep you from experiencing a true acceptance of yourself. You have the capacity to become whole, and to feel the transformational healing power that arises from annihilating the pain of the past and being reborn. You deserve more than mere survival, and you need to convince yourself that you can experience a full and rewarding life. Part of this may come from working with others in some healing capacity. But some of it arises from simply allowing yourself to enjoy the rewards of being alive.

Pluto sextile ASC: Your perceptual awareness and keen insights add a sense of command and power to your personality. If you follow a life path that involves healing or counseling work, you may realize your capacity for reaching into the depths of others and helping them reclaim their power. This role can also be carried out at home, or in the workplace in other capacities. Your ability to regenerate your own body and spirit is powerful, and even if you are ill, you may have energy reserves that allow you to heal more quickly than the norm. You can feel the power of being a woman and are capable of projecting that power in a positive sense that does not intimidate or threaten others. If others are threatened by you, it may be because they know you can sense their insecurity!

Pluto square ASC: An intimidating edge is added to your personality. You are quite likely to operate from a hidden agenda, and even though you may not show your hand, others can feel that there's something going on beneath the surface. You can become obsessed with doing things in a particular way, and can also be quite compulsive in these behaviors. You may have issues about control and power, some of which may be the results of difficulties early in your life. However, you also have the capacity to heal the wounds you experienced, although your emotional attachments to them can make it difficult. Vengeful attitudes sap your own power and energy, and alienate others. If you feel that your path is blocked, or has been blocked, by others who have been in control of your life, your work involves breaking away from those old entanglements and moving ahead. This is much easier said than done, but there are many ways to accomplish the task and break the patterns so that you can finally feel free.

Pluto trine ASC: An aura of intrigue is added to your self-projection. Your self-assurance can be the result of your easy connection to your inner self, and also arises from your ability to read between the lines and see what's actually happening. This energy connection can be further developed through your study of psychology and human behavior, although you may be quite a natural at understanding human nature in the first place. You may also have a dogged persistence when you're on the trail of pursuit—whether you're pursuing a relationship, an idea, or a goal.

Pluto quincunx ASC: You may go out of the way to protect your vulnerabilities. Sometimes, this sense of vulnerability is only a projection that results from an unresolved emotional issue. But many times, the vulnerability arises when you are in an unfamiliar situation or around people who are intimidating. You can react defensively, which adds to the problem, but you can also respond by altering your attitudes to reflect confidence, or at least curiosity. Masking your deeper feelings works in some situations, but can lead others to mistrust you. To change these circumstances, begin to develop your awareness so that you are more confident about what is happening. Allow yourself to probe into unknown territory (like a new relationship) without worrying about outcome—just be in the moment. You are very perceptive, but may not trust those perceptions. Listen, watch, and feel: you always know the truth.

Pluto opposition ASC: You have a real potential for power struggles in relationships. You may not trust the entire process of marriage, especially if it seems to mean that your husband gets the power and you get the laundry—or, in today's world, that you get to work and do the chores while your partner plays golf on the weekends, but you can also be the one who's guilty of wrongfully using your own power, so do be honest before you play the blame game. In most cases, this aspect symbolizes an intense desire to break away from your old life and establish a new order. This can be done without bloodshed and heartache, but only if you're dealing with the issues in a way that allows you to become whole.

The Role of Your Moon in Self-Projection

There are many different facets of the Moon in your chart, and in this book we'll explore many of them. When it comes to identity, your Moon speaks volumes about who you are at the deepest level: the soul of your being. This quality permeates your personality. It is the part of you others "feel." When you stop to reflect, you may also hear your Moon in your words, see her influence in your mannerisms, and show her qualities in your attitudes.

Moon in Aries: Your Aries Moon reflects an attitude of independent thinking and a need for autonomy. Your real self is striving to achieve a true sense of individual identity. The courage that resides deep within your soul helps you get through all sorts of dilemmas and difficulties, although you may resent anything that holds you back or ties you down. You are the Warrior Woman, and have the capacity to meet life on your own terms. You will fight for what you love, and enjoy a life with ample opportunities to experience true passion.

Moon in Taurus: Your Taurus Moon provides a quality of stability and sense of focus. Your real self residing at the core your being is driven to attain a strong sense of security, and your resistance to letting go results from needing to maintain that security base. You are the Earth Mother, and your love for things rich in texture and form is connected to your attunement to the earth itself. Inner strength and calm allow you to face even the toughest challenges, but also provide your solace when you need a break from the everyday grind.

Moon in Gemini: Your Gemini Moon adds a quality of curiosity to your personality. Your real self is driven by a need to experience a wide variety of situations, to explore the world of ideas, and to connect to others through your mind. You are the ever-curious girl, regardless of your age: your mental attitudes can be forever young. Needing plenty of room to try out your diverse interests, you may be difficult to pin down.

Moon in Cancer: Your Cancer Moon radiates a quality of nurturing support to your personality. When you take someone under your wing, they know that you're there for them, but you can be guarded about showing your feelings, since you also feel vulnerable and may be afraid of losing someone or something you love. Once you allow yourself to reach the awareness that everything changes, the fear of loss can transform into an acceptance and support of the true process of growth. It is that experience that feeds your soul and adds grace to your life.

Moon in Leo: Your Leo Moon enhances your personal presence, and you can radiate an exceptional warmth and passion. You love a life filled with rich experiences, and seek out people and situations that stimulate an opening of your heart. Driven by the desire to be recognized, you may also need some time in the spotlight, and will fare best in relationships that allow you to have your moment in the sun. Your loyalty is a matter of pride for you, and it can be difficult for you to let go when faced with change.

Moon in Virgo: Your Virgo Moon strengthens your sense of discrimination and underscores your need for perfection. The problem can be the yardstick you use to measure that perfection, and you may be frustrated with your own humanity and vulnerabilities as a result. You may be sensitive to criticism, but can also be highly critical of yourself and others as a part of this desire to have your life exactly as you feel it should be. By directing your need to make improvements toward positive ends, you'll feel much happier with yourself and with others. That means you may have to let go of the idea that everyone (including yourself) and everything will meet your high standards all of the time.

Moon in Libra: Your Libra Moon is the part of you that feels most alive when you share those special moments in your life with a partner or companion. Somehow, life is better when you have a true, balanced, working partnership, but getting to that point can be a bumpy road. This drive actually stems from the duality that exists within yourself. Your inner self needs as much recognition and support as the part of you that exists in, and is validated by, the outside world. Herein lies your true partnership, and from this point, a relationship with someone else can become a reasonable reality.

Moon in Scorpio: With your Moon in Scorpio, you have a sixth sense about everyone and everything. Your hunger to experience life at its deepest levels adds an intensity to your personality that radiates from the core of your being. You are a healer, a magician with the ability to create and act as a catalyst for change. You may be capable of drawing energy from many sources to create true transformation, but before this is possible you must learn to heal yourself, to let go of the pain you have carried, and to know what it is like to be reborn.

Moon in Sagittarius: Your Sagittarius Moon reflects a quality of wisdom, adventure, and spirituality. Despite all the outside distractions, your real self is striving to achieve a sense of truth, honesty, and integrity. Deep within yourself, you are the Wise Woman, and will open most gracefully to those individuals and circumstances that allow you to express and develop this part of yourself. To do this you need one thing above all else: true freedom. It's easier said than done!

Moon in Capricorn: Your Capricorn Moon is that part of you that stands on solid ground when everything around you is slipping or changing. You can move with change. In fact, you can even initiate changes by continuing your climb. You may be exceptionally ambitious, and need goals in order to maintain your focus. Taking charge is easy for you, but your reluctance to relinquish control can be your downfall. When you sense that things are out of harmony, try to get back to nature—or at least stand on the cool grass. Connecting to the earth is connecting to yourself.

Moon in Aquarius: Your Aquarius Moon stimulates your need to know as much as possible. Because of this, others may see you as an intellectual sort, whether you think of yourself in this manner or not. At the core of your being, you know that you are pure consciousness, and it is that feeling that drives you and keeps you alive. You can feel that part of you that is connected to the whole of humanity, but you may not like what you see when you look at people, since humans are not always humanitarian. Because of this connection, you may sense that your life is not entirely your own, that somehow, you're here to make a difference. And so you are.

Moon in Pisces: Your Moon in Pisces feels everything—the joy of a child petting a puppy, the thrill of a ballet dancer in a perfect spin, and the despair of the lonely and abandoned street person. It's difficult for you to turn off your feelings because they tell you so much, but sometimes you would just love to escape their intensity. To accomplish this, you can retreat into your creativity and imagination, but you can also lose yourself in addictive behaviors. Developing your compassion for others is wonderful, but so, too, is developing a real compassion for yourself and your spiritual essence. By integrating your spirituality into your everyday life, you become whole. Somehow, in the process, the world becomes a much more comfortable place.

～

CHAPTER THREE

UNDERSTANDING YOUR INNER FEMININE SELF

lthough the temptation is to think that just because you are a woman you are in touch with your inner feminine self, this is a much more complicated task than it appears to be! First of all, the model for the true power of femininity has been lost over recent history and is now becoming re-energized. Recovering this power is a personal task for each woman, and learning to use feminine power constructively on a personal and collective level is another story. This process is the cradle of self-healing, and provides the essence of your personal security. It can also forge the path to a profound healing within our society as we accept our strengths and recognize the differences men and women face in becoming whole individuals.

The primary energies traditionally associated with your inner feminine self are the Moon and Venus, but Neptune and Pluto are also significant in your experience and expression of this part of your psyche.

The Heart of Your Feminine Psyche: Your Moon

The Moon is the energy that filters through your subconscious self, and it tells the story of your connection to the part of you that provides nurturing, support, care, and comfort. The person who reflects the model for your Moon energy is usually your mother, and you see her through the lens of your own emotional matrix, signified by the Moon. Sometimes when you learn about your Moon, you may think that these descriptions define your mother, but in reality what they define is what you really needed from your mother. This is, in essence, your projection of your Moon onto your mother. In many cases, a woman's real mother does not seem to actually own the qualities of her Moon, and therein may lie some of the frustrations between mother and daughter! As you mature, you learn to send this energy into the world, but to be truly effective, you must first own this energy and know how to use it to care for yourself.

Moon in Aries: Your Aries Moon stimulates a powerful inner drive to establish your autonomy and independence. Your feminist attitudes result from your independent way of thinking, and may forge new frontiers to advance your position as a woman in the world. Passion is your life fuel, and you need people, situations, and opportunities to feel the rush of energy that arises when you are carried away by passionate desire. You can be quite headstrong when you want something, or someone, and definitely have your wiles. Even though you may have been taught to think of others and their needs first, your need to be in the lead and first on the list is there all the while, and it is definitely okay to feel that way, if you deal with that need honestly. Taking a back seat while a husband achieves his aims and you settle for just a "job" or staying home (when you don't want to) could lead to trouble if you really want to develop a strong career of your own. Yet your support of another can be quite powerful when you feel that you are also getting what you want out of the situation, and you must remember that the choice is yours.

Some type of challenge keeps you alive. Whether you choose a competitive career, participate in your favorite sports or recreation, initiate all the family outings, get involved in politics, or take the lead in community activities—your energy, effort, and excitement can be inspirational and contagious. If you feel penned in, ignored, abused, or excessively limited, you may also be challenged internally by your own anger at not having a chance to prove yourself. This anger can undermine your strength if it is not channeled into something productive. Men may have difficulty dealing with your independence, and even though you may be tempted to prove yourself according to the masculine rules of the game, as a woman, you have some attributes that a man simply cannot employ! Instead of feeling that the game of life is always about winning and losing, try to re-focus on the idea of creating or not creating, and look for some healthy outlets that allow you to win a few and lose a few. You'll always be playing, and may as well enjoy the game according to rules that allow everyone to benefit.

Moon in Taurus: With your Moon in Taurus, you are a woman of substance. Your deep need to feel safe and stabilized may be seen through the way you go about creating your own safe haven in the world. You may love the embrace of your favorite chair, and can feel invigorated when you get your hands in the earth. Even though other people may look to you for a feeling of shelter, you are not likely to resent it, since you feel much more alive when you are surrounded by the people and things you love. The undercurrent of your energy is quite feminine, and your sensuality radiates in everything you do. Taking in love, beauty, and the vital essence of life is easy for you, and when you love someone or something, you are not likely to change your feelings, regardless of what happens over the passage of time.

If you have children, they may sense that you will always be there, unwavering in your support. Lovers, partners, and friends can experience the same security, and you need consistent support from them, too, even though you might deny it! Despite the fact that much of your life is dedicated to producing growth-oriented options for yourself and others, the part of growth that means letting go is not easy for you, and dealing with change is not easy, since you hate the thought of losing anything that has become a part of your life. You may suffer great pain following separation and loss, and may feel quite diminished if love goes wrong. By using your power of perseverance to sustain you, you can accomplish the realization of many hopes and dreams, and experience healing and renewal.

Moon in Gemini: Through your Gemini Moon, your connection to the feminine aspect of yourself arises first through your mind. Mental stimulation keeps your soul alive, and as long as you are learning and feel that you are exposed to a wide variety of options, your sense of wholeness remains intact. Your approach to life may seem out of the ordinary to those who expect stale repetition, since the variation in life experiences you explore out of a need to see and do as much as possible may seem "unfeminine". In many respects, you may present an androgynous quality, and may feel quite at home in situations or attire that incorporate both masculine and feminine elements.

You may love children, and have a special knack for communicating with young people. After all, you are the eternal child, filled with a sense of wonder and delight, and may find that spirit more alive within the young. But your lighthearted spirit can also be uplifting to anyone who shares a conversation or spends time with you. Because you are easily distracted, you might have difficulty maintaining a regular routine, or may even find it impossible to maintain the same relationship for long. A partner who is as open to new experience and exploration as you are can be perfect, but you have little patience for those who lack curiosity or interest. Your variety of friends, lovers, mates, careers, and homes can lead to a feeling that nothing stays the same for long. Yet you can be consistent when something or someone holds your interest. It's a pretty tall order, but after all, don't you deserve something exceptional?

Moon in Cancer: Through your Cancer Moon, you connect to the essence of the feminine soul. You feel the changes pulsating through life. You know the rhythm of your body. Your soul feels the essential shifts of the cycles that are the heartbeat of life. Providing nurturance is as natural to you as breathing, and you have your own special way of making others feel right at home when they're with you. Your emotional sensibilities can be especially powerful, and you may find yourself describing how you feel when someone asks what you think about something. It might be easier to minister to another's needs than it is to ask for help, since you are usually uncomfortable exposing your vulnerabilities. You adore the feeling of being held in a tender caress, and may long for the security that arises when everyone you adore is there, close to home, safe in the nest.

Your reverence for the sanctity of motherhood, home, and family is a powerful driving force in your life. Sometimes it's easier to pull out all your old memories and stay in the safety of the past than it is to move into new territory. Protecting yourself, and protecting those you love, can lead to a kind of stifled existence if you go too far. Learning to get back to that space that tells you that everything is okay, even if you are in the midst of a challenge or crisis, will give you exceptional peace of mind. Opening the doors just a little to allow those under your care to take a few risks on their own can be especially freeing to all concerned. You might also feel much more satisfied when you get out of your own shell and take the risk of letting go of the past and moving into the bright light of a new day. After all, it's only natural to change, just like the tides—everything flows in and out.

Moon in Leo: Your Leo Moon radiates the kind of warmth that imparts the glow of love to everyone around you. You are a powerful woman, capable of asserting your desires in such a manner that others may find it difficult to refuse your requests. Perfectly suited to the role of family matriarch, you take a strong interest in helping to guide and develop those under your care. Although you can be quite comfortable at home surrounded by those you love and adore, you may also crave greater recognition, and definitely need your time in the spotlight. Never lacking creativity, you have many options for self-expression, and need to adopt a way of life that gives you ample opportunity to develop your talents.

The feeling that life is meant to be savored and enjoyed stimulates your desire to play, and you definitely need ample time for recreation. When entertaining, you pull out all the stops, and can be quite lavish with your generosity. Elaborate situations are not likely to intimidate you, but may, instead, be more like a challenge. You can be self-absorbed and self-indulgent, and need to have friends you can trust who will tell you the truth when you've gone too far, and you need to accept that truth, if it does come your way, as a sign of caring and concern. When you're hurt, your sulking can be just as dramatic as your joy when you're happy. During those times when your possessiveness raises its head, try to be aware of the part of yourself that feels threatened. Since letting go is never easy for you, you may simply be responding to a fear of losing something or someone you love, but forcing your will is not likely to make everything better. Surrendering to the love you feel might, however, make an exceptional difference!

Moon in Virgo: Your Virgo Moon strengthens your sense of connection to your feminine self, and adds a steadiness to your emotions. Your instincts about the best ways to do things are usually right on the mark, which can be a little irritating to those who would take a more haphazard approach. As a woman of discriminating taste, with an eye for quality, you're not likely to settle for anything that falls below your standards—including a mate. The high standards you set for others are nothing compared to the standards you hold for yourself. In fact, you might gain great relief by simply giving yourself a break from time and time and letting your hair down. Otherwise, you can become nagging and hypercritical, just because you are concerned about getting everything done in the best possible manner.

You may have a particularly powerful sense of body awareness, and may go out of your way to maintain your physical health. Eating a natural foods diet that centers on simple nutritional balance may even help you maintain your emotional balance. For you, the mind-body connection is especially crucial, and taking steps to keep your spirit, soul, and body in healthy condition will definitely improve the quality of your life. Although you can accept most physical limitations with a matter-of-fact kind of attitude, you are not likely to appreciate being sick, since you are oriented toward producing something at the end of the day, but you can also adapt when necessary. Striking a few requirements from your list of expectations may have a marvelous healing effect on your life as a whole, and finding a reasonable outlet for your critical sensibilities is necessary to help you maintain your sanity. Developing greater tolerance for yourself and for others is your key to finding greater joy.

Moon in Libra: Your Libra Moon shapes your attitudes of femininity in a very special sense: for you, being a woman is a beautiful experience. You may love the essence of feminine grace, charm, and delicate beauty, and your ability to radiate those qualities can be easily developed. Your ideals are quite high, though, and you may have a sense of impatience with yourself when you fail to meet your own ideals, and can be especially dissatisfied when you feel that someone else is unhappy with you. When external standards become too important, even your own faith in your inner beauty and personal worth begins to wane. Once you've fallen into the trap of trying to please, you can lose your sense of yourself, but you have a gift. You are capable of regaining your balance and getting everything back into perspective, and you are quite capable of standing your own ground and waging battles when necessary.

You may yearn for a partner, someone with whom you can share your life. Feeling like Cinderella, hoping that somewhere there is your dream lover and partner, you may dream that somehow you will be beautiful and lovely enough to have him: the perfect man who will respect your needs and honor your individuality. However, fairy tales can be the source of your greatest pain. There is nothing wrong with wanting a partner, but expecting another to be your salvation can set you up for disappointment! You have the power to change the outcome by changing your focus. Creating your inner partner can be your greatest challenge, and it is not until you have accomplished that aim that you will feel like a whole woman. Deep within your soul, you know that you will never have the perfect partner until you accept yourself as perfect. Oh, yes, that includes embracing your shortcomings, and it includes accepting the human foibles of everyone else you love. Then, and only then, will the beauty, peace, and harmony you hope to find in the world shine through you, and the Universe cannot help but reflect it back to you.

Moon in Scorpio: Through your Scorpio Moon, you hold the kind of feminine power that is purely charismatic. Your sensuality radiates through the way you move, speak, and express yourself. You know the ebb and flow of emotion, and you also feel the intensity of emotions ranging from biting rage to pure ecstasy. With such all-consuming power, you approach life with a fervor that is unrivaled. There's nothing halfway about the way you feel about anyone or anything, although you don't always expose the full measure of those feelings. Your shadow insists upon dancing with your lighter side, and once you've embraced the entirety of your inner being, you have unmatched power. You are definitely a force, and your ability to instigate change reaches into many dimensions of life experience.

As an agent for metamorphosis, you can bring healing where there is pain and suffering. Whether a wounding of the heart and spirit, or a trauma to the body, your touch and support can help bring transformation into the lives of others. Those in your care have an unrelenting ally. Those who have hurt you or someone you love may face an unparalleled vengeance. Sometimes, though, you may hang onto old pain like a trophy, and at some point in your life you may find that carrying your medals around slows you down or impedes your ability to experience the full measure of love and happiness. Although it is more difficult to open to healing energy for yourself, it is necessary to occasionally clear out your emotional closets and release old pain, resentment, and guilt. Guilt is your greatest enemy, not the situations or people who have caused you pain, and love is the key that opens the door to your power.

Moon in Sagittarius: Through your Sagittarius Moon, you yearn to find your sense of home, comfort, and inner peace through developing knowledge. You may hope to experience horizons that reach beyond what you knew as a child. Your mother may have inspired you to reach beyond your limitations, or you may have seen her as a teacher who seemed to have the answers for everything. Even as a young girl, your mind could reach into the possibility of what life was like in other parts of the world, and as you are becoming a whole woman, an interest in other cultures may even stimulate your desire to travel to other lands or to learn different languages.

The real thirst you feel is to know Truth. Your search for truth may be found through your dedication to building a strong spiritual foundation in your life, but you may also find that truth resides in accepting and embracing cultural diversity. You're most comfortable when you can be candid, and may surprise people with your brash and outgoing nature. Sometimes, you may feel that femininity is the last thing you possess, but your brand of feminine self is comfortable standing toe to toe with men in the world—so what if you have lace on your boots! Your moods are usually optimistic, since the future is a promising consideration for you in any situation. Isn't that what your Mom might have said?

Moon in Capricorn: The energy of your Capricorn Moon supports your need to accomplish your goals. You may be driven to succeed, and whether you are focused upon attaining that sense of accomplishment through a career or within a family setting, you are not likely to cease your pursuit until you are satisfied. You place a high value on hard work, and do not mind burning midnight oil if it means that you will achieve your aims. This drive is impossible to miss. Your sense of responsibility has always been there; even when you were a little girl you may have felt an obligation to achieve, and may have placed great emphasis on pleasing your parents and gaining their accolades. As a woman, you may be so focused on achievement that you have little time for such frivolous pleasures as romance and recreation, but the little girl inside you still wants to get out and play. Did you ever get a chance when you were small?

Crying in public may simply be unacceptable to you, but so may be holding hands with your sweetheart while you're walking into your favorite restaurant. Perhaps excessive emotional displays do seem to waste your energy, but until you let your feelings out, you will always have a wall between your heart and the soul of life. Perhaps it's the guilt that keeps you from walking away from the job at noon on Friday and taking a long weekend—or perhaps it's fear.

Dealing with fear is a primary factor for you. You are a realistic thinker, and may "know" what could happen if you're not planning for contingencies or calculating risks. Consequently, you are also a prime candidate for depression. Once you've fallen into a depressive rut, your melancholy can invade your sense of personal power, and you may feel that you've lost everything. Where is your salvation? It is in the space just next to your fear: your sense of humor. You see the ridiculous part of life that is also the struggle, and you do know how to laugh at it all. Make it a point everyday to read the funnies, to see the humor in the news, to find the joy in the eyes of a child. When you're smiling, so much more is possible.

Your sense of responsibility may be so powerful that you attract people who need to be parented. Always caring for the needs of everyone else can sap your vitality, and you may ultimately grow to resent the fact that everybody is so dependent on you to always be there to bail them out. It will never change until you can relinquish your need to be in control of everything (and everyone), just so you can feel safe. Let go. Give your husband or kids a chance to be responsible for themselves, and ask for support when you need it. You need to feel the tender touch of love, so give it a try on a regular basis. Hug therapy may be just what you're seeking. Maybe you could sneak a teddy bear into your briefcase.

Moon in Aquarius: Through the energy of your Aquarius Moon, you have your own unique style of expressing your femininity. You can be outspoken, and may express attitudes that go against the grain of conservative thinking. You've never liked the thought of being saddled with traditional roles, and even if you have children, you're not likely to take on the job of mother in a conventional manner. As a revolutionary type of woman, you might prefer to be considered for who you are as a person. Your feminine self is not necessarily crippled by this attitude, but you may have a little trouble expressing your tender emotions or giving in to your feelings, even when they are overwhelming. What you dislike most about emotionality is the fact that emotions do not make sense. Well, it's the truth, but everything in life is not logical, Ms. Spock. You feel the way you feel, and expressing those feelings does not diminish you or your power. In fact, it is through that very expression that you may become fully authenticated!

Your unpredictability is rivaled only by your need for personal space, and you may be uncomfortable in relationships that have a lot of requirements. Unconditional love and acceptance are your watchwords, but you may not always find this, even from yourself, once you cross the threshold of intimacy. If you feel you've gotten in over your head, your attempt to stabilize yourself may be a bit radical, and your lover or partner may experience your withdrawal as aloofness or coldness. Unless you want to underscore this impression, you must clarify that you simply need a little time and space to get clear about your feelings. Then, be honest with yourself about what precipitated your bolting through the door. That fear of losing your independence and autonomy may have grabbed you by the throat. You may also simply need a change. Trust your intuitive sensibilities to guide you. Be honest about the way you feel, and give up on the idea that you will always understand your emotions. They simply are, and they are an important part of you.

Moon in Pisces: Through your Pisces Moon, you express a profound sense of Divine Feminine energy. The Source of All Power definitely has a feminine side, and you are quite capable of harnessing that power. It flows through your imagination and creativity. It sings through your love and compassion. It dances through your joy. You know that strength for you is not about controlling, but it is instead about surrendering. You surrender to divine compassion, and your heart fills with love. You surrender your fears, and your imagination takes you on a journey into the spaces of pure beauty. But surrender does not mean that you give up your own needs and feelings. Nor does it mean that you have to place everyone else (including "The World") above your own needs. Selfless compassion is one thing. Martyrdom is another. To avoid becoming victimized, you must learn to recognize abuse of power when you see (or feel) it. Although you may want to provide help and rescue to others, you may not be adept at sheltering yourself from being victimized by those you're helping. In psychological terms, you need to learn to set some personal boundaries. You are especially prone to co-dependent behaviors: situations in which answering the needs of others completely overtakes your own needs. You may also fall into the trap of addictive behaviors as a means of escaping the pain of life in the real world. Ultimately, either of these options can lead to your becoming the victim once again. But here, you may actually victimize yourself. Suffering needlessly is highly self-destructive. In truth, you are seeking to return to the Source from which you came; and when you go inside yourself, you may discover that you've never lost contact after all. You just have to wake up to an expanded reality and renewed vision.

Aspects from the Moon and Your Feminine Self

The aspects from your Moon to the Sun and planets in your chart add a special dimension to the expression of your feminine energy. When the Moon connects to other energies, she brings the receptive, intuitive, and receiving qualities of her nature to the nature of the planet aspected. Sometimes this can be helpful, but in other situations these combinations create an inner conflict. Delineation of lunar aspects in regard to embracing your femininity are discussed in the following pages.

Conjunctions from the Moon

Moon conjunct Sun: Through the energy connection between your Moon in conjunction with your Sun, your willfulness is expressed is a more sensitive manner, but your emotional sensitivity can get in the way of your need to be direct about your feelings. You can lack objectivity, and can become overly attached to a situation because of your feelings about it. Instead of trying to act like a man in a man's world, allow yourself to function as a whole woman. You'll be much more effective, and may even bring about a change in the way things are done!

Moon conjunct Mercury: The Moon and Mercury conjunct in your chart can bring a positive enhancement to your intuitive sensibilities, but when you're emotionally involved with someone or attached to a particular outcome, your emotional needs can block the clarity of your intuitive self. Your feelings about something can also get in the way of your objectivity when you need to make a rational decision, and sometimes your attempts to be purely rational can block the expression of your deeper needs. Just remember that how you feel about something might be just as important as weighing the "facts" in a situation, although you may have to set your feelings aside in some circumstances. Finding ways to remain emotionally centered can be of great benefit to you.

Moon conjunct Venus: With your Moon conjunct Venus, your feminine self gains strong momentum. You can project the power of being a woman in a very convincing and positive manner, and it can be difficult for others to attack you without drawing fire from your supporters and allies. Your natural beauty radiates clearly, and you may have a gentility that inspires peace and harmony. In social situations, you may be the one who knows how to provide the right things for everybody, and who can create a wonderful atmosphere for sharing and comfort for those who are your guests.

Moon conjunct Mars: With your Moon conjunct Mars, you're likely to be quite direct about expressing your feelings. Assertiveness is not likely to be a problem for you, and you may sometimes seem more like one of the guys than a "lady." You can develop an excellent acceptance and understanding of men, even though you may prefer the fact that you are a woman. Your concern for the way others may feel when you take action can be a good thing, in that you may actually consider the outcome of a situation before you act, but sometimes the impulse to express yourself is too strong to think first. When you're going for it, it's probably a good idea to send a signal so that anyone who wants to avoid getting toasted by your afterburn can get out of the way. You can also be somewhat manipulative, so try to be aware of when you're attempting to control the way another person responds to you. Passive-aggressive behaviors will usually work against you.

Moon conjunct Jupiter: With your Moon conjunct Jupiter, you are a die-hard optimist, and your energy can inspire and encourage others, too. More likely to think
about conquering the horizon ahead than staying in the present moment, you are
also quite independent and don't like to think about setting personal limitations.
Consequently, it's easy to overdo it. Whether you make promises that are later difficult to fulfill, or indulge yourself too frequently, you can get in over your head
before you know it. Try to stay in the present moment some of the time. You can
be difficult to pin down, and your adventurous spirit may be more at home when
you're on the move than when you're in the kitchen.

Moon conjunct Saturn: Through the conjunction of your Moon and Saturn, you may
try to be in control of your feelings too much of the time. Always concerned about
appropriateness, you can limit yourself by becoming too judgmental, or you may be
too concerned about whether or not you will be accepted by the "right" people. You
may also be too self-critical, and may resent being a woman—especially when it
comes to advancement in the world. It's easier for you to take responsibility for
things than to ask for help, which can leave you with a rather heavy load. If you're
convinced that hard work makes the difference between happiness and despair, you
are certainly the perfect candidate for Workaholic of the Year. If you are going to
work so hard, tell yourself that it's a good thing to be proud of your accomplishments and allow others to show appreciation for your efforts. Try to get a handle on
whom you are trying to please. If it's you, perhaps you can lower your standards just
a little in order to indulge yourself from time to time.

Moon conjunct Uranus: With the Moon in conjunction with Uranus, you may feel
that you are riding an emotional roller coaster. Your highs can be very high, and
your lows, very low. Your hormonal cycles may also be rather extreme, and you
might benefit by taking a very careful look at holistic ways to handle PMS, and
may need to review your dietary habits to be sure that you're getting appropriate
nutritional support. Your independent spirit plays a definite part in your resistance
to taking on the traditional roles of a woman, although you can be a trendsetter
when you're simply doing things your own way.

Moon conjunct Neptune: With your Moon in conjunction with Neptune, your
emotional sensitivity is exceptionally heightened. Your psychic sensibilities can
be immensely powerful, especially in regard to sensing what others are feeling.
This can be quite helpful in some circumstances, but can be a liability in situations that require your objectivity. Because of this quality, you may end up being

the expressive partner in your relationships—you may even find that you are responding to and expressing what your lover or mate cannot express. This is frequently a problem in male-female relationships, since men are often uncomfortable expressing feelings, but if you are the one who does all the emotional work you will eventually become exhausted. It is crucial that you develop some type of emotional filter to avoid depleting yourself entirely. Work on co-dependency issues can also be highly beneficial to your growth, and will help you create healthier relationships with everyone, including the men in your life. This should not get in the way of your compassionate nature, and may even enhance your clarity when it comes to your psychic impressions.

Moon conjunct Pluto: With your Moon conjunct Pluto, your emotional intensity is difficult to miss. You can be quite compulsive, and when you are in a "groove" may find it difficult to get out. Men may be especially intimidated by your sensuality, and if you have control issues, you may even project an aura of power that can overwhelm any man who gets close to you (at least occasionally). You may also be somewhat intimidating to other women, especially if you harbor a mistrust of women. The connection you feel with your mother may be especially strong, and it is quite possible that you felt inundated by her emotional needs in a very powerful way when you were younger. If your mom had difficulty handling her own emotions, you may have some leftover resentment toward her that needs to be released in order to heal that relationship. Conscious awareness of this aspect of your part can make a big difference in the way you relate to others, and if you sense intimidation or blocking, you can back away a little to help diminish the intensity of your own energy—if you really want to let someone into your inner sanctum.

Semisquares from the Moon

Moon semisquare Sun: Since your Moon and Sun are in tense semisquare aspect to one another, you have some conflict between the feminine and masculine elements of your psyche. You may have grown up in a home in which your parents seemed to be at odds with one another, or in which you were caught in their conflict. In your own struggle to determine the strengths of being a woman, you may sometimes feel that your inner sensibilities are overridden by your need for recognition. With maturity, you are learning that you can use your awareness and respect for your deeper emotional needs to act as a springboard for accomplishment and personal recognition.

Moon semisquare Mercury: Your Moon and Mercury are in semisquare aspect, stimulating frustration between your thoughts and feelings. It can be difficult for you to express your deeper feelings verbally without feeling overly exposed emotionally, and you can also have trouble separating your feelings about someone or something from your need to make rational decisions. It's important to acknowledge your emotional sensibilities, but learning to distinguish your own anxieties or prejudices from the facts can be a truly anxiety-provoking situation. By maintaining deep levels of emotional stability through self-awareness, meditation, or even in counseling situations, you may finally be able to give each part of yourself credence when it comes time to make those major life choices.

Moon semisquare Venus: The conflict between what you need and what you want is signified by the energy of your Moon in semisquare aspect to Venus. Creating an awareness of your deeper feelings is the only way out of this conflict, especially when it comes to relationships. In other choices, like career decisions, this tension arises when you have to face something like asking for a raise, changing jobs for personal reasons, or climbing up the ladder in a manner that seems personally awkward. Although you may sometimes think that it would just be easier to let somebody else tell you what to do, you are not likely to be satisfied with the end results unless your own needs and list of preferences are carefully considered.

Moon semisquare Mars: Feelings of underlying agitation and frustration are indicated by the semisquare between your Moon and Mars. These energies are not really compatible with one another, since one is about going inside and the other is about directing your energy outward. Consequently, your turmoil can spill over into your relationships, feelings about yourself, and inability to allow some things to take their own course. Although it may be your preference to satisfy everyone, that's not always possible, and sometimes when you take a stand for yourself, other people may seem to be hurt or insulted. The manner in which you do this makes all the difference, and learning to observe reactions and alter your attitudes and behaviors accordingly can afford the opportunity to make a great deal of headway. You don't like staying stuck in situations that are not working, but if you feel that you cannot leave, you can make yourself and everybody else miserable until some solution is reached. Handling feelings of anger more directly is a good first step to becoming more emotionally stabilized, and learning to step out of the way when someone else is angry or upset is step number two.

Moon semisquare Jupiter: Setting limits just seems frustrating with your Moon in semisquare aspect to Jupiter, but setting limits is necessary if you are to experience what you want from your life without stretching yourself too thin. When you're feeling insecure or vulnerable, you may also suffer from low self worth that seems, for the moment at least, to be relieved by overextending yourself in some way. If you're tempted to spend or buy when your funds are low, it's that need to feel better that may be prompting you to pull those credit cards from your wallet. If you're tempted to say "yes" when you really want to say "no," it's the same stimulus. You need to know that your life is filled with promise and possibility, but you also need to safeguard that promise by knowing where to draw the line.

Moon semisquare Saturn: If you wonder why you keep repeating the same patterns of holding yourself back when you really want to move into something new or different, part of the stimulus may arise from the energy of your Moon in semisquare aspect to Saturn. Deep inside, you may mistrust yourself as a woman, or may feel that being a woman is second rate in some way. If these attitudes are present, they may be learned behaviors and feelings that were incorporated into your psyche through exposure to other people who taught you to mistrust yourself! Most of the time, these teachings are not intentional—they can occur from the things you hear or observe in society. Even if you did experience intentional inhibition of your self-expression when you were a young girl, you are not destined to stay that way forever. You have the power to use these old messages as a springboard to a different point of view. You can decide that this is simply not true, or that your needs radiate differently now. When you are tempted to compromise on things, and your feelings tell you that you are working against yourself, you can stop yourself before you give away your needs. When you feel that you're holding back, resisting getting close, or mistrustful of your own needs, you can also change these attitudes—a little at a time. The key to success is in pacing yourself according to your ability to move forward. Rushing headlong into something before you're ready will just set you back again.

Moon semisquare Uranus: The energy of your Moon in semisquare to Uranus adds a rebellious quality to your femininity. You cannot maintain situations that are personally inhibiting without running headlong into your own needs for independence. The manner in which you stage your rebellions makes all the difference in whether or not they support your growth or undermine your effectiveness as a whole woman.

Moon semisquare Neptune: Setting emotional boundaries is difficult for you, since the influence of your Moon in semisquare to Neptune opens your energy to everything and everyone around you. Your emotional sensibilities can add amazing qualities to your creativity, compassion, and desire to make a difference in the world, but if your energy is being misused by others, the effect you hope to achieve may never be realized. You may feel that being a woman means that you are cursed with too much sensitivity, but it really has nothing to do with being female. You can create emotional filters by learning to discover the difference between what you see when you look into someone's soul and their actions or attitudes in the world. Those who have potential to change certainly need to be encouraged, but not at the expense of your own soul or sanity! You may also have a strong desire to withdraw, which can be seen through addictive behavior patterns. Whether these addictions manifest through your personal relationships with other people or your relationship with substances, they can undermine your sense of personal worth as a woman.

Moon semisquare Pluto: With the energy of your Moon in semisquare to Pluto, you may have an underlying mistrust of your own femininity. This can be the result of early abusive situations, or a series of relationships that have undermined your trust in yourself and your needs. However, you can change these hurtful patterns and are capable of transforming your life into one of wholeness and personal satisfaction by releasing your old attitudes and accepting yourself and your needs. Learning when to hang on and when to let go of feelings and emotional attachments is one of your biggest lessons.

Sextile Aspects from the Moon

Moon sextile Sun: With your Moon in supportive sextile aspect to your Sun, you may enjoy a positive blending of the masculine and feminine elements of your psyche. As a result, your ability to enjoy and relate comfortably to both men and women can function more easily. With your subconscious, emotional nature in harmony with your will power, you can also be much more confident about seeking out experiences and relationships that fulfill your needs. You're less likely to allow the needs and demands of others to overwhelm your sense of self.

Moon sextile Mercury: Your Moon in sextile aspect to Mercury indicates a positive blending of your mental and emotional energies. With your ability to include both your rational thinking processes and your emotional sensibilities in decision-making, you can face the challenge of choices with greater confidence. You may feel comfortable integrating your intuitive sensibilities with rational thinking, and can be an especially effective counselor and communicator. Other people trust you to be thoughtful and fair-minded.

Moon sextile Venus: Your Moon is positively supported through a connection to Venus, strengthening your ability to express your feelings and needs, and stimulating an enhanced social sensibility. A genuine concern for the welfare of others is quite easy for you, and your protective, caring nature leaves a lovely impression. Shows of affection are part of your identity, and your friends and family are likely to look forward to your smile and hugs. Your beauty shines through in your words, actions, and attitudes, and you may demonstrate true grace under pressure when you're faced with challenges. In relationships, your openness stimulates intimacy, and you trust your feelings to help guide you.

Moon sextile Mars: Your Moon is positively supported through a connection to Mars, increasing your courage, emotional stamina, and self-assertiveness. Instead of waiting for your needs to be fulfilled, you are likely to do something about it. You appreciate people and situations that provide excitement and challenge, and can handle competition quite nicely. In fact, you may actually be at your best when you're feeling a little pressure. In difficult circumstances, you have the ability to continue on, since you know that everything changes. Relationships with men are not likely to be especially difficult, since you are strong enough to attract men who are sure of themselves. You're likely to be bored in a relationship with a man who has little drive, and will be much more attracted to someone who knows what he wants. Your women friends also appreciate your straightforward, shoot-from-the-hip type of attitude, and may look to you for leadership and support.

Moon sextile Jupiter: With your Moon in a supportive aspect to Jupiter, you can develop an emotional resilience that will help you maintain your positivity and optimism despite any challenges you may face. Laughter and good humor may be among your trademarks, and you may thoroughly enjoy intelligent wit and insightful comedy. It feels good when you extend generosity toward others, and you can be quite appreciative when you are the beneficiary of good will. Your tolerance toward others stems from your desire to experience a life that is uplifting, and you may be quite comfortable around a wide variety of people and in different situations. The air of excitement that permeates your personality can be quite attractive, and can open many doors. Since you tend to see potential in other people, you can be an inspiring teacher or mentor, and may even act as an agent or guide for those who need your assistance.

Moon sextile Saturn: Your Moon and Saturn are in a supportive aspect to one another, indicating that you have an excellent ability to focus your energy. Taking responsibility is easy and natural for you, and you may have always been quite willing to deal with taking care of yourself. You're not looking for a man to rescue you, and even if you marry are likely to prefer to maintain your personal autonomy. You prefer the way you feel when you've done your job well, and shirking responsibility or scapegoating will always leave you feeling personally depleted.

You may be somewhat reserved in the way you express your feelings, although you strive to achieve an understanding of your emotions. When approaching emotional difficulties, you are more likely to try to find solutions, and can be especially understanding and supportive. As a mother, you can be unwavering in your consistency and support of your children, and as a partner, can demonstrate a reliability and respect for yourself and your mate. In the workplace, you can be an excellent manager or leader, and men and women alike can respect your integrity, determination, and practicality.

Moon sextile Uranus: With your Moon and Uranus in supportive aspect to one another, you demonstrate a strong ability to express your individuality, and appreciate that which is unusual in others. You may have a special affinity for creative, ingenious self-expression, and are not likely to fit into anybody's preconceived ideas about what a woman should be. You are creating yourself, and your image and personality can sparkle through the expression of your special talents and abilities.

You can be somewhat distant emotionally, especially when you're involved in one of your projects, but may just need to remind yourself that you need the connection to those you love just as much as they need their connection to you. In relationships with men, you may not be interested in playing the traditional roles, and need a mate whose intellect and passion for life are well-developed. You may have friends from all walks of life, and might even prefer to be around people who are unusual. Your friendships with other women can be one of the most cherished experiences of your life. Since you can see the uniqueness in everyone, you are an excellent candidate for helping others identify and develop their positive, distinguishing attributes, but you're not likely to want to baby-sit them—just give them a good jump-start.

Moon sextile Neptune: Through the flowing energy between your Moon and Neptune in sextile aspect to one another, your sensitivity and imagination are strengthened. Your compassion extends to all forms of life, and you may display a profound reverence for life. Your spirituality is an integral part of your life, and you may need time each day to reach within and connect with your deeper essence. You can be quite sensitive to the feelings of those you love, and may respond before they even have a chance to verbalize their needs. As a mother, your connection to your children can be quite profound, and you can be a powerful force in helping them discover their own creativity.

Others may rely on you to provide help and support when they are in need, and you are usually happy to accommodate them. Getting involved in your community may seem quite natural for you, and the spiritual support you feel when participating in a project that positively alters the quality of life is wonderful fuel for your soul. If you take everyone at face value, you can be victimized, since unscrupulous individuals are likely to recognize your vulnerability. Even in legitimate circumstances, you may end up giving more than your fair share, simply because you have difficulty walking away when someone is in need of help.

Moon sextile Pluto: With the easy flow of energy between the Moon and Pluto indicated by their sextile aspect to one another, you can be quite adept in your understanding of human emotion. In many ways, you are a natural psychologist since your insights into the inner workings of the psyche can be quite powerful. But that insightfulness also works to your benefit in the world of business and within your personal relationships. Whether in work or your personal relationships, you can be highly expressive of your opinions and feelings, and appreciate the same honesty and expressivity from others.

There is a healing quality about you that may draw others into your life who are seeking support and understanding. As a mother, you can be deeply connected to your children and may even find that their friends come to you for your sincere understanding and insight. In your intimate relationship with a partner, your passion can be immense, and you may experience a level of unity and bonding that completely transforms your life. Since you're not likely to do anything halfway, you usually take the time to be discriminating in your choices. Leaving yourself vulnerable is simply not your style.

Square Aspects from the Moon

Moon square Sun: With your Moon and Sun in a square aspect with one another, you may feel that you are constantly having to make choices that compromise your needs in order to get what you want (or vice versa). You may feel caught in the trap of being a woman, and may resent the fact that your opportunities seem limited or thwarted as a result, but the trap is much deeper than that. It actually may stem from a desire to have complete autonomy, in conflict with your need for someone to care for you. The trade offs are rarely satisfying when you compromise, and you may feel resentful toward or hurt by what you chose to give up.

You may be responding to behavior you learned as a young girl, when you had to choose between the disparity of your mother and father. Their conflicts may not have been drastic, but you certainly received different input from each of them. When you study the basic essence of your Moon and Sun, you can see the difference between these energies, and may wonder if you can ever achieve any type of inner peace and harmony. What is required is a powerful dedication toward understanding your real needs, and the determination and will power to be sure that these needs are met. You will always be tested, but may find that the tests themselves provide the very structure you need in order to succeed. Now that you are a woman, you do not have to continue to please mom and dad or seek their approval, but you do have to attain your own.

Moon square Mercury: Your Moon is in a square aspect to your Mercury, indicating possible difficulties in your ability to be rational. First of all, you do not have to be completely rational all the time—it is simply not possible. Now that's said, when you do need to make an objective or impartial decision, you need to be very careful in your considerations. Those people in your life whom you've learned to trust and value can also be helpful sounding boards when you're facing an important choice or dilemma. You must also give yourself a chance to grow up and take the heat for your own feelings and needs. The problem is that your feelings run very deep, and if you hold a particular prejudice, you may find it quite difficult to release it.

When someone or something challenges the way you feel, you can be threatened. Criticism can be very wounding, and you may never recover if you cannot objectify a situation in which you are being critically assessed. If your attitudes remain stubborn and unyielding, you may become quite lonely. Spending time with children and dealing with their honesty can be exceptionally healing for you, and you may find that you really mature once you've taken on the role of mother.

You may always feel stressed around people in authority until you become more flexible in your attitudes and less sensitive to the idea that you might occasionally be mistaken about a few things.

Moon square Venus: The energy of your Moon in square aspect to Venus stimulates a feeling of discontent. You feel internal conflict when you want what you cannot have, and can be caught in the throes of emotional turmoil when you are faced with letting go of one situation in order to move into something different. That old adage, "you can't have your cake and it eat, too," applies to the type of dilemma you frequently face, especially in the realm of relationships. When faced with compromise, you feel depleted. Yet you may also fail to allow yourself to really go for the things you want, since the fear of losing something that valuable can be overwhelming. You are highly susceptible to emotional blackmail, and may be reluctant to admit it when you feel strongly for someone because you don't want to be vulnerable. All these attempts to keep yourself protected act like a barrier against your happiness, and until you address your fears of intimacy, you may never have a fully functional relationship.

You could gain exceptional benefit from studying human psychology and learning about human behavior. Working in a therapeutic group situation could also provide methods for you to understand the manner in which you relate to others and they relate to you. Then, you can ultimately risk developing a gradual intimacy. A female friendship provides a safe starting place, since part of your frustration arises from a lack of trust in yourself as a woman. Sharing your feelings and thoughts with a friend, and taking responsibility for becoming a good friend yourself, will help you overcome the barriers that may have been in place since you were a young girl. Jumping into an intimate relationship before you've learned to trust yourself and your feelings can leave you vulnerable, and may even expose your mate to your unresolved issues.

Moon square Mars: With your Moon in square aspect to Mars you can be emotionally volatile. You may feel overly defensive, and can react to others in inappropriate ways when you feel insecure. Your lack of trust for men can be extremely marked, and you may also find it difficult to trust assertive and powerful women. Any emotional trauma you experienced as a young girl is likely to have penetrated your psyche like an irremovable shard of glass. Your own assertiveness seems to come out in bursts of anger or volatile temperament, attitudes that can alienate others and create a general atmosphere of mistrust and hostility. People may treat you with kid gloves for a while, but ultimately, if you are going to have any type of harmony in the world, you must find a healthy way to deal with your feelings of agitation and frustration. By dealing with your feelings when they arise, you are on the right track. Owning your anger is also important, and by finding positive ways to release anger and hostility, you will finally remove that piercing pain you've experienced every time you've tried to open your soul. Because you are crisis oriented, you might find a wonderful outlet for this energy in some type of crisis intervention work, emergency medicine, sports activities, or the like.

Moon square Jupiter: With your Moon in a square aspect to Jupiter, you may feel restless, and may not be entirely at home with the idea of limitation—any type of limitation. You expect a lot from yourself, and when you're feeling low, can overindulge in spending, eating, or playing just to get that feeling of fullness that seems to be lacking. To develop the strength of your femininity, you need to have ample outlets through which to express your generosity and caring, and must also learn that nurturing yourself does not always mean overdoing it. You also need ways to sustain your enthusiasm, which means learning to pace yourself so that you are still excited about a project (or relationship) long enough to sustain it.

Moon square Saturn: Your tendency to hang onto every emotion is underscored by the square aspect between your Moon and Saturn. You can easily become overwhelmed by your fears, and may sometimes feel so anxiety-ridden that you are paralyzed. It's easy for you to become overly dependent upon others because you may be afraid of taking responsibility for yourself. It is important for you to feel needed, and in order to accomplish this in a healthy way, you need to understand the true nature of control. You are a prime candidate for a co-dependent relationship in which you set the limits for others because they refuse to set limits for themselves. There is a difference between guiding, helping, and teaching others, and taking responsibility for them when they need to carry their own burdens.

If you have children, you may find it difficult when you need to let them go during different stages in their growth. Your fears about the harm they could experience can thwart their ability to live full lives. These fears may be the result of the things you learned from your own parents, although you have the power to break this chain of family fate. If you gradually begin to create situations that allow children to develop their own ability to make good decisions and fend for themselves, you can release your protective grasp more easily. Teach your children to trust their own instincts, and learn from them the healing power this can bring.

Your depression and anxiety may be related to a biochemical imbalance, and you might want to discuss your concerns with a physician or holistic health practitioner. If you are depressed, a physical condition in which seratonin levels are blocked, you may experience a miraculous shift in your attitudes and energy levels when these blocks are removed. You can also help to facilitate a change by staying physically active, eating healthy whole foods, and getting plenty of rest and relaxation.

Moon square Uranus: The tension produced through the square aspect between your Moon and Uranus creates an unpredictable quality and can lead to emotional instability. Your rebellious attitudes can have a positive effect in stimulating change, and you may be quite ingenious. Not only are you likely to resist falling into a rut, you may rebel strongly against any conditions that inhibit your personal freedom and autonomy. For this reason, marriage can be a difficult option, especially if you're trying to hold to the old traditions and play the role of dutiful housewife, or other roles that do not suit you. However, you can sustain a relationship if it is open, exciting, and growth-oriented—and if your partner is as independent and experimental as you are! You can be drawn to an alternative lifestyle, and may have attitudes that fly in the face of convention when it comes to love, relationships, children, *and* career. In many ways, you are a trendsetter, but if you wish to be respected and to have your talents as a woman taken seriously, you must utilize your resources to their fullest and allow yourself to shine as the individual you are. Trying to shape yourself into something that you are not will destroy your soul.

Moon square Neptune: With your Moon in square aspect to Neptune, your imagination is highly active and your emotional responses can be especially dramatic. Your emotional sensitivity can range in extremes from ecstasy to despair, and you can respond just as powerfully to an imaginary stimulus as to a "real" one. Your idea of reality can be somewhat different from the norm, because you feel the vibrations of everything around you. But since you are functioning on the physical plane, it is important for you to learn to distinguish physical reality from the reality that is beyond the physical. Once you've accomplished this, you can draw more reasonable emotional boundaries, and can feel much more in control of your life. You also need these boundaries in order to avoid being used or abused by others in your life.

Your compassion can be a wonderful thing, and ministering to the needs of others does, indeed, fill your soul. But you may have difficulty separating your feelings from the emotions and feelings of others, and can find it difficult to walk away from the situations that you must leave behind. Your yearning for a soul mate can lead you to see only what you want to see in the man you love, instead of accepting him for what he is. In relationships, you are quite prone to high levels of co-dependency or addictive behavior patterns, and may be the one who ends up falling victim to another's emotional instability unless you learn to give yourself some psychological space. This is not as easy to do as it sounds, because when you are attached to someone, you can be very deeply attached. Sacrificing yourself to the needs of another, especially if the person is self-abusive or is abusing you, can destroy your spirit. Developing skills in meditation, contemplation, and other self-reflective techniques can help you feel more connected to the core of your inner self, and may impart the objectivity you need to determine if you are in a situation that can allow you to make your dreams come true, or if you're in a living nightmare. Spending time developing your creative or artistic interests can have a similar strengthening effect upon your psyche.

Moon square Pluto: Through the tense square between your Moon and Pluto, your emotions are extremely intensified. You may hold some deep-seated resentments, and can hang on to guilt eternally unless you make an effort to release it. Your trust of your own power as a woman can be undermined, especially if you felt emotionally abused as a child. It is quite possible that you were mistreated because one of your parents resented your being there, but you may also have been simply struggling for survival in a situation that provided little emotional nurturance. Regardless of the particulars of your early conditioning, you do have the capability of healing these old wounds through the same energy that has sustained their pain.

You may be drawn to relationships for the pure physical pleasure and stimulation they provide, but may not want to feel emotionally close due to your lack of trust. Yet deep within your soul, you may long for that bonding that results from the alchemy of two souls merging. Since you were not issued an instruction manual on how to deal with people when you entered this life, you need to give yourself plenty of time and room to research human nature and human emotion. Safe circumstances, like a friendship with someone who shares your interests, can give you a chance to learn about trust—but you must be honest about your feelings! Even though you might think that you would prefer to live apart from society, filtering into social situations can help you trust yourself more fully, because interacting with others helps you develop objectivity. To have the love and tenderness you need from others, you must learn forgiveness, too. That forgiveness begins within yourself, and releasing tension and stress while letting go of the burdens from your past will help you feel much lighter, more alive, and free. Then, and only then, can you feel good about the power of being a whole woman.

Trine Aspects from the Moon

Moon trine Sun: With your Moon in a supportive trine aspect to your Sun, you may be quite capable of integrating the masculine and feminine elements of your psyche. This indicates that your experience of relationships between men and women has not been especially difficult. In fact, you may have a strong connection to both your mother and father. Your experience of life as a woman is not likely to seem especially limited, since you may be quite comfortable dealing with the world on your own terms without feeling that you have to be in conflict on gender issues. Self-respect and sincerity radiate through your personality, and men and women alike may respond to your requests or leadership. You may not feel particularly motivated to achieve high levels of success, since it might seem easier to take the easy road. This is fine as long as you're happy with your life, but if you feel you want or need more, you may simply need to get moving and set your sights on options that will allow continual growth on every level.

Moon trine Mercury: With your Moon in supportive trine aspect to Mercury, you are an exceptionally perceptive woman. Your desire to learn, communicate, and accumulate knowledge are ever-present, helping you maintain an open mind and youthful spirit. Communicating your thoughts and feelings is easy, and your sincerity and sympathetic nature encourage others to be open with you, too. Whether you choose to pursue a career or focus on family concerns, your problem-solving abilities always work to your advantage. Part of your strength arises from the fact that you may be able to trust your "sense" of things as much as you trust the data about them. When you say that you have a "feeling" about something, it is unlikely that anyone will accuse you of being silly, since your sensibilities are usually right on the mark!

Moon trine Venus: Through the supportive connection between your Moon and Venus in trine aspect to one another, you express a quality of beauty, grace, and emotional strength that is highly attractive. The fact that you are a woman works to your benefit because you are comfortable with yourself and love the softness, gentility, and level of creativity that are so much a part of you. Your sense of color, style, and form can be applied in vast situations—from the way you dress, to your design of an office, to the creation of a highly successful business venture, and your ability to deal with people may be legendary. Whether you're reading bedtime stories to your children or making a presentation at work, your warmth, imagination, and refinement are a pure joy. You're the perfect person to influence positive change in others, because other people are likely to trust that your motives are pure.

Moon trine Mars: With your Moon in trine aspect to Mars, you can be quite confident about expressing your feelings and asserting yourself in a positive manner. Your knack for dealing with people is excellent, and you can be quite effective dealing with men on your own terms. You are likely to find the male-female dance quite interesting and enjoyable, and the differences between men and women are more intriguing to you than they are perplexing. As a mother, you can be especially supportive, since you enjoy dealing with your children on their level and generate an atmosphere of safe support, creativity, and fun. In relationships, you are not likely to hesitate about expressing the way you feel, and can show all your emotions, including anger, without worrying if they are "acceptable." Since you take yourself at face value, you may also have the same approach to dealing with others, which makes for a great ingredient in any relationship.

Moon trine Jupiter: Through the energy of your Moon in trine aspect to Jupiter, you have exceptional emotional resilience, which is primarily supported by your sense of optimism and confidence. You are more likely to feel that being a woman is an asset, and may find it easier to flow with the emotional tides and cycles of change that are a normal part of your life. Generosity is natural for you, and you have an excellent ability to attract abundance. Nurturing others may flow quite readily. However, it is also easy for you to take things and people for granted, so it's a good idea to take stock of your good fortunes and remind yourself to show gratitude and grace. This can be an aspect of laziness, since positive changes of fortune may seem to occur quite naturally, but if you recognize and develop your strengths, this same energy can provide an endless reservoir of emotional and spiritual strength.

Moon trine Saturn: Your emotional stability is strengthened through your Moon's trine aspect to Saturn. This connection gives you an ability to accept yourself as you are, and your personal honesty with yourself about your needs helps you approach life in a responsible manner. You can accept those special qualities that arise from being a woman, and can even find ways to use the power of being a woman to your advantage! You may feel that it is important to strive toward achieving respect, and can readily gain the respect and admiration of others because they can count on you. Although you may not be looking for a man or partner to take care of you, you can appreciate the importance of mutual support. As a mother, your stabilizing force can be invaluable, and you may gain exceptional joy from teaching and guiding your children. In the workplace, you are likely to be the one others turn to when they need an honest opinion and responsible attitude. You are a teacher, whether or not you work formally in this position in society: your life is your lesson plan.

Moon trine Uranus: With your Moon in trine aspect to Uranus, you present an exceptional level of independence and autonomy. You're the kind of woman who prefers to develop your own path, to do things your own way, and to experience a sense of absolute freedom. This does not mean that you prefer to be alone. In fact, you may be continually surrounded by friends and family. You just like to have plenty of room! Your approach to dealing with the men in your life is likely to be at arm's length until you develop a sense of trust and understanding, and you may have a variety of experiences in relationships. You are most open with a man who can be your friend first. In your relationships with women, you may have a number of friends, and they are likely to be remarkably different. Since you're a feminist at heart, you appreciate women who are developing their own paths, but you may also find that those who are as yet unsure of themselves are drawn to you as a mentor and friend.

You may have mixed feelings about being a mother. Although you might think you would be happier if children were born walking and talking, you can thoroughly enjoy the experience and pleasures of motherhood. You'll seek the most innovative ways to approach caring for your children, and may even be quite inventive in dealing with their needs. Your intuitive sense is a plus in dealing with your kids, and if you are a mom, you've probably discovered this more than once! You're quite adept at handling teenagers, since you can identify with their rebellious attitudes and their need to develop unique identities. Because of this, you may always seem younger than your years, and you like it that way.

Moon trine Neptune: Through the trine aspect between your Moon and Neptune, you are capable of developing an exceptional level of compassion. Your sensibilities are quite remarkable, and this awareness is likely to extend into the realm of strong psychic sensitivity. You may "feel" something long before you get the physical evidence! Your imagination and sense of artistry may be quite evident in your life, and your hypnotic qualities can be alluring. Since you may also be sensitive to the feelings of others, you may be continually drawn into situations where others pour out their hearts to you, and you have the ability to accept and support them in a special manner. Becoming aware of your emotional boundaries is important, and you may naturally do this by seeking out time alone, periods of meditation, or a comfortable quiet space to relax. You may be adept at caring for others, but may also develop a strong awareness of your inner self and needs. You may even find that using the changes in awareness associated with your menstrual cycle helps you enhance your strength, creativity, and emotional resilience.

As a mother, you may be especially sensitive to the needs and emotions of your children, and can provide a heavenly sense of comfort, but because you innately know these things, you may also tend to do too much. You cherish relationships of all types—friends, family, and lovers—and you may feel that your life is incomplete without an opportunity to share the deep compassion you have for the sanctity of life. You are definitely capable of expressing the true power and energy of the Goddess: the feminine aspect of All That Is. Anyone who looks carefully can see it reflected in your eyes.

Moon trine Pluto: Through the connection of your Moon and Pluto in trine aspect, your emotional sensibilities are intense. Your ability to sense things below the surface is amazing, including the way others feel—despite what they may say! You can be an intimidating woman, although you don't try to be, simply because you possess a level of awareness that is absolutely penetrating. Your embrace of the true essence of feminine power is remarkable, and your ability to bounce back in the face of challenge or adversity is directly linked to this power. With a high capacity to create and transform, you are capable of returning life to the lifeless and purpose to that which has grown stale. You are innately aware of and connected to the powerful changes that occur throughout your menstrual cycle, and by working with these alterations in your body, mind, and soul, you can become a much more effective woman.

Others may be drawn to your healing quality, and you can open your soul in such a way as to allow others to find their own strength. In intimate relationships, you have the ability to achieve a level of bonding that transcends the ordinary. Your sexuality and sensuality are special keys for your achievement of ecstasy. As a mother, you have a phenomenal link to your children, and can be especially effective in helping them develop a trust and understanding of their deeper needs and feelings.

Quincunx Aspects from the Moon

Moon quincunx Sun: With the energy of your Moon and Sun in quincunx aspect to each other, you may feel that you are constantly frustrated with your needs to remain autonomous while still wanting to be comforted or supported. Although you may intellectually understand that these experiences are not mutually exclusive to one another, and that you can have both, you tend to overcompensate emotionally! In most instances, you find that fulfilling your deeper needs for closeness, tenderness, and support can actually strengthen your sense of personal autonomy. You can have a little trouble achieving balance in your relationships, and will be most successful when you allow room and time for the effects of change and growth.

Moon quincunx Mercury: Through the quincunx aspect from your Moon to Mercury, you may have an ongoing and frustrating argument within yourself about what you think and what you feel. Sometimes you can relax and allow your emotional sense of something to flow easily and freely, and sometimes you can make a perfectly logical decision without having to deal with your feelings about it. But since life is a complicated series of events and experiences, you usually need to incorporate both in some manner. Your argument may be more centered on what you've "learned" about what is logical and what is not. Rational thought processes can involve and incorporate your "sense" of things, and still be rational! However, you can fall victim to that accusation that being a woman somehow impairs your judgment. Now, isn't that a silly idea? Seems that the truth is more along the lines that being human impairs judgment, but who wants to argue?!

Moon quincunx Venus: With your Moon in quincunx aspect to Venus, your sense of your own worth and beauty fluctuates. Once you get used to the idea that your changeability is a part of something positive, you can reflect a more positive level of self-esteem. It's like remembering to avoid trying on a swimsuit when it's two days before you start your period. You know you'll look and feel better about yourself in another week! This same energy is at work in your relationships. A healthy relationship is not the same from day to day, and if you expect that everything, including your feelings about someone, will always be the same, you will never be satisfied. Once you realize that you may appreciate yourself, someone else, or your life situation in a cyclical or changeable manner, you can make the adjustment, and your happiness is much more consistent!

Moon quincunx Mars: With your Moon in quincunx aspect to Mars, you may feel a continual level of agitation, especially if you've failed to process feelings of anger or negativity. You may have mixed feelings about being a woman, and may sense that men have more power, control, or influence—and you may even give up some of your own power to men in relationships in order to maintain the "peace." This does little to resolve the conflict, which involves your need to allow your own assertiveness, strength, and drive to work to your benefit when you are striving to fulfill your needs. Perhaps your relationships can give you the perfect stage for dramatizing this inner conflict, and if you can play out some of your own frustrations with a supportive partner, that feeling of agitation may take a vacation.

Moon quincunx Jupiter: Through the influence of your Moon in quincunx aspect to Jupiter, you may feel a profound sense of discontent with yourself and your life. If you feel that your expectations are never fully realized, maybe you need to adjust your expectations, or abandon them altogether in some instances! Begin by taking a careful look within yourself to determine the center of your feelings of emotional lack. You may vacillate between loving the feeling of being a woman and resenting the fact that you are a woman. You may be torn between your obligations to care for someone and your desire to have someone take care of you. You may compare your home, life situation, relationships, or family with others and feel that you come up short. Or you can overcompensate and do whatever you feel is necessary to make sure that you are ahead of the "Joneses" in the contest of who is better. The key to resolving these conflicting circumstances may reside in accepting yourself and your situation, and then working toward improvements within realistic limits.

Moon quincunx Saturn: With your Moon in quincunx aspect to Saturn, you may feel an undercurrent of instability and insecurity. Vague fears can leave you with a feeling that you will never be quite settled or satisfied, and can inhibit your free expression of your power as a woman. You may have absorbed an attitude of fear or mistrust through the things you learned from your family or your mother, and may not trust your own ability to make your way through life. If you try to inhibit your feelings and needs, and operate from a sense of lack, then your frustration grows. If you give your power to someone else by allowing them to make the decisions, take control, and rule over your life, you may feel secure, but the security is false, since you do not own it.

To change this unsettling tide of energy, you must spend some time reflecting on your deeper needs, and may have to take a few risks by going outside the boundaries of your comfortable prison into the clear air of freedom. Finding your own power as a woman, accepting your strengths and limitations, and fully embracing your needs is not an easy task, but it is possible. Determining what you need to feel stable, alive, and comfortable may also require that you let go of some of the traditions you've held close to your heart. It feels like unlacing a corset: you do, after all, need to breathe!

Moon quincunx Uranus: The quincunx aspect between your Moon and Uranus indicates an unpredictable quality and can show a tendency toward emotional instability. Your rebellious nature usually emerges when you're faced with a situation that requires you to conform to standards you find unbearable. Otherwise, you are more likely to make the necessary adjustments to get by or keep moving, just to keep things simple. When you do compromise and lose something precious, your discontent can be overwhelming and your rebellion can be far-reaching. You may vacillate between enjoying your experience of life as a woman and resenting the fact that you have to deal with the issues surrounding being a woman, or the physical experience of cyclical change that accompanies womanhood. If your hormonal levels seem to be inconsistent or highly variable, you might benefit from a holistic approach to your physical dilemma.

Intimate relationships are important to you, but you may have little tolerance for situations that are too inhibiting. Although you may complain that you seem to attract others who are not available in one way or another, ask yourself how open you are to making a commitment. Until you're ready to settle down, you're more likely to send mixed signals yourself.

Moon quincunx Neptune: The energy of your Moon in quincunx aspect to Neptune indicates an enhanced emotional sensitivity. Sometimes you may be quite clear about the way you feel, but this influence provides a level of occasional confusion due to the difficulty you may have maintaining your emotional boundaries. You may feel that you sometimes just want to escape from it all, and during these periods can be rather distant and hard to reach. If you're uncertain or do not want to make a commitment, your vagueness can be very effective, although frustrating to those who would like to hear a definitive answer from you, but then there are those times when you open the doors to your soul and cannot give enough of yourself.

There is a corresponding cycle involving the amount of influence you experience from others, too, and you may fall victim to deceit or illusion. It is this experience that yields a feeling of mistrust of yourself, but it is counterproductive to close away or deny the truth. If you've learned denial from your early life experiences, that may seem to be the most plausible manner of dealing with personal tragedy or challenge. Yet you feel extremely uncomfortable when you fall into the trap of denial, because you can never hide from yourself. Fortunately, you have the capability of rising to the occasion and extracting yourself from emotionally destructive situations, but you have to see them first!

Moon quincunx Pluto: Your Moon is in quincunx aspect to Pluto, which can indicate a sense of mistrust of yourself as a woman and of your deeper feelings. You may have had early experiences that led you to believe that anyone who is close to you will ultimately abandon you, undermining your sense of emotional trust. Whether this was a hugely significant event, like the loss of someone close, or what appeared to be insignificant to the observer, like a puppy running away from home—your tendency is to hang on to the trauma rather than letting it go. Then, when you begin to feel close to someone, your subconscious self remembers that pain and pulls up all your barriers. It's almost as though you are in conflict with some internal, overly protective mother. You may also hold resentment toward yourself for being a woman, and need to seriously question whether or not this is the case. If so, determining what is at the core of those feelings might help you let go and move forward. You have the capacity to understand and experience true healing and transformation, but if you keep hanging on to things you no longer need, that transformation never seems quite complete.

Oppositions from the Moon

Moon opposition Sun: Your Moon is in opposition aspect to your Sun, adding emotional intensity to your personality and stimulating a strong sensitivity to your environment and those within it. You are also face to face with yourself and may struggle to remain aware of who you are and what you need, especially in your relationships. Sometimes, it may seem that you are striving to achieve some type of balance between what you want and what others want from you, but if you are connected to the center of yourself, this task becomes much easier. Even though you may think life might be simpler if you did not have to consider how you feel about things, removing this sensitivity would diminish a powerful level of awareness. You have the capacity to develop high levels of objectivity, since your intuitive insightfulness can work to your benefit. Your emotional sensitivity can also get in your way if you get out of balance or if you allow someone else's needs to overwhelm your own.

This aspect indicates confrontation between the masculine and feminine elements of your psyche, and this can be played out in your relationships until you gain an awareness of how you work on the "inside." You may even find that you play the roles of both father and mother to your children, although your mothering nature usually overwhelms your more assertive side. In intimate relationships, you may attract men who want a mother, but you want, most of all, to be a true partner. Certainly there is a level of nurturing that occurs in close relationships, and there's nothing wrong with becoming "mommy" and "daddy" in your roles. Caretaking is part of your identity as a woman, but the levels at which you accomplish expressing this tenderness are up to you.

Moon opposition Mercury: With your Moon in opposition aspect to Mercury, you can use your feelings about something to add a different level of objectivity to your decision making, but it is also easy to let your feelings and your thinking conflict with each other, and you may sometimes feel torn between being logical or rational and being sensitive. It probably upsets you when someone calls you overly emotional, since you really want to be clear and rational. but your feelings are your feelings, and finding a way to allow your feeling nature to play a part in your life is one of your challenges. One of the key qualities associated with this energy connection is an ability to find the common ground, or at least the joining point, of rationale and emotions. You'll also find that your ability to speak with conviction makes you a very convincing woman. When you believe in something, when your heart is in it, there's no stopping you. Who can argue with that kind of power?

Moon opposition Venus: The opposition between your Moon and Venus stimulates a need to become aware of your feelings of self-worth. All the things that go into creating self-esteem are important for you to understand, and foremost among them is an awareness of your true needs. Your wants and needs can definitely be in conflict with one another, and you can fall victim to feeling that having someone else love you, or having certain things or a particular station in life, defines your worth as a person. Finding the common ground between meeting your needs and satisfying your wants is not always an easy task, but you can do it if you practice the art of self-awareness. Then your relationships will improve dramatically, too.

Part of your conflict can arise from accepting the true nature of being a woman— and that includes the process of change. Allowing yourself to express who you are at any given time in your personal evolution enhances your self-acceptance. This allows you to embrace those you love more fully and freely while you feel a more profound opening of your own heart. Loving in a truly soulful manner is much easier than loving from a distance, and you do need to know how it feels to be fully immersed in the process of being, creating, and sharing the essence of love.

Moon opposition Mars: Your Moon is in opposition to Mars, stimulating a need for excitement. You may also feel that you are a magnet for conflict and crisis, and your life may seem to be somewhat crisis ridden. Others may think of you as a temperamental woman, and you can certainly be rather expressive when you want to be. Your anger can reach the point of overwhelming you, and you may find that when you do express excessive anger, you become emotionally exhausted. Yet you cannot resist getting things stirred up a bit, especially if you are ready for things to change. It's finding the balance point that's difficult, since going too far one way really causes problems.

Relationships with men can be quite interesting, since you are capable of being just as assertive and may not be willing to wait for them to act (or react!). The old model of the man in pursuit would be okay with you if the man would act when you wanted him to act, but you have little patience, especially if you want something right now! You do like the idea of knowing that you are also desirable, and that is the rock versus the hard place. You may also find it difficult to avoid getting others emotionally stimulated, especially if you know that there's a fight in there somewhere—so watch the way you handle being emotionally manipulative. This is true in your intimate relationships, with your children, and with your friends. Passive-aggressive maneuvers will get you into trouble, and it's a good idea to at least strive for honesty, especially if you want to walk away on good terms.

Moon opposition Jupiter: Your Moon is in opposition to Jupiter, adding a strong sense of optimism and a desire to see life get better and better. You can also get yourself into trouble if your expectations are not fulfilled, and need to learn the importance of setting reasonable limits. This includes limits on eating, spending, and doing things for other people. Now, you don't have to become a miser—in fact, you probably could never carry it off, since somewhere, somehow, your generous nature would spill out. You've probably learned that excessive restraint is not particularly effective for you either, since you need a few indulgences here and there.

Finding the balance point is the key: and that depends on your setting those limitations. Yes, you can move the limits if you discover that you can handle it; and you really have to remain alert to your expectations about yourself and others. It's easy to feel that you would be happier if only you had more, or if only you could do more, become more, or experience more. Finding a positive channel for this need to push the limits is absolutely necessary, or you may discover that you are never satisfied with yourself. As a mother you can be an amazing and inspiring guide, supporter, and teacher, but you need to remember to allow your children to grow at their own rate, and to live their lives in a manner that fulfills their needs for personal expression.

Moon opposition Saturn: Your Moon is in opposition to Saturn, which can add a level of seriousness or strictness to your personality. It may seem that you've always had to be responsible, and you may have carried responsibilities that were beyond your years when you were younger. You may also have felt some disappointment when you were a young girl, and might have sensed that you were not good enough unless you followed a particular set of rules of behaviors. As a result, you may be overly cautious when it comes to allowing yourself to be emotionally open. You can also be too judgmental, of yourself and of others, and can block your feelings quite effectively when you are in a vulnerable situation. However, you may realize that what you thought to be a satisfactory control of your feelings was instead a repression of your deeper needs. It is here that you have your work cut out for you.

Determining what is right and wrong at a deep level of truth, instead of at a level of fear or prejudice, requires a great deal of courage. This is especially true when it comes to knowing what you need, because you may feel that there is something wrong with being who you are or with satisfying your needs. You may also feel that you have been shortchanged by being born a woman. If this is the case, try to determine where you learned this. In your relationships, you may opt for what is practical, and that may seem much safer than being too experimental. That's okay, as long as you can still express your needs and fulfill them. You may find exceptional healing through your experience of becoming a mother, but only if you can remove any resentment you may feel about the process! You can be a wonderful teacher, a protective guide, and a steadfast shelter for your children, and may, through the experience, find that you are giving yourself that same support you so desperately needed when you were a child.

Moon opposition Uranus: Your Moon is in opposition aspect to Uranus, adding a high level of unpredictability to your emotional nature and a need for personal independence. You need excitement, change, and distraction, but at levels you can tolerate without totally disrupting your life. You may also be more comfortable when you're independent, instead of being tied to a set schedule, a certain role, or a particular list of demands. As an independent woman, you are more likely to tolerate commitments, but if you're expected or demanded to do certain things, you may just rebel for the sake of rebellion. After all, you're an individual! There may be other planetary aspects in your chart that add a level of focus and stability to your life, but this influence alone can disrupt even the best-laid plans! At the level of your soul, you cry out to be seen and accepted for who you are, unconditionally. That acceptance must first come from within yourself.

This influence also indicates the possibility of higher than normal fluctuations in hormonal levels, which can stimulate more profound emotional changeability. Those who are close to you probably recognize a cyclical level to your alterations in mood, and you can tie them to a cycle yourself if you pay attention. You may or not may not decide to choose motherhood as an option, and may be more comfortable in non-traditional relationships. To maintain a relationship, you need plenty of room to be yourself, and to be the kind of mother you want to be, you need to develop a supportive relationship with your children that has some level of consistency. You may relate to teenagers more easily than to small children.

Moon opposition Neptune: Your Moon is in opposition to Neptune, indicating that you are profoundly sensitive at an emotional level. Your imagination, creativity, and spirituality are important elements in your life, and you need ample outlets to develop them. Although it may be somewhat difficult for you to maintain your emotional boundaries, you do need to find a way to determine the difference between your real feelings and the feelings you have because of your association with others. Your sensitivity draws others into your life who may be in need of acceptance, support, and rescue. In fact, you may feel that you are a magnet for people who need help, and may be drawn toward work that allows you to give of yourself to the world. You are a woman who feels everything, and your compassion can be immense. In order to avoid drowning in the woes of the world or in the miseries of life, you need to develop an emotional filter. Part of that filter is structured through your creative expression, since when you're flowing with this energy, you can release and open your energies toward healing. Another element of your filter can be strengthened through meditation, or taking time to separate yourself from the demands of the world.

In your intimate relationships, you are a prime candidate for co-dependency, so be on the alert. You may always be working to keep your awareness levels clear so that you know your real feelings, and it is so tempting to rescue others. Before you dive into the turbulence, can you swim? Sacrificing yourself can be costly. If you are confused about what you need, you are likely to be too deeply immersed in something or someone, and can benefit from developing some outlets that provide objectivity. As a mother, you may be especially sensitive to your children and their needs. In fact, your psychic sensitivity to their feelings can be amazing. Your spirituality and compassion can be a wonderful comfort for them, but you can also allow them to take advantage of you, since you are susceptible to their emotional blackmail—so be on the alert, especially when your children get older.

Moon opposition Pluto: With your Moon in opposition to Pluto, you feel everything at a deep, intense level. You rarely wade in the shallows, since immersing yourself in whatever you're doing is much more gratifying, but your intensity can also stimulate compulsive or obsessive levels of behavior. You can also be an intimidating woman, especially when you're focused on something or someone, and can become completely absorbed in your own feelings. This energy is wonderful for healing, since you have the capability of penetrating into the depths and releasing blocks; although it may be easier to direct this energy toward someone else than it is to direct toward yourself.

Anyone who is uncomfortable with his or her emotional nature and personal vulnerabilities may feel exposed when he or she is around you. Even though you may not intend to overwhelm them, you sometimes do. In your close relationships, it is crucial to allow others to be themselves, warts and all. Your tendency might be to transform them, and that could be dangerous. However, if a person is working toward change, you can certainly be helpful, and you may be the catalyst for change in the lives of many people. As a mother, you can be extremely attentive and aware, but you can also be overly protective and can create an atmosphere of claustrophobia for your kids if you go too far. Use your sensibilities to determine how your children are responding, and allow yourself to back off when necessary. Otherwise, you may reach a point where it feels that you are abandoning ship in the midst of a storm.

Moon Phases and Your Feminine Sense of Self

The Moon's aspect to the Sun corresponds with a particular phase of the Moon. Most people are aware of New Moons—when the moon is beginning a new phase—and Full Moons—when the Moon is brightest and most intense, but there are also other increments in the phases of the Moon. Your Moon phase shows specific qualities that emerge from your deep emotional nature and is quite important when defining the archetypal qualities you project into the world through your feminine essence.

To determine your Moon Phase, look to the degrees separating the Moon and Sun. Some computer-calculated charts indicate the phase of the Moon. I have also noted the degrees of separation from Sun to Moon, and you can easily perform this calculation yourself. For example, if your Moon is between zero and 45 degrees away from your Sun (moving forward through the zodiac), you were born at the New Moon Phase.

New Moon (0 – 45 degrees ahead of the Sun)

Your Moon is in the New Moon lunar phase, indicating that you approach the fulfillment of your desires and needs in an immediate manner. Your impatience with yourself and with everyone else around you can stand in the way of true fulfillment, but it is that same immediacy that is part of your chart. Your impulsiveness can seem quite

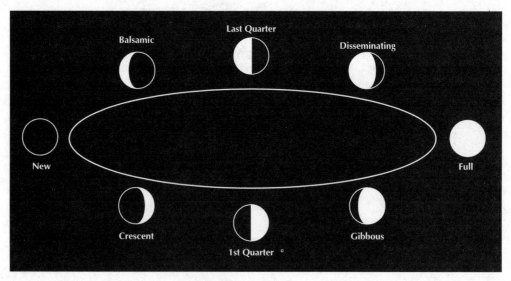

Illustration 6

**New Moon
0°**

"unfeminine" at times, since the old myth of femininity had much to do with "waiting for the prince," but you are here to form a new quality of relating to life: the quality of fresh expression and spontaneity. You are here to project a powerful sense of identity, and achieving a sense of wholeness between your inner and outer self is an important part of your self-development.

The archetypal quality of "The Mother" represented by this moon phase elicits your strong connection to the natural rhythms of conception, creation, and birth. You may even enjoy a positive element of freshness and new life in your projection of yourself as a woman. You'll not appreciate others trying to shelter you too much, but may need to find a few touchstones that will allow you to rest until you venture out into your next experience with life, love, and happiness. Your weakness may be a lack of objectivity, and it can be difficult to find and own your power until you have mastered some skills that add greater objectivity to your sense of self and reality.

**Crescent
Moon
45°**

Crescent Moon (45 – 90 degrees ahead of the Sun)

Your Moon is in the Crescent Moon phase of the lunation cycle, indicating a tendency to struggle against yourself in some way. Life itself can seem to press against you, and you may need to spend some time in reflection to understand that you are not really under attack. Your refusal to do things the way they have always been done arises from your need to feel that your life is moving forward, and that your potential for growth is unchecked. Your old conditioning may have seemed worn once you reached puberty, because once you began to be aware of what it means to be a woman, you had your own ideas of the kind of woman you wanted to become. The archetypal quality associated with this moon phase is "The Maiden," the young girl coming into her womanhood and experimenting with her individuality.

Your need to develop a strong awareness of your spiritual and sexual identity is a strong element of your growth into wholeness. Since you can be quite assertive when you need to be, you may have relationships that intensify your inner struggle until you learn to accept your individuality and know that it is a positive part of your true self. As your faith in yourself as a woman of substance and power becomes better integrated, you will find that it is easier to develop the self-assertiveness that is at the core of your being and trying to get out.

**1st Quarter
Moon
90°**

First Quarter Moon (90 – 135 degrees ahead of the Sun)

Your Moon is in the First Quarter Moon phase of the lunation cycle, indicating that you approach the fulfillment of your desires and needs by taking action. The frustration of waiting for someone else to get something started may leave you feeling that you're always the one who blazes the trails, but you do get a rush from forging ahead, and may even accomplish greater growth in the process. The frameworks you are creating can not only sustain you, but may also become part of the social system. The archetypal quality associated with this moon phase is that of the "Wild Woman," a quality that is expressed in an uninhibited form of sexual and spiritual energy. Through this quality, your passion drives you to experience life as an erotic, satisfying experience, unfettered by the restraints others may so easily embrace.

Your willfulness may also be rather intense, and sometimes you may feel that you are at odds with yourself. Many of the old habits, attitudes, and teachings you learned as a young girl may seem obsolete, since you're more likely to want to create your life on your own terms, but there is a thread that continues throughout your life that binds you to all you have been and to the traditions that forged your foundations. Crisis is definitely something you understand, since you not only experienced it in your early years, but seem to attract it now. You may have a healthy respect for the power of crisis—which is the peak moment of change—since you know it leads to a new phase of experience and opportunity.

**Gibbous
Moon
135°**

Gibbous Moon (135 – 180 degrees ahead of the Sun)

Your Moon is in the Gibbous Moon phase of the lunation cycle, indicating that you are continually striving to reach your goals, and that you are definitely growth-oriented. Even when you've accomplished one achievement, you may feel an immediate discontent, because you can see that there is yet another possibility or pathway. In relationships, this can create a frustrating series of power struggles, especially when others are content to leave things as they are. You need and want to be perfect, and that ideal of perfection is also evolving as you mature. It is crucial that you maintain an awareness of your feelings and needs, and that you spend some time in introspection in order to gain the level of perspective necessary to help you maintain your equilibrium.

The archetypal quality associated with this moon phase is that of "The Muse," stimulating your creative self-development. This is a cycle of blossoming, and you need to feel that your life is an experience of opening up. As you work to create the experience of yourself as a whole woman, you may begin to realize that what you see within yourself is much more valid than the images, ideals, or expectations projected by society—especially those that are false and that do not support the true nature of womanliness. Your devotion to finding this quality within yourself can, indeed, sustain you and may inspire others as well.

Full Moon (180 – 135 degrees behind the Sun)

Full Moon
180°

Your Moon is in the Full Moon phase of the lunation cycle, signifying that you are in pursuit of illumined consciousness. This phase stimulates a quality of idealism, and you may feel most alive when you are connected to the world around you in some way. Your objectivity may be one of your strongest qualities. The archetypal quality associated with this phase of the moon is that of "The Lover," the part of you that knows and shows the power of attraction, sensuality, and desire. Through these qualities, you can create a level of eroticism and high romance.

This sense of relatedness can stimulate a powerful desire to find your soul mate, and you may be more driven than many women to make that connection. It goes beyond a singular relationship, since you are also capable of becoming intimately connected to the world in some manner. Communal experiences are quite empowering for you. Whether you're participating in rituals in church, sharing a group consciousness experience at a retreat, or caught in the thrill of cheering for your favorite team, you can ride the wave of energy, and add your own vitality and strength to carry it further. The process of evolution and growth are extremely important, and despite your biological age, you will be most satisfied when your days and nights create a rhythm of continuity, completion, objectivity, and connection.

Disseminating Moon (135 – 90 degrees behind the Sun)

Your Moon is in the Disseminating Moon phase of the lunation cycle. The idea behind this lunar phase is that of broadcasting seeds, and although there is a masculine quality implied, this phase is definitely one that requires yin, or feminine, levels of continuity. You may feel driven to teach others, to share what you know, and are comfortable in the

**Disseminating
Moon
225°**

role of mentor. In fact, your mentoring flows so naturally that others may not realize that you're passing on to them a truly powerful depth of knowledge and understanding. Your own understanding of yourself and life experience can be enhanced when you open yourself and release your power, creativity, and understanding into the world.

The archetypal quality associated with this moon phase is that of "The Companion," the essence of equality, trust, and sharing. It is crucial that you maintain a strong connection with the core of your being, so that you remain aware and awake, instead of allowing your own direction to be shaped by beliefs, ideals, or attitudes that seem more powerful than your personal focus. Instead of being driven by these beliefs and ideals, you grow more fully into yourself when you add your ingredients to the soup and alter the outcome. Your crusade can be quite exciting.

**Last Quarter
Moon
270°**

Last Quarter Moon (90 – 45 degrees behind the Sun)

Your Moon is in the Last Quarter Moon phase of the lunation cycle, symbolizing an element of conflict that is at the core of your personal growth and understanding. This cycle has often been described as a crisis on consciousness, since you may feel that you are turning away from the old and moving toward a new level of inspiration and understanding. The archetypal quality associated with this moon phase is that of the Warrior, stimulating a passion for existence that allows you to develop clarity, liberation, and self-confidence. Through "The Warrior Woman," you learn about fervent sensuality, courage, and sexual freedom. Your experience of this ideological conflict may arise through your need to break away from false ideals and to reorient yourself to a new way of being, thinking, and living.

What you learned from your mother and her generation about being a woman may not fit with what you are experiencing, although some aspects of your experience from her may ring true. The tricky part is finding your own way without totally destroying the path you've been taught. You are a revolutionary, and although revolutions can be radical and extreme in their outcome, they do not have to be entirely bloody! It is as though you have a fragile egg that needs to be moved to a different nest. First, you must create the new nest, then you must make the journey without breaking the egg, then you must settle in for a time. After that, it's up to the egg.

Balsamic Moon 315°

Balsamic Moon (45 – 0 degrees behind the Sun)

Your Moon is in the Balsamic Moon phase of the lunation cycle, symbolizing a powerful process of distillation within your soul and spirit. You can taste the future, but may be caught in present circumstances that make it difficult to fully realize your vision. Nonetheless, your vision remains, and inspires you to hold fast in your quest for wisdom and understanding. The archetypal quality associated with this moon phase is that of the "Wise Woman," whose intrigue and consciousness are expressed through mystical vision. This quality allows you to explore the far reaches of your inner self, including your shadowy side, without fear, because you hold the candle of illumined understanding. As a prophetess, you are a woman whose sense of what is to come may be clearer when applied to others than it is when you try to figure out your own pathways.

Emotionally, it is important to discriminate between the people and situations that are part of your growth and are in harmony with your needs, and those who would take unnecessary advantage of you—because you can project a martyr-like quality. You can also be tempted toward fanaticism if you're too emotionally attached to an ideal, belief, person, or situation. Personal sacrifice does not mean that you cannot attain a sense of happiness and joy, but instead may mean that you have to let go of some of your prejudicial viewpoints or attachments in order to fully surrender to the power of your own creativity. You may be the artist or performer, caught up in the experience of your creativity so fully that you do not realize that the building has just collapsed around you. Somehow, the essence of what you create survives and sustains you.

Venus: Your Feminine Goddess Self

The energy of Venus is multifaceted. We have seen her depicted as a beautiful goddess. She exudes love, sensuality, and the ideal personification of attractiveness. Your Venusian energy is an expression of your personal self-worth, your values, your expression of artistry, your sense of love. You allow your Venusian self to emerge when you do things that make you feel pretty, when you play the game of attraction, and when you indulge yourself in the things that give you pleasure. Through Venus you seek harmony and learn to give and receive love. Venusian energy is also part of your connection to other women, and the placement of Venus in your chart can tell you a lot about your openness and acceptance of your own femininity. Although your Moon may indicate your basic emotional nature, the manner by which you express your feelings is frequently through Venusian energy. To understand the facets of Venus from the perspective of her role in your feminine nature, study her sign and aspects.

Venus in Aries: Through the energy of Venus in Aries, you project a special flair and can be quite effective initiating romance and sending out the right signal when you're attracted to someone. You love the rush of passion that ignites at a moment's notice, and are more inclined to follow those feelings than to ignore them. It's unlikely that you have ever accepted the idea that it's the woman's place to wait for a man to take the first steps in a relationship, since when you experience attraction you can be quite driven to pursue your feelings. This directness can be intimidating to those who are reticent about expressing themselves or their feelings. For you, the feelings of the moment are extremely important, and you're most comfortable when you can address them immediately. If this sounds as though you are impatient, well, you already know that story. Waiting is not your style. You enjoy being noticed, and may look great in bright colors, especially red shades, which enhance your fiery energy. Getting somebody's attention, after all, is the first step!

Venus in Taurus: Through the energy of Venus in Taurus, you express an earthy type of sensuality and a deep appreciation for natural beauty. You seek out experiences that speak to the beautiful side of life: music, the arts, and creative expression are all important to you. You also have a special affinity for the earth and her life forms, and may enjoy a lifestyle that makes you feel in harmony with the earth. Colors of the earth enhance your own beauty, especially greens and rich earth tones. Touch is an important factor in developing a strong bond, and you may have difficulty feeling close to someone unless they are nearby. Surrounded by the things and people you love most, your own beauty radiates a glow that is difficult to ignore. Once you've found your own particular style in your manner of attire, hair style, or other forms of self-expression, you're likely to stay with it. You do allow room for improvement, however, but are more open if it's your idea!

When you're loving, you love completely and deeply, and have little tolerance for anyone who provides only lip service. You may expect that your lover will be as committed as you are, and can be sorely hurt if your trust is betrayed. You know what you like, and may not be open to trying something different, and you prefer to savor life, love, and the things you enjoy. You can be a patient and understanding lover, although you can be quite possessive.

Venus in Gemini: Through the energy of Venus in Gemini, you express a fun-loving and youthful beauty that shows in your demeanor, your personal style, and your approach to relationships. Your mannerisms, gestures, and voice say a lot about you. You may take great pride in your education, and might go out of your way to make sure that others understand you. Your ability to relate to people from many backgrounds gives you a cosmopolitan air. A well-developed mind is truly beautiful to you, and you may love to read and converse with others who are knowledgeable or interesting. In your desire to experience many different levels of love, you may appear somewhat fickle, since you can change your focus so easily. You do have the capacity for long-lasting relationships, but only if you're still interested in the person and stimulated by the energy of the relationship. Your experience in a career may satisfy many of your desires, and can add a strong level of fulfillment to your life.

Your personal style and expression of beauty may change at different times in your life, although you may always be able to wear the fashion of the time. Bright greens, blues, and yellows have an enlivening effect, and may be good choices for your environment or personal attire.

Venus in Cancer: Through the energy of Venus in Cancer, you experience beauty at a deep, emotional level. You love things that make you feel comfortable, warm, and secure, and appreciate people and surroundings that make you feel at home. You also have the knack of generating a warm, protective environment, whether at work or at home. Music may be an especially important part of your life, and if you sing, you may have a soothing voice. You innately know how to utilize the beauty that arises from being a woman, and may have a special appreciation for the feminine qualities of life. Watery colors compliment your energy—greens and silvery blues—and feel good in your environment, or you might like wearing them. Flowing, soft clothing styles allow you to express your easy grace, and you enjoy wearing skirts and pants alike, as long as they're comfortable. Babies and children may always be drawn to you, because they can feel your nurturing energy.

In your close relationships, you can be quite the caretaker, and might even enjoy the domestic side of life. At the least, you enjoy eating good food, and if you have the time and inclination may become quite a good cook. Tender touch and warm embrace have a powerful effect upon you, and you need to receive as many hugs as you give. You can be somewhat protective and possessive of those you love, and may have difficulty when your children leave the nest—that's okay. Your love can reach beyond the barriers of time and space.

Venus in Leo: Through the energy of Venus in Leo, you radiate a powerful, attractive energy. Your flair for the dramatic may be seen in your elegant manner and sense of style. Although you can be at home in casual attire, you can wear the most luxurious evening attire in grand fashion, and certainly look marvelous in jewels. Your warm smile lights up your face, and you may also enjoy being in the spotlight. Certainly in your close relationships, you like being the center of attention, and may pout if you are ignored. It's unlikely that such a situation will last long since you love life and live to enjoy yourself. Indulging in your favorite forms of entertainment (and you may be quite entertaining yourself!) adds energy and power to your life.

You are capable of standing up for yourself, and probably have a high level of self-esteem. Even if other factors in your chart diminish your self-worth, you rise above them by tapping into the source of love that burns deep in your soul. However, you can be a bit lazy and self-indulgent, and if you're feeling hurt can go overboard in this regard. Although you may take your time opening your heart, once you allow yourself to love, you are not likely to change your feelings. Even if a relationship ends, you may still hang on to it, although some of this can be a matter of pride. Anyone who has been the recipient of your warm hugs is not likely to forget you, since you do have a big heart and generous spirit.

Venus in Virgo: Through the energy of Venus in Virgo, you love the simple things of life. Your delight in the beauty of spring flowers, a kitty's warm purr, a baby's soft skin, and the wrinkled smile around your lover's eyes make life worthwhile. Little escapes your eye for detail, and you appreciate excellent workmanship and self-expression. Your own natural beauty radiates best when unencumbered by excess, and you may sparkle in soft colors and elegantly tailored attire. Comfortable, soft, flowing garments may be your preference whenever possible, but you can also look great in a gabardine suit.

You may have little time or tolerance for excess, and although you may enjoy romance, may not go out of your way to create it. However, you do know what you like, and once you've developed trust in a close relationship, may be quite open about your preferences. It's easy for you to be overly critical of yourself and others, partly because you notice everything and have such definitive taste and favorites. You can be tolerant, although you have to work to develop this skill to its fullest extent. You may find it difficult to experience the love you dream about, especially if the guy who catches your eye turns out to have dirty fingernails. Give him a bar of soap and see how he cleans up before you strike him from your list entirely.

Venus in Libra: Through the energy of Venus in Libra, you express a sense of refinement and grace in your mannerisms and demeanor. You can be quite at home in social situations, and may have an excellent manner of expression. You may feel very comfortable surrounded by blue tones, pinks, and mauves, and probably look fabulous in tasteful color combinations. You're drawn to the beautiful, and enjoy opportunities to dress in your finest attire. Others may comment on your style, charm, and attractiveness, and you need to realize that although you may be physically beautiful, what radiates most powerfully is your inner beauty. Music and the arts are an important part of your life, and you may enjoy artistically talented people. In addition to your own artistic sensibilities, your eye for color, form, and style may be your trademark.

You like to think of relationships as egalitarian, but may tend to give more than you receive—especially if you're trying to please someone. However, you will thrive best in a situation that is truly balanced and where both people can stand on their own. The idea of love may seem much easier than the experience you have in loving, especially if you're in the wrong situation. For you to love, you need a circumstance that is harmonious and non-threatening, and where you are not tempted to fall into judgmental attitudes.

Venus in Scorpio: Through the energy of Venus in Scorpio, your open expression of love and passion may be quite limited in comparison to the depth of your feelings. Only when you've learned to trust another will you open your heart, and even then, you may hold back a little just to protect your vulnerabilities. You approach love with passion, and have a profound sense of what lies beneath the surface. You may be an expert in human behavior, since you can "feel" where someone is despite what they may say. Because you sense these feelings, you may begin to respond accordingly, but can be caught in this awareness, since some people will not allow themselves to act on their deeper feelings. You, of all women, should understand that, since you may hold back if you fear you might be hurt.

The magnificence of opening the heart is unmatched for you, and when you can unleash your own longings, and express your own sense of beauty, you can be exceptionally charismatic. In fact, you can be positively enticing, and you know it. Your ability to use your sexuality as a plus is almost magical. You look great in intense colors: deep reds, purples, burgundy, indigo, black; and when you're feeling a little low might be able to pull your spirits out of the dumps by getting into your favorite sexy attire. When you love, you love completely, and forever. When you're hurt, you can be unceasing in your vengeance. Nothing is halfway for you. It's all or nothing.

Venus in Sagittarius: Through the energy of Venus in Sagittarius, you can be quite direct in expressing your feelings. Your playful spirit and fun-loving sense of adventure plays a large role in your relationships, and you may be most expressive when you're having a wonderful time. You can also be highly spontaneous, almost combustible, when you're attracted to someone. Then, if you act before you think, you may get into trouble. You're almost just as talented at getting out of tight spots—probably from your experience! You adore men who are intelligent and thought-provoking, and can enjoy people from a wide variety of cultures and backgrounds. Venus in Sagittarius definitely has a sensual side, and you can be rather indulgent, almost hedonistic, in your attitudes. Your live, love, and be merry approach is fun during the dating scene, but when you decide to settle into a relationship or family-oriented lifestyle, you can change your focus.

Your deeper side is looking for a partner whose philosophy and attitudes toward life are similar to your own, and who appreciates and practices truth and integrity. You find the beauty of life in nature's own bounty, and may have a powerful appreciation for the wild. When you're out in nature, communing with the trees, mountains, streams, oceans, and wildlife of the earth, your own creativity comes alive. It is your own wild beauty, that sparkle in your adventurous eyes, and your contagious laughter, that make you truly attractive. When you have to be in the "real" world, you may still sport attire that would allow you to take off on an exploration at a moment's notice, and if you have to "dress up," you're at least likely to wear comfortable shoes!

Venus in Capricorn: Through the energy of Venus in Capricorn, you may be somewhat reticent about expressing your feelings, and may shy away from appearing vulnerable, but you do have a strong sense of the feminine element of yourself. This restraint may be lodged in what is "proper" and "acceptable," and getting away from stereotypes and into your real preferences can be a slow process. Once you find your own style of expression, you'll feel much more confident in your self-worth and comfortable with your image as a woman. When you accept yourself as you are, your beauty radiates throughout your being, and others may find it easier to experience the profound nature of your love. When you're in natural surroundings, your best attributes may shine through. Muted earth colors may have a soothing effect on your psyche, and are likely to compliment your appearance, but you may also look great in black.

You appreciate people and things that are tried and true, and may not be entirely confident about your softer side, until you know its strength. The last thing you want is to appear helpless or needy. Although you may sometimes dream of what it would be like to have someone take care of you, you're quite unlikely to allow it! When you're in a committed relationship, the mutual support and care that can develop can be truly sweet.

Venus in Aquarius: Through the energy of Venus in Aquarius, you harbor a sense of unconditional love, and need love relationships that allow you to feel free, open, and expressive. Your capacity for friendship is immense, although you may have only a few special friends who share your intimate thoughts and secrets. Yet everyone who meets you may feel that they have found a friend, and you are likely to be sincere in your desire to acknowledge the humanity in everyone. Although your feminine nature is quite strong, in some respects you may feel almost androgynous, since you may be able to relate to both men and women with a clear understanding and connection. You may have quite a broad appeal, and if your career places you in the public eye, men and women alike may respect and admire you. Your sense of personal style is likely to be quite unique, and you may look great in clothing that is trend-setting or unusual. You may even create some of your own styles, or have someone create them for you alone. Translucent colors like violet, turquoise, and purple stimulate your energy.

In relationships, you may find it difficult to focus on just one person until you know for sure you've found someone who understands and accepts your uniqueness and individuality. The man who is looking for a "regular" wife has not found his answer in you! You are most likely to exchange vows you've written yourself than to feel at home with the old standby of "love, honor, and obey," and certainly would leave out the obey part. You may also prefer to avoid marriage altogether unless it serves a reasonable purpose and is addressed on your own terms.

Venus in Pisces: Through the energy of Venus in Pisces, you can develop a powerful sense of compassionate love. Your expression of your deeper feelings vibrates through everything you do, sometimes strongly, and sometimes in a more subtle manner. You are deeply sensitive, and unabashedly romantic. All the romance novels with the perfect love that takes you away from the cares and trouble of the world were written for you! That sense of the romantic goes beyond man-woman relationships. It permeates your expression of yourself as a woman. Your own beauty shines brightest when you are at peace with yourself. Your energy needs to flow, and you may be most comfortable when you're dressed in loose-fitting garments in soft colors, but you can also wear striking colors when you need energy.

You need to flow through life and with life, and you need to satisfy your faith in what is good and perfect. You need something that can stand up to your devotion and adoration—whether that is an artistic form of expression, a family, a spiritual path—you need to put your heart and soul into your life experience. If all this seems idealistic, well, it is! You are filled with ideals: ideals that will never be satisfied until you test them against the experience of life itself. You're a woman filled with so much compassion that if you cannot express it, you will wither away. You can also be vulnerable, and may fall victim to unscrupulous individuals if you trust absolutely everyone at all times. This is the hard part of the story, and the part of life that can sometimes be discouraging and leave you feeling sad. That still will not stop you from finding the beauty in life. You see it in the eyes of the children; and along with the despair that seems to be everpresent in today's world, you see the hope and hold faith in the dream for true peace.

Venus Aspects and the Expression of Your Feminine Self

Conjunctions of Venus

Venus conjunct Sun: The conjunction of your Sun and Venus represents a very powerful expression of your feminine creativity. You can radiate love. Your sense of personal value and self-esteem is enhanced through this blending of energies, and you can be especially effective in developing your natural beauty. This aspect adds charm, grace, and magnetic attraction to your list of personal attributes.

Venus conjunct Mercury: Through the blending of Mercury and Venus energies in conjunction with one another, your manner of speaking and communicating is enhanced. This aspect influences your ability to develop excellent people skills, and you may be a gifted speaker, writer, or lyricist. These qualities may emerge through your manner of speech, which can be quite elegant and charming. Your sensibilities toward others, and the care you take in striving to create a feeling of peace and harmony, can be seen in your personal relationships as well as within the work environment.

Venus conjunct Mars: With Venus and Mars in conjunction aspect with one another, you may have an especially active expression of your emotions and artistic sensibilities. Even though you may want to assert yourself in some situations, this blending of energies indicates that you are likely to consider the effect of your actions prior to initiating them. This sense of consideration can work to your benefit, but can also be somewhat frustrating if you're trying too hard to please someone else. You may be driven toward developing relationships and might find it difficult to feel comfortable when you feel you're alone, especially in social situations. That rarely lasts long, since you're probably quite charming and hard to resist.

Venus conjunct Jupiter: The conjunction of Venus and Jupiter stimulates your generosity and ability to attract high levels of abundance. It may appear that you are quite lucky, and, at the very least, these qualities attract good fortune. Yet if you direct all this energy toward yourself, you can become quite spoiled. Your sense of "I want" can become rather self-indulgent, especially if you take people or situations for granted and expect that you will always have everything without having to assert much effort. If you allow this energy to flow in and out, giving and receiving, you'll discover that you not only experience greater satisfaction, but that you know the true essence of an abundant life.

Venus conjunct Saturn: Venus and Saturn are conjunct in your chart, stimulating a feeling of restraint in expressing your emotions. You have high standards for yourself. In fact, you may have a long list of qualifications for yourself and others that must be met before you can be on on the receiving end of the goodies. Although that may seem like a practical approach, it can be a bit frustrating. Your feminine self-expression can be quite powerful through these energies, but you're not likely to be flowery and silly. Instead, you prefer a mature approach to love and emotions, and can be quite matter-of-fact about what you do or do not like. You have a well-defined taste and sense of style.

Venus conjunct Uranus: With Venus and Uranus in conjunction aspect, you are attracted to the unusual, and may be somewhat experimental in your sense of style. This includes your style in relationships, which is definitely centered around a need to break some of those old outmoded ways of loving and being loved. Taking on subservient roles or giving up your independence could be impossible for you. You may also prefer to dress in a manner that flies in the face of convention, and it probably looks good on you. After all, you are doing this to attract what you want. The only problem is figuring out exactly what (or whom) that might be—since your feelings could change tomorrow.

Venus conjunct Neptune: The conjunction of Venus and Neptune stimulates an amazing creative and artistic sensibility, but, more importantly, allows you to experience and express a true sense of compassion. The essence of The Goddess is quite powerful for you: you can float into the heart of divine love and bring that quality into your life. You may project a mystical, magical quality of beauty. Your desire to make the world a better place can lead you to spend time doing things for others, which is, in itself, an expression of divine love. Allowing some time each day to reflect and meditate is important in helping you maintain your personal boundaries, since you feel everything. You may dream about the perfect love, and have high hopes that you will one day be carried away. However, you may be disappointed when Prince Charming arrives, especially if he turns out to have stinky feet.

Venus conjunct Pluto: With Venus and Pluto in conjunction, your expression of love, and desire to be loved, take on a powerful intensity. This adds an amazing dimension to your feminine essence. Your charisma can be intriguing, and your aura of mystery, enticing. Your embrace of the strength of being a woman gives you a special edge, and when you are focused on giving energy and love, can be the catalyst for true miracles of transformation—including your own. Comfortable with your sexuality and sensuality, your relationships allow you an opportunity to express deep levels of love and passion. And your creative energies are just as potent.

Venus Sextiles

Venus sextile Mercury: With Mercury and Venus in sextile aspect, your grace in communicating and relating can be quite effective and may endear others to you. You probably avoid crass and rude individuals, since you are not comfortable in distasteful circumstances. Ladylike behavior is much more your style. Refined mannerisms and speech may be among your trademarks—or at least, you're known to have good taste!

Venus sextile Mars: Venus and Mars in sextile aspect add to your attractiveness. You feel confident asserting yourself, especially if the object of your desire is close at hand. You're the type of woman who knows how to send the right signals, but you also know when to take action. Even in competitive situations, you can be charming, which may give you an interesting edge. You have a way of making others feel comfortable when they're around you, and may be adept at dealing with situations that require peace-making or intervention.

Venus sextile Jupiter: Through the sextile of Venus and Jupiter, you express a heightened sense of confidence in yourself as a woman. Your feminine attributes work to your advantage, even in business circumstances, where your artistic sensibilities and taste may be quite attractive. You may also appreciate and support the efforts of other women, and can work well in concert with others focused on a similar goal or cause.

Venus sextile Saturn: With Venus and Saturn in sextile aspect, you possess a well-defined sense of taste and personal style. You are capable of applying your creativity and artistry to a number of situations, including those in the working world, and may be adept at making the best choices when it comes to business decisions. Your reasonable judgment in matters of the heart allows you to deal with relationship issues without throwing your life into a tailspin. Emotional maturity has always been one of your strong points. You know that some things take time to reach their best levels, and you have the patience to wait when you know it will be worthwhile.

Venus sextile Uranus: With Venus and Uranus in sextile aspect, you can be quite provocative. Your unique way of expressing yourself draws attention, and can work to your benefit when you're feeling good about yourself. You're the type of woman who prefers to do things your way and to have a strong level of autonomy in relationship to others. And you're quite willing to offer the same to others, and may encourage your friends and family in their efforts to develop themselves. You like being an individual, and enjoy doing things that amplify your uniqueness.

Venus sextile Neptune: Venus and Neptune are in sextile aspect to one another, adding a sense of mystical imagination to your expression of love and beauty. You are an enticing and romantic woman, and love indulging in your favorite fantasies. Your creative and artistic sensibilities may be especially important, and you may be artistically gifted. Employing these qualities within your relationships and career allows you to rise above the everyday and mundane.

Venus sextile Pluto: The sextile aspect between Venus and Pluto indicates a strong level of charisma. You can fully embrace and appreciate the power of being a woman, and know how to use it to your advantage. Understanding the deeper essence of emotions, you are capable of experiencing profound change and growth through opening your heart and allowing love to flow unencumbered through the totality of all that you are. This strengthens your personal artistry.

Venus Squares

Venus square Mars: Venus and Mars in square aspect indicate an inner conflict between your desires and your ability to attain or satisfy them. Part of the problem may be impatience with yourself and with others: you want it now. You may also feel some level of resentment or frustration with your inability to gain the full measure of what you feel you deserve, and this, in itself, can impede your progress! The core of this conflict can center upon a battle between your feminine and masculine inner self. It can manifest in ways such as sexual discrimination or sexual harassment, and if you stand up to these types of injustice and abuse, you'll find that you feel much more powerful and at peace with yourself. You must be attentive to the ways you give away your power, because this is the key to understanding how to resolve this conflict.

Venus square Jupiter: Your expectations of yourself are quite powerful. Stimulated by the square between Venus and Jupiter, you may be rather flamboyant in your manner, and may not know when you've had too much of a good thing. Setting limits is difficult and frustrating, since in your heart you may believe that anything is possible. If you see yourself in unrealistic proportions, or if you expect impossible things from life, you may feel continually disappointed. You might even try to make up for the deficiencies by overindulging yourself or overspending. There's nothing wrong with optimism, but there is a difference between optimism and unrealistic expectations. Learning that lesson is one of your challenges, and if you are to have the faith in yourself that you deserve, you'll have to face it. Believing that having enough money or status will make up for a lack of personal worth can get you started on the wrong foot. Try again. You are a creative, witty, and visionary woman with a lot to offer. Now, that's a good beginning.

Venus square Saturn: With Venus in square aspect to Saturn, you may close away your feminine vitality and block your power of attraction. Your mistrust of your own worthiness is related to a feeling of frustration that comes from being a woman. In fact, you may even resent being a woman some of the time, or may mistrust other women. You may feel you've been shortchanged, or that you are not getting what you deserve. But you may also project an attitude of critical restraint that stands in the way of your ability to express your own worth and beauty. Sometimes, this aspect indicates that you resent being valued for your beauty, or fear that if your physical beauty fades or does not meet the "standards," you will be worthless. Once you fully realize that the energy of beauty has little to do with the facade, it's easier to radiate your true worth, and to attract what you really need. Otherwise, you may feel that you are continually faced with disappointing compromises.

Venus square Uranus: With the energy of Venus in a square aspect to Uranus, you have a rebellious spirit that shows in the way you present yourself as a woman. You may choose unusual forms of dress, different hair styles or colors, or other forms of adornment that fly in the face of convention. Sometimes you do it for effect. Other times, you're just feeling experimental. Your approach to relationships may have much the same effect, and you're not likely to settle for playing the roles traditionally delegated to women. If your actions or attitudes alienate others, this energy becomes counterproductive. What you really need is to be accepted for your uniqueness.

Venus square Neptune: The energy of Venus in square aspect to Neptune stimulates your imagination and romantic spirit. You love delving into fantasy, and can be quite dramatic. You may also be tempted to wear a mask in order to cover your feelings of vulnerability. This mask can be in the form of make-up, manner of dress, or different forms of escape. You are sensitive, and have such idealism that you may feel true pain when reality slaps you in the face. The problem you may face in creating your true expression as a woman is discovering what it is you truly want and need. The vague sense that it's out there somewhere does not convince you that you'll ultimately find the right image or step into the magical spotlight. You need to find a way to allow romance and imagination to blend with what is truly possible. Using this energy to envision yourself as the woman you want to become, and then gradually altering your life to "test" your vision can allow you to determine the differences between what you do and do not really need. Keeping your emotional boundaries intact is one of your greatest challenges, especially once you fall in love. You can accomplish it by remaining mindful.

Venus square Pluto: You may feel a deep undercurrent of vulnerability when it comes to allowing yourself to embrace the fact that being a woman means something positive. This feeling, stimulated by the square aspect between Venus and Pluto, may have very deep origins. Whatever the cause, you may feel compelled to prove that you are powerful, worthwhile, and worthy. For some reason, you may feel ashamed of yourself, and cannot allow your beautiful essence to shine through. You may even resent being a woman, especially if you've been deeply hurt. If you dig deep enough, you'll find real treasure at the core of your being, and that treasure is hidden in the heart of a magical woman: you. This is the part of yourself that can heal and regenerate your spirit, allowing you to be totally transformed as you embrace a new essence of your powerful self.

Venus Trines

Venus trine Mars: Your ability to integrate and utilize your powers of attraction in harmony with your sense of assertiveness is enhanced through the trine aspect between Venus and Mars. When you know what you want, there's no stopping you, although your approach may be tempered by charm and sophistication. Your confidence in yourself shines through in a beautiful way, and can be extremely attractive. When you're in relationships, it's unlikely that you'll feel threatened. Men may be especially comfortable around your easy grace.

Venus trine Jupiter: You love the elegant, beautiful, and finest things life has to offer. Your self-assured and cheerful attitude is very attractive, and works like magic when you're in a pinch. Somehow, you can always pull out of a tight situation, a result of the power generated by your deep sense that you truly deserve to have your needs fulfilled. With Venus in trine aspect to Jupiter, you are the eternal optimist, and may have an excellent vision of what the future can bring. Others may be drawn to you for this reason, especially when they are at a lack for ideas or options. Social gatherings may be your forte, since you definitely know how to entertain in a grand manner, but you're the woman who can accomplish the same results in a business setting, too. With classy appearance and intelligent grace, you're the woman everybody notices and enjoys.

Venus trine Saturn: When you're committed to something, you put your heart into it. The influence of Venus in trine aspect to Saturn indicates that you take a straightforward approach to expressing your feelings. You're willing to give yourself time to determine what you want and how you feel, and this enhances your emotional maturity. Sometimes, you may take yourself a little too seriously, but you rarely go overboard. Although you prefer to be around others who are personally responsible, you may discover that you are the one who understands the bottom line and ultimately carries through. Men may be attracted to your impeccable manner, but may appreciate you most for your helpful support. As a mother, you provide a wonderful, steady support for your children, and understand their needs for continuity and responsible tolerance. These energies are a plus in all your relationships, because you have an honest grasp of the importance of longevity and the passage of time in developing an abiding and trusting love.

Venus trine Uranus: You're happy about the things that make you different, and you may be highly creative and artistically gifted. The trine aspect between Venus and Uranus adds a dimension of innovation and uniqueness to your self-expression. Although you may be a feminist at heart, you're not likely to take a radical stance that alienates those who are less broad-minded, unless you're forced to do so. Instead, you can help to bring about the types of changes that allow old, outworn attitudes to fall by the wayside. These same energies are responsible for a certain type of magnetism that seems to put you in the right place at the right time to take advantage of unusual opportunities and good fortune. Thank your lucky stars!

Venus trine Neptune: If any woman has vision, it is you. Your grasp of the essence of what is and what can be is reflected in your imaginative artistry and gift for adding a special dimension to whatever you do. With Venus in trine aspect to Neptune, your awareness can transcend the ordinary, and you feel it through your heart. You believe in love and know its power. Sometimes, others may think you're an angel, and that's okay with you! Of course, you know that you are only human, but may long for the perfection you sense in the spiritual realm of reality. In your self-expression, through music, the arts, drama, and even common everyday experiences—you can take your life one step closer to paradise. Your emotional sensibilities are heightened through this connection, adding a level of compassionate love to your life. Sometimes, you may feel disappointed in human nature and the human condition, but by opening your heart to those around you and developing your connection to the truth of love, you can make a difference.

Venus trine Pluto: You've experienced the powerful transformation love can bring into your life. In fact, you may live to re-create this magic over and over again. Whether it's in your relationships, through your connection to your children, in your work with others—you are capable of acting as the catalyst that brings renewal, healing, and rebirth. Through the energy of Venus in trine aspect to Pluto, you express the essence of healing. That "medicine woman" role does not have to be anything strange. In fact, it may be just as easy as making a pot of chicken soup! This quality is also part of your charisma, and you are quite capable of understanding how to use your sensual and sexual qualities to your advantage. You know that being a woman is a powerful experience, and you're probably quite content in that knowledge. After all, would you have it any other way?

Venus Oppositions

Venus opposition Mars: If any woman feels the dance of love and the intensity of the power of attraction, you do. You can be especially magnetic. The energy of Venus in opposition to Mars indicates an internal conflict, however; and it is the conflict between the masculine and feminine elements of your psyche. You may want to experience life and relationships to their fullest, but can get in your own way if your attitude becomes belligerent or selfish. You can become competitive with your own needs, especially if you feel you're weak, or that being a woman makes you the weaker sex. Then, you can overcompensate by becoming too aggressive and wonder why nobody likes to be around you. When you go too far, men will think you are a "ball-buster."

You may be very sensitive to criticism, and jump to a defensive attitude before you've had a chance to hear the entire story. But there is a strong possibility that you can move beyond these limitations by using the very same energies that get you into this pickle. When you take the time to objectify what is going on, you can see both sides. You do understand that there is a definitive difference between men and women! Because you need some competition and crisis in your life, your relationships will fare better if you find a positive outlet like sports, games, or other pursuits that allow you to feel challenged. If you fail to develop other ways to direct this energy, you may be stuck in situations that seem one-dimensional or filled with conflict.

Venus opposition Jupiter: You love the side of life that is filled with fun, games, and enjoyment. Your playful attitude can be quite endearing, except that you have trouble knowing when it's time to grow up. With Venus in opposition to Jupiter, you can be very self-indulgent, and may appear to be greedy or gluttonous in your desires. You may also live under the mistaken impression that if you achieve enough status, have the right clothes, live in the best neighborhood, or have the most influential friends, you will be accepted and loved. As a woman, you are especially vulnerable to the illusions perpetrated by advertisers who play on these desires, so remember that the next time you go shopping! What you need in your life is an outlet that allows you to give of yourself and share your resources. The joy you gain from helping others enjoy the good things in life may be more exciting than having it all yourself.

Venus opposition Saturn: You may long for the kind of love, support, and acceptance seen in the movies—where, no matter what happens, a man will do anything for the woman he loves, but deep in your heart, you may feel that it will never happen, or worse yet, that you do not deserve that kind of happiness. "It's all make-believe," you might say. With Venus in opposition to Saturn, you close the doors to your heart and inhibit the fulfillment of your own desires. All that fantasy stuff does not sit well with you. You want something real, lasting, and satisfying, but may not be willing to give enough of yourself to have it. It is imperative that you get in touch with your fears and anxieties, and that you face your real needs. Otherwise, you may feel that you are always compromising or getting the hand-me-downs. Take the time to look at yourself and change your image: amplify your best qualities instead of trying to shape them in a way that is satisfying only to somebody else. You may be stunningly beautiful, but may not trust your own beauty. Or you may feel plain and ordinary, and sense that this means you are an undesirable woman. What makes you desirable is your own acceptance and joy in being yourself.

Venus opposition Uranus: Do you remember the line in Peter Pan, "I won't grow up!"? Well, in your heart of hearts, you would prefer to remain as free, experimental, and playful as you were when you were a young girl. In many respects, that independence and "catch me if you can," attitude is always a part of who you are now, as a woman. With Venus in opposition to Uranus, you have little interest in being a cookie-cutter image of anybody. You may dress in a bodacious manner, and may feel uncomfortable with "traditional" hair styles, clothing, or jewelry. You can actually create your own look, which ultimately expresses the truly beautiful qualities you have to offer once you've gotten beyond the need to shock everybody. You are an individualist, an experimenter, and need lots of room for self-expression. But sometimes, in creating all this room, there is a big empty space inside your heart where you want and need someone else to be close. Your friendships are a good beginning for understanding the way you need to be accepted and supported in your life. You're learning that there is a difference between unconditional acceptance and irresponsibility. You may have to give a little more of yourself, however, before you have the life situation, relationships, or happiness you hope to achieve.

Venus opposition Neptune: Knowing yourself as a woman can be a little difficult, since you may try on a lot of images before you see yourself reflected back in the mirror. With Venus in opposition to Neptune, you may reflect more of what others see in you than what you see in yourself. Sometimes, when you try to get a grasp on the parts of yourself you value most, you may come up with empty hands, groping in the mist for a vague and fleeting connection to the core of your being.

You do have an answer to this frustration, and it lies in the experience of delving into your inner being. Whether through creative, artistic, or musical expression or meditation—you need to know your inner self. It is here that you have clarity, and here that your true essence of beauty and identity through love emerges. There will never be anyone "out there" to rescue you and return you to yourself. You must do that for yourself, or you will, instead, end up the victim of illusion or deception. No amount of make-up, no perfect screen role, no Prince Charming, will ever be the answer. The answer is already there, hidden in your heart. It is true, compassionate love for life.

Venus opposition Pluto: At first, when you were grappling with the experience of becoming a woman—during the time of hormonal rushes, physical changes, and powerful urges—you may have resented yourself, your body, or your lot in life. Deep within yourself, you knew that there was a power, and that it was centered in the fact that you are a woman. With Venus in opposition to Pluto, you can be the reflection of the positive, transformational, and healing power of being all that is woman. However, you may have to experience a few changes within yourself before you get there. It is imperative that you face the pain or hurts you have experienced through loving, loss, and disappointment. Hiding behind an impenetrable shield will only block your ability to attract what you need from life. It is crucial that you deal with any feelings of shame, guilt, or hatred—especially if they are directed toward yourself. Forgiveness is not an easy task, but you deserve a chance to live your life to the fullest and to experience the true essence of love, beauty, and harmony. In metaphysical teaching, there is an old concept called "harmony through conflict." You know what that means. It is the essence of your life, and the path you are following in discovering who you are as a whole woman.

Neptune, Pluto, and the Dream and Power of the Feminine

Although the planets Neptune and Pluto move very slowly and are generational in nature, the do have an influence upon your psyche. These energies define much about the collective experience that shapes your inner self. You're experiencing Neptunian energy when you're in the midst of reverie, when you're deep in dreams, and when you're feeling compassionate. Neptune drives your imagination, the realm of illusion, and your psychic sensibilities. Because Neptune is difficult to grasp on a physical level, there is a lot about this energy that can be problematic, and when you are caught in the negative grasp of

Neptune, you can give in to addictive behaviors, escapism, and deception, but you do have a way of channeling this energy. It is through Neptune that you find the heart of compassionate love and understanding. This is the doorway to your inner self.

Neptune remains in a sign for a long time, and its influence has an impact on your expression of personal femininity. You'll also experience Neptune on a broader scale. Neptunian images impact the collective, and the filter (the sign Neptune is in) says a lot about what the collective views as the personification of an ideal. By understanding how this energy works on both a collective and individual level, blend the concept of Neptune with your Moon and Venus. Think of Neptune's energy as the background color and lighting in a painting, with Moon and Venus providing the features in the foreground.

Neptune's Sign in Your Chart and the Ideal of Femininity

Neptune in Cancer: With Neptune in Cancer, you are part of the generation of women who walked across the threshold of the twentieth century (1901–1916). You hold the sanctity of the family as a primary feature in your life, and have a deep reverence for the things you learned from your mother and grandmothers about what it means to be a woman. Your spirituality may be an important mainstay in your life, and the protection you feel by connecting to the spiritual essence of life has been extended from you to those in your care. Even though you may not have been taught that God has a feminine side, you've always known it was there because you can feel the support and love from Divine Mother.

Neptune in Leo: With Neptune in Leo, you are part of a generation of women who felt it was important to assert personal autonomy and who needed to be recognized as individuals in their own right. Although you may have a strong appreciation for the men in your life, you are part of the generation, born from 1916 to 1929, that brought women into the spotlight. Personal image has also played a powerful role in your sense of individual identity, and you understand the importance of feeling strong within yourself. The changes initiated by your generation, such as women's suffrage, are still extremely influential in the shift in attitudes that is continuing to evolve in today's society.

Neptune in Virgo: With Neptune in Virgo, you are part of the generation of women, born from 1928 to 1943, who have understood the importance of developing and maintaining sound minds and bodies. In the perfect world envisioned by your generation, health, good education, and clean environments are extremely valuable—and you have, individually and collectively, instilled this attitude into the developments of modern society. Your role as a woman in the world has also been influenced by a strong desire to learn and to become proficient in dealing with the world. The vision of sound health on every level held by your generation is still powerfully influential in the development of educational models, health facilities, and other institutions that support the betterment of life on earth.

Neptune in Libra: With Neptune in Libra, you are part of the generation that has been fascinated with beauty, the idea of peace, and the hope of a perfect world. Perfect relationships are part of the perfect world, but it is your very generation that has blasted through the illusion of dysfunctionality. Your role as a woman within a relationship is one you are creating along with the other women of your generation born from 1942 to 1956. By holding a collective image of truly egalitarian and fair-minded relationships, where each person can fully express themselves, you have been part of a global change. The effects of this change are still manifesting.

Neptune in Scorpio: With Neptune in Scorpio, you are part of the generation of women born from 1955 to 1970 who are forging new frontiers in the sexual revolution. This is not only in terms of human sexuality, but also in the roles men and women play in regenerating society. You are the generation that will grapple with issues of control and whose influence in the arenas of human rights will cover the entire spectrum from conception, to birth, to sexual lifestyles, to choices in death. As you are maturing and making these choices, you may resist the idea that some belief system or government should dictate the choices you make in these intimate situations, but you must also create a vision that goes beyond these old systems and encompasses a true compassion for the experience of life and the pain and joy of choice on every level.

Neptune in Sagittarius: With Neptune in Sagittarius, you are part of the generation of women born from 1970 to 1984 who are just coming into maturity. Your influence in the realms of education, government, and politics will be immense, and as an individual member of this generation, it is imperative that you discover and employ the things you are learning about truth. You were born at a time when media had a profound influence upon society, and you will find ways to use the technologies that are developing to shape the lives of people on earth. You may grapple with the differences between "truth" and "facts" and can either fall victim to false belief systems or create better ones. Women of your generation may rise above the limitations of their mothers and grandmothers because of their educational opportunities, but also because you and they will not accept the same limitations.

Neptune in Capricorn: With Neptune in Capricorn, you are part of the generation of young women, born from 1984 through 1998, who will carry the torch for the new structure of modern society. It may be your job as a collective to bring order out of chaos. One of the primary dilemmas you will face involves the importance of productive lifestyles and responsible choices. You will also be surrounded by a large number of people who are of the "older" generation. Institutions (including government and educational institutions) can be especially powerful during your lifetime, so when you're creating them, try to be aware of the functions they can serve within society that will further the development and evolution of humanity.

Pluto's Primordial Beauty

Pluto represents the primordial essence. It is from this level that all transformation occurs: birth, death, illness, healing, and it is here that the powerful kundalini force continually regenerates itself. This is the space of all creation and all power. It is the space of origin: the Great Mother. In mythology, one of the most powerful stories relating to Pluto is the story of Persephone, who is transformed by being taken into the underworld. It is here that she finds her place, but her power cannot be fully expressed until she learns how to equalize it with the experience of life on earth.

Pluto's Sign and Your Feminine Power

Pluto in Gemini: With Pluto in Gemini, you are part of a generation of women born from 1884 to 1913 who have had to learn about the importance of developing the mind and creating positive avenues for communication. You have seen the explosion of the information revolution, and have witnessed the powerful influence of the exchange of ideas on a global level. You may feel as an individual that one of the sources of true power resides in developing your own mind through education, outreach, and tolerant understanding of the diversity of life on earth.

Pluto in Cancer: With Pluto in Cancer, you are part of a generation of women born from 1913 to 1938 who have had to learn about the importance of strong families and what it means to be tied to a particular family heritage. You have been alive through the challenge of hate mongers like Hitler who violated the very sanctity of human life. You have been part of the powerful woman's revolution, even if you were not actively burning your bra, which has altered the very nature of families and women's roles in society. These things have had a powerful influence upon your own psyche as an individual, too. You have learned that the sanctity and power of life may rest in finding a true sense of home within yourself.

Pluto in Leo: With Pluto in Leo, you are part of a generation of women born from 1938 to 1957 who have had to learn about manifesting power and breaking the illusion of the patriarchy. You are among the women who have reshaped society. If you've developed a career, you may have done so against an old system. Instead of destroying that power base, your task within the collective is to change the nature of power through love and creativity, and through honoring the sanctity of life.

Pluto in Virgo: You are part of a generation of women born from 1957 through 1972 who have Pluto in Virgo. It has been your challenge to develop a true awareness of the relationship between mind, body, and environment. You've blasted through many of the mysteries of the way humans function—at physical, psychological, and sociological levels. Additionally, you may be seeking a way to improve the quality of life and are likely to be dealing with repairing mistakes and fixing things as much as you are creating new options. At an individual level, this energy prompts you to determine ways to improve yourself.

Pluto in Libra: You are part of a generation of women born from 1972 through 1984 who have Pluto in Libra, and are challenged to break down the barriers within society that inhibit growth and free expression of the human spirit. You may also find that you must tear down old structures that have determined the nature of human relationships in order to heal some of the problems existing among human beings. This can reach from marriage contracts to international relations between governments.

Pluto in Scorpio: You are part of a generation of young women born from 1984 through 1995 who have Pluto in Scorpio, and will play a key role in understanding the true nature of healing. The advances in medicine developed by your generation will have far-reaching effects on the quality of life. You must also heal the environment, and may feel that you're spending a lot of time cleaning up the mess wrought by the generations that preceded you. In order to assure the survival of humanity, you may have to face exceptional challenges, but you're up to it!

CHAPTER FOUR

OWNING YOUR INNER MASCULINE SELF

For centuries, women were not allowed to assert themselves in the world, and carefully learned the role of supporter of their "men." Those who failed to respond in this manner were frequently shunned or punished, although there have always been women who defied convention! During this century particularly, women have broken out of their strictly "conventional" roles, and have been making their own way in the world. As a collective, the women's movement of the twentieth century has brought women into positions of strength in Western society, especially in America, through obtaining the vote and programs like affirmative action, which have helped women move into positions of strength through better education and greater opportunity. Issues surrounding everything from birth control to family leave have offered women new alternatives and broader choices. Because of these changes, women have been successful at fulfilling more of their needs and owning their own power more readily.

As a result, a woman's relationship with the men in her life has also changed. Despite women's collective knowledge about the need to be whole persons, it is still sometimes easier to allow men (fathers, brothers, lovers, and husbands) to "own" certain qualities (They, in turn, prefer that women own certain qualities—like emotions!), but to become truly whole and functional, it is necessary to find and incorporate your inner masculine self into your sense of wholeness instead of projecting that part of yourself on others (most usually men) in your life. This will allow you to feel more confident about stepping into the world and will also lead to improved and more honest relationships in every part of your life.

Shining Your Own Light: Your Sun's Energy

Through the process of becoming at home with your ego, you gain a true sense of personal strength and power. To own this power, you must learn to acknowledge that it is okay to be recognized for who and what you are. Your Sun energy is the primary factor in the expression of ego needs. As a young girl, you may have seen your father through the filter of your Sun. His power of getting out into the world, and the manner by which he did it, shaped your own sense of personal identity. When reading about your Sun, you may find characteristics you recognize in your father, or that you hope to find in the significant male relationships in your life, since the Sun in your chart also symbolizes significant men. This energy is, in itself, the core of your spirit and the flame that burns deep in your heart.

Your Sun's Masculine Voice Through the Signs

Sun in Aries: Through your Aries Sun you have the capacity to develop a strong level of autonomy and self-direction. You may be a self-starter, and will prefer to address life on your own terms. However, you can have a little difficulty trying to figure out how to go after the things you want without alienating others. If your approach is too brash or abrasive, you'll meet with resistance and end up feeling that you're always defending yourself. Despite being a woman, you may be okay in situations with "the guys," especially if you're involved in sports or other activities in which there are more men than women present. Since you can be competitive, you may set up situations that provide a challenge, but do not need to feel that you're always doing battle. You need some positive outlets through which you can develop your willpower, and may enjoy a career path that requires you to forge into new territory from time to time. You're an excellent leader, and whether you're working in the world, guiding your family through a crisis, or seeking spiritual clarity, you can forge a path that others readily follow.

Sun in Taurus: Through your Taurus Sun you experience a sense of continuity and stability, and can express your masculine side through establishing a secure place in the world. Whether you choose a career path or family structure as your focus, you are like an anchor and have the ability to provide strength and consistency. It may be important to you to create a home base, and the energy you put into building your home includes both house and family. Your special sensibility toward the environment can grow as you mature, and you may find that your awareness of the importance of preserving the environment and making the best use of resources is behind your most powerful drives.

As a woman, you will take great care to build upon the foundations in your life, and may prefer to assert yourself in a slow, steady pace. Your career path needs to provide opportunities for you to establish yourself and grow steadily. Regardless of your marital status, you function best when you have your own money and resources. Although your father may have been the breadwinner and financial mainstay when you were a child, you may prefer a different situation with a husband or partner. Allowing the man in your life to control your finances will ultimately result in a power struggle, if not externally, then certainly within yourself. You can work cooperatively with a partner toward joint ventures, financially and otherwise, and can feel willing to share and contribute to the financial and other needs of your family, but you will feel greater autonomy if you also have a separate fund that you control for yourself.

Sun in Gemini: Your expression of your masculine sensibilities through your Gemini Sun is filtered through your intellect. Your admiration for others who are knowledgeable and communicative is a direct result of your own desire to know as much as possible. If your early impulse was to think that a man might be a more knowledgeable authority than a woman, that has probably changed radically as you have matured. In fact, you may even challenge that assumption through your choices in career. However, you may not think in terms of man versus woman: you're more into dealing with people for who they are, and may assume that others will also take that stance. You may even have a knack for communicating quite effectively with both men and women, and may make strides in bridging the gender gap. You can waffle a bit in situations that require you to take control, and may sit on the fence a bit too long some of the time—it just takes a little objectivity to get this under control, especially in new circumstances. Once you know how things work, you can be the maven of juggling priorities.

Sun in Cancer: Even when you're expressing your assertiveness and will, your emotional sensitivity acts as a filter. You innately know that expressing your masculine side has nothing do with acting like a man, but that instead, you can assert yourself and enjoy the edge that being a woman confers. Your projection of the masculine has a feminine quality—Cancer is a feminine water sign! Before you can readily assert yourself, you must "get a feeling" for the person or situation; it's almost as though you turn inward before you turn outward. It may be difficult for you to stand up to boisterous, power-hungry individuals, and your shields are likely to go up when you're confronted with circumstances that seem to assault your vulnerability. However, once you're more at home with a situation, your sensitivity will help you navigate through it more gracefully than some of those rowdy types of individuals. You appreciate sensitive men, although you may attract men who need to be mothered. As you've discovered, there are many ways to nurture. However, you may also think you need a man to protect you. When you step back and look at it, who is protecting whom? Your drive to accomplish recognition may be stimulated by your need to create the security you need for yourself and your family, and once you have children, they may take first priority.

Sun in Leo: Since you're no stranger to the spotlight, you've probably had ample opportunities to express your assertiveness and personal strength. Your Leo Sun is a magnet for attention, and your actions and attitudes determine whether or not that attention is helpful or detrimental. You have the potential to radiate a powerful energy, and may be an inspiration to those who need a stable source of confirmation that life is, indeed, okay. You can be intimidating to men who are unsure of themselves, and may even take advantage of this; just try to remember your own insecurity when you first faced raw power! Taking on the challenge of leadership can be one of your most fulfilling experiences, although you can be quite domineering in some situations. If you've been giving away your power to the men in your life, you have probably attracted strong-willed individuals. To become truly complete, you must learn to embrace and express your own individuality in a manner that opens your creativity and fills your heart.

Sun in Virgo: You may be glad you're a woman. In fact, some of the more brutish aspects of manhood may hold absolutely no enticement to you whatsoever. As a Virgo woman, you're not interested in expressing your masculine side as a man might—you would prefer to own your identity and express it just the way you want it! But face it, you can be intimidated by men, and may have given away some of your power because you don't feel very comfortable tooting your own horn. There is a difference between appreciating yourself and standing up for the recognition and advancement you deserve, and letting someone take advantage of you. Unfortunately, you may not really want to do battle, and might prefer to just do your job or attend to your duties and let the blowhards have their fun. You also get in your own way by being too critical of yourself, or feeling that you are not really "perfect enough," to have all the glory. It's possible that you felt a strong sense of judgment or criticism from your father, and learned to be Little Miss Perfect in order to gain his approval; but that was when you were a little girl. By applying your powerful sense of discrimination and critical judgment to determine if you're getting what you need from your relationship, your job, or your family, you can make an honest assessment of your life situation. Then you can forge a plan of action that will assure that you achieve a better pathway for your personal fulfillment.

Sun in Libra: Claiming your sense of individual autonomy may not be an easy task with the influence of your Libra Sun. Since you tend to think in terms of relativity, it's difficult to extract your own assertive self in a confident manner, especially during your early years. You may have learned to place great importance on your physical appearance or on proper social behavior, learning to behave like a young lady, assuming that if you were pretty and charming enough, all the other things would just fall into place. Stepping out into the world and discovering that you needed to be known for more than your looks may have been your first reality bite. Your sense of relativity can be one of your best assets, however. By making harmonious choices of partners—whether they are friends who share your interests, lovers, or husbands—you can get the type of feedback you need to see yourself more clearly. Then your autonomy and individuality are strengthened through greater objectivity. However, if you seek a partner or husband who will take on the tasks you don't feel prepared to handle, like dealing with the demands of the world, you will be continually frustrated and will frustrate your partner, too. Additionally, developing social relationships that support and reflect your true values will help you feel more confident about your identity, instead of just seeking situations that increase your social standing or status.

Sun in Scorpio: A deep craving for power, that you feel but others may not see, accompanies the energy of your Sun in Scorpio. Your father may have seemed somewhat omnipotent when you were young, and he may also have been difficult to understand at times. You have a greater respect for men who can stand up to their own power, and who can respect the unique power of women, too. There is a part of you that will always be fascinated by superheroes and superheroines that stems from your fascination with alterations in energy and transformational change. Throughout your life, you may be drawn into situations that need to change, and in which you provide the catalyst for the transformations. In many ways, you are a natural healer, and you can bring this quality of regeneration into your relationships, your work, and your creativity. Embrace the fact that you are a Goddess! Live to create, and own your ability to use the magical ingredients that bring power into your life and that affect dynamic shifts in the world around you.

Sun in Sagittarius: Since you've always wondered about everything, a certain level of personal assertiveness has always been part of your personality. Your Sagittarius Sun energy is a powerful driver, stimulating your sense of adventure and endless questioning and giving you an air of excitement. You're the woman who has been comfortable venturing out on your own, particularly if you have a strong interest driving you. As a young girl, your experience of your father may have been especially connected to his interest in learning, or his philosophical or religious teachings may have been a stronghold in your life. You may also have a desire to develop these elements of your life in your own way, and in searching for the truth of yourself are likely to discover some differences from your upbringing. Developing your individual identity may be easier said than done, because you may always have a tendency toward extreme reverence for your teachers and may take the teachings too literally. Task one: separating the teacher from the teaching will allow you to gain confidence in your individual ability to develop a connection to divine truth. Then, as you explore the vast nature of spirituality, you may discover a path that is uniquely your own. This, in turn, influences your sense of who you are, not just as a woman, but as a human being on a quest for the ultimate.

Sun in Capricorn: You've rarely felt satisfied unless you have a sense of accomplishment. Embracing the drive of your Capricorn Sun is a huge challenge because once you've set your sights on something, stepping back or stopping your steady progress toward your goal is almost unthinkable. If you learned as a young girl that it was the man who could accomplish absolutely anything in the world, you may have resented that fact, because you've always had a yearning to be recognized and respected. If your relationships have supported the theory that it's a "man's world," you may not trust your own sense of who you are. It's a question of learning about the nature of reasonable control. As a woman, you will express control differently from the way a man might. You may not care so much about submission of will. Instead, you may be most interested in asserting your will in a manner that will give you the ability to direct your own life and through which you can positively shape the lives of others.

Sun in Aquarius: The most friendly path toward developing and expressing your willpower and personal drive may be that of education. As an Aquarian woman, you appreciate a well-developed mentality, and may feel most confident when you are comfortable in your knowledge about a subject or situation. However, you may have felt as a young girl that the people who knew the most were men, and you certainly may not have questioned whether or not a man had the right to be different. Although you have felt the impulse to be different, you've never been entirely comfortable with the idea of alienating yourself from the society of which you are a part, and as you've developed your own individual identity, you may have sensed that becoming who you are might not exactly fit the model your father had in mind for you. If you're owning your personal power, you're confident about expressing your uniqueness and meeting the world on your own terms. If you've not yet embraced this part of yourself, you may be trying to accomplish it through projecting these qualities on your husband or partner. Let him be the genius in the family! Your own genius may not fully emerge until you've consciously determined that you, too, deserve to be seen for who you really are.

Sun in Pisces: Your own sense of identity and strength alludes you, especially if you feel confused about your place in the world. The influence of your Pisces Sun stimulates marvelous dreams about what life could be, but you may not fully realize those dreams unless you can find a way to create positive personal boundaries. This is first accomplished by becoming acquainted with who you are, especially on an inner level. You may feel a special fascination with men, and may believe that they have more influence and power than you. It's tempting for you to project the qualities of power and control onto the men in your life rather than taking the risk of standing up for yourself and your needs. It's also possible that you will unconsciously seek out men who are wounded and need your compassionate support. In truth, you have exceptional strength through your resilience and adaptability. You can flex and bend with the changes happening around you and within you, and emerge quite nicely, thank you! However, in order to fully own and express your will, you may have to struggle with the feelings and sensibilities that make you vulnerable to being victimized by those who would take advantage of your gentle spirit. It's also tempting to allow men to see in you whatever they wish, instead of establishing an identity that is more readily definable on your own terms. It is this challenge that tests your ability to embrace and fulfill your own needs.

Sun Aspects: Inner Harmony and Conflict

The aspects between the Sun and other energies in your chart defines the flow or frustration of your expression of your solar power. These aspects help to define the issues you have with men, too, and you may recognize some of the strengths you possess through understanding and developing the qualities energized by the Sun's aspects.

The Sun's Conjunctions

Sun conjunct Mercury: The conjunction of your Sun and Mercury adds emphasis to your need to be recognized as a thoughtful or intelligent woman. The value you place upon learning, knowledge, or information can be rather intense. You may also be under the impression that if you're smart enough, you'll get what you want from life. That may be true, but there are many levels of intelligence. One of those levels involves knowing when to stop talking and start listening, so remember that when you feel that you're not really being heard.

Sun conjunct Venus: The influence of your Sun in conjunction to Venus adds a glow to your self-projection, and may soften the impact of your assertiveness (the iron hand in the velvet glove). This can be a plus, and can stimulate an energy that readily endears you to others. You may be able to use your charm and good taste to your advantage, too, especially in business and personal situations that call for a touch of class, but you can also become too self-absorbed, and may tend to think that just because you like or want something that you should have it. Careful: you could develop a princess complex!

Sun conjunct Mars: Adding to your need for recognition is a drive to accomplish the things you want to do. The combined energies of the Sun and Mars in your chart function like a supercharged turbo engine. That sounds a little masculine, doesn't it? More power!! Well, how do you handle the need to compete, on your own terms, without igniting too many fights? First of all, give up the idea that every-thing must be peaceful all the time. Accept the fact that you are somewhat crisis-oriented, and that you need situations that allow you to drive yourself. Avoid getting yourself into circumstances where you are ruled or controlled by others. If you give in, you might turn that energy inward and undermine your physical vital-ity. Look for challenges, and have some fun with them, and find a man who is strong enough to stand the heat of your passion. Just agree on the rules before you start playing any games!

Sun conjunct Jupiter: Staying in one place seems terribly limiting to you, and you may always be one to test the limits or to go beyond the realm of expectation. Your Sun in conjunction aspect to Jupiter is an energy of pushing limitations in order to experience a broad range of options and opportunities. You may be quite comfort-able taking on roles that in the past were traditionally dominated by males, and may be quite adept at handling positions that represent the interests of a company or even a nation.

Sun conjunct Saturn: You're strongly influenced by a need to do things properly and correctly with your Sun in conjunction with Saturn. Your need for self-respect is quite strong, and you may also seek others as teachers and guides who are worthy of your respect and admiration. If you are ignoring your own needs to take posi-tions of strength or control, you may attract others who will simply overwhelm you with their own power. This can be especially true in relationships with men, since you may project your own need for control onto the men in your life, and then wonder why you never have what you really want. Once you take steps that help you establish your own aims and ambitions, however, there's no stopping you! With this aspect, you can either take charge of your life or be controlled, but either way, learning about control is paramount.

Sun conjunct Uranus: The influence of your Sun conjunct Uranus stimulates an immense need to develop your self-assertiveness and individuality. Finding your-self may involve taking a path that is out of the ordinary, but that's to be expected since you're an extraordinary woman! You may wonder why you seem to attract men into your life who are unattainable or distant, and it could just be that the root of the problem is that you do not want to be tied down. Part of owning the masculine element of your psyche is the experience of allowing yourself to be a woman on your own terms.

Sun conjunct Neptune: You are a dreamer, and your ability to visualize yourself and the world as you wish them to be is exceptional. Through the influence of your Sun in conjunction to Neptune you can also create a special connection between your inner self and your experience of the world. This is a tricky aspect to handle because it's tempting to hide from yourself or to simply play roles instead of finding the part of yourself that is real and expressing that to its fullest capacity. Your "sensitive" side may try to be a martyr some of the time, but you'll quickly learn that this path will only cost you time, energy, and creative vitality. You must also learn to avoid the trap of over idealizing men, including your father. When you're taking this view, you are more likely to be projecting your sense of identity on the men in your life instead of working toward establishing your own. Once you can see the men in your life as they are, in the truest sense of themselves, you will also be free to express the essence of yourself more fully.

Sun conjunct Pluto: You may be tempted to allow your life to be absorbed by the will and expectation of the men you love, from father to lover to husband. You may even have had an experience early in your life that tested your ability to survive. In truth, the conjunction between your Sun and Pluto indicates that you need to know what it is to express the charisma and intrigue that are the essence of your power as a woman. Men may be both fascinated and overwhelmed by your intensity, and you're likely to stir up a bit of controversy with anyone who is uncomfortable with their emotions, including their sexuality. As you fully integrate the essence of your will and drive with your need to create change, you can become an effective healer and powerful catalyst for growth.

The Semisquares

Sun semisquare Mars: With your Sun in semisquare aspect to Mars, you can be strongly aggressive at the wrong times. If you've not accomplished integrating your own needs to take charge of your life, you may attract men who are overly belligerent, strong-willed, or too controlling. It's important that you learn how to handle anger, whether it's your own or somebody else's. Finding healthy ways to express your personal assertiveness can open a lot of doors, but there will be times that you seem to break down a few doors just because there seems to be no other choice! Knowing that you can't always control or change the actions of others will also help you determine when you need to step out of the way of another person's anger or aggression. Sometimes the winning posture is stepping aside with dignity.

Sun semisquare Jupiter: The frustration of your Sun in semisquare to Jupiter arises when you feel that you've disappointed somebody. Your own expectations of yourself need to be carefully evaluated, too. There's a strong tendency for you to project high levels of expectation onto the men in your life, and to then feel frustrated when they fall short. Although you like to approach life with optimism, sometimes you are blindly optimistic, and learning how to balance your hopes with realistic possibilities is part of owning your own sense of identity.

Sun semisquare Saturn: You tend to give away too much power to the men in your life with your Sun in semisquare aspect to Saturn, and every time you do, you feel regret. The problem is experience: over time, you learn to alter your fear of being in control and gradually accept more and more responsibility for yourself and your happiness. As you do this, you will take a more measured approach to dealing with the men in your life. You may feel that you have to prove yourself in some way, and that's okay as long as the motivation rests in your need to satisfy yourself, but if you're swallowing your personal pride just to please some man, you still have work to do.

Sun semisquare Uranus: You may be inconsistent in owning your personal masculinity with your Sun in semisquare aspect to Uranus. When you're confident in your abilities and expressing your individuality, you can relate to men on an equal level (your preference) and remain in the moment quite easily, but when you're feeling overly rebellious or taking actions that undermine your personal stability, you may discover that you're attracting situations that leave you feeling rather out of place and men who are simply flakes. Finding ways to express your uniqueness without turning over the apple cart requires finesse, and through listening to your intuitive self more readily, you'll become much more adept at staging revolutions where everybody benefits.

Sun semisquare Neptune: You really don't have to fix all the men in the world, but with the influence of your Sun in semisquare aspect to Neptune, you surely can attract needy, addicted, or unreliable men. The more aware you are of your needs to take charge of your personal identity, the less you will project onto men. Strangely enough, you'll also begin to attract a different quality of men, who may still be needy or wounded, but who are working on themselves. You may feel most powerful when you're playing the role of either victim or rescuer, but be careful—in these scenarios, there are usually no winners.

Sun semisquare Pluto: You need to know what it's like to feel a sense of strength and influence. With your Sun in semisquare to Pluto, you may attract men who have major control issues, and until you learn how to be in control of yourself more positively, you may feel abused, abandoned, or wounded through your relationships with men. Your inner relationship with your psychological masculine self may be stuck in old patterns that you learned from your early childhood experiences, believing that men are somehow more powerful or that you don't really deserve to live life fully and well. You can harness the power necessary to leap beyond these old messages into a brighter sense of yourself, transforming your life, and consequently healing your relationships.

The Sextiles

Sun sextile Mars: The ease of expressing your will power and assertiveness is enhanced through the energetic sextile between your Sun and Mars. Your comfort with the need to make your own way may be apparent in the manner in which you approach everyday matters, but you can shine when you're faced with a challenge. In fact, challenges that ignite your desire for achievement or recognition can stimulate you to go the extra mile. You may not find it necessary to compete with men, since you can be quite comfortable with yourself and your abilities, and it is likely that you will feel capable of pursuing the fulfillment of your desires for a satisfying career and healthy personal life. In the face of competition, regardless of who or what is on the other side, you are capable of holding your own.

Sun sextile Jupiter: Your confident, optimistic attitude supports your ability to express your personal assertiveness. The energy of the Sun in sextile to Jupiter strengthens your ability to act with conviction and hopefulness. You may also be quite accessible—comfortable with yourself, radiating a friendly, easygoing attitude. Both men and women may find you easy to be around, although you may be more interested in some of the pursuits considered "masculine," like politics, sales, or sports. You like your masculine side, and that works to your benefit.

Sun sextile Saturn: You're probably ambitious, since the energy of your Sun in sextile to Saturn stimulates your need to gain respect. Taking responsibility for yourself seems only natural, and you are likely to feel that you do not need anyone, including a husband, to take care of you. You enjoy relationships that provide an opportunity for each person to succeed and develop. Your attitude toward men is probably healthy, although you may be quite happy that you are a woman.

Sun sextile Uranus: Independence and individuality have always been among your trademarks. Your ability to express what is unique about you is strengthened through the sextile aspect between your Sun and Uranus. You can relate to almost anyone, anywhere, and this universal appeal can broaden your options in career and relationships. Not only are you a woman who believes that each person should be considered on his or her own merit, you may be revolutionary in changing social systems or business practices that discriminate against this fundamental principle. For you, a person's gender may have little to do with whether or not they are capable or competent—and that applies to your opinion of yourself!

Sun sextile Neptune: Even when you are in a circumstance when you need to take charge or assert yourself, your gentility and compassion radiate through your actions and self-expression. Through the influence of your Sun in sextile aspect to Neptune, you have the capacity to accept yourself and others, and may be very open in your expression of faith in the principle of universal love. For you, embracing the masculine element of your psyche may be as simple as riding a bike—you just do it. Any other conflicts that you may have within yourself in this regard can be easily resolved through making an effort to integrate your spiritual and physical needs. You may over-idealize just a bit, so do remember that blind trust can be a problem.

Sun sextile Pluto: At least some of the role models you've followed have known how to use their power positively, and your admiration for this quality arises from your own desire to establish yourself as an influential and healing woman. Your will power is supported by your ability to embrace and utilize change through the sextile aspect between your Sun and Pluto. You realize the importance of owning your strengths, and may be instrumental in helping others do the same. Psychologically, you are likely to feel good about embracing your need to be assertive and strong—your masculine side—but you know that this does not mean you have to take control of someone's life, and you're not willing to allow that to happen to you, either!

The Squares

Sun square Mars: You may feel an undercurrent of anger that rarely loosens its grip on your psyche with your Sun in square aspect to Mars. This can be especially true if you've failed to address your needs to direct your own life. It is crucial that you come to grips with your feelings about the men in your life, including your father. You may be fighting battles that are already won, and can be belligerent or hostile, which can be alienating and self-defeating. Finding positive outlets for your need to be challenged, like sports or other competitive games, will make a huge difference in the quality of your life, but the critical factor is knowing that you can get what you want once you've entered a level playing field.

Sun square Jupiter: For many years, you've felt driven to be better than you think you are. This is the influence of your Sun in square aspect to Jupiter. It was important for you to feel that your dad was proud of you when you were a little girl, and you may still not feel that you've quite succeeded unless you gain the recognition of the man who is important in your life. Although you have plenty of optimism and confidence in yourself, in fact, you may sometimes go beyond your limits. But you'll never be satisfied until you know that you've reached the horizon of your dreams on your own merits.

Sun square Saturn: You may feel less than you are, especially if you've given too much control to others. Your self-will is frustrated by a feeling that you are inadequate through the influence of your Sun in square aspect to Saturn. Even as a little girl, you may have felt required to meet impossible or difficult demands. This influence could also represent great self-restraint and a tendency to limit your own opportunities, especially if you are constantly undermining your options by failing to take responsibility for yourself. It is conceivable that you feel saddled with too many responsibilities, or that you have difficulty saying no because you do not want to be rejected or limited. In order to fully claim this part of your masculine psyche, you must accept yourself and break the habit of negativity. It is also important to address your fears and to confront the fact that you may simply be afraid of allowing yourself to have the respect you deserve. Once these self-limiting attitudes are addressed, you can concentrate on dealing with life's challenges from a much better perspective.

Sun square Uranus: You're a revolutionary, although you may feel that you're ahead of your time with your Sun in square aspect to Uranus. In connecting to the masculine part of your psyche, you're likely to reject any of the images of self that have been created by someone else. You'll simply rebel against any man who tries to tell you what to do or whom to be. If you're resisting establishing your own identity in the way you intuitively know you must, you're actually rebelling against yourself. Instead of just going for shock value, you may actually find that you can integrate your unique qualities into an exciting expression of yourself that gives you an excellent edge in a world of otherwise mundane possibilities.

Sun square Neptune: Experiencing an honest connection to the true essence of your spirit is not easy with your Sun square Neptune. In order to integrate or express this masculine element of your psyche, you first have to find it! Your tendency to project your sense of identity onto the men in your life is heightened under this influence. If you've been in situations with men that have left you feeling deceived, then you may be the victim of your own inability to see yourself and others clearly. The undercurrent of this energy is a lack of trust within yourself, and it is that quality that needs to be healed in order for you to move forward. Your compassion for life and need to feel spiritually connected are basic requirements if you are to embrace your ego, but you're caught in a true Zen experience: you must first surrender your ego in order to find it! The key is knowing where and to what that surrender must be directed.

Sun square Pluto: You may feel that if you can annihilate the power of control men have over your life that you will then own yourself. With your Sun square Pluto, you've always struggled to be in control, and much of the time, you've struggled against yourself. What you are seeking is transformation, not destruction. If you felt that you faced strong survival tests in the past, you may believe that your identity and will are damaged, but you have the most amazing ability to regenerate yourself, and you can do it consciously. That means you can determine who you want to become during your rebirth, and that is truly phenomenal. You're also challenged to be aware of the manner in which you handle positions of influence, since your own misuse of control or judgment of others can easily backfire.

The Trines

Sun trine Mars: Your ability to assert yourself and pursue the fulfillment of your needs and desires is strengthened through the energy of your Sun in trine aspect to Mars. When you find yourself in situations that require you to take positions of leadership, you are quite capable of rising to the challenge. When you feel you need support, you can also reach out to others who will enjoy sharing the experience with you. Understanding that you are a strong woman, and allowing yourself to test your strength in pursuit of your aims, brings renewed vitality into your life.

Sun trine Jupiter: Your optimism and confidence penetrate into the essence of your spirit. You believe in yourself with the Sun trine Jupiter. You may also attract influential men into your life whose standing and success allow you to enjoy more of the good things life has to offer. Your ability to attract abundance is amazing, but you may not feel complete until you realize that you are the magnet for your own good fortune! By expressing your generosity toward others, you gain strength and will also feel more complete.

Sun trine Saturn: As a realist, you understand that you have certain responsibilities as a normal part of life. With your Sun trine Saturn, you may be quite happy to accept those responsibilities, instead of expecting that someone else must carry your burdens. Your relationship with men and with your father may be quite good, especially in business circumstances. You express a positive sense of your inner masculine when you are in control of your life circumstances.

Sun trine Uranus: You don't have to fit in with everybody else in order to see and accept yourself. With your Sun in trine aspect to Uranus, you are most confident when you are expressing yourself in your own unique manner. By developing your special talents and individuality, you will be ahead of the game of determining where you want to go with your life. By allowing yourself ample opportunities to show your independence and exercise your autonomy, you will become whole.

Sun trine Neptune: Through the influence of your Sun in trine aspect to Neptune, you may express the masculine qualities of your ego self by directing your energy toward helping others. You may not need the recognition or the spotlight, although you can be quite gracious in its glow. Your need to integrate the spiritual and creative aspects of your self-expression flows much more easily when you are in harmony with the rhythm of life. Your way of developing your identity may be connected to creating peace and making a difference in the quality of life.

Sun trine Pluto: Although you may be fascinated by powerful and influential men, you know that you also possess a strength of your own. You have the ability to use your influence to create healing and renewal through the flowing energy of your Sun in trine aspect to Pluto. Regardless of your beginnings or of your current situation, you are capable of initiating and accomplishing great change when necessary.

The Quincunxes

Sun quincunx Mars: Learning when to take an assertive stance and when to let the dust settle is a tricky proposition for you with your Sun in quincunx aspect to Mars. Sometimes, you may feel out of step with your own internal rhythm, and can push too hard or exhaust yourself physically and spiritually. The manner in which you handle anger is critical to your strength as a whole woman.

Sun quincunx Jupiter: Before you know it, you can get in over your head. The influence of your Sun in quincunx aspect to Jupiter stimulates a powerful restlessness and desire to push beyond your limits. The problem is seeing the limits in the first place! For you, they need to be made out of rubber in order to stretch as frequently as you would like.

Sun quincunx Saturn: You may underestimate yourself and your abilities, especially if you feel that you are being judged by those in superior positions. Your ego self is sensitive to being tested with your Sun in quincunx aspect to Saturn, but you know that you need the tests in order to become stronger. Allowing yourself to be noticed can be especially anxiety-provoking, and you may benefit from developing your ability to be comfortable in front of other people.

Sun quincunx Uranus: Knowing when to let your wild and zany self emerge and when to try to fit in is tricky with the Sun in quincunx aspect to Uranus. Sometimes, your timing seems to be off, but that's only when you're not paying attention or listening to your intuition. When you're on, you're phenomenal; but when you're off, you can feel very unsure of yourself. Try not to be so hard on yourself. Sometimes the fun of the experiment is worth the embarrassment!

Sun quincunx Neptune: You may think you have a special talent for getting off track with your Sun in quincunx aspect to Neptune. The problem is one of focus: integrating who you are with where you are. Your imagination and creative sensibilities are especially strong, and sometimes your "consciousness" can seem to be in one place while some other part of yourself is in a totally different zone. As a result, you can present a confusing image to others, and may not feel particularly confident about the image you want to present, period. By spending some time each day in meditation or contemplation, calming your mind and centering your energy, you will be more capable of balancing these inner frustrations. Then, the peace, compassion, and love that resides in your heart can shine through all that you are much more easily.

Sun quincunx Pluto: Sometimes, you're just too intense. Although you seem quite normal to yourself, the influence of your Sun in quincunx to Pluto indicates some inconsistency in your self-concept. When you're feeling uncertain of yourself or insecure, you can overcompensate by becoming too compulsive or obsessive, and it is this intensity that can get in the way of your progress. By becoming more aware of the things, people, and situations that trigger your vulnerability, you can compensate and become more consistently sure of yourself.

The Oppositions

Sun opposition Mars: Do you seek out conflict? Sometimes it may feel like you are a magnet for competitive or conflicting situations with your Sun in opposition to Mars. Testing your strength can be a positive challenge, but your tendency to present an image or attitude that challenges others can result in great discord. You may also attract men who are abusive in some way, especially if you are not asserting yourself when necessary. You need healthy outlets for your drive, like sports, and you feel more alive during high activity periods or in a crisis-oriented career like emergency medicine.

Sun opposition Jupiter: It's easy for you to overdo it. The influence of your Sun in opposition to Jupiter stimulates your tendency to overexaggerate. Sometimes, you do have bragging rights, but during the times when you feel rather ordinary, you may stretch the truth just a little. Learning about limitation is one of your lessons, since you prefer to think optimistically, and with the sense that there are only horizons without fences. You may also expect too much from others, or feel that they should do more for you—and this can lead to great disappointment. To achieve the balance you seek, you need ample opportunities to move beyond your current circumstances while still maintaining your equilibrium.

Sun opposition Saturn: You may be afraid to allow your ego its moment in the spotlight with your Sun in opposition to Saturn. After all, what would happen if you made a mistake? Your early conditioning may have included strong criticism or endless rules about how you were supposed to behave in order to be acceptable. Gaining acceptance from your father may have been very important, although difficult to realize. Even today, you may attract controlling men. That same critical attitude may permeate your sense of yourself, and you may be holding yourself back just because you fear the unknown. There will be different times in your life when this self-limitation will be tested and you will be forced to take a look at who you are in truth, versus who you have become in order to survive. As you become more aware of your own nature and needs for self-expression, you will gradually bring these two points closer together.

Sun opposition Uranus: You really do like to be different, and may have a knee-jerk response of rebellion when anyone uses the phrase, "You can't do that!" The influence of your Sun in opposition to Uranus is about breaking through the barriers of the ordinary and allowing your individuality to shine through. You insist upon liberation, perhaps too much sometimes, and as a result can appear distant or aloof to the very people you might like to impress. Your challenge to be different may influence your choice of partners, and until you come to grips with what you need and who you are, you may simply attract a series of flakes. Finding the ways to express your freedom urges without burning all your bridges before you cross them is an amazing challenge to your ingenuity.

Sun opposition Neptune: Have you ever wondered if you simply live in another world? The influence of your Sun in opposition to Neptune stimulates an amazing challenge: you have to find yourself beyond the illusion, yet you must know how to use illusion to express yourself. One of the greatest potential traps you face involves your tendency to project your sense of identity onto the men in your life. It can be difficult for others to see who you really are, especially if you are not clear about it yourself! You may think of yourself as an actress playing many roles, but when the curtain closes, you feel lost and confused. Who are you? Sometimes taking on different roles can help you find yourself, but you will never find your salvation trying to save everybody else. Nor will you know yourself if you give your power to somebody and allow them to shape your life. Creating a safe haven for yourself that allows you to get away from the pressures of the world is crucial. Just remember that you cannot stay there all the time and really find yourself. You need to reach out and make tangible connections.

Sun opposition Pluto: You may continually run into power plays—situations in which you feel overwhelmed. With your Sun in opposition to Pluto, your identity is continually evolving, and your search for yourself may seem to be endless. In some respects, that can be a positive experience, particularly if you are probing into your psyche and releasing the elements you've outgrown or no longer need, but you can also become obsessed, and may not know when to stop turning over rocks or looking for bad guys. You are a powerful woman, capable of stimulating growth and change. Sometimes, you expose corruption in the process, but other times, you find an absolute treasure.

Mars and Your Self-Assertiveness

Mars energy is assertive, aggressive, and combative, and can be angry. These are not concepts that come to mind when identifying "feminine" qualities. In fact, women who possess and project these qualities from within themselves often get bad names, and may be called "ball-busters," or other expletives, by the men who are dealing with them. To become fully whole, you need to accept the manner in which you can utilize your Mars energy so that you are confident and strong with it, and so you can get into the world and make things happen for yourself! This is your drive and the manner in which you assert yourself. Accepting and expressing your drive adds a greater sense of personal satisfaction to your life.

Mars Signs: Identifying Your Drive

Mars in Aries: Pursuing the fulfillment of your needs and desires is something you do with great courage and strong assertiveness. With Mars in Aries, you learned early that you like to do things that are challenging. Whether you're involved in sports, career pursuits, or building a family—you're the woman who will forge ahead despite the odds. You may also be quite comfortable expressing your anger, openly and directly. Who say's it's not ladylike?

Mars in Taurus: Although you may be stubborn, when you want something you can be relentless in your pursuit of it. Through your Mars in Taurus, your embrace of the assertive side of your masculine psyche projects a powerful steadfastness. You may not want to turn the world upside down. In fact, you may do your best to make sure that those things that are important to survival remain. You may also be more comfortable projecting your fighting spirit on men who seem to enjoy that type of thing. Through this part of your masculine self, you prefer to maintain the status quo.

Mars in Gemini: With Mars in Gemini, you can be a bit of a mischief-maker. Sometimes you may not mean to get things stirred up, but you have a knack for igniting action with words. Getting out into the world is relatively easy for you, and you can connect with your assertive masculine drive by developing an understanding of your psychological nature. You may feel at ease in the company of men and women alike, since you present a generally non-threatening quality.

Mars in Cancer: Although you can be assertive when you have a stake in something, your indirect approach may lead others to believe that you are passive. With Mars in Cancer, you do need to watch a tendency toward passive-aggressive behavior and may have to consciously avoid emotional manipulation. For you, getting out into the world is easier if you have a reason or a need. Otherwise, you may be just as comfortable focusing your energies on things closer to home. It is crucial that you become aware of how you handle power and the manner in which you deal with situations where you need to be assertive. Your first response may be to back down, or to wish that there were a man there to defend you. Learning to stand up and be counted is the first step toward fully embracing your masculine psyche, and when you do, your conviction alone will be your shield.

Mars in Leo: When you want something, there's little to keep you from getting it. With Mars in Leo, you may radiate a strong sense of confidence when you're putting on your assertive face, even if you feel like Jell-O inside. The key to your will lies deep within your heart. When you love something or someone, your willing courage is always there, helping you forge ahead or provide protection. You've stood in the center of the storm before, and will probably do so again. And you may have learned how to be firm in your strength through the love and support of some powerful men in your life. However, you're more alive when you know how to harness that same power for yourself.

Mars in Virgo: Harnessing your assertive self is rarely your first priority. With Mars in Virgo, you're usually focused on getting the job done in the best manner possible. Although your work may be meticulous and the things you produce awe-inspiring, you may have difficulty standing up for yourself and making sure you get the attention you deserve. It may be much easier for you to allow someone who seems more powerful to fight the battles while you plan the strategy.

Mars in Libra: With all the press about Libra being peace-loving, you may assume that your Mars in Libra would prefer not to fight. Well, all the nasty parts of a fight may not be your style, but you certainly know how to inspire a good battle! The truth of the matter is that you are a fighter, and you know how to go after what you want. It's just that, if at all possible, you'd prefer to do it in good taste!

Mars in Scorpio: With Mars in Scorpio, you're determined to fulfill your desires, and you can be unstoppable in your drive to achieve your aims. You're not likely to deny your sexuality as part of your personal magnetism, and can be strongly aggressive when you know what you want in any circumstance, including the bedroom, but you are also the mistress of control, and can be cold as ice when you've been hurt. You understand the power that surges in the soul of a woman, because you've harnessed it more than once.

Mars in Sagittarius: You can be a bit sassy with Mars in Sagittarius and certainly have no trouble at all setting out on your adventures. Even as a little girl, you were probably on the go, and now that you're a woman, you may have a restless energy that is only satisfied when you're on a quest. Your confidence and optimism may be radiant when you're in pursuit, but you can become frustrated if you have to stay in one place too long.

Mars in Capricorn: If you've been accused of being too controlling, it was probably true! With Mars in Capricorn, you may be at your best when you're in charge of something, but trying to take charge of someone else's life will only get you into trouble! This is *not* the positive expression of your masculine psyche asserting itself. You can be a wonderful teacher and guide, and will find that you prefer a life filled with people who are learning or who know how to take care of themselves. Taking control of your life is a result of accepting and fulfilling your personal responsibilities, and it is this fulfillment that helps to strengthen your assertive self in the most positive manner.

Mars in Aquarius: As an independent-minded woman, you assert yourself most easily in situations that will provide you with more freedom. With Mars in Aquarius, you carry the spirit of liberation, and may forge a pathway that allows you to express yourself as a unique woman. You may feel most confident when you're working with friends or others who share your ideals. When you're frustrated, you can become stubbornly rebellious. Yet you are usually willing to try something different, or to be a little experimental in your approach to doing things. However, you can get stuck in an attitude of wanting to do everything your way, so be on the lookout for it!

Mars in Pisces: Although you are sensitive, you are by no means weak! With Mars in Pisces, your resilience is one of your strengths, and your flexible approach to handling challenges allows you more room for maneuvering through difficult territory. You may not always trust your assertive ability, and may feel that it would be better if somebody stronger were there to defend or protect you. Your key to your assertiveness and power is in your ability to visualize and create your own strength. You may learn by watching someone else, but when you dance for yourself, it's wonderful to watch, and frees your spirit!

Mars Aspects: Keys to Getting What You Want!

The Conjunctions

Mars conjunct Jupiter: On the move with an eye toward the future, you possess the confidence to accomplish almost anything. The conjunction between Mars and Jupiter in your chart stimulates a positive attitude, and adds a special element to your ability to deal with and enjoy challenge and competition. It's easy for you to pursue your interests and desires, and you're most likely to be at the head of the line instead of waiting to see what happens.

Mars conjunct Saturn: Your desire to achieve respect and to perform well is very strong, and with Mars conjunct Saturn, you have the ability to develop the self-discipline you need to get the job done. Although you may handle your responsibilities adequately, you may resent their infringement on your "free" time. You can attract restrictive relationships and circumstances in which you have little freedom, but once you become aware of your real needs and responsibilities, you're likely to grow beyond needing this type of external restraint. Self-control is much more your style than accepting control from others.

Mars conjunct Uranus: Sometimes you may feel like a time bomb, ready to go off at a moment's notice. With Mars conjunct Uranus, you like that kind of excitement and anticipation, although other people may feel nervous wondering what you'll do next. Your need for freedom is immense, and you perform at your peak when you know you can do things your own way. Your explosive energy may not seem particularly "feminine," but this is part of your assertive self—it's not supposed to be!

Mars conjunct Neptune: Sometimes, your imagination just takes over, and you have to go with the flow! With your Mars conjunct Neptune, your key to success in any endeavor involves surrendering to the flow instead of pushing against it. The problem with this energy bond is that your actions can leave an impression of vagueness. In your attempts to evade situations you'd just as soon avoid, you may be accused of being deceptive. You can also be the mistress of mixed messages, so try for clarity if you want to create a position of strength. One other dilemma: you can project too much onto the men in your life. If you do not want to be disappointed, don't make them more than human!

Mars conjunct Pluto: You may never take "no" for an answer, especially if you're set on pursuing something or someone you really want. The influence of Mars conjunct Pluto adds an amazing level of intensity to your assertiveness. In fact, you can become obsessive if you've lost your objectivity. Releasing anger and hostility instead of repressing it will afford you a much greater level of personal freedom.

The Semisquares

Mars semisquare Jupiter: Knowing where to draw the line is frustrating under the influence of Mars semisquare Jupiter. You like to feel that you're free to experience total spontaneity in the moment, but discover that just jumping into situations before you're ready leaves you feeling depleted. Until you've developed a positive sense of your inner masculine strength, you can experience some of the frustration of these energies through your relationships with men, who may consistently disappoint you. If you're wondering why you seem to attract men who have simply not grown up, well, you love that little boy quality—it's fun! That is, until, you need to count on him for something. Creating long-term relationships may be difficult, and that includes the long-term discipline necessary to complete projects. Think of those difficulties as bumps in the road of life instead of excuses to walk away before you've honored your promises.

Mars semisquare Saturn: You may be very disciplined, at least some of the time, with Mars semisquare Saturn. It's that "some of the time" that is at the core of the problem. Consistent effort is not your strong suit, unless you really want what you're going after. When you want something badly enough, you can be persistent, sometimes to the point of compulsive. If you expect that men are the only ones who are supposed to be responsible for the difficult concerns in life, you'll be frustrated when you realize that he is taking charge. You can be good at being in charge once you learn the difference between focus and restraint, and until you are taking responsibility for your own actions, you are functioning in a limited capacity. Fearing the effects of taking assertive action is a denial of your own power and stifles the development of your inner masculine strengths.

Mars semisquare Uranus: The energies of Mars and Uranus are in semisquare aspect, illustrating one dimension of your rebellious personality. You may wait until you've had it to the brim before you act, which can be quite disruptive to your own life and to the lives of those around you. Learning to express your discontent or frustrations when they arise can help you vent your anger more effectively and may even confer a more positive sense of self-direction. If you're around angry males, you may feel a lack of control or direction because of their disruptive actions and attitudes, but once you begin to exercise your needs for autonomy and independence, you'll see your relationships changing. Taking a stand can be very empowering, and initiating change will free your spirit.

Mars semisquare Neptune: Sometimes you cannot locate your assertive self with Mars in semisquare aspect to Neptune. This is particularly troublesome when you really want something, but do not know how to go about making it happen. Focus your actions by becoming aware of your tendency to vaporize your own energy when someone else more influential than you enters the picture. That's just an illusion anyway: you are the one creating your life; how much more influential can you get? So, when you're involved with a man and lose yourself in his desires and attitudes, you're giving away your power. There is a big difference between adding your support and losing your own life direction. Your struggle is very centered around this issue.

Mars semisquare Pluto: With Mars semisquare Pluto, you may be fascinated by powerful people, and your desire to feel your own competence emerging is quite strong, but the way to handle power and influence correctly is not easy, since so many hidden issues come to the surface when power situations are foremost. Whether you're dealing with men who are obsessed with their own need to control everyone and everything, or you find yourself driven by your own compulsions, you're struggling with defining the true nature of power. There are beneficial ways of exerting dominance, and when you experience the reward of bringing healing into your life, you'll be able to direct differently your own need to be in control.

The Sextiles

Mars sextile Jupiter: You get an extra boost of confidence and courage with Mars in sextile aspect to Jupiter. You may find it much easier to take a stand instead of relying on someone else (like a man!) to fight your battles. If you have something to say, you much prefer to speak your mind, although sometimes actions do speak louder than words.

Mars sextile Saturn: Your ability to channel and focus your energy is amazing, and when you need to apply yourself to a task, you can achieve excellent results. Through the influence of Mars in sextile aspect to Saturn, you are capable of developing excellent self-discipline—a beneficial expression of your inner masculine psyche. You also can use positive restraint when necessary, allowing you to take advantage of the growth and maturity that occurs over time, instead of just opting for the thrill of the moment. The bottom line: you're good at being in charge. In fact, you really like it that way!

Mars sextile Uranus: Directing your energy toward achieving the freedom and autonomy to express yourself as you will is a result of your Mars in sextile to Uranus. You're definitely a liberated woman, although you may not have burned your bra to prove it. By exercising your ingenuity and taking advantage of your talents, you've learned to carve a path that is uniquely yours. You're not finished yet, and need plenty of room to try a few more experiments in creating life on your own terms!

Mars sextile Neptune: You are an exceptional visualizer: you've always known that if you can get a clear picture of what you want to do, you can probably do it. The energy of your Mars in sextile to Neptune helps you blend your ability to work from more than one level at a time. The effect you have on others can be purely mesmerizing. This magical quality can extend into your career, adding a gentility to your power and influence.

Mars sextile Pluto: Directing your energy toward the things you want is no problem for you with Mars in sextile aspect to Pluto. When you're focused on something, your energy can create something akin to a "tractor beam." You know how to use your sensuality to your advantage, and men may find you difficult to resist. Owning your power as a total woman capable of transforming the circumstances of your life through your own actions, you can be especially influential within your relationships and successful in your career endeavors.

The Squares

Mars square Jupiter: Knowing when to stop can be a problem for you, since the influence of Mars in square aspect to Jupiter can feel like a runaway train. Your enthusiasm can sparkle, but you can also be carried away by a need for adventure, to explore and experience as much of life as possible. You may be attracted to men who promise more than they can deliver, and wonder why you are frustrated with them. Learning to channel your optimistic attitude toward realistic possibilities will not only afford you a more satisfying life, but will allow you to waste less energy on things that are simply wild goose chases.

Mars square Saturn: You can hold yourself back by giving in to your fears and anxieties. The influence of Mars in square aspect to Saturn prompts you to distrust your own abilities, and you may feel frustrated by your personal limitations. Getting stuck in your personal limitations can be virtually paralyzing, but you do have options. If there is something you really want, you can break the inertia and move gradually and steadily toward achieving it, but first you must release yourself from the fear that is blocking your path. It may be the result of feeling too limited by the men who've controlled your life, whether they were father, brother, teacher, or lover. Learning to satisfy yourself is not easy, but it is a strong desire. That desire alone can blast through the wall of fear that has penned in your energy. Memories of failure are the past. You're creating the present and future!

Mars square Uranus: You can be somewhat inconsistent in your assertiveness with Mars square Uranus. Your need for excitement can stimulate your pursuit of experiences that may be thrilling, but dangerous. You can also waste a lot of energy pursuing those thrills instead of creating what you really need. Freedom of expression is high on your priority list, and you may be attracted to people who also love freedom but have difficulty making commitments. For you, commitments may seem more momentary than long term, but until you can focus your energy on what you truly need, you may always feel as though you are dangling in midair.

Mars square Neptune: You can fool yourself by setting off on unrealistic paths with Mars square Neptune. Learning to trust yourself is not easy, since you may feel that your dreams are so far away you might never reach them. If you try deceptive means of achieving them, they are never real enough, but your hunger to reach them can be immense, and you can trust the wrong people, indulging falling for the wrong guy, hoping that you'll get there sooner. Carving a more realistic path is possible, but it takes abandoning false hope for true faith in yourself. Use your ability to envision your life as you want it, and then apply your energy to make it happen, instead of just hoping you'll get there—someday.

Mars square Pluto: No doubt about it: you are intense. With Mars square Pluto, you can be relentless in your pursuit of the things you want. But deep within yourself, you may hold resentment or disappointment that stand in the way of projecting the confidence and courage you need. This can be the result of old emotional wounds that still stab into your soul. You may have a deep distrust of men, which can consequently rob you of the ability to direct your life as you desire. Sometimes you can become so caught up in getting even when you've been hurt that you lose track of what you really want. You can appear threatening to men until you no longer feel threatened by them. By setting your focus on situations that are in harmony with your higher needs, you can break any patterns that may have become vengeful or hateful. You can also use this same energy to release the things you no longer need and become whole—a much better choice than dragging around a lot of baggage!

The Trines

✓**Mars trine Jupiter:** You may wonder what you've done to deserve some of the breaks you've experienced: just when you're in hot water, you find a way to get out. With Mars trine Jupiter, you definitely get into a few circumstances that are over your head, but you can make the most of them, and somehow can come out smelling like a rose. Your confidence and enthusiasm attract many opportunities, although you may not take advantage of all of them. You can be a little lazy with this aspect, particularly if you have access to sources of support that make it easy for you to coast through life. Through applying yourself, you can go further and make an amazing difference in the lives of others who may truly need and appreciate your generosity or spirit.

Mars trine Saturn: Getting things done is usually not a problem for you. With Mars trine Saturn, you like to accomplish what you set out to do, and may do it with room to spare. This aspect symbolizes a positive, supportive connection between yourself and the men in your life, since it also shows that you can be self-reliant when necessary, something anyone else will appreciate. You may also have excellent timing, but have to exercise it if you're going to make the most of it!

Mars trine Uranus: Your independent spirit works to your advantage with Mars trine Uranus. You've always liked to do things on your own and in your own way, and you are quite adept at most things you attempt. The blending of your intuitive self with your assertive and physical ability also adds a special edge, whether you're tackling a project or learning a new aerobics routine. You can project your independence without threatening the men in your life, and will appreciate relationships with men who are self-reliant. You may also expect a lot of yourself as a woman, and have a tendency to hold a superwoman image of yourself because you know you are capable of so many things. Life is much simpler when you allow yourself to be just a woman who is occasionally a superhero.

Mars trine Neptune: You can be a little lazy with Mars trine Neptune. After all, why should you go to all that trouble when what you want is only an arm's length away? It can also be easy to allow others to do things for you, instead of doing them for yourself. Through this energy, you attract many of the things you want, especially if you've clearly visualized having them. When you do want to accomplish something, you also use your inner sense to help you be more finely tuned. You know how to play the "inner game" to get what you want from life. Whether in athletic pursuits or preparing to make a presentation at work, when you see yourself doing it, your actions automatically follow through. However, you must assert action to create response from the world.

Mars trine Pluto: Your intrigue may be due to the influence of Mars trine Pluto, which stimulates your ability to blend your magnetism and charisma with action.

You are a powerful woman, with the ability to direct your energy toward healing and transformational change. Men may be captivated by you, even when you're not doing anything out of the ordinary—for you. You can employ your sensuality to your advantage, and you know what turns people on.

The Quincunxes

Mars quincunx Jupiter: You may spend too much time backtracking, since you occasionally go over the limits and have to regroup with Mars in quincunx aspect to Jupiter. This can be seen in the way you use your physical energy, but you may also have evidence from your relationships: jumping in too quickly. When you're pursuing your aims in your career, your enthusiasm about all the possibilities can cloud your ability to adequately evaluate what will actually be required from you. The tendency to try to wiggle out of tight situations can get you into trouble, but you generally prefer to do what you can to get your life back on track. It just may seem like there are a lot of detours.

Mars quincunx Saturn: Trusting your own ability is not always easy for you. The influence of Mars in quincunx aspect to Saturn indicates a strong tendency to feel that you are either inadequate, unprepared, or afraid when you need to assert yourself. Getting your energy "out there" can be anxiety-producing, and because of the frustration you feel, you create unnecessary limitations for yourself. Taking responsibility for yourself is important, but you may also take on responsibilities that belong to others. By learning to focus your energy and develop the skills and talents you need to accomplish the realization of your desires, you can be successful. You may sometimes just need a little confidence booster!

Mars quincunx Uranus: Scattering your energy might be one of your specialties with Mars in quincunx aspect to Uranus. It's sometimes difficult for you to focus on doing one thing at a time, and consequently, you may not accomplish what you want. This can leave the impression that you are a flake, and you may find that you are not trusted with important projects or new responsibilities if you've been too scattered. However, you do have the capability of juggling quite nicely, as long as you're not trying to keep too many things in the air at once.

Mars quincunx Neptune: You may have an indirect approach toward asserting yourself with Mars in quincunx aspect to Neptune. Your evasive tendencies can undermine your ability to accomplish what you want, especially if you are sending mixed messages through your actions (or lack thereof!). Men may seem difficult to pin down or understand, and part of the problem could be that you have trouble letting them know what you want or need. Try taking the risk of sharing your dreams with someone you trust, and find ways to approach manifesting them instead of hoping that someday they will just happen. You'll be much more satisfied when you've been instrumental in creating your own happiness.

Mars quincunx Pluto: You may be under the mistaken impression that you are not capable of standing up to people or situations who seem more powerful than you. Your uncertainty can stem from the influence of Mars in quincunx aspect to Pluto, especially if you've always adjusted what you want in order to satisfy somebody else. As a woman struggling with the best ways to make your life your own, you have an interesting hurdle to clear: you may have to abandon many of the things you've learned and replace them with new beliefs. Standing up for yourself will not always be easy, but with practice, you can become quite good at it!

The Oppositions

Mars opposition Jupiter: You may love the feeling of exhilaration you experience when you're screaming down the highway at ninety miles an hour with your hair on fire! Oh, you're not that wild and crazy? With Mars in opposition to Jupiter, you may not always be pushing the edge of your limits, but chances are, you'll do it most of the time! Being a woman rarely gets in your way; in fact, you may find people frequently shake their heads and wonder how a woman could do what you just did. Your impulsiveness can get you into hot water, although you might be quite adept at coming out okay, anyway. Finding healthy outlets for your need to experience the exciting adventure of living will allow you to live a longer, safer life. That's why bungee jumping has an advantage over just jumping freely off a three-hundred foot cliff!

Mars opposition Saturn: When you want to assert yourself or pursue your desires, you may run into a solid wall of fear or anxiety. With Mars in opposition to Saturn, you continually face the prospect of what could go wrong, how you could make mistakes, or why you cannot do something. Some of this is early conditioning, and you may honestly believe that because you are a woman, you cannot do what you want to do with your life. If you have physical limitations, you may be caught in the trap of using them as an excuse instead of finding a way beyond them. Your inner drive is very strong, and you have the capability to move beyond these limitations by getting in touch with your fears and standing up to those who would hold you back. Try taking small steps at first, just to get used to forward motion. Before you know it, you'll be sprinting across the finish line with a new record!

Mars opposition Uranus: You are a rebel. As a woman with Mars in opposition to Uranus, you're more likely to do things your own way, and may even energize revolutionary change in your life through taking action on something you believe in. Your preference for being around others who enjoy freedom may lead you into many different friendships and relationships over your lifetime, and there can be many people who seem to enter your life only temporarily. As an innovator, you may be unmatched, but you do not like the idea of being held back.

Mars opposition Neptune: You can be a hypnotic and captivating woman with Mars in opposition to Neptune, but you can also attract men who are not what they seem to be (you may see only what you want to see!). Your actions and energy can be difficult to pin down, and you can be rather evasive if you don't want to be committed. Sometimes, you expend so much energy on your dreams that you exhaust yourself, but you know that you need your dreams as a focal point. By balancing your inner self with your aims, you can create true magic in your life. But if you simply try to escape or put all your energy into illusion, you'll feel depleted. Try looking into the mirror before you take action, and remind yourself who you are and what you want to achieve.

Mars opposition Pluto: It's easy to be overcome by your compulsive desires with Mars in opposition to Pluto. You can be a relentless woman, never ceasing in your pursuit until you are satisfied, but you can also give your power away to others by allowing them to dictate what you can and cannot do. If this stems from your survival needs, ask yourself if you deserve more than just surviving. It may be the result of not knowing how to trust yourself and your own abilities, or you could be trapped by your own shame or guilt. You have the capability of creating real healing and transformation through your actions. By clearing out your old traumas, you may even amaze yourself with the results you see. Start by saying good-bye to that wounded little girl inside yourself who could not defend herself or her desires, and show her what she is capable of achieving.

~

CHAPTER FIVE

DEVELOPING YOUR MIND

*E*ducation and learning are lifelong processes. Your approach to developing your intellect is multifaceted, but there are special indicators in your astrological chart that help you understand the best ways to develop your mentality. Improving and strengthening communication skills is also part of developing your mind, since connecting to others is certainly improved if you can effectively illustrate your point of view! There are several planetary energies and astrological houses that are connected to your mental and intellectual growth. Together these form the matrix of your intelligence.

Mercury: Expressing Your Ideas

Although the energy of Mercury is traditionally considered to be the main indicator of your mentality, there are also other qualities that are part of your mental and intellectual self, but it is through Mercury's energy that you link your thoughts and ideas with others. This energy forms the cornerstone of your intellectual development. Through Mercury you express your thoughts. It is Mercury's sign that shows your approach to listening and learning, and how you are likely to communicate.

Mercury's Signs: Your Mental Signature

Mercury in Aries: You're always ready to take on a few mental challenges, and have a very active mind with Mercury in Aries. An independent thinker, you may prefer to study at your own pace rather than be slowed by those who do not move at your speed. You can be a good communicator, but do not like to spend time beating around the bush. You're a "just the facts, please" kind of woman, who would prefer to determine how you feel and what you think about something instead of listening to a long diatribe about anything.

Mercury in Taurus: When you have ample time to spend exploring an idea, you are much more comfortable. The influence of Mercury in Taurus adds a quality of well-considered thinking to your mentality. You seek out practical ways of doing things and are interested in the way something can be utilized instead of spending time with theoretical possibilities. Common sense is much more your brand of thinking, and hands-on learning has always been your forte. You have a great sense of structure, which may stimulate an interest in building things or working with crafts. Your ability to remember can be exceptional, and you rarely let go of an idea that is important to you. You can be stubborn and tend to close your mind if you don't want to deal with something, but if you have an interest in anything, your curiosity about it may never be completely satisfied!

Mercury in Gemini: Your quick wit and intelligence are strongly evident in your manner of speaking and writing with Mercury in Gemini. Diverse interests keep you busy, and you may enjoy a wide variety of friends, too. Always on the lookout for something different, you can be easily distracted, especially if you're not particularly interested in your current focus or situation. A flexible thinker, you may be capable of listening to diverse points of view and finding the common ground. Your interest in human nature may prompt you to study psychology, literature, or sociology, but you can also operate very nicely in any situation requiring good people skills. You have a special affinity for understanding and communicating with young people, and may always project an attitude that belies your age. You may be quite adept in abstract thinking, but probably prefer ideas to numbers.

Mercury in Cancer: You are a receptive thinker with Mercury in Cancer, and you can use your convictions and personal feelings about someone or something to your advantage when you need to express your ideas. You may have a photographic memory, with outstanding abilities to recall anything you've seen or learned. If you really want to remember something, when you can see it in your mind, your ability to recall the details can be amazing. Although you can be a little sentimental, and may love romantic stories and songs, you can be objective when necessary. You may be a first class storyteller, with an excellent ability to use different inflections in your voice.

Mercury in Leo: When you want an audience, you can be quite magnetic in your manner of speaking and presentation with Mercury in Leo. You can also be an attentive listener when you are interested in anyone or anything, and definitely enjoy being entertained. You're a woman who commands attention through your elegant style and presentation. Sometimes though, your own opinions can get in the way of learning something new or different. It is rare that anyone will ever be able to convince you to change your mind unless you want to do so, although you may not be able to take "no" for an answer when you're on the other side of the picture!

Mercury in Virgo: Your analytical powers can be highly developed through your Virgo Mercury, and you have a wonderful ability to maintain a practical perspective. Learning is easiest for you when you have practical experience and a hands-on approach to assimilating new information. You may also enjoy sharing what you know, and can become an accomplished teacher. Although you may be somewhat critical in your judgment or assessment of people or situations, you may not intend to be nit-picking. Your eye for detail simply makes it difficult to ignore anything that is out of place or below standards. As a rule, you try to keep an open mind, since you enjoy the experience of learning and discovering how things work.

Mercury in Libra: Developing your intellect is probably a high priority for you with Mercury in Libra. Part of your desire to learn is stimulated by your need to become a better communicator, since you enjoy socializing and making connections with others. You may love fine literature, and may even express your own talents in writing or public speaking. You can also be an effective counselor, since you're adept at seeing both sides of any situation. Situations that tolerate and support the development of new ideas stimulate your learning, and you may enjoy group circumstances that have the added benefit of the blending of ideas that arises when several people are exploring together. You also need ample room to develop your own ideas, and will appreciate work circumstances and relationships that support your intellectual growth.

Mercury in Scorpio: Ever-curious about what lies beneath the surface, you are prompted to become a deep thinker with Mercury in Scorpio. You may enjoy studying nature, and your fascination with the mysteries of life can also prompt a keen interest in fields like medicine or metaphysics. It's not likely that you have ever been satisfied with simple explanations, and with your ability to grasp hidden meanings and to develop a broad perspective, you can gain an understanding that is much more gratifying. You can also be rather stubborn, and may hold to your ideas with an emotional fervor that makes it difficult for you to get out of some of your ruts! When faced with the challenge of learning something entirely new or different, your first response may be to balk; but if you're given time to adjust, once you become involved in the learning experience, you're likely to seek out every detail.

Mercury in Sagittarius: With Mercury in Sagittarius, you will always be interested in learning. You're not likely to be satisfied until you've opened many doors to knowledge. The grand adventure of life challenges your mind, and your philosophical outlook may allow you to investigate some subject that others find off limits. When it comes to ideas, you think in terms of possibilities, not limitations. You learn best when given the freedom to explore at your own pace, but you can become distracted from your mental focus. Remember that you need a few breaks to operate at your top mental proficiency, so incorporate them into your schedule to avoid mental burnout.

Mercury in Capricorn: Your practical approach to learning is stimulated by your Mercury in Capricorn. You prefer to deal with the facts, and may be uncomfortable when faced with purely theoretical possibilities. For this reason, you're more interested in knowing about things you can grasp with your physical senses. Participating in learning is crucial for you, and situations that give you a hands-on opportunity will afford faster, more efficient assimilation of information. You can also be an exceptional teacher since you know how to structure the presentation of material and information in a manner that will build a solid foundation for understanding. Earning respect for your knowledge may be important to you, and you may be drawn toward developing a definitive career path that affords you the respect you desire to achieve.

Mercury in Aquarius: Although you have a very active and curious mind, with Mercury in Aquarius you may be most interested in learning about things that are at the leading edge. Your fascination with technology and your inventive mind may lead you into areas that are off the beaten path, but you're also in touch with social issues, and may have a desire to understand human nature and society that takes you into some very interesting fields of study. You definitely prefer to learn at your own pace, and may balk at learning about things that are not particularly interesting to you. As a little girl, you may have responded to your parents and teachers by saying, "I know," a lot, and that reflex remains strong. Intuitively, you do know about everything, but in the practical sense, you may not have had the time or opportunity to experience the development of that knowledge! By listening to your intuitive voice and blending the insights you experience through your intuitive awareness with practical experience, your intellectual development can be unparalleled.

Mercury in Pisces: Your impressionable mind opens your consciousness to a high level of imagination and creativity with Mercury in Pisces. Although you may have a little trouble distinguishing the difference between what you feel and what you think about something, this is unlikely to get in the way of your learning what you need to know about life. You can be an insightful thinker, and may be able to rely on your sixth sense to help you when making decisions and judgments. It may be easier to communicate some of your ideas through art, photography, dance, or music than through words, since the depth of your perceptions may seem inadequately expressed in words alone.

Mercury Aspects: Mental Triggers

The Conjunctions

Mercury conjunct Venus: You may enjoy learning with Mercury conjunct Venus. However, you're likely to be a little lazy in your approach, and may not like the disciplinary side of school as much as you like the socializing. With an excellent ability to relate to people, you can be an open and effective communicator.

Mercury conjunct Mars: With Mercury conjunct Mars, you may have little patience when it comes to learning new things. You like to get to the point. Although you can be argumentative, sometimes you take the other side of a subject just to keep the conversation moving. Exciting communication is much more your style. Your mind may never seem to stop.

Mercury conjunct Jupiter: You think big with Mercury conjunct Jupiter, and may have a wide variety of interests. Your fascination with languages, cultures, and lifestyles other than those you know so well may prompt an interest in continued education or travel. Learning is likely to be a lifelong passion for you.

Mercury conjunct Saturn: You're a serious and critical thinker with Mercury conjunct Saturn, although you may have a well-developed sense of humor. Sometimes your dry humor is misunderstood, especially by those who take you too seriously. You have the ability to discipline your mind and focus on whatever you're studying. As a result, you may be a good student, but perform best in subjects that hold your interest and have a practical application to your life.

Mercury conjunct Uranus: You're an inventive thinker with Mercury conjunct Uranus, and may be fascinated by new ideas and unusual people. You may learn best in an open environment with few restrictions, and prefer to operate independently in your career. Sticking with the same old routines everyday is boring, so you're probably quite good at creating distractions.

Mercury conjunct Neptune: Your psychic awareness opens your mind to a different realm of thinking with Mercury conjunct Neptune. Your imagination and creativity flow readily through your communicative self, and expressions such as writing, music, and photography provide excellent outlets for you. You may love poetry and are fascinated by anything spiritual or otherworldly. Acting is a good outlet since you have the ability to immerse yourself in the development of a character.

Mercury conjunct Pluto: You are a perceptive thinker with Mercury conjunct Pluto, and can be intense when you're focused on something or someone. An excellent researcher, you like to probe beneath the surface for the information you need and may be fascinated with subjects like psychology, metaphysics, or life science.

The Semisquares

Mercury semisquare Venus: Your need to be socially correct can get in the way of saying what you really want to say with Mercury in semisquare aspect to Venus.

You may also be too sensitive to the way others communicate with you, and if confronted with harsh or abrasive behavior, may have difficulty dealing with the person or situation. However, this influence stimulates an interest in developing your communicative and social skills.

Mercury semisquare Mars: You can be quite abrupt with Mercury in semisquare aspect to Mars. When you're eager to say something, you may just blurt it out without thinking. Although this can add a quality of spontaneity to your personality, you may sometimes feel that you've just put your foot in your mouth! Jumping to conclusions can also interfere with your learning process, in that you may sometimes find it difficult to complete a task or finish an assignment.

Mercury semisquare Jupiter: You may be easily distracted with Mercury in semisquare aspect to Jupiter. It's also difficult to set limits, and saying "no" can be rather difficult, since you certainly do not want to think you're missing anything! Knowing when to stop, when to be quiet, and when to slow down can be important lessons in your personal development. Setting reasonable goals is a good beginning, since having a definite target will create the focus you need to bring more balanced judgment.

Mercury semisquare Saturn: You may be reluctant to speak up or share your thoughts with Mercury in semisquare aspect to Saturn. This may stem from fears that are the result of difficult learning situations when you were a young girl. You may also not trust your intellectual abilities. Finding your own way of learning, approaching problem-solving in a manner that allows you to confirm your abilities, and gradually gaining faith in yourself will likely prove to you that you are not only capable, but quite a good thinker after all!

Mercury semisquare Uranus: You've always liked to do things your own way, and your approach to problem-solving may be outside the realm of tradition. With Mercury in semisquare aspect to Uranus, your manner of communicating is one of the expressions of your individuality. You learn best when you have a good balance between structure and freedom, and in your career you'll function at the highest level when given opportunities to demonstrate your independence. Staying focused on anything for a long period of time can be difficult for you.

Mercury semisquare Neptune: You may sometimes have trouble maintaining your focus, especially if your imagination is stimulated! With Mercury in semisquare aspect to Neptune, your mental impressionability is high, which can be beneficial in circumstances that require you to be creative, but you can also be mislead and can become confused when you're overwhelmed with too much input, and may tend to miss critical details. In important matters, double-check all information in order to make sure you're clear about it.

Mercury semisquare Pluto: With Mercury in semisquare aspect to Pluto, you can become obsessive in your thinking. You may fret over details that make very little difference and miss information that is critical, especially if you've closed your mind or become distracted by your emotions. Sometimes this aspect indicates difficulty processing information, although it also indicates that you are capable of adapting through training yourself to approach things differently.

The Sextiles

Mercury sextile Venus: Your enjoyment of learning and sharing ideas is stimulated by Mercury sextile Venus. You may have good writing abilities, too, and are likely to perform best in situations that require good communication and people skills. Although you might be okay learning on your own, the social aspect of school, conferences, and community gatherings has a boost all its own.

Mercury sextile Mars: Your ability to grasp information quickly may be heightened with Mercury sextile Mars. One thing is sure: you like to get to the point! You may have little patience with slow decision-making processes. Your quick wit may be one of your trademarks.

Mercury sextile Jupiter: Learning about life, people, and possibilities can be a passion for you. With Mercury sextile Jupiter, you're always interested in finding out more, meeting different people, or traveling to new places. Your curiosity is heightened by this aspect, and so is your communicative ability. You may be a gifted writer, public speaker, or teacher.

Mercury sextile Saturn: Disciplining and focusing your mind is supported by the energy of Mercury in sextile aspect to Saturn. You learn best in situations that follow a pattern and allow practical experience to play a part in developing your understanding or skills. When necessary, you can also do very well studying a subject on your own, although you may truly appreciate the guidance of a dedicated teacher or mentor.

Mercury sextile Uranus: New ideas are not only interesting to you, but your own originality is strengthened through Mercury in sextile aspect to Uranus. You may have a knack for working with technical equipment, and can be quite adept at grasping abstract ideas. Futuristic concepts are more reality than fiction to you, since you can see new avenues readily.

Mercury sextile Neptune: Your imagination is easily stimulated with Mercury in sextile aspect to Neptune. Self-expression flows readily, and writing, music, painting, and photography can all be worthwhile avenues for you to express your ideas and view of the world. You may be an excellent mimic and talented actress.

Mercury sextile Pluto: Probing into the depths is fascinating to you. With Mercury sextile Pluto, you're rarely satisfied with what you see on the surface. Consequently, you are inclined to research, investigate, and question. Complex ideas appeal to you, and you may enjoy subjects that challenge your mind.

The Squares

Mercury square Mars: You may feel that your mind is constantly whirring with Mercury square Mars. As a result, focusing your mental energy can be a bit difficult, but when you do concentrate, it is with intensity. Although you may complain about mental challenges, there is a part of you that enjoys them. You can be argumentative or confrontational in your manner of speaking or communicating, which can create turmoil or alienation if carried too far. Healthy debate is different from hostile accusation.

Mercury square Jupiter: Learning may never seem to have an end point for you. With Mercury's energy in square aspect to Jupiter, you have a deep need to expand your understanding, but unfortunately you may never be satisfied with what you learn or know. It's all too easy to scatter your energy or lose your mental focus by becoming too easily distracted. This state of divine discontent arises from your own expectations that sometimes exceed your abilities of the moment. As a result, you can become discouraged if you fall short of the mark or may be disappointed when learning or completing a project takes longer than you had expected. That's not likely to stop you, however, since these energies together keep your mental abilities strong and your desire to know always alive.

Mercury square Saturn: Your tendency to take things too seriously can result from the influence of Mercury in square aspect to Saturn. You may have a mistrust of your own intellectual abilities, fearing the outcome of wrong answers or poor judgment. This can lead to an inhibition in your self-expression, and may also result in your appearing to be too critical or judgmental of others. However, you may also be driven to learn, which can be a good thing if you are in an environment that gives you an opportunity to truly develop your mind.

Mercury square Uranus: Staying focused is very difficult with Mercury square Uranus. You may be very intelligent, but can still have trouble staying on track, which can inhibit your full grasp of a subject. However, if you are stimulated by and interested in something, you will stay with it because of your fascination. You need career opportunities and learning situations that allow you to do several different things at your own pace. Repetitive activities may just drive you nuts!

Mercury square Neptune: Your fascination with beautiful, imaginative, and out-of-this-world experiences is powerful with Mercury in square aspect to Neptune, but you can also be distracted from your ability to focus or concentrate by your need to escape. Listening can be difficult, especially if you are not interested in the person or subject, and paying attention to details can be bothersome. However, these elements are important, and incorporating them into your self-expression and intellectual development may even add to the effect of your creative and imaginative abilities!

Mercury square Pluto: You can become quite obsessive in your thinking with Mercury square Pluto. Although this can be useful when you're involved in an investigation or research project, it can be overwhelming when you're trying to relax at the end of the day. Your need to know what is at the core of everything can drive you to explore things that frighten some people, and you may make important headway. Knowing when to give yourself a break is another story.

The Trines

Mercury trine Mars: Your ability to accomplish the things you set out to do is enhanced with Mercury trine Mars. You may be quite adept at learning new things rather quickly, and are not afraid to investigate new subjects. Mental challenges are positively exciting for you, and you may always be studying or investigating something just because you love the challenge. You may also be confident when addressing groups or presenting your ideas, and can stimulate others to follow your leadership.

Mercury trine Jupiter: Your interest in learning, exploring the adventure of life, and increasing your understanding is stimulated by Mercury in trine aspect to Jupiter.

You may always be on a quest for greater knowledge, and you seek out inspiring people and experiences. Your tolerance and acceptance of different viewpoints are enhanced through this quality.

Mercury trine Saturn: Your ability to discipline your mind and complete projects is strengthened through Mercury in trine aspect to Saturn. This influence is helpful in educational pursuits, and you probably value the importance of education for yourself and for others. You may be a gifted teacher, and can be a strong role model for those under your guidance.

Mercury trine Uranus: Your inventiveness and unique approach to life strengthen your intellectual development and ingenuity with Mercury in trine aspect to Uranus. Technological advances are both useful and interesting to you, and you may be quite adept at integrating new methods into existing systems or situations. You may be a gifted writer or public speaker, and may also have a knack for reaching the masses through media such as radio or television.

Mercury trine Neptune: Your imagination and creativity enhance your intellectual development with Mercury in trine aspect to Neptune. You may be a gifted writer, artist, actress, or photographer—and whether or not you develop these talents, you have an excellent eye for that which is beautiful and enthralling. You perform at your peak in an environment that is serene and inspires your visionary manner of thinking.

Mercury trine Pluto: Mercury's trine aspect to Pluto adds a special depth to your thinking abilities, and may stimulate a desire to look beneath the surface for answers. You may feel most comfortable working in an area that allows you to probe. Metaphysics, medicine, and the healing arts can be especially appealing to your way of approaching questions. There is also a special psychic ability associated with this energy connection.

The Quincunx

Mercury quincunx Mars: Sometimes you just seem to get ahead of yourself with Mercury in quincunx to Mars. Your eagerness to rush into the most exciting element of a subject or situation can cause you to overlook important details or miss necessary information. Consequently, you may spend a great deal of time retracing your steps. By taking a more evenly paced and attentive approach, you can save yourself a lot of time, and reach your desired goals much more quickly.

Mercury quincunx Jupiter: You have big ideas, and may overestimate your abilities or underestimate the requirements of a job or situation with Mercury in quincunx aspect to Jupiter. Jumping into an experience with inadequate preparation can be a problem with this aspect since your eagerness can outweigh your abilities. This rarely dampens your enthusiasm, which is one of the qualities that keeps you interested in life and gives you the energy to stand up and start again.

Mercury quincunx Saturn: Mercury's quincunx to Saturn provides a bit of friction when it comes to learning. You may frequently second guess yourself, and can undermine your own effectiveness if you're constantly chipping away and never quite satisfied with your own ideas or answers. This can be helpful when you're finishing something and you want everything just right; but that nagging sense that you're missing something, or that you don't know quite enough, was probably amplified in your early learning experiences. Maybe your way of looking at things was simply different from your parents or teachers. Now you are allowed to have your own ideas!

Mercury quincunx Uranus: Knowing how to incorporate what is unusual or different into your intellectual development experiences can be difficult with Mercury in quincunx to Uranus. It's like trying to keep up with the fast-paced changes in technology—you may feel that you're always a little behind. But you're not running a race! You're seeking ways to express your unique ideas and inventive concepts so that they are understandable, acceptable, and useful. Learning how to deal with your need for distraction is important, since you may never get anything finished if you change horses in midstream too often.

Mercury quincunx Neptune: It's easy for you to become lost in the maze of details with Mercury in quincunx aspect to Neptune. You may prefer to maintain a state of tranquillity, and certainly communicate and perform best when you are clear, but you can be distracted by outside influences. Finding that quiet space within yourself is the key to coping with outside distractions. You need circumstances at home and at work that give you a chance to exercise your imagination and creativity.

Mercury quincunx Pluto: Sometimes it's important to be completely immersed in what you're doing; but other times, you need to know what's going on outside your own sphere. With Mercury in quincunx aspect to Pluto, you may be constantly making adjustments, although your obsession to do things as you wish is usually the overriding influence. You need to know how things work beneath the surface, but may not always know how to get into the core of something without destroying it. This is particularly true when you're learning something new or researching something out of the ordinary. Gradually opening a door rusted on its hinges may not always work, but trying it first might be better than knocking the wall apart in order to get in!

The Oppositions

Mercury opposition Mars: You are an intuitive thinker, but sometimes you drive your intuition instead of allowing it to open the doors to your mind for you. With Mercury in opposition to Mars, you may literally attack new ideas or circumstances, but you also have the courage to explore areas that others may find impossible or difficult. When confronted with new situations or ideas that you find disagreeable, you can become belligerent or argumentative, especially if you feel insecure. Developing your mind can be a positive challenge for you, but you can make it a battle.

Mercury opposition Jupiter: You may always feel that you want to know more than you do. The influence of Mercury in opposition to Jupiter stimulates a powerful desire to gain greater understanding and to improve your intellectual abilities. It also stimulates a sense that you will never reach the horizon. In some respects, this influence can be helpful because you will always be seeking new information and inspired by new circumstances. However, the restlessness associated with this influence can lead to a kind of wanderlust, in which you are never quite satisfied with your knowledge or abilities.

Mercury opposition Saturn: You can be strongly focused and disciplined in your thinking with Mercury in opposition to Saturn; but you can also be too judgmental or restrictive in your thinking. It's easy to get stuck in the rut of approaching things the same way all the time, or you may think that your ideas and opinions are the only way to do things. Okay, so you acknowledge that there are other ways to do things, but that your way is best. By consciously working to maintain an open mind, you may even improve upon yourself. Imagine that!

Mercury opposition Uranus: Your distractibility is enhanced with the opposition from Mercury to Uranus, and your patience with slow-paced educational pursuits is likely to be close to nil. You are an intuitive thinker, and will never fully develop your mind unless you can build an effective bridge between rational and intuitive thinking processes. You need both in order to achieve your highest intellectual potential. You are, at heart, a scientific thinker, but may not follow the old paradigms. You're here to create a few models of your own.

Mercury opposition Neptune: The realm of imagination captures your mental focus much more easily than mere reality with Mercury in opposition to Neptune. If you have a good focus for your ideas and viewpoints, like a creative outlet, this aspect can work quite nicely. You may be adept at writing, performing arts, acting, visual arts, cooking, crafts—anything that allows you to express your fascinating and magical point of view, but if you become caught in despondency or dependency, or trapped by illusion, this aspect of yourself can be difficult.

Mercury opposition Pluto: You can become obsessed with an idea or way of doing things with Mercury in opposition to Pluto. When you're focused on something, you're focused. There's no halfway. You don't just wade into an idea, you immerse yourself. This quality can be especially useful in research, investigation, or spiritual questing, but you can also get stuck, close your mind, and lock away the possibility of change (even though transformation in your thinking is your goal). When you refocus your mental energy toward that end, you can even change the obsession!

Your Moon: Thought Patterns

The energy of your Moon also has a mental component. The Moon is the realm of thought, the process of subconscious thinking, and plays a strong role in intuitive thinking. Your Moon describes your "state of mind," which certainly can have a lot to do with your ability to think clearly, learn, or communicate. Consider the Moon as the symbol of your thought patterns.

The Mental Influence of the Moon by Sign

Moon in Aries: You like to learn about things that get your energy moving. Through your Aries Moon, your learning filters are more stimulated by exploring ideas that are challenging and that require some creative thinking. You also prefer to learn at your own pace, and may not like the idea of being held back because somebody else has not quite reached your level of understanding.

Moon in Taurus: You're a "show me" kind of woman, and learn most easily in situations that allow you to be involved. The influence of your Taurus Moon in developing your mind adds a practical sensibility to the things you're most drawn to study. If you see that you can use something to develop your stability or strengthen your long-range growth, you may study it even though you do not particularly like the subject! When you do enjoy an area, you can be a very studious individual, indeed, and you rarely forget anything.

Moon in Gemini: Developing your mind is a high priority with your Gemini Moon, and your need for diversity can be a plus in learning situations, but you can also have trouble focusing your energy, and your distractibility can get in the way of learning. You can use this to your advantage by juggling your priorities, as long as you don't let your distractions become more important than your responsibilities.

Moon in Cancer: Your thinking processes are comprehensive, and, through the influence of your Cancer Moon, you tend to think in terms of continuity. This allows you to grasp the deeper meanings of history and to develop an appreciation for the ever-changing development of humankind. You may also have excellent powers of mental retention. Your teachers will always be an important part of your life, and your appreciation of their efforts is not likely to go unnoticed.

Moon in Leo: You're drawn to learning about the things and people you enjoy, but can be stubbornly resistant to ideas that are foreign to you with the Moon in Leo. Your preferences are quite strong, which is okay, but can get in your way when you need to make adjustments or embrace new information or experiences. You learn best in an environment that affords you a little attention, since praise and recognition for your efforts will stimulate you to go further.

Moon in Virgo: Since you appreciate well-educated individuals, you are likely to make an effort to improve your own understanding and knowledge. The influence of your Virgo Moon in your intellectual development is strong, and you may always be reading or studying something just because you want to know how things work. You may also be open to new ideas, although you'll probably test them before you accept them.

Moon in Libra: The social part of learning is important to you, and your Libra Moon may influence you to develop your social skills more fully. Your love of cultural expressions, such as the arts and literature, is quite evident, and you are drawn to refined people and situations. Your learning environment is important, and you'll find that you're more open-minded and mentally focused in a beautiful or serene setting.

Moon in Scorpio: Since you usually have strong feelings about most everything with your Moon in Scorpio, you'll find that this influences your intellectual interests and development. Your fascination with the mysteries of life can lead you to study subjects such life science, psychology, or metaphysics, and your innate sense of healing energy may lead you to study or develop your skills as a healer, regardless of your career path. You can be resistant to new ideas, and have a tendency toward prejudicial thinking since you can be emotionally tied to those ideas and ideals you hold sacred, but when you do decide to explore something new or different, you're thorough about it.

Moon in Sagittarius: Through your Sagittarius Moon you are most drawn to subjects that appeal to your higher nature. You cannot separate your feeling for the natural order of things from the way you learn. You may be most interested in subjects that are philosophical and that provide pathways to understanding the greater truths of life and the laws of nature and the universe. Always on a quest, you may be fascinated with knowledge and wisdom, but can be uncomfortable if you have to focus on any one subject for too long.

Moon in Capricorn: Your practical nature permeates your approach to learning with your Moon in Capricorn. Your sense of structure stimulates your need to have a definitive path in your learning experience, and you may feel especially close to the teachers who have strongly influenced your life. Your need for respect may prompt you to pursue educational options that underscore your capabilities and give you a stable platform for personal and professional growth. Discipline is probably not a problem for you, although you may resist being restrained by the "system."

Moon in Aquarius: You're fascinated by unusual ideas and unique individuals, and may enjoy learning about anything that takes you into the realm of the future. The influence of your Aquarius Moon in your intellectual growth and development is quite remarkable. You look for possibilities, and prefer learning situations that allow room for experimentation. You may learn best in an environment that is open and allows you to grow at your own pace and perform at your peak when you have the freedom to express your ideas and talents.

Moon in Pisces: Although you may not enjoy the structure of academia, you love to open your mind to the realm of possibility. Your Pisces Moon functions much like a mental sponge: you take in everything! When you're emotionally drained or upset, you're likely to function less clearly on a mental level, but when you're centered, your perceptions are amazing. It's important that you give yourself time and room to process your feelings about something before you dive into it, since your own reticence can block your ability to learn.

Jupiter and Education

Jupiter also plays an important role in learning, stimulating you to look ahead into the realm of possibility, beyond the horizon of the now. Through the energy of Jupiter, you enthusiastically share what you know with others. As a woman, you are likely to feel most at home when you use this energy to encourage and support others, but you can also apply this to yourself—it just takes practice! Jupiter's energy illustrates your approach to philosophical thinking, religious study, and spiritual law. This energy also prompts your interest in higher education, and is connected to institutions like universities and colleges. Your philosophies and ideals definitely affect your choices and preferences when it comes to learning.

Jupiter's Sign and Learning

Jupiter in Aries: Your quest for knowledge may be a challenge with Jupiter in Aries. You're like an explorer, ready to go at a moment's notice, looking for the answers to life's mysteries; but you'd like to get there quickly because there could be something else more exciting waiting around the bend. Your philosophy is "here today, gone tomorrow," and your life experience has taught you that if you fail to take advantage of opportunity when it knocks, you may not hear it knocking again!

Jupiter in Taurus: Your philosophy of building on a solid foundation is influenced by Jupiter in Taurus, and you probably approach learning in this manner. You look for situations that will provide practical knowledge, and information that will strengthen your sense of safety and stability. You may also be somewhat fixed in your ideas about the best ways to learn, or about the way education should be structured or delivered. You learn best in situations that allow you to put your knowledge to use: you're result-oriented. That's good, because then you feel you're on solid ground. But some things do not have tangible results, and that's where your measurement of value may need some readjustment!

Jupiter in Gemini: Your philosophical approach to life and learning is rather eclectic with Jupiter in Gemini—a "live and let live" attitude. You may also appreciate the diversity of ideas and cultures existing on the planet, and can benefit from exploring them. Sometimes you may think you have to know about all of them, but the important part may be to discover the link between the many schools of thought and cultures of our world. Oh, that's right, you're not limited to this world—what about life in other galaxies? How do they run their cities? Now, that should really get you going!

Jupiter in Cancer: Your philosophical approach to life and learning may be very much like mother taught you with Jupiter in Cancer. Your adherence to some of the attitudes that shaped earlier generations has great value for you, and you may have a keen understanding of the importance of learning from history. Sometimes, however, your emotional attachment to your philosophies can get in the way of the essence of how and what you believe.

Jupiter in Leo: Your philosophical approach to life and learning involves experiencing the true essence of self-expression with Jupiter in Leo. You may take great pride in your educational accomplishments, and may like to be noticed. Your generous spirit extends into all areas of your life, and you may feel that giving of yourself by sharing your talents and abilities is important to your personal development. You can be very attached to your beliefs and ideals, and may not appreciate others who find fault or who disagree with them. It's not likely that you will change your idealistic viewpoints unless you are personally motivated to do so.

Jupiter in Virgo: Your philosophical approach to life has a practical leaning influenced by your Jupiter in Virgo, and you are likely to learn easily and function best in an environment that has a sense of organization or pattern. You are naturally inclined to teach others, but need to watch for a tendency to expect others to move at your pace. Learning tolerance can be quite helpful if you are to achieve the success you desire (and that includes tolerance for yourself!).

Jupiter in Libra: You've adopted a philosophy of fairness, and may believe that life should always be just with Jupiter in Libra. Although you've seen evidence to the contrary, your ideal life would involve situations where everyone is treated fairly and equally. You function and learn best in an environment that is beautiful and peaceful, and if you're involved in education, will include social skills in your teaching practices. You may also have an interest in the law and the social practice of other cultures, and may be an expert in diplomatic or social relations.

Jupiter in Scorpio: You can be very attached to your ideals and philosophies with Jupiter in Scorpio, and may have very definitive feelings about your educational endeavors. You can be quite shrewd, and may even be secretive about what you know. It's like having the prize-winning recipe and only giving a few of the ingredients to those who would like to duplicate your efforts. You should never underestimate your influence on others, especially in learning situations.

Jupiter in Sagittarius: You're open to learning all kinds of things with Jupiter in Sagittarius. You may even make learning your lifelong pastime, although not necessarily within an institutional setting. You appreciate the value of travel, connecting with people on a cultural level, and understanding the different viewpoints and philosophies abundant in the world. Your enthusiasm for life inspires others, and you can be an excellent leader, teacher, or executive because you inspire confidence in those who work for you or learn from your instruction.

Jupiter in Capricorn: Your belief that you can only count on what you have in front of you can restrict your opportunities. With Jupiter in Capricorn, you may think you're a realist, although some people might call you a pessimist. The truth is probably somewhere in between the two, since you do look at life in a very practical sense and have learned that you rarely experience change or advancement unless you work for it. Once you discover the importance of giving of yourself, sharing your talents, and opening your mind to new possibilities, you may finally stumble into true abundance.

Jupiter in Aquarius: You may embrace a philosophy that advocates the diversity of humankind with Jupiter in Aquarius. Developing your mind is an important priority in your life, and you can be quite intellectually adept. Your original ideas are part of your charm, and others may be impressed by your ability to integrate new concepts into existing structures. Your interest in other cultures and ability to relate to people from many walks of life may lead to your study of human relations, sociology, or business management.

Jupiter in Pisces: Your quiet enthusiasm can be charming. With Jupiter in Pisces, your beliefs and ideals are an integral part of your life, and you may find it impossible to separate your spiritual needs and expression from other aspects of your life experience. You function best in environments that allow you the freedom of your beliefs and that encourage you to develop your compassion.

Jupiter's Aspects and Learning

Aspects from the Sun to Jupiter

Sun conjunct Jupiter: You're confident in yourself and your ability to understand and learn with your Sun in conjunction to Jupiter. Your enthusiasm for your ideas and philosophies is evident in the way you live, and others may learn from your example. It's easy for you to give of yourself, share what you know, and extend your generosity in other ways. Sometimes, however, you may not know when to stop, and can overdo it!

Sun sextile Jupiter: Confidence in your ability to learn is stimulated through the energy of the Sun in sextile aspect to Jupiter. This can indicate a positive relationship with your teachers, and may stimulate your own desire to share what you know with others. You enjoy the feeling of reaching beyond your limitations through developing your understanding.

Sun square Jupiter: Your educational background may be of concern with your Sun in square aspect to Jupiter. Somehow, you may feel that you are less valuable if your education falls short of what you think it should be. However, you are also adept at learning from life experience, and need to learn to credit your life experience, and the things you have produced through your life, as truly valuable.

Sun trine Jupiter: You may have a lot invested in your educational endeavors, and take pride in your beliefs and ideals with your Sun in trine aspect to Jupiter. Your interest in improving your standing in your community or within your profession may also stimulate a need to continue your education. Since you probably enjoy learning, and certainly appreciate the opportunity to share your own ideas, this can be an excellent option. Consequently, you may want to seek out career situations that give you a chance to advance and allow you to learn.

Sun opposition Jupiter: Your expectations of yourself are always high, and this may extend to your need to learn as much as possible with your Sun in opposition to Jupiter. However, you can also overestimate your abilities and may jump into situations ill-prepared or overly confident. This can lead to a tendency to underachieve, because you have not thoroughly prepared yourself. To create the balance in your life that will allow you to grow on every level, you need to determine a reasonable set of goals and then apply yourself to the efforts required to realize them.

Aspects from Mars

Mars conjunct Jupiter: Your enthusiasm about anything can be quite strong, and this extends toward learning and new experiences. With Mars conjunct Jupiter, you can also jump into situations before you're aware of the details, and may feel overwhelmed when you discover what you've gotten yourself into. That is not likely to stop you, especially if you find a challenge in the process. Learning about law, religion, politics, and philosophy can benefit your life.

Mars sextile Jupiter: With Mars in sextile aspect to Jupiter, your eagerness to explore new vistas is strengthened. This is literally a courageous approach to learning, and you might even enjoy pitting your ideas against another, just for the fun of it. After all, that sense of expansion through competition is what this aspect is all about!

Mars square Jupiter: You can become easily distracted from your focus with Mars in square aspect to Jupiter. The distractions arise from your need for action and high levels of activity; if something gets stale or boring, you'll get nervous! In order to successfully complete projects, you may actually need to have more than one thing happening in your life, so that you have a healthy diversion when you begin to feel stuck. You can also try different approaches to the same idea or material in order to grasp it more fully. It's also crucial that you set your sights on goals that you can actually achieve, instead of always shooting for the record! Achieving a sense of completion is important, or you may lose an element of self-confidence.

Mars trine Jupiter: Your enthusiasm and confidence help you tackle most any task and accomplish your aims. The influence of Mars in trine aspect to Jupiter adds a special spark to your desire to reach beyond your limitations, and can spur you to follow many pathways in your search for excellence. You may also have good luck, seeming to be in the right place at the right time. Part of this arises from your ability to trust your own sense of vision for the future: you can see the path and then you take action and follow it.

Mars opposition Jupiter: You may be strongly goal-oriented with Mars in opposition to Jupiter. However, you may set goals that are very difficult to achieve, or that require you to reach beyond your own limitations. You love a good challenge, including challenges in learning. It's possible you could reach burnout before you complete the task, however, especially if you're pushing too hard too soon. Learning to pace yourself is crucial if you are to achieve the success you desire.

Aspects to Saturn

Jupiter conjunct Saturn: Although you may have great admiration and respect for yourself and others who achieve their goals, you may have a tendency to underestimate your own abilities with Jupiter conjunct Saturn. This influence provides a need to accomplish focus and outreach at the same time, quite a task, but there are situations that will allow you to do just this. Educational pursuits fall within this framework, particularly the pursuit of professional accreditation or accomplishment in your chosen field. However, this aspect can also represent a tendency to avoid challenges and to take the easy way out.

Jupiter semisquare Saturn: Making the best use of your assets is important since you have Jupiter in semisquare aspect to Saturn. In learning situations, you sometimes compromise, or may not be motivated at the right times, resulting in a feeling of underachievement. You do need discipline and focus, but that is different from setting yourself up by getting into circumstances where you cannot realize your potential.

Jupiter sextile Saturn: The vision of what you hope to achieve and what you can accomplish can be very clear with Jupiter in sextile to Saturn. Goal-setting is an important part of realizing your dreams, and you can be confident about creating goals that are within your grasp. You may also be willing to work hard to achieve your aims, and in educational pursuits as well as life challenges, your efforts make a significant difference in the outcome. Your educational choices may have a practical basis, and you'll enjoy knowing that you're learning something you can actually use!

Jupiter trine Saturn: Learning can be easy for you, since your desire to reach beyond your limitations blends very nicely with your ability to discipline and focus your energy. Your sense of judgment can be quite well developed with Jupiter in trine aspect to Saturn. Creating educational goals may have played an important part in your life when you were younger, and you still enjoy learning and expanding your grasp of knowledge about the world. You may consider yourself a lifelong student, always seeking, constantly building your understanding. This is the seat of true wisdom.

Jupiter quincunx Saturn: With Jupiter in quincunx aspect to Saturn, the continual juggling between your priorities and your desire to expand your horizons may manifest through such activities as working and going to school. Once you've accomplished your goal, you may then feel that your life is out of balance because the stress factor is lower, and it is crucial that you find a positive replacement for the stress—like enjoying the fruits of your labors!

Jupiter opposition Saturn: Sometimes you may feel that you're pulled between two polls with Jupiter in opposition to Saturn. On one side is your desire to do everything according to the rules, and on the other side is your desire to feel free as a bird. There is a middle ground, but it can seem like an unhappy compromise if you are trying to satisfy too many other people. Your need to establish your expertise is important, but you may also want to carry yourself further than your teachers or guides taught you. That's okay. It's called progress.

Aspects to Uranus

Jupiter conjunct Uranus: The idea of being unusual seems just fine to you, since you feel much more like yourself when you're expressing your individualism. With Jupiter conjunct Uranus, you have a very high level of perception, and need to trust your first impressions. Your religious beliefs or spiritual ideals may play an important role in your life, and you may be more attracted to a spiritual path that allows room for your individual growth at your own rate.

Jupiter semisquare Uranus: Interruptions in your educational endeavors can occur with Jupiter in semisquare aspect to Uranus. You may also change your mind about your educational or professional goals, and start over on a new path. If so, you lose a little time, but if you're focused on the changes that are in harmony with your real needs, then at least you'll be on the right path! But jumping from one thing to another simply because you are bored is another story.

Jupiter sextile Uranus: Your joy in discovering new ideas is one of your strongest motivations with Jupiter in sextile aspect to Uranus. You can take advantage of technology within personal and professional situations, and may have a knack for understanding new ideas. You may seek out unusual people and may be strongly drawn to ideas that are geared toward evolutionary growth and change. Out-of-the-ordinary opportunities are likely to manifest during different times in your life, and by taking advantage of them, you can completely alter your life. In many ways, your life can be quite serendipitous.

Jupiter trine Uranus: Your ability to attract invaluable educational opportunities has always been part of your life with Jupiter in trine aspect to Uranus; whether or not you've pursued them is another story. However, you may experience a series of fortunate options throughout your lifetime, especially in the realm of learning and personal development.

Jupiter quincunx Uranus: Jumping into situations with inadequate preparation can be a problem with Jupiter in quincunx aspect to Uranus. In educational pursuits and career development, you may always feel a bit dissatisfied unless you have ample freedom to do things your own way. You may need a bit of structure, however, to avoid becoming too distracted, and therefore accomplishing very little.

Jupiter opposition Uranus: Your strong will and independent way of thinking may have made it difficult to adhere to the educational plan set forth by traditional society. With Jupiter in opposition to Uranus, you need to learn in the school of life, although you can also accomplish an education within the system if you must. Your need to break free of dogmatic thinking is powerful, and you will probably rebel against any school of thought that tries to label you in any way. After all, you're here to break the mold, right?!

Aspects to Neptune

Jupiter conjunct Neptune: In learning situations and in circumstances that require clear judgment, you can get into trouble when your idealism and imagination cloud your thinking. With Jupiter conjunct Neptune, you visualize a life filled with peace and opportunity, and may have difficulty accepting the more tragic elements of life. You must also avoid a tendency to try to "fake it" when you don't really know something. This aspect is helpful to actors, although there is a tendency to overdramatize!

Jupiter semisquare Neptune: You may have a tendency to overestimate your abilities or overexaggerate what you've actually accomplished with Jupiter in semisquare to Neptune. Bringing harmony between what you dream for yourself and the actual opportunities you experience can be frustrating. However, this frustration can be diminished by developing an honest and powerful connection between your inner self and your outer life. There is a powerful difference between using visualization and action to change your life and just pretending that it is something other than it has become.

Jupiter sextile Neptune: Your interest in spiritual and metaphysical teachings can be quite powerful with Jupiter in sextile aspect to Neptune. With an ability to accept the differences between cultures and belief systems, your efforts toward developing harmony among the diverse factions can be quite significant. Most important, your own openness to understanding both universal and manmade laws allows you to transcend ordinary judgment and become more aware.

Jupiter trine Neptune: With Jupiter in trine aspect to Neptune, your desire to learn may be focused on a need to understand the mystical side of life. Your education may be strongly influenced by your religious or spiritual beliefs, and it is through these ideals that you may also experience some of your most profound opportunities for personal growth.

Jupiter quincunx Neptune: You can be quite unrealistic in your thinking and judgment with Jupiter in quincunx to Neptune. It's easy to be influenced by others who impress their will or opinions on you, and standing up to their demands may be difficult. You may not even be aware that you've been influenced or manipulated until the source of the manipulation is out of the picture.

Jupiter opposition Neptune: You're an idealist with Jupiter in opposition to Neptune. Since you want to believe the best in people, you get into situations where you are deceived, especially where legal agreements are concerned. It's crucial that you consult an impartial third party on any decisions that affect your long-term future, and especially in circumstances that involve finances. In learning situations, you have difficulty separating the teacher from the teaching, particularly in spiritual teachings. Your emotional attachments get in the way of your clear judgment.

Aspects to Pluto

Jupiter conjunct Pluto: You can be doggedly persistent in achieving your hopes with Jupiter conjunct Pluto. However, you can also become too compulsive or obsessive in your beliefs or ideals, and need to learn how to temper your idealism. Otherwise, you can become overly zealous in your attempts to influence others.

Jupiter semisquare Pluto: Your deep curiosity about the way things work is stimulated by Jupiter in semisquare to Pluto. You're not likely to be satisfied with blanket explanations of anything. You want to turn over a few rocks, particularly in the philosophical department, and find out what's lurking underneath. This is okay, but the manner by which you do it makes all the difference in the results!

Jupiter sextile Pluto: Your perceptive abilities can be highly developed with Jupiter in sextile aspect to Pluto. This can be quite helpful when you're involved in research or investigation, since your sixth sense may lead you to discover things that the cold facts might ignore.

Jupiter trine Pluto: Your curiosity about the mysteries of life may stimulate your desire to further your education. Jupiter's trine aspect to Pluto stimulates a deep sense of yearning to understand the larger questions, like "why am I here?," and may prompt you to continually seek these answers throughout your lifetime. However, you may also find that others seek your wisdom and guidance since you have the capacity to listen and accept them on their own terms, without judgment.

Jupiter quincunx Pluto: You may not trust belief systems, especially if you feel that your life has been negatively manipulated by someone posing as an ultimate authority. Finding your own path can require a series of shifts in consciousness, but as long as you know you are on the path of personal discovery, you'll welcome the transformation.

Jupiter opposition Pluto: Your desire to expand your mind can be especially powerful. The influence of Jupiter in opposition to Pluto creates a strong need to probe into the mysteries of life. You can be mislead by those who would misuse you by trying to control your freedom of decision and power of independent action. Adapting your own ideals to the beliefs or ideals of others can be dangerous. In learning situations, you can run into difficulty with teachers or professors whose approach challenges your beliefs or ideals.

Saturn's Role in Learning

The purpose of Saturn is to provide clarity, structure, form, and discipline—elements that are certainly important to learning. Saturn functions primarily as your inner teacher. Mothers are the most influential Saturnian models in western society. They typically provide the structure, guidance, and support for their children in the realms of learning, socialization, and personal growth. Once you entered society as a child, teachers played the Saturnian role; but the role of mothers and teachers in relationship to Saturn is to help you define the structure upon which you will build your life. You eventually learn to "own" your Saturn, and know how to discipline and focus your own energy. In essence, Saturn is the energy that helps you identify your priorities, and it is through this energy that you develop the skills that will serve you as you learn throughout your life.

Saturn's Signs and Your Approach to Learning

Saturn in Aries: With Saturn in Aries, your ability to reason can be quite strong. You may have good powers of concentration and enjoy a stimulating debate. In learning situations, you may have had trouble dealing with your teachers when you were a little girl. Your desire to be accepted can overwhelm your need to express yourself, resulting in an inner conflict. Once you determine your own direction, it is important that you follow your path with confidence and courage.

Saturn in Taurus: You may not enjoy school with Saturn in Taurus. Better yet, you probably do not enjoy tests, but when you have a chance to prove yourself, you can be stubbornly persistent until you've achieved satisfaction. Your sense of structure is amazing, and you may be quite adept at growing things. Try to apply your understanding of the processes of nature to your own development.

Saturn in Gemini: Achieving a sense of intellectual strength is important to you with Saturn in Gemini. This influence actually adds mental stability and focus, although you have a wide variety of interests. Your ability to adapt is one of your strengths, but you must be careful to avoid undermining the integrity of the structures you've built by failing to be attentive to your responsibilities. You may be a very good teacher since you have an excellent understanding of the way the mind works.

Saturn in Cancer: With Saturn in Cancer, you may have a strong affinity for history. Your reverence for the past, and your ability to connect what has happened before with what is happening now, makes you a prime candidate to teach or guide others, or to get into politics. Whenever you are involved in teaching, you learn more. Although you may find a few particular teachers who inspire you throughout your life, you are most inspired by those who have held tenaciously to other goals until they've seen them accomplished. Sounds like what you wish for yourself.

Saturn in Leo: You have a strong appreciation for many of your teachers with Saturn in Leo, especially those who have helped to foster your self-expression. Although you can be somewhat reserved and may be reluctant to fully express yourself when you know you're being evaluated, once you get over your stage fright you can become a very effective communicator. Your mental intensity can be quite strong, and you may gain momentum when you've accomplished an important goal.

Saturn in Virgo: Your approach to education and work are very much alike: keep everything in order and on track. With Saturn in Virgo, you function best when you have a plan. You can be overly critical of yourself and others, especially if you're taking life too seriously and cannot see the humor in the midst of your challenges. You may actually enjoy attending to the details and learning the facts about different things, but can become too caught up in the minutia. Remember the old adage: can't see the forest for the trees.

Saturn in Libra: You may hold education in high regard with Saturn in Libra, and understand the importance of becoming part of the social structure. Even if a part of you feels comfortable operating outside the realm of convention, your basic sense of stability and confidence is supported when you know you fit in with society. You may enjoy learning about the law, sociology, and cultural anthropology, but your natural talents may reside in human relations.

Saturn in Scorpio: You can be a resourceful student, and adept in research and investigation with Saturn in Scorpio. You may learn better and perform at your peak when you feel safe and well-protected. Circumstances that leave you feeling exposed are threatening, especially if you're working on something important or developing a creative project or idea. You prefer to work in relative secrecy, and do not appreciate having your efforts exposed without your permission. Life science, medicine, psychology, and metaphysics are good areas for your study and focus.

Saturn in Sagittarius: Education can be a lifelong pursuit for you. The influence of Saturn in Sagittarius stimulates a strong need to explore the world of philosophy, religion, and culture. You may also enjoy the sciences and can feel quite at home in academic surroundings. Teaching may be a natural outlet, and will provide an endless opportunity for you to continue learning. You may also enjoy travel and independent study.

Saturn in Capricorn: You're likely to do whatever is necessary to help you accomplish your aims with Saturn in Capricorn. If that includes extensive education, you're on track, but you may also discover that the things you need most to learn are in the school of life. You can be highly disciplined, and have a desire to achieve mastery in your chosen field. You also appreciate the practical side of life, and enjoy learning skills that help you maintain control over your life—like knowing how to change your own tires or repair a leak in the kitchen sink.

Saturn in Aquarius: Your interest in learning may be quite genuine with Saturn in Aquarius, although you might have strong opinions about the needs for educational reform. You may do well learning about scientific fields, although you can be rather rigid in adhering to certain theories. Abandoning old ideas may not be as easy as you would like, since you prefer the sense of security you gain from thinking that you might be able to predict a certain outcome because you're using something tried and true. You cannot help but carve out a few new pathways, since true genius rarely repeats a worn-out pattern.

Saturn in Pisces: In learning situations, you may feel a little uncomfortable, especially if you're put on the spot. With Saturn in Pisces, you can be quite conscientious and devoted to your subject, but you can also become too emotionally attached to things being done in a particular manner. You may feel too self-conscious when you have to stand up for your ideas, but if you are in the company of others who understand and support you, you can actually perform quite well and with great conviction.

The Houses Associated with Intellectual Development

The areas of your chart that are connected most strongly to mental and intellectual development are the 3rd, 9th, and 11th Houses. The 3rd House deals with communication and the development of concepts. It is here that you learn the basics, and it is here that you develop the rudiments of language and communication skills. The sign on the cusp of your 3rd House indicates how you approach linking your ideas with others, and planets in this house indicate the type of energy that can be applied in a special way to help you develop your communicative and writing skills.

The Sign on the 3rd House

Aries on the 3rd: Your approach to communicating and making contact with the world is direct and to the point with Aries on the cusp of your 3rd House. Your mental activity level can be consistently strong, and you have the potential to be a dynamic speaker or writer. Mental challenges, such as puzzles and brain teasers, can be enjoyable, but you may also get fired up in a good debate. You can be argumentative with Mars ruling your 3rd House, and are uncomfortable when you have to stay on a schedule. Learning things on your own and striking out on an individual path can be very exciting, and may be the most mentally stimulating challenges of your life.

Taurus on the 3rd: Your approach to communication and sharing your ideas may be somewhat reserved with Taurus on the cusp of your 3rd House. Although you may seem reluctant to open up and share your thoughts or make connections with others, you're actually just getting a feeling for the situation before you open up. Once you do get moving and start communicating, you are usually quite impressive with your well-formed opinions and ideas. Your mellow manner of speech may be reflected by a beautiful, soothing voice. With Venus ruling your 3rd House, you enjoy learning about things that have value in your life. You may have a good head for business, and a good eye for quality workmanship.

Gemini on the 3rd: Your insightful intelligence is influenced by Gemini's rulership of your 3rd House. Your multifaceted way of thinking is quite an asset when problems need to be solved or people need to be contacted. An exceptional negotiator, your ability to bring people together by opening lines of communication is one of your greatest assets. Mercury's rulership of your 3rd House adds a special ability to get along with others on an everyday basis, since reaching out and making contact is also self-confirming for you. You like to get to the point, and prefer to deal with factual evidence when making important decisions. Learning may be rather enjoyable for you throughout your lifetime.

Cancer on the 3rd: It's easier for you to communicate and share ideas about things that stimulate your emotions with Cancer ruling your 3rd House. You may also have a high memory capacity, thinking in terms of whole pictures. However, you may not be a good student, because you would prefer to "absorb" information; it seems so much easier that way. You do absorb a lot, but when you need facts, you may regret that you neglected to fire up the old brain cells. With the Moon ruling your 3rd House, you are most likely to share your ideas with people who feel familiar and safe, but you also prefer to communicate with passion and feeling. Stale numbers may never appeal to you.

Leo on the 3rd: You may be a passionate communicator and an intuitive thinker with Leo ruling your 3rd House. Once you set your mind on anything, you can become strongly focused, and you may take great pride in your intellectual accomplishments. However, you may not appreciate others who correct you or make light of your ideas, even though you can appear to be quite gracious about it. Your thinking may be influenced by your family more than you realize, especially by siblings, and if you maintain an active relationship with siblings, you may find that their opinions mean a great deal to you. With your Sun ruling the 3rd House, your ego is tied to your intelligence. You consider yourself worthwhile only if you've developed your mind or achieved some type of recognition for your ideas.

Virgo on the 3rd: Your approach to thinking, learning, and communicating is analytical with Virgo ruling your 3rd House. You may enjoy learning, and can develop a good relationship with your teachers. However, you are quite sensitive to criticism, and can be too critical of yourself or your own intellectual abilities. You're probably more intelligent that you realize! Your ability to illustrate detail is evidenced by your writing and speaking, and you may be a consummate storyteller and convincing reader (ask your children!). With Mercury ruling your 3rd House, you enjoy the support and interaction created through networking with others, and may have a special interest in education or children's issues.

Libra on the 3rd: You learn best in situations that are peaceful and non-confrontational with Libra ruling your 3rd House. You may enjoy experiencing beautiful music, fine literature, browsing museums and galleries, exploring anything that appeals to your sense of refinement and grace. In school, pleasing your teachers may have been important, and in life, you prefer to think that others are happy in your presence. Although you can be strong-minded, you may not like to argue, since it throws you off-balance. With Venus ruling your 3rd House, you may enjoy the company of others, and can be quite at home in social situations. School and work may be most enjoyable because you like to be around others and to share your ideas.

Scorpio on the 3rd: You are definitely opinionated with Scorpio on the 3rd House, and may have a biting wit. However, it's not easy for you to speak up in defense of yourself. You appreciate having things your way, and learn best in situations that allow you to have some measure of control. An excellent student and unparalleled researcher, when you're interested in something, you will probe to the depths. Your interest in life science, medicine, psychology, and metaphysics may be quite remarkable. With Pluto ruling your 3rd House, you have the capability of getting to the core of anything, and may not stop your search for answers until you've turned over every possible rock looking for clues.

Sagittarius on the 3rd: You may love the adventure of learning with Sagittarius on the cusp of your 3rd House. You can see the big picture, and enjoy situations that allow you to participate in decision making. Travel and reading may be important pastimes, and provide you with continued opportunities to learn and expand your mind. With Jupiter ruling your 3rd House, you may be drawn to study religion or law. You can easily become an excellent writer and dynamic public speaker.

Capricorn on the 3rd: With Capricorn on the cusp of your 3rd House, you have a serious approach to your mental development and learning. You learn best when you can add practical experience to the process, instead of just dealing with abstracts. With a natural inclination toward business, you can become adept at handling and understanding money and finances. Saturn's rulership of this house adds a strong desire to learn about things you can use, and you may also have an exceptional sense of structure and design.

Aquarius on the 3rd: Developing your mind is a very high priority with Aquarius on the cusp of your 3rd House. Although you love to learn, you may not enjoy adhering to a particular structure in your education: you have your own ideas about what is important! However, you can follow the program if necessary, especially if it means you will ultimately be able to become more independent as a result. You can be opinionated, although you may like to think of yourself as humanitarian, and frequently take an idealistic stand (at least according to your family). With Uranus ruling this house, you are concerned for the welfare of humanity, and you also enjoy reaching out to make contact with people on the planet. You're also interested in making contact with beings living beyond the bounds of earth. Here on earth, you may be fascinated by technology, and be a whiz with computers.

√ **Pisces on the 3rd:** You have a very insightful and creative mind with Pisces on the cusp of your 3rd House. Your imagination may work overtime, and when you're involved in a creative project, you may become totally absorbed in it. You may be somewhat sensitive to criticism, although you can usually keep it in perspective, especially if you can use it to shape your personal expression more clearly. You're also likely to show sensitivity to the feelings and needs of others in your manner of speech and action. With Neptune ruling this house, your vision can be far reaching, and your psychic sensitivities may also be especially powerful.

Planets in the 3rd House

Sun in the 3rd: The influence of the Sun in your 3rd House shows that you literally shine as a communicator. As a young girl, you probably enjoyed school and the experience of learning, especially if you gained positive recognition for your efforts. The energy of the Sun here adds to your abilities as a speaker, writer, and conversationalist. Your people skills may be among your greatest assets. The sciences can also be interesting to you, and you may have a special ability to shed light on subjects that are difficult for many people to understand.

Moon in the 3rd: With the your Moon's energy in the 3rd House, you have an impressionable mind and are capable of absorbing a great deal of information. However, recall can be a little more difficult, especially if you were daydreaming when you were listening to that lecture; if you are attentive, you can remember quite vividly. You may never have enjoyed studying, although you can be a very effective writer and communicator. Emotional sensitivity plays a powerful role in your thinking processes, and if you're upset or vulnerable, you can be easily swayed by the influence and opinions of others. It can be difficult for you to separate your feelings from your thoughts, and as a result, your decision-making processes usually incorporate both.

Mercury in the 3rd: Mercury's influence in your 3rd House adds a strong intellectual objectivity to your mentality. Your love of ideas, interest in virtually everything, and ability to connect with people from all walks of life adds a vibrant quality to your personality. You may enjoy learning, and can have a special ability to understand and relate to children and adolescents. Manual dexterity can also be quite well-developed, and activities like playing instruments or working with your hands can provide a special sense of fulfillment. You may also be a gifted writer and have a yearning to be constantly on the go or traveling somewhere.

Venus in the 3rd: You can be a persuasive communicator with Venus in your 3rd House. Although you may not like to exert a lot of effort toward structured learning, you do enjoy the arts and music, and may expend extra energy learning about and experiencing such refinements. Your own artistry is evident in your interests and abilities, and you may communicate most effectively when you're expressing yourself creatively.

Mars in the 3rd: You can be assertive as a communicator with Mars in your 3rd House, but need to watch a tendency toward impulsive decision making. You have a very active mind and need direction for your mental energy in order to feel satisfied with yourself. Speaking or acting before you've had a chance to think things through can result in trouble, accidents, or quarrels. Although you may not mind a debate, when you're angered, you can become hostile in your speech and manner. You can also be an irritating tease and need to know when to stop to avoid generating hostility from others.

Jupiter in the 3rd: With Jupiter in your 3rd House, you may really enjoy education and learning. Your memories of school are likely to include good experiences and positive social interactions. You may also enjoy travel as a means of learning, and may always find ways to incorporate travel into your life experience. Work that keeps you on the move can be satisfying, but you may need to learn to focus your energy to avoid becoming too scattered. Your ability to acknowledge other cultures and diverse ideas adds to your development of true wisdom, and you may always be seeking to find those links between the diversity present in human existence. You're optimistic about the prospects for your own future and for the future of humanity.

Saturn in the 3rd: You may be serious about developing your mind with Saturn in the 3rd House, although you may not like being tested. When you're prepared, you usually perform quite admirably on any type of examination, including the tests of life. You need to be attentive to a tendency toward worry and negative thinking, which can sap your vitality and weaken your ability to think clearly. This influence adds a strong ability to discipline your mind, and you can certainly study when necessary. Regardless of your experiences in school, you are likely to be a lifelong student of the things you love and enjoy.

Uranus in the 3rd: The energy of Uranus in your 3rd House adds a special ingenuity to your thinking. You love projecting yourself and your thoughts into the future, and may be quite inventive and visionary. Although you may be a rebellious and revolutionary thinker, you are a natural scientist, always seeking the yet undiscovered truth. Maintaining your concentration can be difficult, and you need ample opportunities to work at your own pace. However, some structure will help you avoid scattering your mental energy. Leaving room for your spontaneous urges to get up and go is very important, and anyone who is in a relationship with you needs to understand that you can change your mind or decide to do something at a moment's notice.

Neptune in the 3rd: You are a dreamer and a visionary. With Neptune in the 3rd House, you think in terms of what could be, and you have a powerful imagination. This sensibility can be readily translated into writing, music, and artistry, but does not necessarily aid your concentration when you need to learn something like algebra. Mental focus can be difficult, unless there are other aspects that aid you in this regard. As a result, you can feel insecure about your intellectual development and ability. Meditation or participation in a disciplined type of creative activity can help you channel your artistic manner of thinking into productive areas.

Pluto in the 3rd: Looking beneath the surface and searching for what lies beyond the facade is stimulated by the energy of Pluto in your 3rd House. You can be an avid researcher or scientific thinker, and may be adept at understanding many of the mysteries of life. Your interest in subjects that are somewhat taboo, like sexuality, birth, and death, adds a special dimension to your personality. Your ability to concentrate can be good, although you can be obsessive in your thinking. Since you may not realize the extent of your own mental intensity, you wonder why some people have difficulty being around you. They may be uncomfortable with your penetrating insight (especially if they have something to hide), but may also feel that you know more than you do. You rarely let on about everything you know or think, and can be secretive about anything that is important to you.

The 9th House and Higher Learning

Your 9th House shows your approach to higher learning, which is usually accomplished through a college or professional degree program. Subjects like philosophy, religion, political science, cultural pursuits, and the like are strongly associated with this facet of your development. Travel and languages are also extensions of this part of your chart. The sign on the cusp of your 9th House shows your approach to higher learning, and planets within the 9th House stimulate this area of your chart according to their expression.

The Sign on the 9th House

Aries on the 9th: You pride yourself on your original ideas and may be quite successful in your educational endeavors because you are willing to take a chance and express yourself! With Aries on the cusp of your 9th House, you may thoroughly enjoy learning through your life experiences, but school can also be a worthwhile endeavor. Your curiosity about the laws of life may lead you to forge into the study of metaphysics and philosophy with great passion. The influence of Mars as ruler of this house adds strong courage to your convictions, and a powerful faith in yourself and your ideals. You can be an ardent defender of the law, and may also be quite adept at standing up for yourself and your beliefs.

Taurus on the 9th: You have definite viewpoints about the way life should be with Taurus on the cusp of your 9th House. You may appreciate the value of higher education, especially where you see that it has practical value. Your curiosity about the wide-ranging differences in philosophies and religions may prompt you to study them, although your own philosophy may be more down to earth. With Venus ruling your 9th House, you enjoy the social elements afforded through education, and are more connected to people who share your artistic or creative interests.

Gemini on the 9th: Your powerful curiosity about life on earth and the people who inhabit the planet may stimulate a desire to learn through institutions of higher learning and travel. The influence of Gemini on the cusp of your 9th House adds a powerful need for logic and reason in your life, and you may extend your education in order to strengthen this aspect of your understanding. You've always asked "why?" about everything, and may be ever-seeking to answer some of those unanswerable questions. The influence of Mercury as ruler of this house adds a desire to connect your thoughts and share your ideas about religion, philosophy, and culture with others.

Cancer on the 9th: You have strong feelings about education with Cancer on your 9th House cusp. Your love of travel and desire to embrace an understanding of the world and her people is very powerful. You may also have great devotion to your spiritual path, and your sense that there is much more beyond the mere "reality" of the physical plane drives you to probe into the mysteries. You may also have a strong affinity for understanding history and human development. The influence of your Moon as the ruler of this house adds a special dimension of intuitive insight to your understanding and development of awareness. Your nurturing support of others under your guidance makes you a very good teacher, guide, and mentor. You believe that education should nurture the mind and spirit and foster a desire toward continued learning.

Leo on the 9th: The influence of Leo on the cusp of your 9th House adds a powerful sense of confidence to your ability to develop your understanding. Your search for and love of Truth drives you to study a broad range of material, but you also enjoy learning about some things just because you like them! You have a bit of wander-lust, and love to travel and experience the wide diversity present in life on earth. The Sun's rulership of this house adds a sense of pride to your educational accomplishments. You can be sensitive to criticism from others about what you know, how you say things, or the manner in which you do things.

Virgo on the 9th: Your approach to higher education is practical with Virgo on the cusp of your 9th House, and you appreciate learning experiences that allow you to apply what you know. In matters of religion and philosophy, you prefer a path that makes a difference in the quality of your everyday life, although you probably appreciate the experience of ritual as a means of focusing your energy. The rulership of Mercury in this house indicates a strong mental objectivity about belief systems, and you try to understand everything through a purely mental frame of reference. Some things, like faith, may not fit into this framework and can be difficult for you to understand, and you may simply have to learn to accept them!

Libra on the 9th: You may see education as a means of refining your innate ability to learn and understand with Libra on the cusp of your 9th House. Your love of literature, philosophy, and fine arts may lead you to study them further, or to become adept at developing your own aesthetic abilities. The social aspect of higher education may have been quite enjoyable during your college days, and you may still love to be around others who are fascinated by ideas. Study groups, community or church activities, and politics may allow you to further your interests. With Venus ruling this house, your own sensibilities may be a bit more refined. Coarse speech or destructive behavior may fly in the face of what you feel is proper and socially acceptable.

Scorpio on the 9th: The influence of Scorpio on the cusp of your 9th House stimulates your desire to find the deeper meanings of life. You may pursue this through educational endeavors, but may also learn from travel and independent study. The intensity with which you approach learning can be amazing, and your intuitive sensibilities may guide you into paths or areas that logic alone would ignore. Your ability to probe and research can be exceptional, and with Pluto ruling this house, you're not likely to leave many stones unturned in your search for the truth.

Sagittarius on the 9th: The influence of Sagittarius on the cusp of your 9th House stimulates a strong desire to open your mind and find the truth. Your quest may lead you to travel, study, converse, write, read, and explore. Nature is fascinating to you, as is human nature. You enjoy the experience of competition at the philosophical level: something like the Olympics is appealing to you, where people from all parts of the world come together to strive for excellence. Jupiter's rulership of this house stimulates a prophetic and visionary ability, and encourages you to reach beyond your current limitations toward horizons that are yet undiscovered.

Capricorn on the 9th: You may take education seriously, and are likely to prefer learning things that have a realistic basis with Capricorn on the cusp of your 9th House. A practical approach is much more suitable than abstract learning. You may be very much the "show me" type of woman, who prefers to have evidence for all the theories. With Saturn ruling your 9th House, you are a prime candidate for academia, and might fit into the academic pattern quite nicely, including becoming a teacher. Regardless of your aims, your education needs to provide a reasonable option for making a living. This energy also stimulates a somewhat orthodox approach to religion and philosophy, although you may have a strong affinity for nature religions and ritual.

Aquarius on the 9th: You live in the world of ideas with Aquarius on the cusp of your 9th House. You love to learn and explore a wide range of experiences. Travel to unusual places, meeting unique people, spending time with good friends may all play a part in your learning and the development of your mind and consciousness. Your fascination with futuristic ideas and unconventional thinkers stems from your desire to develop your own unique philosophies, but you can be somewhat reluctant to do so. The influence of Uranus as the ruler of this house stimulates a strong humanitarian nature, but you may feel somewhat disappointed in human nature itself, which never seems to meet your high expectations.

Pisces on the 9th: You are definitely an idealist with Pisces on the cusp of your 9th House. Your vision of the world as a better place with opportunities for true peace and harmony can be a powerful driver in your quest to improve your own life. In higher educational pursuits, you may be more inclined to study philosophy, religion, political science, and the arts than math or science. It's tempting for you to impose your ideals or beliefs on others who may seem less "enlightened," but you may need to show some restraint in this regard if you are to experience the peace you dream of. With Neptune ruling this house, you can use your ability to visualize to aid you in your learning pursuits, and to help you create the world as you desire to experience it.

Planets in the 9th House

Sun in the 9th: Your affinity for philosophy, religious study, teaching, and higher learning is no accident. With your Sun in the 9th House, you feel powerfully drawn to study higher truths and to invest much of your life in pursuit of excellence. You are an eternal student and can be a profound teacher. In many ways, you feel that your life is a journey, and whether you travel on the face of the planet, into space, or simply on the inner realm, you are always seeking to understand the greater meanings of life. A sense of higher moral law pervades your identity, and you may, in all your endeavors, strive for the path of true righteousness.

Moon in the 9th: The influence of your Moon in the 9th House adds an intensive receptivity to higher learning and enhances your ability to connect through your spiritual self to divine understanding. Your spiritual life is strongly important, and you may also strive to improve your understanding of life through education, travel, and cultural explorations. You may be capable of adapting to living in cultures other than that of your birth, especially if your Moon is in a mutable or cardinal sign. You may always feel that you are somehow protected by a higher power, and may feel closely connected to your spiritual guide, angels, or divine presence. Your love of philosophy and devotion to your ideals is quite genuine, and plays an important role in your sense of security. You may interpret Higher Power in terms that are both masculine and feminine, but your connection to The Goddess quality is your bridge between your human consciousness and the consciousness that radiates from The Source.

Mercury in the 9th: Your continual need to learn is enhanced with Mercury's placement in your 9th House. Instead of just learning facts, you can be drawn to gain a deeper understanding, and it can be natural for you to pursue higher education or lifelong studies. Your ability to expand your consciousness is enhanced through this influence, and you may be visionary and strongly intuitive. Travel, writing, teaching, or publishing may be of interest and can add a sense of adventure to your experience of life.

Venus in the 9th: Educational pursuits, extensive travel, and exploring cultural diversity can be among your greatest pleasures with Venus in the 9th House. You may be interested in living abroad, and can easily adapt to different cultural and environmental influences, especially if your sense of aesthetics is heightened from the new experience. Your appreciation for the art and culture of humankind can be powerful, and your own growth and sense of personal artistry and creativity are strengthened through your exposure to a wide variety of options and influences.

Mars in the 9th: You're excited by the experiences of travel, and may have a passion for learning with Mars in the 9th House. This placement also stimulates a mental restlessness, and can indicate some difficulty in focusing your mind. You need some distractions in your life, but can disrupt your flow and concentration by adding too many options. Your enthusiasm and zeal for your beliefs and ideals can be quite intense, and you can be effective stimulating the interest of others through your own devotion and the strength of your convictions. You may need to guard against a tendency toward trying to influence others to change their own ideals against their will, since you can be extremely persuasive.

Jupiter in the 9th: Continuing education is absolutely natural for you with Jupiter in the 9th House. If you are not in school, you are likely to be exploring new vistas through travel, personal study, or enthusiastic discussions with others who share your quest for understanding. You may be involved in teaching, writing, or publishing, and can have a special affinity for religious or metaphysical studies. An enjoyment of the diversity of cultural expressions across the globe may prompt you to live abroad, and you may have friends in different countries. Ultimately, you may hope to have friends in other galaxies! This placement indicates a keen intuitive ability and sharp awareness of the larger scheme of things. As a result, you may be able to blend your logical and intuitive processes during decision making, thereby enhancing your judgment.

Saturn in the 9th: Saturn's influence in your 9th House enhances your desire to learn and strengthen your understanding. You may have followed strict religious teachings when you were a young girl, and may still have powerful beliefs. Your fears can stand in the way of moving beyond your early training, but your desire to know and understand the truths of life on your own terms is also powerful. As you've matured, you have learned ways to expand your spiritual understanding and are developing a very workable spirituality. Your philosophical outlook is based on practicality and usefulness, and you have a powerful work ethic. You must be careful to avoid becoming a workaholic, although your precision and attention to detail are appreciated by those who utilize your talents or employ your expertise. You can be an exceptional teacher, but may be too critical when your students fail to meet your expectations. High standards accompany everything you do, and you insist that your own children follow a high moral code. Your lessons in life may involve learning greater tolerance and acceptance of each individual for her- or himself, although those who are close to you know that your desire for excellence can prompt anyone to accomplish more than they dreamed possible.

Uranus in the 9th: You're a trail blazer with Uranus in the 9th House, and can have a life filled with unusual experiences and rare treasures. Drawn to unorthodox philosophies and eccentric ideas, your views of life can encompass a true sense of unconditional acceptance. Your unique ideas and unusual manner of expressing them can be quite beneficial to your success in writing, speaking, broadcasting, publishing, teaching, diplomatic relations, and ventures not yet tested. You may have an unusual education, and may not follow traditional methods of learning, but you can still develop your own special genius as long as you remain mentally active and experimental. Your ideas about education can stimulate revolutionary changes, and you may be active in doing just that through your local school board or participation in the field of teaching itself. Travel on the physical plane and within the inner realms can open new vistas of awareness. You may even have some connection to the aerospace industry, a fascination with life on other planets, and a wonderful ability to envision alternate realities.

Neptune in the 9th: Your consciousness may be highly impressionable with Neptune in your 9th House. A mystical quality permeates your awareness, and you may be strongly visionary. Your idealism can be exceptionally powerful, and your devotion to your beliefs can influence every aspect of your life. Although this placement does not necessarily encourage strong intellectual or educational pursuits, your desire to bridge the connection to higher knowledge can be powerful. There can be a nebulous element to your mentality that can create confusion when you're trying to express your ideas or philosophies, especially if you are out of balance or unfocused. Since you can be easily influenced by others, you need to safeguard against falling victim to unscrupulous teachers, and will always benefit from maintaining a connection to your inner self and a means of determining your deeper understanding. You need a philosophy that is worthy of your profound devotion.

Pluto in the 9th: With Pluto in the 9th House, you can be quite dogmatic in your ideals and beliefs, but you are also likely to completely transform those belief systems at least once during this lifetime. You understand the power of the mind, and the importance of educational excellence, and may pursue educational endeavors that will allow you to strengthen your own understanding. An avid researcher and careful investigator, you are more likely to expose corruption and abuse, and can create powerful changes through sharing your discoveries.

The 11th House: Goals and Hopes for the Future

Through the 11th House, you learn from peers and connect with your community. The 11th House involves your special interests, too. This is very much the school of life because this is the area that relates to developing your goals. The sign on the cusp of your 11th House influences your attitudes about what you want from life, and planets within this house show the type of energy you have available to you that will aid you in reaching your goals.

The Sign on the 11th House

Aries on the 11th: Although you may be somewhat involved in your local community, you're happiest when you're in the lead or left alone to do things your way. You may not always set strict goals for yourself, since sometimes getting through the moment seems like enough of a challenge. But when you do set goals, they are most effective if they stimulate action. With Mars ruling your 11th House, you can be unstoppable. If you're curious about something, your exploration may not cease until you've reached the summit of the experience.

Taurus on the 11th: Your interests have a practical focus and you may limit your community involvement to matters that affect you directly. Goals can be especially important to you, and are usually tied to stabilizing your life, especially financially.

It's important that you explore your deeper motivations, and that your goals reflect and support a true sense of personal worth. Although it's tempting to think that money can answer your needs for acceptance, it's rarely enough unless you can fully embrace yourself. Your interest in investments can play an important role in your life. With Venus ruling your 11th House, you may look for an easier path to realizing your dreams. You may be able to attract the right people and situations, and may feel that the right partnership and most prestigious friends can open doors for you. In the end, you really want to be the one who has the influence.

Gemini on the 11th: You're probably surrounded by friends who share your interests, and those interests usually involve enjoying life. With Gemini on the 11th House, maintaining contact is important, and you may feel that you need a lot of gadgets, like telephones, computers, cars, or other devices that help you stay in touch. Your goals may include accumulating these things, but your larger goal is staying connected! With Mercury ruling this house, you may think of a lot of goals you would like to follow, but may not stay focused upon them. You may understand that you become what you think, and as you mature, are realizing the importance of focusing your thoughts more clearly in order to create a life that reflects your true values and needs.

Cancer on the 11th: Since your primary drive is to create a true sense of security, your goals will be set to accomplish that aim. With Cancer on the cusp of your 11th House, you definitely feel that it is important to do things that will keep you and those you love safe. You can also be successful in achieving your aims because you know how to put more energy behind your objectives: you can both visualize and emotionally connect with your affirmations. The influence of your Moon is connected to attaining your objectives, and stimulates a powerful interest in family values, women's issues, historical preservation, or collecting (among other things!).

Leo on the 11th: The goals you set for yourself may be impressive with Leo on the 11th House cusp. You need life experiences that provide you with positive recognition for your efforts, and that begins with your feeling good about your choices and accomplishments. In community activities, you may take a role of leadership, and can inspire those around you to strive for excellence. With the Sun ruling this house, you may spend a lot of time and energy developing your special interests, and can be quite strong about setting and pursuing your goals.

Virgo on the 11th: The overall organization of your life may be centered around the things you are striving to accomplish. With Virgo on the cusp of your 11th House, you function best when you have a plan of action. You're the one who is prepared for contingencies because you're likely to have given some thought to the possibilities of what could happen. You can also be flexible when you have to alter your course, but only if you can see that you will still arrive at your goals. Change for the sake of change may seem like a waste of time for you. The influence of Mercury, which rules this house in your chart, adds an analytical and rational quality to your approach to creating and setting goals. You may try to be logical whenever possible, but practicality is also important.

Libra on the 11th: You may wish that life would just provide the right situations, and that by living a just and harmonious life, you would get where you're trying to go. With Libra on the cusp of your 11th House, you may not always have definitive goals, like a list of objectives; but when you think about it, you do have preferences, and those preferences frequently act as the anchor for your goals. The influence of the energy of Venus, which is the ruler of this house, adds strong values to your aims and objectives. You may also like the idea of achieving a certain amount of prestige and social status, and may even take these considerations into account when organizing the overall plan of your life. This may function subconsciously, but when you get inside yourself, you can probably see how these needs drive you to make some of your choices.

Scorpio on the 11th: Although you probably have rather well-defined goals, you don't always let other people know about them with Scorpio's influence on the cusp of your 11th House. You have a lot invested in achieving your aims, and may not welcome the emotional input others have to offer, particularly if it undermines your plan of action. So you've learned to give only so much information about where you're going, and to keep the rest to yourself. Pluto's energy rules this house, adding an intensity to your focus when you're on the path toward realizing your accomplishments. Sometimes you can be so obsessed with getting there that you miss something else along the way. It's probably a good idea to step back and alter your perspective from time to time.

Sagittarius on the 11th: You aim high with Sagittarius on the cusp of your 11th House. "The sky's the limit!" may be your approach to pursuing your goals, and you see no reason to limit yourself to known horizons. You need to explore the ultimate, to experience the unusual, to find adventure, but if you become too distracted from your path toward achievement, you can undermine your ability to reach those ultimate heights. Jupiter's energy rules this part of your life, and adds a sense of expansion and optimism to your goals. Because of this, even when you do experience setbacks, you're quite capable of retreating and starting again with even more enthusiasm than you possessed before.

Capricorn on the 11th: You're capable of putting a strong foundation underneath your dreams with Capricorn's influence in your 11th House. You may find it easier to accomplish your aims when you have a well-defined path, and that path can be clarified by setting goals. You need long-term and short-term goals, since you can become discouraged if you're simply aiming for something that will happen many years in the future. Those short-term goals will also act as stepping stones toward the summit! Saturn's rulership of this house shows that you need clarity when working toward your aims, and that you might appreciate guidance or support from a friend or mentor to help you maintain your focus.

Aquarius on the 11th: A strong factor in your spirit of adventure is related to the influence of Aquarius on the cusp of your 11th House. Sometimes you can lose track of your goals or aims because you project too far into the future; but you are a "futurist," you like to think about the possibilities for change. You also feel good about the idea of forging into untried territory, or trying different approaches. As long as the possibilities seem somewhat logical, you'll give them a shot! The energy of Uranus, which rules this house, adds a fascinating dimension to your personal objectives. You need to be different from the rest of the crowd, and your personal aims are centered around employing and improving your special talents and gifts.

Pisces on the 11th: Your desire to have the things you want and to experience a life of true security begins with your dreams. With Pisces influencing your 11th House, your dreams play a major role in accomplishing your aims. Your ability to envision what you want from life can be quite empowering. If you can do something that confirms the probability of making your dreams happen, you can be even more successful. Although you have to start with the dream, at some point you need to touch the physical reality. It's like career day at school. You may think, "I'd like to be a doctor," but until you follow a doctor around for a few hours and get a sense of what it would be like, you may wonder if it actually fits. By making some physical connection to your dreams, you can become a masterful creator of your life. Neptune's rulership of this house adds a desire to make a difference in the world. You know that you can be part of the change that will add meaning and compassion to the experience of life.

Planets in the 11th House

Sun in the 11th: With your Sun in the 11th House, you need goals that will give you an opportunity to gain recognition. You may have interests in community affairs, politics, or professional development that can ultimately take you into positions of leadership. Your personal development and educational endeavors may include public relations, management, or counseling skills, and you may find that you become a role model for others who wish to follow in your footsteps.

Moon in the 11th: The influence of your Moon in the 11th House draws your attention to the need to be involved with others. Your goals, interests, hobbies, and professional development may be more enjoyable if you're sharing them with special friends. You may feel a strong connection to your women friends, and may even have a special affinity for political issues that are connected to women. Your work will be more satisfying if you feel that it helps you accomplish something deeply meaningful, instead of just spending your time making money doing a job that means nothing to you personally. So when you're setting your personal goals, take your feelings about your choices into consideration. Listen to your soul's voice.

Mercury in the 11th: Your ability to use your mental energy in a direct manner when working toward your goals is highly accentuated with Mercury in your 11th House. Networking with others who share your interests, making connections with people in your community, staying in touch with professional friends—all these activities are driven by the energy of Mercury in this house. Your speaking and writing ability can aid you in achieving your goals, and by developing your intellect and understanding, you can rise further, faster in your personal and professional growth.

Venus in the 11th: Learning the social skills necessary to further your pursuits of personal and professional growth is important with the influence of Venus in your 11th House. You know the significance of knowing the right people, making connections, and developing the pathways that will help you achieve your aims. Although you may enjoy the experience of community, political, or social interaction, you may not appreciate the feeling that you have to please others in order to have what you want. If this arises, it could be that you have made choices that are designed to satisfy someone else, and that it is time to re-examine your values and set goals that allow you to feel more worthwhile on your own terms. You can actually be quite adept at choosing the right friends and associates whose values reflect your own, and whose influence helps to forward your own aims. Conversely, your influence can have the same effect in the lives of others!

Mars in the 11th: When you have a goal, your action, energy, and courage play a significant role in achieving it with Mars in your 11th House. You may enjoy challenges, and can accomplish more if you are met with situations that require you to rise to the occasion. You may also prefer to stir up activity levels when things start to get a little boring or stale. Choosing the outlets within your community and among your friends and professional associates that allow you to make a difference can be very important. You may find that you become too involved in the social side of life and lose track of your larger goals. When you focus on your aims, you have no trouble doing whatever is necessary to make them happen.

Jupiter in 11th: Jupiter's influence in your 11th House adds strong optimism and confidence to your ability to set and achieve your personal aims. Your vision of the future may always drive you to improve your life, and you may feel that setting limits will only get in the way of achieving the possibilities! You can become quite adept at public relations and community affairs, and may enjoy politics or spending extra time developing your special interests. Friends play an important role in helping you achieve your goals, and you can also benefit from staying active in professional and political associations. You may need to learn how to say "no" to some of the requests that come your way since you can become overly involved and thereby fail to accomplish half of what you hope to achieve.

Saturn in the 11th: With Saturn in your 11th House, you operate best when you have a plan. Setting realistic goals and working toward making them a reality gives you a way to focus your energy and forms the basic structure of your life. You may appreciate an approach toward education that provides ample opportunities to achieve excellence, and in your profession, you will look for a career that allows you to achieve greater influence over the passage of time. If you're involved in political or community activities, you're likely to take on roles of leadership and responsibility, since just sitting back and watching may be a bit uncomfortable for you. In your work, you need to earn respect, and prefer recognition that arises from a job well done.

Uranus in the 11th: Your approach to goals is stimulated by a need to express your individuality with Uranus in the 11th House. You may take an unconventional approach to achieving your aims, and operate best in situations that allow you plenty of freedom and room for independent action. Political and community affairs may be of interest to you, and if you become involved in such activities, you may be responsible for stimulating revolutionary change. Your choice of friends and associates, personally and professionally, is likely to be diverse.

Neptune in the 11th: The influence of Neptune in your 11th House can create a lack of direction. You may not be sure of your goals, although you do like to dream about possibilities. Setting goals can seem like a waste of time because you can also lose track of your aims and then feel that you have somehow failed. If you apply this energy in its fullest strength, you can use your inner vision to manifest changes in your life. Your ability to visualize what you want can be exceptional. The problems you encounter may concern whether or not your dreams are within the realm of possibility, and whether or not you can put the necessary action behind your vision to make it a reality.

Pluto in the 11th: With Pluto in your 11th House, you need goals that will help you change your life. You may be drawn into groups of people who share your interests or profession, and are not likely to enjoy just sitting back if nothing is happening. You prefer to become involved in using the power of the collective to create change, and you can be quite influential when you wish to be. You may be fascinated by politics, and if you choose to become involved in political or community affairs, can become a catalyst for far-reaching change.

～

CHAPTER SIX

YOUR SPECIAL EDGE

What you've heard is true. Women are definitely the intuitive sex. The process of intuitive awareness may be more developed for you as a woman because you are more cyclically aware, thanks to your anatomy and hormonal changes. In the twentieth century, studies have confirmed that there are significant differences in the way men's and women's brains operate. Women have the ability to tap into their intuitive consciousness and act in accordance more readily than men, but there is something more. As a woman, your natural affinity with the energy of the Moon increases your receptivity, which is an important ingredient in opening to the intuitive process. Intuitive awareness is multifaceted. You can use it when you're dealing with emotional and psychological issues, you can apply it to your creative expression, and you can take advantage of your intuition in your work as part of your decision making. Developing your intuitive process is like strengthening any other sensibility—you have to concentrate some time, effort, and energy in order to finely hone this part of your psyche. Although some quality of intuition may be there innately, to make the most of it, you must learn to trust, listen, and incorporate it into your life. Your spiritual focus may also have a lot do to with whether or not you're comfortable developing your intuitive sensibilities, since it is through expanding your awareness that you become more spiritually adept.

The Water Houses: Your Intuitive Sensibilities

The parts of your chart that are most strongly associated with intuitive sensibility are the water houses: the 4th House, the 8th House, and the 12th House. The 4th House is connected to your soul history. It is here that you seek a sense of home, a connection to your family, and a feeling of safety and comfort. It is here that your soul remembers your past, even if your conscious mind cannot fit the pieces together.

The Sign on Your 4th House: Remembering Your Soul's Intention

Aries on the 4th: You are striving to complete the mission of your soul with Aries on the cusp of the 4th House. Your struggle to create the security you need may sometimes test your inner courage, and you may feel that you are doing battle with the physical plane. In many respects, you are a spiritual pioneer, venturing forward into life driven by the deep needs your soul remembers, but that you may not consciously recall. With Mars ruling this house, you can allow feelings of anger or frustration to block your ability to surrender to the peace you work so hard to achieve. You need to take an active approach toward fulfilling your soul's destiny while still allowing your creative mind to listen more carefully to your inner voice.

Taurus on the 4th: With Taurus' influence on the cusp of your 4th House, you may feel a powerful drive to create a stable, secure base of operations. Sometimes, however, you can be so focused on external values that you forget the importance of forging a meaningful connection to the deeper purpose of your life. With the energy of Venus influencing this house, you are learning that one of your keys to unlocking the mysteries of your soul history is through your heart. When you can open to the essence of love that resides in the center of your being, and allow this love to flow into your environment and those within it, your soul is nourished and you are whole.

Gemini on the 4th: You may be quite curious about the nature of your soul with Gemini on the cusp of your 4th House. Sometimes, when you try to force spiritual issues to fit into a logical framework, a part of you may scream out that you can't get there that way! You can also become distracted from the yearnings of your soul in favor of exploring the world, and, after all, you are here on the physical plane and need to understand the nature of things. You have a powerful sixth sense, especially in matters that affect your family. Mercury's rulership of this house adds the potential of blending your intuitive and rational processes.

Cancer on the 4th: Your connection to your soul may be centered in your sense of being rooted to your family with Cancer on the cusp of your 4th House. You may feel an urge to explore family history or genealogy, and in the process, may discover some exceptional information about yourself that seems to ring a very deep chord. You have a compelling sense of knowing when things are right, which is more like a "feeling" than a thought. With your Moon influencing this house through its connection to the sign of Cancer, your needs to establish the right home environment may go deeper than just wanting to live in the right neighborhood. You need a place where you feel connected at the most profound levels.

Leo on the 4th: With Leo on the cusp of your 4th House, you may feel that your family fate is indeed tied to your own. Yet you may also feel drawn to break away from the restraints that are implied in your family history, and to do things that support your individuality and autonomy. You may nourish others by example: in fact, your example can have a greater impact on your family than you may realize! By listening to your intuitive voice concerning the best way to handle family needs and developing a true sense of security, you may be able to set your ego aside. With the Sun ruling your 4th House, you may find that sometimes your ego can get in the way of your intuitive process. It's important to define the difference between selfish desires and true inner guidance. Strive to avoid trying to control the yearnings of your soul. Sometimes you may have to tell your ego to sit quietly and listen to the part of you that speaks in a quiet whisper.

Virgo on the 4th: The sign of Virgo on the cusp of your 4th House adds a sense of order to your desire to discover your soul's history. It is through your mind that you will make the connection to true understanding, although your mind is only the link. Your deeper consciousness carries you past the gates into true wisdom, and you have a deep understanding that this is a long-term process. Sometimes you may try to analyze the yearnings of your soul instead of just allowing that energy to guide you through your life, but it's hard to ignore your curiosity with Mercury ruling this house.

Libra on the 4th: Your soul yearns to find true peace with Libra on the cusp of the 4th House. You are, by nature, a restless woman, and may not find that peace simply by getting everything right "in the world." Your inner harmony depends on your ability to strengthen your real values, and these may have a very long history. The influence of Venus on this house is also powerful through its connection to the sign of Libra, indicating the importance of establishing a clear connection between the love you need and the love you express through your actions, words, and creativity.

Scorpio on the 4th: Your soul is dealing with the quest to achieve harmony through conflict with Scorpio on the cusp of your 4th House. This influence may draw you into several crisis periods over the course of your life, and you may have to cope with experiences of loss or feelings of abandonment that can leave a very deep wound in your psyche. What you are experiencing may not even seem to be that big or important, but your soul remembers power struggles that have gone on for centuries. During this life, you need to know true healing, which begins with your release of old pain. The energy of Pluto influences this house, adding a high level of intensity to your quest to understand the deeper meanings of life and to discover the mystery of your soul.

Sagittarius on the 4th: Your soul yearns for understanding with Sagittarius on the cusp of the 4th House. You have very high standards for yourself and everybody else, and if you can develop tolerance, you can become an inspiration for others through your quiet sense of determination to do things right. You have a following, which can be a holdover from your soul's history of teaching and guiding others to find the truth. Your desire to explore the earth and her people stems from your own need to assimilate as much information as possible in your quest for true wisdom. Jupiter's rulership of this house adds an energy of expansion and desire to share and experience honest understanding between yourself and those who are part of your life. By tapping into your intuitive insight you can become clearer about what others need from you, instead of just assuming that you know what's best for them!

Capricorn on the 4th: The influence of Capricorn on the cusp of your 4th House adds a need to feel centered and stabilized. Your soul may yearn for a solid foundation that will allow you to grow and change while still on solid ground. The influence of your family can be quite powerful, and you may feel that you were born into your family for very definite reasons. Saturn's connection to this house adds a tendency to hang on to others for support instead of establishing your own platforms for growth, but also can help you discover the importance of becoming self-sustaining.

Aquarius on the 4th: Your soul yearns for absolute freedom and autonomy with Aquarius on the cusp of your 4th House. You may go about achieving this in interesting ways, and sometimes the alienation others feel from you is simply a result of your wanting to do things yourself without their interference. It can be difficult for you to truly cooperate with others, although you do appreciate those who are revolutionary in their attitudes and might join them in a cause from time to time. Your soul lessons center around the need to learn the balance between freedom and responsibility, and until you can be fully responsible for your own attitudes, actions, and desires, your ability to achieve satisfaction will be inhibited. The energy of Uranus plays a powerful role in influencing this house, which can stimulate a tendency toward restlessness and a need for individual recognition. By learning to listen to your intuitive voice when faced with the prospects of change, especially change that seems to come from "outside," you may become quite adept at rejuvenating your life instead of feeling wounded by something you did not want.

Pisces on the 4th: Your sense that your soul has a long and fascinating history is strengthened by the influence of Pisces on the cusp of your 4th House. It's easy to be persuaded by the needs of others, and the beliefs and ideals of your family may be especially powerful for you. Yet you also know that you need to find your own path, and you may hide a secret side of yourself that is quietly journeying toward the summits of understanding and spiritual awareness. Neptune's energy influences this house, adding a deep perceptual awareness that you are much more than "merely human." Your yearning to travel home with your soul drives you to discover the reality of your inner self, which is where you are most alive.

Planets in the 4th House

Sun in the 4th: The Sun's placement in your 4th House stimulates a powerful need to discover your identity through your family ties, and beyond into the history of your soul. You have a very powerful survival urge, and cling to the people and places you know because your identity can be very strongly tied to them. Yet, as you are maturing and growing toward becoming a whole woman, you discover ways in which you are different from the family you knew. Your father and mother may seem to connect to a place deep within your soul, and intuitively, you've always known that the flame of your soul had its individual roots. Weaving together the core of your being with the roots and history that have preceded you is a key factor in achieving the security you so deeply desire.

Moon in the 4th: The energy of your Moon in the 4th House stimulates a strong need for home and family ties; but you can also feel a powerful connection to your soul and need a life that allows you to nourish and support the growth of your soul in whatever you're doing. Getting caught in feelings of selfishness, or opting to do things that serve only your self-interest, will limit your ability to achieve a deep sense of wholeness. Because of this, you may reach to your family, especially to your mother, to both give and receive support. To truly find yourself, however, you may need to break away from your emotional attachment to your family to some extent and forge, instead, a true intuitive and spiritual bond with them. From this perspective, you can respond more appropriately to their needs from a position that allows you to feel comfortable with yourself.

Mercury in the 4th: Mercury's position in your 4th House can stimulate a tendency to become overly concerned with family matters, or to worry too much about what's happening at home. Freeing your mind from your emotional fears or anxieties can be accomplished by allowing yourself to achieve a sense of mental rest: something soothing, like bathing your consciousness in true quiet and clarity. This can be achieved through meditation, and you may discover that everyday acts, like washing dishes or preparing dinner, provide an excellent opportunity to be active yet contemplative.

Venus in the 4th: With Venus in your 4th House, you may love the comfort of being at home. Your inner home, that place where you feel serene and one with yourself, is a place of beauty, and your soul adores basking in that experience. You may also experience a deep sense of satisfaction from the pleasure of being around those you love. Caring for your soul involves creating a space that allows love to grow in your life, and that space reflects your values and personal artistry.

Mars in the 4th: You may feel that your soul is strife-ridden with Mars in your 4th House, and you may experience an undercurrent of agitation or anger until you learn how to deal with your true feelings. You may not know how to deal with feelings of anger when they arise, and you can torture yourself when you repress any emotion, but especially anger. It's important to recognize abusive or difficult situations and take actions to avoid being victimized by another's abuse of power. Dealing with your very active emotional nature involves allowing yourself ample outlets for personal expression. Your instincts push you to achieve a real sense of security, and this is accomplished by asserting yourself in a healthy manner.

Jupiter in the 4th: You need a lot of space and room to move with Jupiter in your 4th House. This includes interior space—room in your psyche—an open mind! You may wonder how you attract good fortune, since you frequently seem to benefit from the generosity of others, but your soul is a generous one, and you may simply be attracting what you project to others. Your desire to learn, to explore the world, and to expand your consciousness is powerful. Whether or not you travel physically, you have the capability of journeying with your soul into the realms of truth and wisdom.

Saturn in the 4th: Saturn's influence in your 4th House may prompt you to operate from a basis of fear and insecurity. This may be an old memory, hidden in your soul from lifetimes past, but it may also be the result of the things you've learned from your parents or family. If you feel that you will never have enough, stop to honestly evaluate your life. What are you seeking? What are your true soul-level needs? Your intuitive powers can be hampered through this placement since you may mistrust yourself or your abilities to attract and create the life you need to experience. By releasing your extreme hold on the past and focusing on the present moment, you may gain a different perspective. You have the ability to build on a solid foundation, and the part of that foundation that is related to your soul growth includes your need to take responsibility for yourself.

Uranus in the 4th: You have a very restless soul with Uranus in your 4th House. Many of the unexpected changes you've experienced have resulted from factors beyond your control, but you've probably been quite capable of dealing with them. In actuality, you need change. Breaking away from your early influences can seem quite natural, since you may have felt a little like an alien as a child! Your intuitive connection can be quite powerful, and your ability to readily shift your focus is the result of your soul-level need to experience true freedom. Although some of your changes may surprise other people, you are aware of breaking free for a longer period: your intuitive self prepares you nicely. Too bad it's harder to prepare everybody else!

Neptune in the 4th: Your soul yearns to escape the frustrations of the physical plane. With Neptune in your 4th House, you're more comfortable when you've moved beyond ordinary reality—when you're in the middle of your favorite creative pastime, listening to beautiful music, watching an enthralling movie—you need to experience transcendence. Unfortunately, this is close to negative forms of withdrawal, and you may push yourself away from the rest of the world in your quest to tone down the cacophony of life. Setting your personal boundaries and creating a strong, yet resilient, emotional filter is crucial if you are to develop a sense of wholeness.

Pluto in the 4th: The influence of Pluto in your 4th House stimulates a powerful drive to uncover the mysteries of your soul. In the process, you may discover old shame, fear, or resentments lurking beneath the surface that undermine your ability to listen and respond to your intuitive voice. If you are to break away from the forces that seem to have an uncontrollable hold over your life and free yourself from these old wounds, you need to find their origins. You must allow yourself to release your attachment to the wounds themselves, surrender to the Healing Woman within your soul, and open your consciousness. Then, free of the guilt that has tortured your inner being for so long, your penetrating awareness can concentrate on creating true transformation.

The 8th House: Transformational Change and Clairvoyance

The 8th House brings you into an awareness of your deepest emotional attachments, and is the space where you are alchemically transformed. This is the seat of your magical power: your ability to change yourself in order to become whole. Here is the heart of healing, but here also you hide your greatest vulnerabilities. Most people shy away from dealing with 8th House issues like sex, death, and taxes. After all, there can be problems with any of them, and they are not easy to explore out in the open. But there is more. For your intuitive development, this area represents the part of you that holds your power, and you must learn to accept and embrace this side of yourself to feel truly satisfied with your life. The particular intuitive element associated with this area of the chart is clairvoyance. Developing the part of your psyche that allows you to probe beneath the surface is one of the functions of your 8th House.

The Sign on Your 8th House and Intuitive Development

Aries on the 8th: Through the influence of Aries on the cusp of your 8th House you may be quite assertive about approaching the mysteries, and may show great courage when exploring the processes of healing and transformational change.

You may feel that your primary thrust in life is to regenerate yourself, to become whole and perfect. Before you can achieve this experience, you may have to venture into some unknown territory: the place that contains your real power. With Mars ruling this house, you may experience some turmoil within yourself, since you may have very powerful physical desires and emotional attachments. You may feel that you have to experience some type of wounding in order to continue in your spiritual quests to uncover life's deeper mysteries. You may even follow the path of the shaman, which requires a level of wounding if you are to travel between the worlds of the inner and outer self, but there is a difference between wounding and self-destruction, and that is the crux of your dilemma!

Taurus on the 8th: With Taurus on the cusp of your 8th House, you may want some tangible proof regarding the mysteries of life that are connected to the experiences of birth, sexuality, death, healing, and the inner nature of the self. To some extent, it is possible to understand the deeper elements of life experience through the physical plane. The processes of life and death may be a profound mystery for you. If you have had children, or if you've been present at a birthing, your life will have been profoundly changed by the tangible experience of such a quickening. Although you may be able to philosophically accept the spiritual essence of yourself, you need to feel the effects this part of yourself has on the other aspects of your life. Adopting a working spirituality makes a lot of sense to you. That means you may need to make the effort to recycle and reclaim, since diminishing resources will not feel okay at the core of your being. With Venus ruling this house, you may become caught in the illusion that locking up your resources will protect you in some way. It's like the old story of the talents: if you don't put them to use, then what good are they?

Gemini on the 8th: Your strong curiosity about the true nature of healing and transformational change is stimulated by the influence of Gemini on the cusp of your 8th House. You can be objective about exploring those "taboo" subjects like human sexuality, death, and dying, and other mysteries that may be deemed occult, but you need to be careful about a tendency to try to put everything into a logical perspective. What you're experiencing is the challenge to create a new paradigm—a new model—for your deeper understanding of life. Mercury's rulership of this house provides an energy of questioning that will keep you always alert to the possibility that there is yet more to learn. You have a keen understanding of the importance of the links between mind, soul, and body, and may have great insights into the true nature of healing.

Cancer on the 8th: You may have a strong feeling about the great changes experienced through life on the physical plane with Cancer on the cusp of your 8th House. This influence strengthens your psychic sensitivity, particularly in the area of clairvoyance, but you can overreact emotionally to your impressions and feelings. Although it's difficult to remain objective, it is necessary to conquer your tendency to let your own emotional responses overwhelm you. The energy of your Moon also influences this house, emphasizing your need to gain an awareness of the manner in which your sensitivity on inner levels can affect your emotional stability. By developing an understanding of the way your inner self operates, and learning to clear your energy when you fall into negative emotional states, you can experience deep healing in your life.

Leo on the 8th: With Leo on the cusp of your 8th House, you may have a lot invested in trying to understand the deeper mysteries and questions that surround birth, death, sexuality, and personal alchemy. You may feel that the importance of developing a connection to these levels will strengthen your personal power, but you must safeguard against trying to control the outcome of things you cannot influence. The influence of the Sun on this house adds a desire to employ your willpower to deal with these ultimate life experiences. Although you know that your energy is responsible for creating your life circumstances to a certain extent, you may not like the times when you have to surrender to a higher power. Yet there is some comfort in knowing that if you release your attachment to your own will as the ultimate and allow a higher will to guide you, you can create an even more rewarding experience of life that affords true healing and regeneration of your spirit.

Virgo on the 8th: With Virgo on the cusp of your 8th House, you may be learning that everything cannot be understood through the mind, although you may try your hardest to make sense of the realm of life that pertains to the ultimate transformational changes—birth, death, sexuality, and healing. You may feel that unless you can grasp an intellectual understanding, certain things are invalid. You want proof that there is life after death, not just theories or stories. You may not be interested in opening your mind to another level of thinking if the science of logic cannot suffice. Yet, if you are seeking to uncover the mysteries, the clues may reside in the obvious. Life itself provides the answers you're seeking, through the continual cycles of nature, which illustrate the patterns of change and rebirth. Mercury's influence in this area of your life can be helpful if you are approaching these needs with an open mind, but you can be overly analytical and forget the importance of opening your heart and listening to your inner voice.

Libra on the 8th: Through Libra's influence on your 8th House you learn about the mysteries of life and those things that are hidden beneath the surface by relating to them. You may have difficulty grasping the essential transformations that occur through the healing process unless you've struggled with illness or injury. If you've dealt with the process, your learning becomes both logical and cellular. You can relate to it. Your yearning for a soul mate or partner who can share the secrets of your soul is prompted by this influence; in this instance, you are seeking someone to relate with you on an inner level. Your awareness of the needs of others is part of your intuitive development, and through this influence you may become quite sensitive to those you love. The energy of Venus is associated with this house in your chart, symbolizing a need to experience the healing qualities of love. It is this influence that stimulates your awareness that love connections are timeless.

Scorpio on the 8th: With Scorpio on the cusp of your 8th House, you have experienced the effects of true regeneration of yourself. Your views of birth, death, sexuality, and healing may be matter of fact—that's just the way things are. Although you can be quite passionate, you may be capable of working with the processes of change that would redirect the focus of your passion. You have a strong flow of energy that aids your own healing, but you can also be effective as a healing channel for others. Additionally, you may be sensitive to the undercurrents of your relationships, although you may not like having to deal with them directly. The influence of Pluto as the ruler of this house strengthens your ability to welcome the inevitable changes and to use them as an empowering opportunity, but if you're too intent on trying to direct the outcome as you would have it, you may be waging war on yourself.

Sagittarius on the 8th: Through the influence of Sagittarius on the cusp of your 8th House, you may have always been curious about what lies beneath the surface. Although you may have accepted explanations like, "That's just the way it is," when you were a young girl you were rarely satisfied with such surface level truths. You want to know the answers to the big questions. However, your approach to delving into hidden territory is often cavalier, and you may not always be aware of what you've jumped into until you're struggling to tread water! Your yearning to know the mysteries will always have a high priority, and you are almost driven, as though on a quest, to find the answers to the ultimate questions. Metaphysical or spiritual studies can offer a pathway. You may also learn a great deal from observing and experiencing nature. With Jupiter's energy ruling this house, you have a powerful sense of the future, and may possess clairvoyance about future events. Your visions can have a prophetic quality.

Capricorn on the 8th: With Capricorn influencing your 8th House, you may have a struggle in matters pertaining to the processes of change and personal transformation. This includes your feelings about aging, and your tendency may be to do whatever you can to avoid the aging process, but some things are inevitable, like physical changes, and living in fear of the things you may not understand, like aging or death, will only block your ability to deal with these changes positively. You can control many of the effects that inevitable changes will have in your life by focusing your mind and energy on constructive possibilities. Saturn's energy is also an important factor in matters of this house, and you are likely to discover that the healing and rejuvenation you desire can occur only when you are taking full responsibility for yourself and your life circumstances.

Aquarius on the 8th: Through the influence of Aquarius on the cusp of your 8th House, you may be exceptionally curious about the experiences of birth, sexuality, death, healing, and human psychology. You may love physical sensations that lead you to the experience of ecstasy, but are also fascinated with the possibilities beyond the physical. Experimenting with different ideas and techniques designed to heighten your awareness can enhance your life, but you may need to exercise some caution to avoid the shock of getting into something when you are inadequately prepared. You may be psychic, and can have an amazing sense of the future. However, the influence of Uranus as ruler of this house adds a sporadic nature to your psychic sensibilities.

Pisces on the 8th: Your awareness that life exists on many levels is related to the influence of Pisces on the cusp of your 8th House. You can flow with the inevitable changes wrought by life—from birth to death and in between. Transcending your fears or anxieties and allowing yourself to flow into the ultimate source of transformational change may lead you to uncover the mysteries of human sexuality, psychology, and healing. You can be highly intuitive, and may gain impressions from people and situations that allow you to penetrate what is hidden beneath the surface. The influence of Neptune as the ruler of this house adds a powerful sensibility to the mysteries of life and allows you to deal with birth, death, sexuality, and healing on a spiritual level.

Planets in the 8th House: Energy for Deep Awareness

Sun in the 8th: The energy of your Sun in your 8th House drives you to experience life with a great deal of intensity toward the ultimate goal of total transformation. Your fascination with what lies beneath the surface stimulates you to delve into human psychology, metaphysics, or research as a means to discover more about yourself. Although you are sensitive on an inner level, your tendency is to try to control things you cannot control, or to fight your need to relinquish your will to things you cannot change. You have the potential to use your energy to bring regeneration and healing into your life and the lives of others, regardless of your professional activities. In order to become the healer you envision, you may have to transform your will to that of the ultimate source in order to be fully effective.

Moon in the 8th: The energy of your Moon in the 8th House draws your emotional focus to the areas of personal transformation and regeneration. Your ability to flow with the inevitable changes you experience throughout your life is continually tested, and if you are flexible in your attitudes, you may find that you welcome the process of release as a means of strengthening your soul. You may be strongly clairvoyant through this influence, although you can have difficulty dealing with your feelings when you sense or see things that can be happening elsewhere or in the future. Because of your capacity to probe beneath the surface, you may be sought after by others who need your insight or expertise. Learning to maintain your emotional objectivity is crucial if you are to become an effective healer.

Mercury in the 8th: You may be extremely curious about what lies beneath the surface with Mercury in your 8th House. Although you can be insightful and intuitive, you can sometimes block your own awareness by trying to make everything logical. By learning to blend your rational and intuitive processes, your thinking can become much more creative, and your insights much more promising. Learning about human psychology, the mysteries of life, and the processes of healing can be especially important. You may be able to articulate and clarify what others need to know and understand about themselves and their deeper needs.

Venus in the 8th: Venus in your 8th House suggests that your experience of love is strongly tied to your ability to heal and transform your life. Your emotional attachments can get in the way of your spiritual evolution if you place too much emphasis on them. These feelings get in the way of your ability to be open to clear intuitive messages. However, you may also find that you are most sensitive to the needs of those you love, and may even feel what they feel. It is through experiencing the depths of love that you will know the greatest transformational changes in your life.

Mars in the 8th: Through the energy of Mars in your 8th House, you are stimulated to dive into the depths of life. Your courageous approach to exploring the nature of personal transformation may lead you into a profound understanding of your own inner psyche, but can also play a role in your ability to help others who are in need of healing, change, and personal growth. Active forms of inner strengthening, such as martial arts, hatha yoga, chi gong, or dance can help you to use your body as a means of discovering your personal power, and lead to total healing.

Jupiter in the 8th: Jupiter's energy in your 8th House stimulates an intense desire to uncover the meaning of life. Your reasons behind delving into the alchemical experiences of life may be centered in a true spiritual quest, and you may be willing to try a number of approaches to finding out what lies beneath the surface. Whether you're attempting to understand how the higher laws work in the experiences of healing, sexuality, or dying, or if you simply want to know what they all mean, you need to look! What you learn may provide exceptional insight, both for yourself and for those who learn from your teachings.

Saturn in the 8th: Saturn's energy in your 8th House encourages you to take a realistic approach to understanding healing and transformational change. You may find that you are fearful of looking beneath the surface, but those fears may be totally unfounded. If you've had experiences that have frightened or harmed you, this influence tends to impress them more strongly into your psyche, and it can be more difficult for you to let go. Old feelings of shame and guilt can also be problematic, and can stand in the way of your healing. These feelings can block your intuitive flow and stifle your ability to experience life to its fullest. You may think that you do not want to know about the meaning of death or the true nature of your sexuality, but that, too, may be based on fear.

Uranus in the 8th: The energy of Uranus in your 8th House strengthens your intuitive sensibilities. You have a keen awareness of future possibilities, and sometimes experience a projection of yourself into a different time. In many respects, this influence is like time travel, although you may not take your body with you! Since there can be an erratic nature to these insights, you may not be able to fully trust changing your entire life based on your flashes. However, if you develop the capacity to blend your insights with the facts or data of the situation at hand, you can make some very meaningful alterations to your life experiences.

Neptune in the 8th: Your psychic impressions can be powerful with Neptune in your 8th House. Your sensitivity is strong in matters that involve health or death, but you may also be aware of the potential for destructive or transformational changes in your environment. If undeveloped, you may just "sense" that things are happening, or your visions may come through your dreams. If you wish to further develop this sensibility, it is important to learn how to create a strong filter so you can become a better "viewer" instead of feeling these things on a personal, emotional level.

Pluto in the 8th: Your perceptive abilities can be strong with Pluto in your 8th House. Not only can you feel what is happening beneath the surface or behind the facade, you may also have a sense of the effects that can occur. Reading between the lines is only the beginning—you are a natural at understanding the subtleties that give away a person's true feelings or thoughts. As a result, you may be an exceptional therapist or healer, but you can also become an amazing investigator and diagnostician. If you choose the path of the Medicine Woman, you can become quite adept at learning how to alter the nature of your physical reality to create and accommodate positive change. You must be clear about your motivations and realize that trying to change or control others for your own benefit will ultimately work against your best interests.

Your 12th House: The Realm of Dreams, the Past, and Imagination

The 12th House is the space of your dreams. Here, you surrender your conscious self and float into the beyond. This is also the place in your psyche that contains your past, and it is where you are one with all humanity. Your superconscious self rests in this part of your psyche—the part of yourself that transcends your everyday reality. Tapping into that part of yourself is not always easy, since you may confuse what you imagine with what is real on a spiritual level. You can find your inner, hidden self by taking an active role and learning to meditate, spending time in contemplation, or watching your dreams.

The Sign on the 12th House: Key to the Hidden Self

Aries on the 12th: With Aries influencing your 12th House, you may have a highly active subconscious self. Your dreams may reveal that you are more temperamental than you appear, and you need a place to channel this fiery quality. By actively participating in understanding your dreams, you may discover a new realm of awareness. With Mars ruling this house, you may be more successful participating in "active" forms of meditation, such as yoga, tai chi, martial arts, or dance. Just sitting quietly trying to gain a sense of what is happening on the inner realm may leave you feeling frustrated, but once you've learned to channel that energy, you can develop a quality of mindfulness that accompanies you in every state of consciousness. You can develop a very powerful intuition, but you may not always listen to it!

Taurus on the 12th: The influence of Taurus on the cusp of your 12th House may interfere with your ability to tap into your dreams. When you sleep, you sleep very deeply and soundly, but you may not have a good recall of your dreams. You can learn techniques that will help you become more in touch with your dreams if you want to know more, and different cycles in your life will enhance your ability to understand this part of your psyche. The influence of Venus as ruler of this house adds a need for harmony at a deep spiritual level, and you may feel most harmonious when you are positively connected to your personal environment. For example, you'll sleep better when you know your actions and efforts strengthen the earth's resources, and your visions for tomorrow will be much more uplifting.

Gemini on the 12th: With Gemini influencing your 12th House, you may be a strong psychic receiver, feeling what others think. In many ways, you are quite instinctual about people and situations. This influence adds to your impressionability, and you may find that you learn best when you're in the presence of someone, or if you're listening to tapes. You can have very active dreams, especially if you're worrying about something. It's important that you learn to relax and let go of the day before you drop off to sleep, or you may experience a restless night. Mercury's rulership of this house indicates some difficulty allowing your mind to rest.

Cancer on the 12th: You are quite sensitive with Cancer on the cusp of your 12th House. Although you may protect your sensitivities with an aura of confidence, you feel everything around you. It is important that you have a comfortable and safe environment for your sleeping and resting periods, otherwise you may not rest at all. Your dreams can be vivid and full of emotion, filled with images of days gone by and people from your past, but your superconscious self may also take you into dream states that are somewhat prophetic. Your Moon is tied to this house, adding a need to become clear about your subconscious motivations and deeper feelings. When using visualization techniques, it is important to allow your emotions to work for you to attain your desires. If you try to repress your feelings about your desires, you will only experience frustration.

Leo on the 12th: With Leo on the cusp of your 12th House, you may have dreams of recognition and accomplishment, but may not always allow yourself to experience the reality of your dreams during the course of your lifetime. Your dreams are important, though, and are the key to your ability to accomplish your aims. To alter the course of your life, you can learn to use visualization to strengthen your sense of yourself and to allow yourself to accept greater recognition for your efforts. Your Sun influences this house, adding a tendency to feel somewhat uncertain about your own worthiness. You may feel that you are more comfortable maintaining a powerful presence behind the scenes playing supportive roles. If you can be more effective allowing yourself to gain recognition, you may have to release your tendency to martyr yourself when it is unnecessary.

Virgo on the 12th: The influence of Virgo on the cusp of your 12th House shows a need for purity of thoughts. This includes a clear and compassionate acceptance of yourself and others, and may involve developing tolerance for the imperfections that exist in everyone. You relish the times you spend in quiet contemplation, and may become adept at using meditation techniques that help you clear your mind. Removing mental clutter is important since Mercury rules this house, and you may fritter away too much energy on unnecessary thoughts or ideas. Your physical health is closely tied to your emotional and spiritual harmony. If you are prompted to serve the needs of humanity, you may spend much of your time in service to others. This can be accomplished in many capacities, but the best choices will arise from your deep sense of awareness, which is guided by your intuitive self.

Libra on the 12th: Libra's influence on the cusp of your 12th House adds a need to be intuitive about your personal relationships. If you feel insecure, you may unconsciously try to adapt yourself to fit the needs of those around you instead of listening to your own inner voice. Establishing a strong sense of personal worth and a good perception of your true needs will help you feel more comfortable when you're alone with your thoughts. It's tempting to see others only as you wish to see them, especially since you may have the ability to look into the souls of those around you and feel what they are capable of becoming. With Venus ruling this house, you can experience true transcendence through love, but you must first realize that love begins in your own heart.

Scorpio on the 12th: With Scorpio influencing your 12th House, you may have a deep inner struggle in your quest to fully acknowledge and express your true strength. You have the capacity to develop an intense awareness of the inner planes, and can be

strongly connected to the collective unconscious. If you use your enhanced awareness for positive healing and as a catalyst for regeneration, your soul is empowered,
but if you direct your energy toward vengeance or become filled with resentment,
you can literally destroy yourself through this influence. Pluto's rulership of this
house adds a powerful intensity to the force of your subconscious mind, which, if
surrendered to the guidance of your superconscious self, can be transformed.

Sagittarius on the 12th: Underneath it all, you have a deep faith in the natural order
of things with Sagittarius influencing your 12th House. Although other elements in
your personality may prompt you to fight against your sense of a higher power,
when you surrender to life's flowing energy, the struggle becomes much easier. Your
ability to look back into history, human history and your own, and learn from your
trials and errors, can give you a remarkable edge in your determination to transcend
the ordinary. The energy of Jupiter rules this house in your chart, adding a capacity
for vision and broad-minded confidence to your subconscious self. You intuitively
know that when you are focused on Truth, everything else pales in its light.

Capricorn on the 12th: You are fascinated with the idea of trying to control your
subconscious self with Capricorn on the cusp of your 12th House. There is a dis-
tinctive difference between mindfulness, which involves focused awareness, and
negative restraint. Your goal is that of attaining true mindfulness, and you have a
need to overcome selfish desires. Saturn's influence of this house adds a distinc-
tive sense that you are bound by karmic ties to complete certain things in your
life. By focusing your awareness to your inner self and unlocking your fears, you
may begin to release yourself. Your experience of the importance of taking
responsibility for yourself and for the evolution of your soul can allow you to
transcend mere physical attainment and accomplish true spiritual awakening.

Aquarius on the 12th: The influence of Aquarius on your 12th House stimulates a
powerful urge to break free of the bonds of the physical plane. Your urge to return
to the source can prompt you to develop your creative or artistic sensibilities, and
to employ your ingenuity in freeing your inner self. You may be tempted to escape
through negative means, and can develop addictions or become neurotically driven
to insulate yourself from the pressures of life. Your true yearnings are connected to
your awareness that there is a reality beyond the physical plane, but you still have
to cope with being here in order to accomplish the quest of your soul! Uranus rules
this house, indicating that you may follow a rather unique path toward awareness
and awakening. That's okay, as long as you reach the light you're seeking.

Pisces on the 12th: Your inner sensitivity and compassion for others may be quite powerful with Pisces' influence on your 12th House, but you may not openly show it to the rest of the world. Your sensibilities may be so intense that you cannot watch the horrible circumstances presented by the nightly news. You are concerned about human suffering, and feel the pain that radiates through the collective spirit. You may need outlets that allow you to make a difference, defending those who cannot stand in defense of themselves. With Neptune influencing this house, you also need to allow yourself time to rejuvenate and fully recuperate from the stress of the day. Your dreams may show you the way, but it is through your life experience that you make a difference.

Planets in the 12th House: Your Hidden Storehouse

Sun in the 12th: The energy of your Sun in the 12th House can produce a desire to close away from the rest of the world—at least part of the time. You enjoy giving energy to spiritual pursuits throughout your life, and may feel most at peace when you can create a positive filter between your consciousness and the cacophony of the world. Your ability to experience an inner awareness can be quite profound, but you may have a few bumpy paths along the way before you achieve a true peace with yourself. Giving of yourself to the world through healthy channels can strengthen your sense of personal evolution; but simply withdrawing, escaping, or falling into addictive patterns will accomplish little more than wasting your vitality.

Moon in the 12th: With the energy of your Moon in the 12th House, your emotional sensibilities play a powerful role in your intuitive awareness. Your ability to feel the energy around you at a vibrational level is intensified, and you may have difficulty separating your own feelings from those of the people around you. Although this quality can be quite helpful in situations that involve counseling or other therapeutic services, it may add to your emotional fatigue unless you've learned how to create an emotional filter. Clearing your energy through conscious focus, allowing you to release any emotional energy you've absorbed from dealing with others, can make a big difference in your sense of vitality and emotional resilience.

Mercury in the 12th: Sometimes it is possible for you to tune in to the mental energy of others with Mercury in your 12th House. Your mind may act like a receiver—picking up thoughts and ideas. It's not exactly that you're "reading minds," as much as you're connecting to others through the mental plane. You may see this functioning most with those who are close to you when you finish their sentences for them.

You can also project your own thoughts to others quite effectively, but may be a better receiver than sender. This influence is quite helpful in dealing with the collective in such activities as media, advertising, or creative expression, since you have an easy understanding of what interests people as a whole. You know what it is: it's that sense of knowing if something will work or if it will flop. However, you do need to clear your thoughts through activities such as meditation or contemplation in order to maintain your focus and lucidity.

Venus in the 12th: You may have great compassion for humanity with Venus in your 12th House. The stimulation to give loving support arises from this influence, and whether you've chosen to direct this energy toward your family and loved ones or into your community through some type of service, your own heart is filled when you're reaching out. You also have a powerful emotional sensitivity, and when there is conflict, turmoil, or pain around you, can feel it deep within your own heart. This may stimulate your creativity in a particular manner, and regardless of your creative outlets, you have the capability to reach others through your artistry. To maintain your own inner harmony, you need to practice forgiveness of yourself and others, and may become an example of true peace and serenity when you're allowing the currents of love to flow through you.

Mars in the 12th: Part of your intuitive nature is connected to your sense that you need to do something that will make a difference in the world. The influence of Mars in your 12th House indicates that you are quite capable of taking action that can have a powerful effect on the collective. It is your choice whether those actions are constructive or destructive, although you may be most stimulated toward peaceful alternatives. You may also be highly expressive as a dancer, actress, or athlete, and have the capability of allowing your energy to flow with and reflect the environment that surrounds you.

Jupiter in the 12th: When you are uplifted through your faith in truth and justice, your intuitive flow is enhanced. Jupiter's energy in your 12th House adds an important dimension to your spirituality, and encourages you to adopt a philosophy that includes compassion, forgiveness, and tolerance. Directing your generosity toward efforts that benefit the collective may seem natural for you. You may also feel a powerful connection to a spiritual level of protection, such as your guardian angels, knowing that even when you're in difficult circumstances, you are out of harm's way.

Saturn in the 12th: Your desire for solitude may be stimulated by Saturn's influence in your 12th House. You may need ample time to reflect and clarify, and can benefit from regular periods of meditation that allow you to release your anxieties and open to true inner peace. It is critical that you learn how to deal with and address your fears because they can inhibit your ability to remain open to your intuitive and creative sensibilities. Finding your inner dragon and discovering ways to either live with or banish the part of you that is overwhelming will restore your faith in yourself and in the divine order.

Uranus in the 12th: Your intuitive self can be highly stimulated with Uranus in your 12th House. You may have flashes of insight that vanish as quickly as they come, and you may need to develop some manner of focusing your mind in order to take advantage of your sense of knowingness. Your meditations can be freeing, but you may have trouble just sitting quietly. An active form of meditation, such as hatha yoga, tai chi, chi gong, or even dancing can be both inspiring and clearing for you.

Neptune in the 12th: Neptune's energy in your 12th House adds a powerful desire to remain close to the source of your spiritual center. You may be extremely sensitive to your environment, and need to learn how to create filters and personal boundaries, but it is not necessary for you to retreat from the world entirely (although sometimes it may seem like a good idea!). It is important for you to find a positive outlet for making a difference in the world, areas where you can give of yourself and allow your compassion for humanity to be expressed. Whether you work in a helping profession, spend time volunteering, or doing charitable work—the key is to keep the energy flowing from the source, to you and outward into the world.

Pluto in the 12th: With Pluto in your 12th House, you need to be aware of your tendency to become withdrawn or obsessed with thoughts that create strong vulnerability. Although you may benefit from taking some time each day to go inside yourself, holding your energy back all the time can block your flow. The problem you're experiencing is one of heightened awareness—you can sense things on a very deep level, and may sometimes sense too much! By creating a positive energy filter (not letting everything bother you so much!), setting emotional boundaries, and allowing yourself ample time to rejuvenate your spiritual energy and vitality, you can become quite influential in whatever you're doing.

Your Moon and Your Intuitive Awareness

Although we've examined many qualities of your moon already, your lunar energy plays an important role in your intuitive development. Since your Moon is related to your subconscious mind, it should not surprise you that this is the part of you that contains all knowledge about yourself and your life. Occasionally, it's a good idea to purge from your psyche the things you no longer need—much like an internal house cleaning. Your hormonal cycles provide an excellent opportunity to do just that, and by using this natural rhythm to release, you can feel much more open to clearer transmission of intuitive thinking!

Your Moon's Sign and Intuitive Awareness

Moon in Aries: Sometimes you can be too busy pursuing your desires to listen to your intuitive voice with the Moon in Aries. You have a very keen intuitive sensibility, but don't like to listen to it when it means slowing down. You may also be more intuitive about things that are new to you. For example, your first impressions are usually quite powerful. Just because you may lose interest in something, you may think your intuition was wrong. That's just impatience!

Moon in Taurus: Your sensual awareness is part of your intuitive insight, which operates through your Taurus Moon. Your kinesthetic sensibilities can be quite amazing, and you may be able to pick up valuable information from touching someone or something. For this reason, you're usually rather picky about the things you want to have around you. If it doesn't feel right, you are not usually drawn to it. If something does draw your energy, you may have trouble removing your focus until it is yours.

Moon in Gemini: Through your Gemini Moon you can become highly intuitive. It's just that you may not always focus that intuitive energy long enough to fully experience what it has to offer. You may also be tempted to try to make sense out of your intuitive insights, and while you're hammering away at them from your logical perspective, you lose track of their clarity. You're probably clearest when you're open to the possibilities instead of trying to make purely logical judgments.

Moon in Cancer: Since your psyche is rather impressionable with your Moon in Cancer, you may be sensitive to the emotional energy around you. Your intuitive insights are more on an emotional level—like knowing what's happening with your children, or feeling something strange when your mom is not well. These connections are not unusual for you, and if you develop them, they can provide a great deal of comfort and clarity, but if you become too emotionally involved in your personal impressions, you can overreact or become upset. Keeping your emotional boundaries is important if you are to use your sixth sense to your benefit.

Moon in Leo: Your intuitive function operates most powerfully when you're in the midst of doing something creative. Since your need for creativity is strong with your Moon in Leo, you may spend a great deal of time pursuing and developing your talents. While you are in the process of fine-tuning your craft—whether you're becoming a more accomplished singer, actress, educator, or business leader—your intuitive insights about when and how to do certain things will give you an added sheen. This is part of your ingenuity, and it adds a glow that shines from your heart and originates in the heart of divine love.

Moon in Virgo: You have a marvelous intuition about the way things work with your Moon in Virgo. This can be useful in practical matters, like knowing how to repair something. You may also be quite intuitive about your own body, sensing when something is out of harmony. However, your tendency can be to overreact to what you feel (is a headache caused by a brain tumor?!), so you need to work on maintaining a strong sense of emotional balance in order to deal most positively with your impressions about your health. When you have a chance to be more objective, like working on an important project or designing something, your intuition guides you to do things that add special details and high levels of definition. This finesse can be intriguing, and may provide a level of fascination to you as well.

Moon in Libra: Through your Libra Moon you may discover that your intuition works to your greatest advantage when you're dealing with people. This can be especially true if you're involved in counseling or human relations, since you may be able to use your sensibilities to understand the larger picture of what's happening. You can also be artistic, and have a marvelous intuitive sense of color, style, and design. You may be a woman who knows how to fit into almost any situation, and part of that is because you can sense the most advantageous times to talk, listen, or walk away!

Moon in Scorpio: You've always been psychically sensitive. Even as a little girl, your Scorpio Moon was at work pulling in the energy around you and feeling what was really happening. Although this could be advantageous in business negotiations (are they really going to come up with two million dollars?), or in personal circumstances, it takes some adaptation because you may not always enjoy what you feel from other people. Your sensibilities probe beneath the surface, and you may be adept at extracting what exists at the core.

Moon in Sagittarius: Through your Sagittarius Moon your mind is open to all sorts of possibilities. Since your search for Truth may take you on many adventures, it seems natural to you that you might find keys to developing your intuitive self through adopting a more spiritual approach to life. Integrating the spiritual into your everyday life is crucial to your personal growth. You simply cannot abandon your principles in any of your thoughts or actions without feeling strong repercussions.

√**Moon in Capricorn:** Your intuitive sensibilities extend into the realm of the practical. Your Capricorn Moon functions much like an anchoring device, helping you keep your feet on the ground, but you are quite sensitive. You feel things through your environment, and flow a great deal of energy into your environments. That's why it is sometimes difficult to move or adapt to a new place. Gathering your energy to relocate is, of course, possible, but you do it much better when you are in control of the relocation! When you arrive in a new place, it takes a while to grow your roots. The same is true of relationships with people—you need a little time before you open your energy to them, but once you do, your connection is powerful.

Moon in Aquarius: With your Moon in Aquarius, your intuitive self is always prompting you to open the doors to your originality. You may spend a lot of time on the mental planes, skimming around the world of ideas, thoughts, and possibilities; but you can become caught in the world of your own thoughts and may lose track of the needs of those around you. Your ideas can be unique and progressive, and you may feel that you're ahead of your time. You may never be satisfied with yourself until you've learned ways to incorporate both your intuitive and creative processes with your logical and rational processes.

Moon in Pisces: Your psychic sensibilities may be quite amazing. With your Moon in Pisces, your sense of things goes beyond the physical into the realm of vibration. You can feel the energy that emanates from a crowd, the energy left over in an empty room, the energy of emotion that is not expressed. You may also have a powerful connection with the realm of the spiritual, and may be aware of things that many people do not see or feel. It is important that you are attentive to your dreams, and that before you sleep or rest, you clear your energy.

The Moon's Nodes: Secrets from the Past and Keys to Your Life Path

There are other points related to the Moon that you'll find in your chart. They are called the Moon's Nodes. They are not planets, but points in space. The influence of the Moon's Nodes is felt on an inner level. From the South Node, you learn about your past and the natural inclinations that may influence many of your subconscious choices. In some ways, the South Node suggests old habits. The North Node of the Moon suggests a spiritual and emotional challenge, and represents the directions you may feel compelled to follow in your evolutionary path. The houses that contain the Moon's Nodes show the areas of your life, or the types of relationship, that are keys to your spiritual development.

Your Moon's Nodal Axis

North Node in Aries: Your North Node in Aries challenges you to develop your courage, independence, and assertiveness as part of your spiritual growth and self-discovery. You may be drawn into situations that require you to stand up for yourself or to fight for your position, and although your preference might be to allow situations to resolve themselves, it is important to take action. Finding yourself involves finding your convictions and creating your own path. With the South Node in Libra, your tendency to rely on others to take care of you or forge the pathways for your development has to be abandoned in favor of self-confidence, free thought, and action if you are to grow into wholeness. Self-determination is your key to fulfillment.

North Node in Taurus: Your North Node in Taurus challenges you to learn about the true nature of your personal worth as part of your spiritual growth and development. You may become fascinated with the idea of accumulating material wealth, but can then discover that it offers very little if you cannot share it with those you love. However, you must find some type of balance between creating stability on the physical plane and releasing your attachments in the emotional world! Your past soul conditioning symbolized by your Scorpio South Node may feel more comfortable being somewhat secretive about your possessions, and even about your deeper feelings. Until you can open to the pure essence of love, and can embrace the heart of your own being fully and completely, your soul will not know true joy.

North Node in Gemini: Through the path of your North Node in Gemini you discover your personal adaptability and mental ingenuity. Learning to think for yourself and developing your communicative skills enhances your growth and opens the doors of possibility. It is also imperative that you become adept at connecting to others in society, that you build a bridge of open-minded attitudes and responsible thinking. Respecting the opinions and ideas of others will go a long way toward dissolving many of your issues. With your South Node in Sagittarius, you may prefer to gallop away into the sunset without a second thought about the results of your words or actions. Your love of adventure and desire to feel free and untamed can get in your way if you are to make progress within the realm of society.

North Node in Cancer: Although you may think that it is just your lot in life because you are a woman, you are growing through developing your skills and expressions as a nurturer with your North Node in Cancer. Instead of resenting the fact that you may be a caretaker, finding positive ways to care for others and teaching them how to care for themselves can be extremely rewarding. You may discover that you feel more whole and alive when you are devoting yourself to mothering experiences. Your spiritual path may lead you to uncover the true power of The Goddess, whose care, support, and nurture inspire your creativity and inner strength. With the South Node in Capricorn, you need to carefully examine your ambitions for their true motivation. If you are driven to achieve recognition and power just for the sake of being in control, you are not growing—you are standing still.

North Node in Leo: Your task with your North Node in Leo is to develop your leadership and influence in ways that fill your heart with self-respect. Power for its own sake is not your goal. Rather, you are exploring the path of the power that arises from the heart of divine love and inspires your creativity and self-expression. Placing yourself in situations that allow you to radiate power and warmth into the lives of others will always benefit your spiritual and emotional growth. With the South Node in Aquarius, your tendencies toward self-centered independence need to be abandoned in favor of using your sense of humanity as a springboard to experiencing true love and happiness. If you fall into the trap of prejudice or distaste, you will only inhibit the true power that sustains your spirit.

North Node in Virgo: Your challenge with the North Node in Virgo is to develop a clear sense of discrimination and pure thinking. You may discover that teaching or guiding others provides an excellent avenue for personal service, and when you look back over your life, you may recall many incidents of others seeking your judgment, support, or guidance. When you've allowed yourself to surrender to truly serving the needs of the situation at hand, you've found new abilities and strengths. With your South Node in Pisces, your old tendencies to escape the burden of responsibility, or to live in a world of fantasy, will accomplish very little in the realm of personal growth. You are learning to employ your imagination and sensibilities toward the service of humanity.

North Node in Libra: Your tasks that stem from your North Node in Libra are oriented toward developing a true sense of consideration, fair-mindedness, and inner harmony. Although it is important for you to value yourself, you are also discovering the importance of valuing and supporting others. Relationships are your key to personal evolution, and the manner in which you handle them gives you clues about your progress. With the South Node in Aries, you are challenged to abandon selfish desire in favor of cooperation. You may also have to battle your own tendencies toward belligerent or combative attitudes if you are to achieve the inner balance and peace you are struggling to develop.

North Node in Scorpio: Your path toward spiritual evolution involves surrendering to the process of complete transformation with your North Node in Scorpio. By participating in experiences that are geared toward healing and regeneration, you will not only experience personal growth, but will feel your connection to a higher power more readily. With your South Node in Taurus, your tendency may be to pursue avenues that are selfishly possessive or narrowly stubborn. Each time you fall into the trap of extreme willfulness, you may experience profound inner turmoil, since you are learning to surrender to the power of love to resolve crises and achieve true healing.

North Node in Sagittarius: You may feel that you are a spiritual pioneer with your North Node in Sagittarius. In order to discover the truths of life, you may need to expand your understanding through educational pursuits, travel, or cultural exchange. All these things lead you to create a philosophy of possibility and confidence that can be inspiring and rewarding for you personally, and to others who may be drawn to follow. The influence of your South Node in Gemini underscores the temptation for shallow thinking and simple explanation that you may have experienced through the influence of others early in your life. You may also have to safeguard against fickle attitudes in favor of committed ideas that lead to the Truth.

North Node in Capricorn: Challenged with the task of learning to carry your responsibilities in a mature manner, you are learning the importance of sustained effort with your North Node in Capricorn. You may also be fascinated by the processes of aging and the wisdom that requires time to develop, although you may struggle against them to some extent. Becoming involved in activities that allow you to be responsible and positively ambitious, you may discover that you really enjoy reaching the heights of achievement. The influence of your Cancer South Node tempts you to be overly sensitive to feelings of rejection or abandonment instead of learning to stand on your own. The confidence and judgment you develop will not only resolve some of your fears, but may give you the energy you need to become a trustworthy guide of generations who will follow in your footsteps.

North Node in Aquarius: Your spiritual path carries you into a true understanding of the need for the human race to be humanitarian with your North Node in Aquarius. Of course, there is a difference, and your frustration with the fact that people are frequently the problem with humanity can gnaw at your soul. By seeking opportunities to serve the whole of society through your creativity and ingenuity, you grow and experience strong evolutionary leaps. Your South Node in Leo may tempt you to make choices that would give you the glory and tempt you to take it for yourself alone. By developing true unconditional love, you'll experience ample support, and at the same time, will be able to keep your heart open and alive.

North Node in Pisces: Spiritual development may be high on your priority list since you have your North Node in Pisces. Surrendering yourself to the will of your higher self allows you to experience truly divine compassion, and may prompt you to follow a path of service to humanity. The influence of your South Node in Virgo adds a critical nature that sometimes gets in the way of your need to move beyond judgment into tolerance and acceptance. You can change this by becoming more open to your inner voice and by trusting and devoting yourself to a life of true peace.

The Placement of the Moon's Nodes: Balancing Your Spiritual Growth

North Node in the 1st House, South Node in the 7th House: Your challenge with the North Node in the 1st House is to become truly independent while breaking away from a need to satisfy the demands of others. The old pattern of self-sacrifice so that others can be happy (the South Node) will feel hollow, and by learning to keep your priorities of personal growth and development clearly in focus, you will actually improve the quality of your relationships and social commitments. Consider what it means to become "self-full."

North Node in the 2nd House, South Node in the 8th House: With the North Node in your 2nd House, it's crucial that you determine a set of values that resonate with your inner self. Establishing your financial independence may be a necessary part of achieving a sense of spiritual balance, since the old pattern that draws you is one of depending upon others to take care of you (South Node in the 8th). Also take a careful look at your attachments, since determining your sense of worth through another person will never satisfy your inner longings, although that may be your early pattern in relationships.

North Node in the 3rd House, South Node in the 9th House: You're learning to express your ideas and share knowledge with others with your North Node in the 3rd House. Your soul's memory, shown by your 9th House South Node, is of accumulating experiences through wanderlust or academic pursuits, and now it's time to bring your mental focus into more concrete understanding. Developing your communication skills will take you into amazing realms of new experience.

North Node in the 4th House, South Node in the 10th House: Strengthening your foundations is crucial to your total growth with your North Node in the 4th House. Whether through nesting, creating a home, developing positive ties with family, or providing comfort for yourself and those who share your life—if you're taking care of this part of your life, your soul will feel complete. The old pattern from the South Node in the 10th House stems from focusing on the outside world. This lifetime is about inner growth, and even if you become famous, you'll discover that you need that special time away from the hassles of performance to relax and let your soul nest.

North Node in the 5th House, South Node in the 11th House: With your North Node in the 5th House, you're learning how to manifest your creative potential. On a psychological level, this placement relates to the recovery of your inner child, which you may accomplish while mothering other children or which may emerge through tapping into your creative spirit. A deep connection with your muse is part of the challenge you experience. The old patterns stimulated by the South Node in the 11th House center around becoming strongly involved in social or collective activities that excluded your personal growth, and although you may still be politically or communally involved, it is crucial that you allow your creative expression to emerge in the process.

North Node in the 6th House, South Node in the 12th House: Taking care of your body is important with your North Node in the 6th House, and you may discover that developing a broad-based knowledge of health and fitness is the key to your sense of wholeness. It's also important to extend yourself in service to others and to find ways to develop a truly cooperative spirit. Your old patterns symbolized by the South Node in your 12th House center on escapist tendencies and isolation that may be based on irrational fears or tendencies toward martyrdom.

North Node in the 7th House, South Node in the 1st House: With your North Node in the 7th House, you face the lessons of learning true consideration for others, and by developing a fair-minded attitude, you'll feel much more complete. The tendencies spurred by the South Node in the 1st House lend themselves to selfish behaviors and self-absorbed attitudes. Your consciousness expands most readily when you open your life to truly balanced partnerships in your personal or professional life.

North Node in the 8th House, South Node in the 2nd House: The challenge imposed by your North Node in the 8th House is centered around learning to share. Not only are you faced with sharing material things, but opening your heart and sharing your inner soul with someone you love and trust is the key to your soul's yearnings. The trap of the material world, including money issues, is signified by your South Node in the 2nd House. This does not mean you can't have money, but that you have to bring your values to a level that transcends the physical plane.

North Node in the 9th House, South Node in the 3rd House: By turning your awareness toward spiritual and philosophical ideals and opening your mind to include a broad range of possibilities, you're answering the needs of your North Node in the 9th House. The old pattern of frittering away your mental energies through too much emphasis on words (including gossip!), and too little emphasis on the overall meaning and impact of your thoughts, is the trap of the South Node in the 3rd House.

North Node in the 10th House, South Node in the 4th House: Finding your self through surrendering to your true vocation (yes, that does mean your calling) is crucial since you have the North Node in the 10th House. Whether you're working on a career path or giving your time and energy to making the world a better place, you need to feel that you're living a life of right livelihood. The South Node in your 4th House can create a sense of emotional insecurity that makes it difficult to get into the world. You must see the world as a positive place instead of feeling that your roots or your past are blocks to your ability to achieve the realization of your ambitions.

North Node in the 11th House, South Node in the 5th House: In order to reach the heights of spiritual growth, you're learning the importance of establishing goals with your North Node in the 11th House. Your connection to your community is also important, as are your friends. If you're too focused on your love life and exclude your connection to friends, you may feel that your life is somehow missing something. It is! This is the draw from your South Node in the 5th House—it tempts you to be too ego-centered. The qualities of unconditional acceptance are not just abstract ideas—you need to put them to work in your life!

North Node in the 12th House, South Node in the 6th House: In order to accomplish the true inner awareness that calls to you, it's important to allow ample time for reflection, meditation, and reverie. With your North Node in the 12th House, your spiritual life needs to be incorporated into your daily life experience: life needs to become your meditation. The South Node placement in your 6th House can be like the itch that bothers you when you're trying to meditate: it may never stop bothering you until you can rise above it! Learning how to leave some of those details and workaholic tendencies behind will provide just the time and energy you need to become acquainted with your spiritual essence.

Uranus and Insightful Intuition

Uranian intuition is the flash of insight. Sometimes that flash is so brilliant that you change your entire life to follow it's glow. This is the part of you that defies restraint, and certainly your intuitive mind can celebrate that possibility! In other chapters, you'll explore the placements of Uranus, and since Uranus spends about seven years in a sign, you'll share these qualities with other people who grew up with you and who are likely to be your peers. However, the house placement of Uranus tells the story of the areas in your life where you're likely to be more intuitive and where your flashes of insight may be most readily accessible.

Uranus in the Houses and Your Intuition

Uranus in the 1st: Your personality is keyed to breaking through all types of barriers and letting the part of you that is different shine through. The influence of Uranus in your 1st House indicates that you need plenty of room to develop and listen to your intuitive voice. It is this part of you that prompts you to make unusual changes. Your manner of doing things may seem unconventional, and your way of getting there can be difficult to explain, but somehow, you arrive—frequently to the surprise of both others and yourself. The discovery of your real self may be the most serendipitous happening of all!

Uranus in the 2nd: Your ideas about the best ways to use your resources are original with Uranus in your 2nd House. Since you may be oriented more toward futuristic or technological things, you may find that your intuition about how to strengthen your finances is enhanced when you're projecting them with a little help from something like a new computer program! You may also be quite inventive in using everything around you, and that is the influence of Uranian energy, too.

Uranus in the 3rd: You've already discovered that you're an intuitive thinker. With Uranus in the 3rd House, you cannot imagine trying to make decisions without taking your intuitive promptings into consideration. You can also be quite intuitive about the best ways to connect with other people, and you may experience sudden changes in your life due to the influences that occur from networking with others.

Uranus in the 4th: The influence of Uranus in your 4th House has been explored elsewhere in this chapter.

Uranus in the 5th: Your insights and inventiveness work to your advantage through your creative expression with Uranus in your 5th House. You need ample outlets for self-expression that are unrestrained. You may also take a highly unconventional approach to entertaining or recreational activities, and may try things that make others shiver. Your need for thrilling experiences can be satisfied through alternatives that are reasonable and do not risk your life.

Uranus in the 6th: With Uranus in the 6th House, your intuitive insights can be seen most easily in your approach to your work. Since you have a sixth sense about working with technological devices, you may enjoy spending time using computers, playing with gadgets, or developing inventive devices. You may also have a special sensibility to health and healing, and you may gain great benefit from participating in or developing alternative healing methods.

Uranus in the 7th: Your originality and ingenuity can be seen in the way you deal with people in social situations. With Uranus in your 7th House, you can be insightful regarding your social relationships, and may attract people from all walks of life into your sphere of influence. If your actions or attitudes are viewed as somewhat unorthodox by more traditional thinkers, it probably doesn't bother you, since what is most important to you is your freedom to express yourself freely and fully.

Uranus in the 8th: The influence of Uranus in your 8th House was explained earlier in this chapter.

Uranus in the 9th: Your unique philosophies and ideals are stimulated by the energy of Uranus in your 9th House. You may feel strongly drawn toward a spiritual path that is somewhat experimental and non-traditional, since you feel most connected to your higher self when you know that you've gotten there on your own! The development of your superconscious self may include a desire to travel on the inner planes or to learn about and experience astral projection.

Uranus in the 10th: Your intuitive self needs free rein to operate in your professional expression with Uranus in your 10th House. If you feel penned in or restrained by your work, you may become agitated or frustrated and perform below your peak capacities, but when you can use your intuitive sensibilities in your profession, your own genius shines through. You may be especially interested in astrology.

Uranus in the 11th: Your insights may be highly valued by your friends with Uranus in your 11th House. You can also be adept at pinpointing the special talents and gifts of others, which can be quite encouraging when someone is seeking their particular path. Innovative approaches to fulfilling community needs may also give you an excellent opportunity to exercise your ingenuity and intuitive sensibilities.

Uranus in the 12th: The influence of Uranus in your 12th House was explored earlier in this chapter.

Neptune: Heightened Awareness

Neptune's energy takes you into the world of the etheric—the place beyond the physical that is filled with mystical wonder. You surrender to this part of yourself when you meditate, when you give in to your creative muse, and when you give of yourself to others.

In developing your intuitive and psychic sensibilities, Neptune provides a primary ingredient: letting go. Through this energy you surrender yourself to the greater truth, but be careful, you can also surrender your will to the power of deception and abuse through another of Neptune's doorways!

Neptune in the Houses: Where You're Especially Sensitive

Neptune in the 1st: Your compassionate sensibilities can be projected through your own actions and words with Neptune in your 1st House. You're highly sensitive to the vibrations around you, and it is imperative that you live and work in an environment that feels good. Harsh circumstances, negative people, and overly intense situations can have a detrimental effect on your health—on every level. You may be psychically gifted and have a powerful sense of the energy of those with whom you make contact. However, you can be deceived, or may deceive yourself, by seeing only what you want to see.

Neptune in the 2nd: The influence of Neptune in your 2nd House adds a dimension of confusion about the best way to use and handle your material resources. You will become clearer about this once you've surrendered your need to determine your value through outside measurements.

Neptune in the 3rd: Neptune's influence in your 3rd House adds a psychic dimension to your thought processes. You may be adept at reading another's thoughts, particularly if you've developed a close relationship with one another. You need ample outlets for expressing your imagination through communication such as writing, acting, or speaking.

Neptune in the 4th: The influence of Neptune in your 4th House was explored earlier in this chapter.

Neptune in the 5th: With Neptune in your 5th House, it's easier for you to release and open your intuitive mind when you're in the midst of creating. Your imaginative and impressionable sensibilities work to your advantage when applied to self-expression—like music, the arts, dancing, writing—but any creative outlet allows you to open to this flow. Any situation that allows you to open your heart will enhance your psychic abilities!

Neptune in the 6th: Your physical body may be highly sensitive with Neptune in your 6th House. You may feel things in different parts of your body as a means of picking up impressions about other people or your environment. When you're around others who are ill, upset, or negative, you can easily absorb their energy on a vibrational level, and it can affect your own sense of well-being. It is imperative that you develop strong emotional boundaries and powerful energy filters or methods to release energy you may have picked up during the day. Long showers, in which you visualize yourself being cleared from head to toe, within and without, can be quite effective. You should also seek out natural healing methodologies as frequently as possible, since you may be highly sensitive to drugs. Alcohol or drug use is a major no-no for you. You're just too sensitive.

Neptune in the 7th: Your image of a soul mate, or desire to find that perfect person who compliments your every need, is very powerful with Neptune in your 7th House. Sensing that this perfect person is out there somewhere can be comforting, but it may also be frustrating if you feel that you are not perfect enough to attract them. The challenge of this position is to become more sensitive to the part of yourself that is your inner partner, and to develop a clearer projection of yourself. If you are constantly trying to project what others want to see from you, or a confusing sense of yourself, you will attract disappointment. Use this energy to clearly visualize yourself as whole, perfect and powerful, and send the signal to attract that partner who can see you and love you as you are.

Neptune in the 8th: The influence of Neptune in your 8th House was explored earlier in this chapter.

Neptune in the 9th: You have a highly impressionable psyche with Neptune in your 9th House. Your desire to find the spiritual path that will allow you to devote yourself to the truth is extremely powerful. You may be highly visionary about the future, and may have a special sensibility concerning spiritual matters. It is crucial that you learn how to separate the teacher from the teaching, since you may mistakenly devote yourself to a person instead of to the ideal to which that person is guiding you.

Neptune in the 10th: You need a career path that will allow you to show your compassion with Neptune in your 10th House. Although you may sometimes feel that it is up to you to save the world, or at least part of it, you are also capable of attracting others who share your ideals and will work toward similar aims of improving the quality of life.

Neptune in the 11th: Your vision of what you hope to achieve can be the key to realizing success with Neptune in your 11th House, but you have to learn the difference between dreaming and doing. Your intuitive sensibilities can be used to your benefit when you're focusing on your goals. You're the perfect candidate to use creative visualization and affirmation techniques to help you achieve success.

Neptune in the 12th: The influence of Neptune in your 12th House has been explored earlier in this chapter.

Pluto: Deep Psychic Awareness

Pluto's insight is on the deeper psychic level. Through Plutonian energy you can read between the lines. You see the twitch of an eye that tells the truth, you read the movement of hands, the tone of voice that betrays what words fail to say. Developing your Plutonian energy requires that you reach into the very depths of yourself and become familiar with your entire being. Yes, that includes your shadow self, your darker side— and it also encompasses your passion, your strength of survival, and your ability to heal.

Pluto's House Placement: Penetrating Awareness

Pluto in the 1st: You have an in-depth awareness of others and your environment with Pluto in your 1st House, and you may be fascinated with the prospects of developing your psychic sensibilities. Although you may be perceptive, you can also become obsessive, and learning how to pull back on your intensity will allow you to grow more rapidly.

Pluto in the 2nd: You're quite insightful about how to make your resources work for you with Pluto in your 2nd House. You can see ways to restore what seems useless or to extend the energy of what you possess, and may be able to make more things out of a loaf of bread and a can of soup than anybody dreamed possible, but you can also be destructive with this energy, and can undermine your strength by giving in to vengeful or hateful thoughts about yourself or others.

Pluto in the 3rd: You may have a very penetrating mind with Pluto in the 3rd House, and can be a psychically gifted. Your ability to use words to create change can be amazing, and you may also be gifted in using your voice as a tool for healing and transformation. You may be capable of probing into mysteries and finding information long after others have given up on finding anything.

Pluto in the 4th: The influence of Pluto in your 4th House was explored earlier in this chapter.

Pluto in the 5th: Your creativity can stimulate healing and regeneration through Pluto's influence in your 5th House. You may also find that surrendering to your creative flow acts as a positive release for unexpressed or blocked emotional energy. Love relationships provide your most phenomenal opportunity to experience transformational change, and anyone who helps you unlock the doors to your heart will also experience life changes. You can become exceptionally connected to your children and lovers, and may have such insight into their energy that you can feel what is happening to them, but you cannot control the outcome or their choices.

Pluto in the 6th: Strengthen your awareness of your physical body with Pluto in your 6th House in order to avoid making choices that can be physically destructive or harmful. Repressing your emotions or ignoring problems does not cure them. You may also have special healing gifts that can help others experience positive transformation, and you may feel that it is important to work in a profession that allows you to do so.

Pluto in the 7th: You can be adept at helping to bring about social change with Pluto in your 7th House. Whether you accomplish this by challenging outmoded ideas about relationships, getting involved in law or politics, or quietly undermining useless prejudices—you can be a healer of social ills. Finding the direction that will allow you to affect positive growth and change adds strength and power to your life.

Pluto in the 8th: The influence of Pluto in your 8th House was explored earlier in this chapter.

Pluto in the 9th: You may feel close to the power that emanates from the Source of All Life with Pluto in your 9th House. Whether you achieve this connection through religious practice, academic study, or personal investigation is not as important as your need to find a direction and philosophy that allow you to exercise high ethical and moral judgment in your own life. This can lead to your personal evolution and spiritual growth.

Pluto in the 10th: As a powerful investigator and researcher, you can apply your penetrating insights through your life work with Pluto in the 10th House. Finding a path that will allow you to uncover the power at the core of yourself may encompass every aspect of your life, and you can become influential in your career or within your family or community.

Pluto in the 11th: Although you may be aware of the ills that penetrate the social system with Pluto in your 11th House, you may hesitate to become involved in changing them. It is important that you express your views and ideas, especially in a political sense, because your insights may be those that help to change the system and allow it to undergo great improvements. Community affairs can also be a positive outlet, although your ideas may cause some turmoil to those who resist change.

Pluto in the 12th: The influence of Pluto in your 12th House has been explored earlier in this chapter.

CHAPTER SEVEN

NURTURING AND CREATING A HOME

Nurturing. Mothering. These experiences are associated with womanliness, but are not solely responsible for defining your womanhood. Although women are the only ones who can become mothers, it is not necessary to be a mother to become an exceptional nurturer! Nurturing is a natural expression for women—but the manner in which it is done is very individualized. Whether with children, lovers, partners, friends—or even with your own parents—you have ample opportunities to nurture others. The person who needs your nurturing most, however, is you.

Although caring for others can fill a special place in your soul, the way you care for yourself is especially important. You may derive nourishment from developing your talents and skills, or through your work. Study or travel can be nourishing; and something as simple as a long soak in the tub can refill your spirit. Part of nourishing yourself is physical, part emotional and spiritual, and part is definitely environmental: what you create in a home. By linking these factors together you can begin to see the important connections between these different levels of personal fulfillment.

The Moon's Role in Nurturing and Creating a Home

Yet another facet of your Moon beyond what you've already explored is what your Moon shows about your deepest needs. You can feel whole only when these needs are answered and fulfilled. Although it is tempting to look outside, your wisdom tells you that a great part of the responsibility for nourishment comes from within yourself. Staying in touch with your Moon and fulfilling needs dictated by your Moon will give you the strength and emotional resilience necessary for creating a truly satisfying life. You'll also find that your relationships improve when you feel free to express these qualities fully and completely, and if you're also building a career, it is this ability that will provide the inner strength necessary to feel whole in the face of your challenges.

The Moon's Sign and Nurturing

> **Moon in Aries:** Your profound need for independence and autonomy, driven by your Aries Moon, can sometimes lead to the feeling that you're rushing through life. Although slowing down may not be the answer all of the time, allowing ample space in your life for enjoyment can help you put the brakes on. Your playful attitude and love of challenge may encourage you to pursue sports as a favorite pastime, and staying active is one of the most nurturing things you can do for yourself. When you let your energy become stagnant, your emotional vitality sags. When nurturing others, it might be easier for you to play than it is to discipline, and consequently, your children may think of you more in the context of fun. That's okay with you, and you probably feel the same way about your intimate connections— if they're not fun, what good are they? Your passion ignites when you're smiling, and you smile a lot when you're enjoying a challenge. You also have a powerful protective streak, and if anyone you love needs a defender, you're there. You might also need to cultivate relationships that give you a sense that you, too, have somebody on your side. Standing on your own is okay, but your soul fills up when you can share your joy with those you love.

Moon in Taurus: Your Taurus Moon is hungry for stability and continuity. You can nourish that need by creating a safe haven for yourself, and when you're nurturing others, feel that it's important that they are safe and secure as well. Your protective nature is quite prominent, and you feel good when you provide emotional (and physical) shelter for a child, lover, or husband. Sometimes you may feel that you need to hold on to everything and everyone, and can project all your energy into protecting your assets. Learning to trust is nurturing for you, and that means allowing some things and some people to leave your care. You feel most nurtured when you are close to the beauty and harmony of Mother Nature. Gardening and farming may feel good, or you might even enjoy building things, including houses or furniture. When you're feeling low, sitting under your favorite tree with your feet in the grass can be rejuvenating. Or you might prefer the pleasures of a massage. Indulging your sensual needs helps to fill your soul so that you have energy in your own storehouse to give to others. Just remember that the balance between giving and receiving is difficult to maintain.

Moon in Gemini: Since your mind's hunger drives you to explore so many different facets of life, nurturing yourself involves feeding your mind. The choice of avenues upon which you direct your energy can be quite important, since you can exhaust yourself if your energy becomes too scattered. Taking the time to quiet your mind through meditation can be positively nourishing for your soul, and you may also find that journal writing or creative writing can act as a positive way to release and clear your energy. Your need to make contact may prompt you to spend hours on the phone, which can also feel supportive and nourishing. When you're involved in nurturing activities directed toward others, your interest and communication provides a sense that you are there for them, but sometimes you may be inconsistent in your emotionally supportive roles because your own interests are elsewhere at the moment. Spending endless hours keeping your mind buzzing can make it difficult to reach that quiet space you need to rest fully and completely at the end of the day. By making a conscious effort to clear your mind and calm your thought processes before you sleep, you will rest much better and awaken refreshed and ready for a new day of exploration and challenge.

Moon in Cancer: You may enjoy the experience of creating a home, carefully building your nest with a focus on comfort. The energy of your Cancer Moon stimulates a need to be close to those you love, and your soul is soothed when you share a warm embrace. Hug therapy is one of the best ways to nourish your soul. Whether you're cuddling a baby or in the arms of your lover, when you surrender to embrace you feel safe and alive. You can impart the same warmth and support to your family or your lover, and caring for those you love can be mutually nourishing. Wonderful food is also nourishing for you on many levels, and if you enjoy cooking, you may feel especially satisfied when you sit down to enjoy one of your own culinary creations. You may also love eating food grown in your own garden. If a man wants to win your heart, it helps if he knows how to cook! When you need extra support during those times when life is wearing you down, take the time to do things that make you feel warm and safe. Cozy up in your favorite chair with a romantic book, fill your tub with fragrant bubbles and settle in for a long soak, get a massage, have lunch with a good friend—or make a list of your favorite things and do some of them instead of wondering if you're ever going to get a break.

Moon in Leo: You love to be entertained, and when you need to reaffirm that life is worthwhile, it helps if you're doing something that fills your heart. With the Moon in Leo, you hunger most for love, and need ample opportunities to create and experience the many facets of love. To some extent, this may come through your own creative expression, and when you're deeply involved in something, you put your heart and soul into it. On a broad level, then, it's important that you make some choices that allow you to participate in a career or relationship that feels good. When nurturing others, you provide the generosity and support that encourages them to realize their own potential. As a mother, you are quite protective, and will not take it lightly if anyone or anything threatens your child. At home, you need a favorite chair and a place that is yours where you can stop and relish the pleasures of life. Getting outdoors in the sun and feeling that warm glow around you can be nourishing, too, and you may have your favorite outdoor pastimes that add a special dimension to your life. Take time to attend concerts, go to the movies, or get involved in your community theater group and get on stage yourself! You know what they say about all work and no play? Well it applies to you double-time!

Moon in Virgo: Even though you may not like to admit it, you do enjoy just sitting back and taking it easy from time to time. Your Virgo Moon keeps you busy, though. There is always something to do, things to fix, or a situation that needs your attention. Your efficiency helps you manage your time, but you have trouble relaxing if you know that there's a project waiting to be finished or someone needing your help. You nourish others by attending to all the details, and many of your efforts may seem to go unappreciated. After all, you make it look too easy. When you need to refuel your soul, the first thing you may have to get past is your guilt about not producing something. Once that's out of the way, you might make time for your favorite crafts as a means to relax, and you may thoroughly enjoy getting lost in a good book. Doing something good for your body also feels great, and you can really benefit from regular massage therapy or foot reflexology treatments. You may love the feel of an herbal body wrap or facial. By indulging yourself a little from time to time, you are rejuvenated, and your efficiency improves in every area. That alone should be ample reason to take care of yourself!

Moon in Libra: You may adore being pampered. The energy behind your Libra Moon may keep you so involved doing things with others to help them stay happy that you don't always do things that fill your own soul. This is especially true if you have children, since you're likely to do whatever you can to make sure that they have a chance for dancing lessons, school functions, music lessons, sports activities, the best birthday parties, or anything they need to develop their social skills and have a full life. If you're married, you may also do a lot to support your husband's needs. You work, too? Well, then you must have lots of time to indulge your every whim! When you stop to think about it, you may wonder what you really do need for yourself. Start by concentrating on your need for inner harmony, and allow a little time each day for peaceful contemplation. You also need to let your hair down sometimes. If that means popping your favorite CD into the stereo and dancing around the room, then go for it! Or take the time to have lunch with an old friend, make a phone call to your college roommate, or go to a movie with your sweetie. Make it a point to regularly visit your beautician and be pampered a little in addition to having your hair done. Find your favorite spot and read a steamy romance novel. Attend a concert or play or go to an art gallery just to be enthralled with the beauty. Filling your soul in these ways fills your heart with joy and adds sparkle to your smile.

Moon in Scorpio: With your Moon in Scorpio, your intense emotionality needs opportunities for release. Although you may spend time lending your energy to others through your work or taking care of family, you may not find it easy to take care of yourself without feeling guilty. Oh, but you do dream about it. Since you tend to protect your emotional vulnerability, you may find it difficult to open up in just any situation, but your desire to let everything go and experience true ecstasy is definitely there. A passionate sexual relationship can be quite delicious, and may seem to be the best nurturing of all. There are other ways to fill yourself that reside in your creative expression. When you pour your heart into your creativity, you are free. It also feels absolutely wonderful when you tear into a project, restore an old piece of furniture, rebuild a house, or bring a tired garden into its full vitality. But you may find the greatest nourishment of all when you surrender to your needs to find the depth of your soul. Activities such as an intensive spiritual retreat, a vision quest, or self-renewing rituals during the full moons call forth a joining of your soul and spirit, and nourish you at the most profound level.

Moon in Sagittarius: With the Moon in Sagittarius, your drive to satisfy your hunger for truth and freedom leads you into pursuits that develop your mind. However, you have to learn to ask for personal space when you need it, and to respect the same needs from others. When nurturing others, encourage them to develop their own independence. At home, you need a place that provides a real sense of space, and where you also have a place for reflection—a room like a study or library, or an alcove in your bedroom might be just perfect. Give yourself ample time to walk in the woods or a park, to read something inspirational, or to have an open discussion with someone you admire. Take time to travel, even if that means only a different route to work or exploring an unknown part of your home town. Vacations away from home can be positively rejuvenating. When you're feeling low, you might be most recharged by adding these things to your life. They feed your soul.

Moon in Capricorn: Work. Work. Work. That seems to be all you do with your Moon in Capricorn. Since you are always involved in taking on responsibilities, you also can be a magnet for stress. When nurturing others, you tend to take care of everything, and may feel that life is easier that way. You know the importance of guiding your children to be responsible for themselves, and can teach this in many ways. One of the best is to take care of yourself by making sure that you're carrying only those burdens that belong to you, and relinquishing those that do not. At home, you need to feel secure and in harmony with the natural order of things. You enjoy the feeling of being around trees, or surrounded by naturally occurring structures like mountains, hills, or rock formations. Allow time during your busy week to hike in the woods or a park, to get into your garden, to climb a tree with your kids. In the winter, go to the mountains to snow ski. See your chiropractor regularly, get plenty of calcium in your diet, exercise to strengthen your bones if nothing more, and when you vacation, get into nature whenever possible.

Moon in Aquarius: You may think that you don't really need much nurturing with an Aquarius Moon. The truth of the matter is that your soul is hungry for the feeling of freedom that occurs when you rise above the ordinary into the realm of the seemingly impossible. You can experience this transcendent freedom in many ways, but may feel it best when you're actually doing something that allows you to physically move beyond the bounds of earth. Flying, hot air balloon rides, hang gliding, even windsurfing may provide this boost to your soul. You may also love skiing, skating, bicycling, or running—when you feel the wind in your face and reach that point of lifting out of your body—your soul is free. Your approach to nurturing others is to help them find their own inner freedom, and you may encourage your children to feel good about their differences and to accept the true diversity of humanity. Your friends also provide an uplifting energy in your life, and spending time with them nourishes your soul. Sometimes a book is your best friend, and when you need to be alone with your thoughts, reading and contemplating can refuel your soul. Meditation and activities like hatha yoga, tai chi, chi gong, or aikido may also help you maintain your mind/body/spirit connection.

Moon in Pisces: Your Pisces Moon pulls you deep inside yourself and beckons you to find ways to return to the source. You feel continually hungry for spiritual rejuvenation, and need ample opportunities to experience renewal at this level. When nurturing others, you provide a sense of comfort and compassion, and when anyone is suffering, you offer unequaled support. Your sensitivity to the influences around you can leave you exhausted at the end of a stressful day; but when you take the time to connect with the spiritual source that empowers you, you can be revitalized. Sleep is especially important, and the quality of your sleep can be enhanced when you release the tension from the day before you fall asleep. You find sustenance in reviewing your dreams, and spending time reflecting on your dreams can provide an opportunity to understand yourself and your life on a more profound level. Your personal environment needs to be serene, and you'll feel more like letting go if you sense that you are, indeed, removed from the world. You love sinking into a hot tub to relax, and swimming can be rejuvenating. Give yourself time to experience regular body work, have regular pedicures, or foot reflexology treatments. When you vacation, find a place that indulges your fantasies, and when you're just taking time off for the afternoon or evening, let yourself experience some positive escapes at the movies, listening to music, or reading a book. Meditation and spiritual retreats will also provide important emotional and spiritual renewal.

Saturn's Support in Nurturing

Saturn also plays a positive role in nurturing. Despite the bad rap Saturn sometimes receives, this energy is necessary to your stability and growth. Through Saturn you learn to take responsibility for yourself and your actions. Saturn also functions as the repository of your fears, and it's important to understand and deal with these emotions in order to be whole. Trying to repress such feelings blocks your ability to feel the positive, supportive energy that life has to offer.

In many respects, the energy of Saturn is played out in your life by your experience with authority figures. Your mother and father, extended family, and teachers were your primary Saturnian influences when you were a young girl, and their direction and guidance still whisper in the way you approach establishing your personal security. As an adult woman, you express Saturn through the manner in which you take responsibility for yourself and your needs for stability and security.

Saturn in Aries: With Saturn in Aries, you may prefer to take on the role of guide and supporter to your children and those in your care in a rather independent manner. You believe in personal autonomy, and will work to be sure that anyone you influence develops it. A competitive spirit may drive you to try to be on the top, first, or the best, and you're not likely to be afraid of starting something new, but you can lose your drive if a situation seems to grow stale, and it's important to clear barriers from your path on a regular basis. Then you'll avoid the traps of repeating the same mistakes or staying in a rut. Either of these concepts just simply does not fit with your model of who you want to become. As a result, you may be tempted to jump into something new or different just for a change of pace, but if you still have unfinished business elsewhere, you may have jumped from the proverbial frying pan into the fire! Creating your own traditions within your family may satisfy your yearning to establish a difference between the way you're doing things and the way mom did it.

Saturn in Taurus: You have definite ideas about the way things should be with Saturn in Taurus, and your manner of supporting and caring for others can be quite stabilizing. You don't enjoy sudden change, and would prefer to follow a traditional path, especially when dealing with your children. Tried and true methods somehow seem safer to you, although anything that adds an element of protection may seem like a good idea when it comes to those you love. Other aspects of your chart may indicate that you like to forge ahead of the times, but in your heart, you can do it only if you see some continuity. With continuity, you can be comfortable and confident with experimentation; but just jumping into something without some proof or connection does not sit well with you.

Saturn in Gemini: You show your protection and care for others by sharing your thoughts and ideas. If it makes sense, you may be interested in trying it. With Saturn in Gemini, you put great stock in logic and common sense, but watch out for distractions. You may be going along, right on track, when suddenly there's an opportunity to try doing it another way. Take your work, for example. If you're bored with it, you may have little energy left to put into it. You're best suited to situations that involve fluctuations and you'll enjoy stimulating mental challenges in your career. The same may be true of your commitments in relationships, so those old "traditional" roles of wife and mother may not be your cup of tea. You'll have to reach a different type of agreement.

Saturn in Cancer: With Saturn in Cancer, you need a home and sense of family in your life in order to feel secure. This is the structure upon which your overall stability rests. The trap of this placement resides in hanging on to the past, including old emotional trauma. Some of that trauma might not even be your own—many of your anxieties are definitely tied to the things you learned from your parents and grandparents. Remind yourself regularly that you are safe, strong, and secure. You may have always been drawn into situations where you're taking care of somebody, but you don't really have to prove your self-worth based on how much you do for everyone else! Even in business settings, you display a caring quality, and can have trouble with a mechanized approach to business. It's easier for you when the people you work with are treated more like family than mere employees. You're definitely capable of bringing a woman's touch into a man's world, and may, in the process, teach others about the positive quality of honoring humanity in the workplace.

Saturn in Leo: You have a definite way you like to do things, and function best when you're in charge. Whether in personal relationships or at work, you utilize the energy of Saturn in Leo to bring things into focus and set definitive priorities. You can be rather stubborn, and may have trouble getting out of your own way, especially when there might be a better way to do something. You're also willing to adapt to change if it will make your life function more smoothly and afford you more time to enjoy the things you truly love. You can be a warm and supportive parent or partner, and take commitments seriously. Your protection and warmth can be steady and strong; and you don't think of yourself as secondary to any man in your life, although you may still be a little intimidated by those you respect!

Saturn in Virgo: It's clear that you have preferences, and you may even be a bit fanatical about setting up a plan of action or organizing your life. With Saturn in Virgo, you have a very critical eye, and may see the problems before you find the strengths. In expressing your nurturing side, this influence supports your desire and ability to teach and guide others; but you must always remember to tolerate the differences between individuals and to allow them to grow at their own pace. The pattern of your life may be the beginning for others who will ultimately go their own way with greater confidence gained through your example.

Saturn in Libra: You are always aware of a set of standards, and you may feel that some of the standards set by others are more important than those you determine for yourself. The influence of Saturn in Libra challenges you to develop a quality of refinement and social skill that will allow you to deal with anyone or any situation in a rational and balanced manner. You may even go out of your way to try to make things fair, and may complain that life itself is not fair. Well, that's the truth! This standard of fairness should also apply to the way you treat yourself, by the way. In expressing your care for others, you may feel that it is important that they learn good social skills, and you can be an excellent role model in this regard. You may feel insecure when you're functioning entirely on your own, and might be much more at ease dealing with the challenges of life if you have a partner.

Saturn in Scorpio: Your interest in restoration permeates every part of your life and is strongly influenced by your Saturn in Scorpio. Even if you sometimes fall short, you understand the importance of making the most of your life and its resources. Your influence on others who cannot see the value in something on the surface can be immense, because you are the master of removing the crust and exposing the jewel at the core. You may also know when there's nothing there to expose, in which instance, you can take what is useless or outworn and recycle it in the best possible manner. This attitude may be especially emphasized since you are a woman and experience the variations related to the cyclical changes within your own body. You can learn to make use of the different levels of energy that occur at different times to become more productive, more secure, and more confident in the natural order of things.

Saturn in Sagittarius: The importance of the spiritual essence of your life cannot be overstated: you need to find a philosophy and way of approaching life's larger questions that provides a sense of stability and security. In your quest, you may explore many teachings and may travel or study different cultures. With Saturn in Sagittarius, you also need to develop an acceptance and tolerance for different beliefs and ideals in order to safeguard against becoming too self-righteous. Your quest for knowledge may prompt you to stay connected to learning institutions, whether as a teacher or student. Learning is your mainstay and source of strength. Your ability to share your life experience with others, especially your children, can inspire them to discover their own quest.

Saturn in Capricorn: You may be most comfortable with a predictable pattern and schedule, and are definitely at ease when you're in charge of a situation. With Saturn in Capricorn, you're a capable teacher, and may achieve the greatest success in situations that allow you to create a structure or plan for others to follow. You may be right at home in traditional roles of wife and mother, but you can also do quite well following a career path. You need to achieve, and may be driven by a desire to gain respect. A common sense approach to dealing with life's challenges is your mainstay, and if you're balancing many roles, you can carry through successfully by keeping your priorities clearly in order.

Saturn in Aquarius: Your need to be around other people is stimulated by a penetrating sense of feeling alone. With Saturn in Aquarius, you realize more than others that becoming a functional part of the social system is a key to humanity's survival. Your hope may be that, through cooperation and hard work, the world can become a better place, and so you become involved in community activities, special interests, or other situations that involve working toward an ideal in order to make a difference. If you begin to feel hopeless, you can just as readily withdraw, but you will not feel satisfied. Developing a special and close friendship is key to your survival as a woman, even if you have periods of separation or live miles apart.

Saturn in Pisces: Although you may sometimes be afraid of it, it is crucial that you explore your inner self and the world of your psyche. With Saturn in Pisces, your spirituality can be the mainstay of your security. Allowing time and space in your life for meditation, creativity, or retreat will not only add to your ability to deal with the problems of everyday life, but will inspire your faith in the greater order of things. You're the woman others turn to when in need, and you can always make a place for someone who needs support, but you can also fall into despair if you see only the problems and troubles of the world, or if your ideals are somehow shattered. Through devoting yourself to a life that becomes your meditation, you can develop a true inner peace and harmony that calms turmoil and soothes pain.

The 4th House and Your Personal Environment

Your 4th House illustrates what you need in a home environment, where you will feel most comfortable, and how you like to live. It is here that you create a feeling of safety, where you can let your hair down and simply be yourself. The sign on the 4th House cusp, and planets in this house, provide important clues about what feels best to you when you're creating a home. You can extend these concepts to include the general type of environmental area you might like best (near mountains, lakes, in cities, close to the ocean, etc.). Additionally, this part of your chart indicates what you need in your haven.

The Sign on the 4th House: What Makes You Feel at Home

Aries on the 4th: Your home may be one of your favorite playgrounds. Although you may also think of your home as a protection from the rest of the world, you need space in your home environment for playful activities. You might enjoy living in a community or complex that affords such amenities as tennis, swimming, golf, or sports clubs, since having these options readily available would be convenient. You may also be on the go a lot, and are capable of enjoying the places you're in temporarily. In your personal environment, you'll enjoy having space around you, and may not appreciate cramped quarters. Shades of red will be appealing accent colors, and you'll add your personal touch to your decor. With Mars ruling this house, there may be lots of activity at home. You may also remember a sense of turmoil or unrest from your early upbringing. When you're unhappy, you're most likely to lash out at your family, but there are other avenues if you want to avoid strife at home.

Taurus on the 4th: A stable home life is very important to you with Taurus influencing your 4th House. Your home is definitely your security base, and you may like the idea of staying in one place long enough to build and feather your nest. The energy of Venus adds her influence to this house, adding a need to create true beauty in your personal environment. Surrounding yourself with the things you love, including your collection of sentimental favorites, makes you feel much more secure. You might enjoy living in an environment that seems more natural rather than living in a city. Trees and lots of green and beautiful gardens are nurturing to you. If you live in the city, you'll still need to have something alive and growing around you. Earth colors are the perfect compliment in your decor, as are natural wood surroundings and furnishings.

Gemini on the 4th: The influence of Gemini on the cusp of your 4th House adds a need for open, airy spaces to your list of preferences in your home environment. You're likely to have an interesting collection of personal belongings representing your varied interests, although some of them are probably collecting dust from a lack of attention. One thing is certain, you definitely need telephones in convenient places, since being able to reach out and touch at a moment's notice is very important. In today's computer age, you may also need a place for your home computer system, complete with modem. There may always seem to be children around your household, since you are probably quite happy to be around them. Mercury's influence may indicate that there are people coming and going. You may like having books and magazines around, and may have a diversified library. Lots of windows are a requirement, so you can feel the breezes moving through your living space. As for decor, some splashes of oranges, yellows, or golds can be stimulating accent colors.

Cancer on the 4th: The qualities of Cancer radiate through your 4th House, adding a need for comfort, warmth, and coziness in your home space. You may love being surrounded by things that have sentimental value, and may have an affinity for antiques or vintage furniture. Your kitchen needs to be state-of-the-art, since you may enjoy fine cuisine and will appreciate an excellent place to create it. Hosting family gatherings and providing a safe place for those you love adds special memories and a wonderful at-home quality to your personal environment. A garden can be both beautiful and practical for you, since tending to things that are growing suits many of your needs. The influence of the energy of the Moon, which rules this house, brings a feeling of nurturing to this space, which is the natural place to experience caring and comfort.

Leo on the 4th: The qualities of Leo radiate through this part of your chart, indicating that you need a home that is solid and strong, where you can occasionally hold court! Although you may not always entertain, you love having a place that is warm and inviting to others. Plenty of light will feel most nurturing, so make sure the sun can shine in, and in the winter you'll adore a warm fire. Your decor may range from simple to lavish, although you to love to add dramatic touches. The influence of your Sun in this house adds a need to feel that you are in control of your personal environment. Even though you may be generous and enjoy entertaining, you're not likely to appreciate unannounced or uninvited visitors.

Virgo on the 4th: A place for everything . . . well, you know how it goes with Virgo ruling your 4th House! You need a home space that makes it easy to stay organized—big closets, lots of cabinets, drawers, shelves—it's the only way to stay on top of all the details. You appreciate an environment that is meticulously clean and uncluttered, although you may not like the idea of having to keep it that way all by yourself. Once you develop a system, you like it that way, and those who share your personal space need to learn to cooperate (you know how you like those towels folded). You may love architectural designs that feature clean lines, and appreciate decor that is both functional and attractive. Neutral colors and natural fibers create a perfect comfort zone. With Mercury influencing this house, you may also enjoy the company of others. An evening of stimulating conversation around the dinner table might be the perfect way to cap off a busy week.

Libra on the 4th: Libra's influence on the cusp of your 4th House adds a sense of style and refinement to your home environment. You love being surrounded by beautiful things, and may have a wonderful eye for color and design. Your home may feature works of art and fine decor, and you can be somewhat meticulous about making sure that everything creates a sense of balance. The energy of Venus is associated with this house in your chart, influencing an inviting atmosphere and friendly home environment that probably draws your friends and family. You may love entertaining, and may be quite gracious to your guests, although you appreciate them most when they observe proper rules of behavior and don't mar the furniture!

Scorpio on the 4th: The influence of Scorpio on this part of your chart adds a need for privacy in your home environment. You love being surrounded by things that appeal to your senses—soft fabrics, lush carpets, a fabulous bed—and may feel best around rich, deep colors. You may have a natural sense of the energy of the places in which you live, and might enjoy working with concepts such as Feng Shui to help harmonize and strengthen the energy of your home. Pluto's influence on your 4th House stimulates a need for healing within your personal space, and you may enjoy using some of the features of your home to help you maintain your physical vitality. A spa, hot tub, or sauna would be excellent additions to your home, and you might also enjoy having your own massage table. However, you may have to import the masseur, unless you've gotten a lucky break and discovered a man who loves to share sensual massage. But that's another story....

Sagittarius on the 4th: The influence of Sagittarius on the cusp of your 4th House adds mobility to this part of your chart, which usually relates to stability. You may relocate several times over the course of your life, and although you are flexible in your ability to adapt to new environments, you may not enjoy the disruption moving creates in your life. The idea of having your home on wheels might suit you pretty well, at least part of the time! You love a house with lots of space, plenty of bookshelves, and nestled in an inspiring, natural setting. Wide-open spaces also feel great, although you may love the feeling of being surrounded by trees. When you do settle down, you may look for an opportunity to have your own little wildlife sanctuary, or, if you answer your big dreams, a ranch with all sorts of critters. Jupiter's energy is connected to this house, stimulating your need to bring a sense of diversity into your sense of home. For this reason, you can actually be at home almost anywhere, if you allow it!

Capricorn on the 4th: Having your own home is definitely important for you with Capricorn ruling your 4th House. Whether you have an apartment or a mansion, having a chance to put your personal touch on your environment makes you feel complete. You may have a well-defined sense of taste, although your favorite feeling is likely to be a room with rich wood accents and textured fabrics. Sometimes you can be a bit austere in your choices, and may even wonder yourself why you bought that uncomfortable chair for the living room. Maybe it was well-made; or maybe it was just a good bargain! Family heirlooms may be to your liking, particularly if they've held their value. Saturn's influence in this part of your chart adds an energy of stability to your home environment, and may stimulate your interest in antiques or period furnishings. You may also have a good sense of structure, and appreciate a home that is solidly built and stands on a strong foundation.

Aquarius on the 4th: You are most drawn to home environments that are somewhat unusual with Aquarius influencing this part of your chart. Well-defined ideas about what you want may lead you to incorporate innovative options into your home space, such as a state-of-the-art computer control center or home security system. You may also appreciate living in or near large cities, since having easy access to the conveniences and options can be quite appealing. However, you do enjoy your privacy, and may even be somewhat reclusive or detached. Your decor may lean toward art nouveau, art deco, contemporary, or eclectic furnishings and designs. Uranus has a strong influence on your 4th House, stimulating your tendencies toward lifestyles that are out-of-the-ordinary. Your need for freedom of expression in this area is powerful, and you might hope for the opportunity to design a home exactly as you want it. If you've not yet accomplished this end, you can at least choose (or design) the furnishings!

Pisces on the 4th: The qualities of Pisces influence your personal environment, adding a need for true serenity. Home is your escape, and your need for a place that feels far removed from the pressures of the world can be quite powerful. Neptune's influence on this house may stimulate a desire to live near water. If you have property near the ocean, a lake, stream, or pond, your comfort and inner peace are enhanced; but if you're stuck in an apartment somewhere, there's no need for despair. A small fountain or fish tank can add this energy. Water in the basement does not count, by the way, but may indicate that you need to bring water into your home more directly! Translucent colors are a wonderful touch to your home space, and you may take extra care in furnishing and decorating your bedroom.

Planets in the 4th House: Your Energy at Home

Sun in the 4th: With the Sun in your 4th House, you're definitely Queen of the Castle! You need a home that reflects your personality, not just a place to live. Anyone who visits will see your special touches. You may also enjoy inviting special friends into your personal space, and family gatherings at home can be quite meaningful to you. Family is important, and the creation of your own family may take a strong priority. You may become the matriarchal leader of your family, and your influence and ideas can have a powerful effect. If you feel that you are carrying on the traditions of a long line of influences, it's probably true. If you are inclined to alter or change those traditions, you can probably accomplish your aims as long as your approach flows from love and not unresolved anger or competitiveness.

Moon in the 4th: Family and home are exceptionally important needs for you with your Moon in the 4th House. Regardless of your other priorities and responsibilities, you always operate with an underlying consideration for the needs of your family. The influences of your parents were probably very powerful when you were a young girl, and you may still feel close to them or be deeply influenced by their responses to the way you meet your own needs. This placement can stimulate a desire to create your own family, and whether or not you have children, your nurturing qualities may be quite apparent to anyone who is close to you. You need a home space that provides a true feeling of comfort and support, and may not feel at home unless you have your special things around you. Those things usually considered domestic, like cooking, may be rather enjoyable for you, and can provide a sense of stability and fulfillment. Most importantly, you need a nesting place.

Mercury in the 4th: Mercury's energy in your 4th House adds a liveliness to your home space. There may always seem to be ample communication happening at your house, with either friends or family sharing ideas or someone on the telephone. This placement also stimulates a need to express your feelings, and in your personal relationships, you can be animated in showing your emotions. When you're upset, you can even be a little high-strung. This energy is unsettling in the home environment and sometimes brings frequent moves. Your tendency to worry about family and home matters is also amplified, and if you're fretting over possibilities, you may miss the opportunity to experience what is actually happening. At home, you need a place for reflection where you can write letters, make entries in your personal journal, or read quietly.

Venus in the 4th: The energy of Venus in your 4th House generates a quality of beauty in your personal space. You love being surrounded by beautiful things, music, and colors that make you feel alive. You may also demonstrate your own artistic sensibilities in the way you decorate your home, and may use your home as a base for creating and producing your own works of art. Your love of family can be exceptional, and establishing your own family may be one of your most rewarding experiences. Having people around you who appreciate and care for you is just as important as having people near who need your support and tenderness.

Mars in the 4th: Mars energy stimulates high levels of activity on the home front in your 4th House. Whether there were frequent moves or just much coming and going, home may not have seemed very settled when you were young, and the pattern is likely to continue unless you consciously change it. Having outlets at home for reasonable competitive expression can be especially positive for your personal growth; a rousing family game of cards, tennis with your mom or kids, bike riding, family sports outings—all of these help to satisfy your need for a positively active family life. If there are no options for activity, then the potential for conflict and argumentativeness increases. Home can be a safe place to express anger or a place filled with strife and conflict. If you experienced power struggles growing up, you may attract the same now until you alter your own energy. Learning how to handle your anger and need for assertiveness will have a definitive effect on your domestic tranquility. There's nothing wrong with feeling angry, you just need good outlets to express it.

Jupiter in the 4th: Home can be an uplifting and inspiring place for you with Jupiter's energy in your 4th House. You need room to move and space for expansion, and may enjoy living in an area that offers a wide range of options such as cultural activity, education, and recreation. You also need plenty of room for your storehouse of knowledge—for books, computers, and anything else that helps you keep your mind alive with ideas. You may have a large extended family, although you may not always see them all. Establishing your own family can be rewarding and enjoyable, and being part of and passing on family heritage may be one of your greatest rewards. Your parents may have encouraged you to extend your education or travel, and your influence on your own children, if you have them, may motivate them to fill their minds with knowledge.

Saturn in the 4th: Your home needs to be a place of foundation and safety, but you may feel that you have to create it yourself with the energy of Saturn in your 4th House. Living a simple life may make more sense than striving for excess, and learning to live in cooperation with nature and the environment can be both rewarding and stabilizing. You may have issues with your parents or family, although getting beyond those issues can be much more difficult than it seems. Hanging on to the past seems to provide a stability that arises from familiarity, but can inhibit your growth. If you are to truly break free, you may have to relinquish your old attachments and strike out on your own. Creating your own sense of home and family allows you to recreate the fulfillment of your needs that may have been ignored or stifled when you were a little girl. Be careful that you are conscious about the way you parent your own children and nourish your own family. There's a temptation to repeat the patterns buried in your subconscious mind instead of defining a new paradigm.

Uranus in the 4th: Your need for the unusual extends into your personal environment with Uranus' energy in your 4th House. Playing the traditional domestic roles is not your style, and you may openly rebel against anyone who tries to demand that you do, but you may actually enjoy the experience of family and home if they allow you the freedom to be yourself and to experiment with new models. Your own relationship with your mother may have been somewhat unsettling, and could be the motivator for your insistence that you are different. Although you may move several times over the course of your life, you can enjoy creating a home and may be excited about the prospects or the experience of designing your own home. A restlessness that prompts you to change residence may arise from your feeling of boredom with the same old thing or a feeling that you just don't fit in. If you can find a community that provides ample options for your self-expression and allows you to indulge your unique lifestyle, you may actually settle in quite nicely.

Neptune in the 4th: Neptune's energy in your 4th House adds a need for a home space that is almost otherworldly. Your home needs to be an escape from the everyday, a place where you can exercise your fantasies and open to your dreams. As a little girl, your home life may have been unsettling, particularly if there was illness or some type of family scandal. Uncovering family secrets may, in fact, be the key to freeing your soul of some of those feelings of inadequacy or insecurity. In the process, you must also learn true forgiveness while avoiding tendencies to martyr or sacrifice yourself for the good of protecting the family illusion. By opening to your inner self through meditation, creative expression, and spiritual development, you can finally achieve the connection to a spiritual home that has called to you since your childhood.

Pluto in the 4th: With Pluto in your 4th House, you prefer a home space that shields you from the intensity of the world and protects you from prying eyes. You may have a special desire to restore an older or vintage home, and, if you're so inclined, have a knack for giving new life to a place that appears worn down, shabby, or in a state of disrepair. This talent also extends to your ability to re-establish your sense of security if you've experienced a major change or crisis. Even if your life has taken turns that have left you feeling spent, you can regenerate and begin anew. Your relationship to your family of origin may have its hidden side, but you are the only one who can heal your hurts from the past. One of your tasks may be to transform the old patterns of your "family fate," and take the soul of your family on to a different course. Watch the temptation to compulsively repeat bad habits you learned at home. Some of them may not serve you particularly well now!

～

CHAPTER EIGHT

MEETING THE WORLD ON YOUR OWN TERMS

*C*areer and financial arenas were for many years primarily part of the "man's world." Women stayed at home, cared for children, and took care of the social needs of the family. This model of patriarchal rule was the model for hundreds of years, but revolutionary change occurring during the twentieth century altered the perception of a "woman's place." Now that so many women are in the workplace, and with the advent of more open relationships where both partners are likely to share paying bills and making financial decisions, the world is changing. You can define your identity in the world in many ways today, including developing a career. Meeting the world on your own terms involves uncovering the manner in which you shine most effectively and the way you use your resources and create a pathway that allows you to realize your goals.

The 10th House: Reputation, Ambition, and Public Persona

The arena of public life is seen through the 10th House. Your ambitions to achieve recognition are realized through this facet of yourself. If the energy of the Sun, Moon, and/or planets are contained in the 10th House, you may be more strongly focused on achieving success in a career. The particular planets emphasize the needs that drive your ambitions to succeed. If there are no planetary energies in your 10th House, you may not be strongly driven to focus a lot of attention on building a powerful reputation or gaining recognition through your career. However, in all cases, the sign on the Midheaven, the planet ruling the Midheaven, and aspects to the Midheaven add their powerful influences to this part of your life and will illuminate your understanding of your calling in pursuit of your life path.

Planets in the 10th House: What Drives Your Ambition

Sun in the 10th: With the Sun in your 10th House, you need recognition and are highly ambitious. Your sense of identity is strongly tied to your career, and it is imperative that you develop a career path that looks good on you! You excel in careers that allow you to take a position of leadership and where you can direct things in your own way. The nature of work that suits you best is further defined by your Sun's sign and aspects to your Sun, but the sign and ruler of your Midheaven (explained below) are also influences that you will incorporate into your sense of personal fulfillment through career.

Moon in the 10th: With your Moon in the 10th House, you may have a powerful need to develop a career path that allows you to express care and concern for others. Nurturing careers have a broad range—from child care, to counseling work, to teaching, or even careers in the food industry. But you're also adept at understanding the collective, and may be drawn to a career in politics, advertising, or artistry that has a broad appeal. Your intuitive sensibilities can be a plus in your career, and work that allows you to utilize and develop your intuitive self to its fullest will be most fulfilling. You're capable of enjoying a career that reflects a definite cycle, and can adapt to the ebb and flow of these cycles rather nicely. Work that centers on women, their interests, and the needs of family can be especially rewarding.

Mercury in the 10th: Mercury's energy in your 10th House indicates that you can be highly adept in a career that requires you to develop your mind and communicative capacities. Whether you're writing, editing, teaching, or researching, you'll enjoy a field that challenges your mind. You'll feel at home in a career centered around young people or work that requires keen manual dexterity.

Venus in the 10th: With Venus influencing your 10th House, you may be fascinated with the prospect of a career in the arts. At the very least, your personal artistry needs to be expressed and acknowledged through your career path. Your love of beautiful things can be incorporated into your career, as can your awareness and ability to work in fields that are of interest to women. Relationship counseling, public relations, image counseling, fashion design, the beauty industry, interior decorating—all these areas may appeal to your Venusian energy. Your knack for endearing others to you, and your charm and grace, can be beneficial in almost any career capacity.

Mars in the 10th: The dynamic energy of Mars in your 10th House stimulates a desire for a career that keeps you active. Your drive is matched by the courage to forge a path that allows you to assert your needs and abilities in a strong manner. You're the woman who can be at home with "the good ol' boys" and can match wits (and probably strength of will) with anyone. Work in physical fitness, the military, or law enforcement may be good choices; but you may also be fascinated with medical fields, and in any capacity can take charge or initiate. Developing positive ways to assert yourself may be necessary if you are to experience the success you deserve, since aggression may seem easier than positive self-assertion. You don't mind taking risks to get ahead.

Jupiter in the 10th: With Jupiter in your 10th House, you feel that the sky's the limit in developing your career path. Your desire to work in fields that reflect your philosophies and higher values may stimulate a career in journalism, publishing, teaching, the law, or religious pursuits. A career that involves connections to diverse cultures or that requires travel can be fascinating, and you might be a natural in diplomatic relations, politics, or international business. You're a natural in sales and can promote anything that meets with your high ethical and moral standards.

Saturn in the 10th: Since you have Saturn in your 10th House, you're probably serious about pursuing a career that will confer respect. A professional choice may seem most appropriate—something like a doctor, lawyer, professor, or business owner. You like the idea of being in control at work (which is really an illusion, but you can get away with it). Career paths that involve governmental agencies, educational pursuits, or powerful business ventures may be appealing and fulfilling. You need structure in your career, and may perform best in situations that require a series of tests or that allow you to advance in your expertise in a well-defined manner. However, it is crucial that you determine what is driving your ambitions, since if you are striving to please someone other than yourself, you may feel continually disappointed in their responses to your successes.

Uranus in the 10th: With Uranus in your 10th House, you're most interested in a career that gives you ample room for individual self-expression. In the arts, you may opt for the unusual; in business, you're the perfect candidate to run your own shop or to work independently. You may exhibit special genius in a particular area, and will prosper in fields that allow you to show your outstanding abilities. You're the kind of woman who likes to break through old barriers and shatter old stereotypes, and will be happiest in a career that is out-of-the-ordinary. You can be a rebel or an inspirational revolutionary. You may have a keen interest in astrology, psychology, computers or technology, the television industry, or fields that have not yet been invented! You like being on the leading edge, no matter what profession you've chosen, and by listening to your intuitive urgings will find the perfect outlet for your special abilities.

Neptune in the 10th: Neptune's energy in your 10th House inspires you to work in fields that help to make the world a better place. You need a life path that reflects your spirituality and imagination, and will prosper most fully in a field that is centered on principles of compassionate love. Your special sensibilities may lead you to work as an artist, musician, or actress, but the success you achieve in these areas will be only secondary to the influence you can have on the world around you. Work in the service industries, medical profession, or within charitable institutions can be important to your personal growth. You may also feel confused about which career path to follow, and may not trust your own abilities. Sometimes you may feel invisible, and may wonder when it will be your turn to be noticed. That is pretty much up to you and the choices you make at the various stages of your life. Once you begin to see your life as a process of unfolding and development, you will realize that your career path and life path merge as one, and that at different times you are focused on different expressions.

Pluto in the 10th: Pluto's energy in your 10th House suggests a need to express yourself in a life path that centers on transformational change. The healing arts may be especially important, but you can express your healing energy in many different professions—from cooking meals to hairdressing to music or writing. You need to acknowledge that you have a powerful desire and need to see things change. Your touch and artistry can restore something (or someone) to its rightful valuable place. You're an explorer, a researcher—one who looks beneath the surface to find what lies at the core. You're a natural alchemist and metaphysician. You bump shoulders with many powerful people, since like attracts like. Once you are comfortable with the true nature of your own strengths, you can move into positions of great influence, which need to be driven through a heart of compassion. The type of work you do may not be as important as the manner in which you choose to do it, which must reflect a strong conviction in yourself as a woman of compassionate power.

The Midheaven: Key to Where You're Going with Your Life

The Midheaven (MC), which is usually near the top of your astrological chart, is signified by an astrological sign. This point in your chart represents your vocation, your calling in life, and the sign at the Midheaven gives you several clues about your path in the outside world. Just as importantly, the Midheaven signifies your blossoming into wholeness and the manner by which you might best accomplish this experience. Your 10th House also provides information about your career path.

Aries on the MC: Making your way in the world and establishing your own place is aided by the influence of Aries at your Midheaven. Your keen sense of ambition keeps you moving forward in the face of competition; you're not likely to collapse in intimidation. You need a life path and career that allow you to exercise some independence, and prefer work that is challenging and exciting. You may also forge new territory through your career or volunteer efforts, and can be the woman who makes progress where others have failed. Your key to personal fulfillment rests in your ability to initiate, and you may love a career that gives you the room and opportunity to blaze trails. The energy of Mars influences the manner in which you illuminate your path to success. You may enjoy working in a field that is physically active, and may have a special affinity for working with children. The courage of your convictions provides the strength you need to realize your hopes.

Taurus on the MC: With Taurus on your Midheaven, your life path challenges you to establish yourself. Your career aims may be driven by your desire to build a stable platform upon which you can develop and express your creativity and artistry. You need a career that allows ample room for growth and that will sustain you throughout your life. You may not be comfortable with the idea of changing your career, and if faced with such a challenge, will perform better when you can exercise some autonomy in the process. The energy of Venus has a powerful influence on your vocation, adding a need to be involved in work that is self-expressive. You may enjoy a career in music or the arts, but you also have an excellent head for business and a good sense of value.

Gemini on the MC: The influence of Gemini on your Midheaven indicates a dominant need to communicate and make connections as part of your life path. When searching for career options, you may be drawn to areas such as writing, journalism, broadcasting, teaching, public relations, counseling, politics, or advertising— but the key factor is that you need to be mentally stimulated and challenged. You're also capable of doing more than one thing at a time, and will appreciate career opportunities that allow you to develop diversified skills. The idea of changing career options is probably agreeable to you. The energy of Mercury has a powerful influence on your vocation, strengthening the need to make contact and build bridges as part of your life work.

Cancer on the MC: The influence of Cancer on your Midheaven indicates a need to create security as a primary feature of your life path. You may feel torn between creating a home and family, and pursuing a career because you probably have some strong ideas about wanting to make a difference in the world. It might seem more reasonable to focus more on one for a while, and then pursue the other, instead of experiencing the inner conflict of trying to do everything at once. You are likely to enjoy many of the traditionally considered "domestic" activities, like cooking or sewing, and can be an exceptional homemaker. Even working outside the home, you may find yourself dealing with home-related industries. Your interest in preserving what has gone before may lead you to spend time studying and endeavoring to preserve history through restoration, antiques, or collecting. You have a good sensibility toward social issues, and may be drawn to politics, community development, and businesses that appeal to women and families. Your Moon's energy also has a powerful impact on the choices you make and the path you take toward creating a fulfilling life, and strengthens the importance of choosing a career that feels good instead of just taking a job because you have to work.

Leo on the MC: With Leo influencing your Midheaven, you may enjoy achieving some recognition through your career endeavors, even though you may safeguard your private life. If you choose not to follow a career, you are still likely to desire public attention, and can use your charisma to effect changes in your community. Your life path is focused on connecting to a sense of Divine Presence, and you have the capability to project a power that originates in the heart of divine love. You'll be happiest in careers that allow you to bring focus, strength of character, and a sense of direction. You may enjoy working in the performing arts, although you can also be an effective producer and director. In business, you're a natural leader, and can act as a force to centralize the focus of others. The energy of your Sun plays an important role in the manner in which you perform on your path toward personal fulfillment. You need to allow your brilliance to shine.

Virgo on the MC: The influence of Virgo on your Midheaven stimulates a desire to achieve a sense of perfection by following the path toward your life purpose. Teaching and guiding your children can be an exceptional experience for you, and you may also feel comfortable in supportive roles in business. If you strive to achieve recognition on your own, you may be most successful in the fields of education, communication, the healing arts, or service industries. You may be very industrious and enjoy opportunities to produce something through your efforts. You're quite adept at dealing with the practical concerns of life, and your common sense about your career choices can help assure your success. The energy of Mercury also has a powerful influence on your life path, and adds to your need to utilize your analytical abilities in your work.

Libra on the MC: Libra's influence at your Midheaven adds a sense of social grace to the manner in which you pursue your ambitions. Your sense of fairness may drive you toward particular aims in pursuit of your right livelihood, and you may be adept in situations that require objectivity and fair-mindedness. A career path that allows you to employ your sense of refinement and good taste will be satisfying. Your people skills can open the doors to careers that involve public or diplomatic relations and consulting, and you may have an interest in law or politics. The energy of Venus plays an important role in satisfying your needs for personal fulfillment. It is crucial that you find a vocation that supports your values and allows you to develop your artistry. The way you utilize Venusian energy has a lot to do with your ability to achieve personal fulfillment.

Scorpio on the MC: With Scorpio on your Midheaven, you are fascinated by a life path that allows you to experience transformation, and that supports change and rejuvenation. In your career, you may experience fulfillment in the healing arts, but you can also be a catalyst for change in business endeavors. Whether you're restoring furniture, houses, appliances, businesses, governments, or people—you may gain great satisfaction delving into problems and discovering what lies at the core. You may also prosper from a livelihood that involves mystery, intrigue, investigation, or research. The energy of Pluto plays an important role in your ability to achieve personal fulfillment and recognition, and you may have to deal with power struggles more than once during the pursuit of your aims. Even when power plays arise that you have not created, you always have a choice about your responses.

Sagittarius on the MC: The influence of Sagittarius at your Midheaven stimulates a need to pursue a life based on high ideals. Your philosophical attitudes shape your life path and the quest for Truth and Wisdom may be the keys to finding your right livelihood. You may find great satisfaction working in academia, religion, publishing, the law, or politics, and even if your job does not fall into these areas, you may always be studying something, and definitely have your opinions! You may enjoy acting as an agent or promoting the talents of others. The energy of Jupiter is associated with your Midheaven, adding a need to follow a career path that is in harmony with your sense of ethics. For you, right livelihood is more than a phrase, it's a way of approaching your life so that everything leads to true prosperity.

Capricorn on the MC: You may have very strong personal ambitions with Capricorn on your Midheaven. Your determination can be one of your greatest assets on your path to success. If you are not pursuing a career path, you still have ambitions, and these may be in the form of family position and influence, or through the roles you take in your community. You're not a woman who is waiting for life to pass you by: you like having a few challenges and prefer to have a focus and life direction. Your life path may seem to be filled with struggle or conflict, although you may be responsible for creating some of those struggles. You're actually proving yourself, and life is your proving ground! In career endeavors, you'll be most comfortable with positions that garner respect, and may aim for professional success instead of just working for a living. In the field of education, you may be either teacher or administrator, and in business, you're quite the executive. You prefer to be in charge, and if you're working in business, government, or industry, will probably aim for the top, or for those positions that allow you to be in control. Responsibility and control are key influences in your ability to achieve a true sense of fulfillment. The manner in which you do this is determined by the way you use the energy of Saturn, which is tied to your Midheaven.

Aquarius on the MC: With Aquarius at your Midheaven, your interest in areas that are off the beaten track may be marked, but you may also find science fascinating. You need to be recognized for something unique that sets you aside from everybody else, and you require freedom to get there. For a career to satisfy you, it will have to provide a mental challenge, and it would be even better if you could utilize technological innovations in the process. Your life path may be most fulfilling when you feel that you're on the leading edge, and when you're experiencing a real sense of uplifted awareness. The energy of Uranus influences your Midheaven, adding a need to employ your intuitive insights to your career endeavors. When you're working independently, you're inspired to put forth your best efforts. You may also be somewhat revolutionary in your approach to your work.

Pisces on the MC: With Pisces at your Midheaven, your aim for a fulfilling life path may be spiritually focused and needs to capture your imagination if you are to reach a sense of wholeness. Your dreams can be your beacon to happiness, but uncovering the difference between dream and illusion can be difficult. For this reason, grounding yourself by establishing a sound connection between mind, spirit, and body will help you clarify the dreams you need to pursue. You may feel a deep need to do something with your life that will ease suffering or provide escape from the painful realities of life. A career in the healing arts, developing your talents in performing arts, or otherwise strengthening your artistic expression can provide outlets for an uplifting life. You may be a gifted beautician, designer, decorator, photographer, or counselor! You may also feel that you want to work in one area, but that your ministry to the world is accomplished through other means. Neptune's energy plays an influential part in developing your path toward self-fulfillment.

What's Ruling Your MC?

In the above paragraphs describing the sign on the Midheaven, a planetary energy was noted. This energy corresponds to the sign through rulership and will play a significant role in the choices you make concerning your life path. Look for that planet in your chart, and find its sign. This gives you even more information about your vocation!

The Sun as Ruler of the MC

The Sun rules the MC and is in Aries: With your Sun in Aries, you'll enjoy forging a life path that challenges your sense of personal strength and courage. Your ability to blaze your way to the top in any situation is quite noticeable, although you can be a little abrasive if your eye is simply on the prize and you fail to pay attention to others around you. When a situation calls for leadership, you're the natural choice.

The Sun rules the MC and is in Taurus: With your Sun in Taurus, you may take a deliberate approach to achieving personal fulfillment through your career. You function best when there is continuity, and may be quite conservative in your attitudes about business. You'll appreciate the opportunity to work in fields that support the best use of the earth's resources.

The Sun rules the MC and is in Gemini: The influence of your Gemini Sun adds a need to pursue a life path that provides ample input! Your mental agility can stimulate your desire to write, work in communication fields like broadcasting or journalism, teach, or pursue a career that utilizes or develops technology. You're also well-suited for any endeavor that involves human relations—from secretarial work to psychological counseling to politics.

The Sun rules the MC and is in Cancer: With your Sun in Cancer, you are drawn to work that provides support and understanding, and you may have excellent

| THE SIGNS AND THEIR RULERS ||
Sign	Planetary Ruler
Aries ♈	Mars ♂
Taurus ♉	Venus ♀
Gemini ♊	Mercury ☿
Cancer ♋	Moon ☽
Leo ♌	Sun ☉
Virgo ♍	Mercury ☿
Libra ♎	Venus ♀
Scorpio ♏	Pluto ♇
Sagittarius ♐	Jupiter ♃
Capricorn ♑	Saturn ♄
Aquarius ♒	Uranus ♅
Pisces ♓	Neptune ♆

Table 6

opportunities in fields that require a good understanding of the collective. In sales, you excel because you create comfort with your clients. In teaching, you rise to the top because you provide nurturing encouragement to your students. In politics, you are a magnet for those who are concerned about home and family.

The Sun rules the MC and is in Leo: With both your Sun and Midheaven in Leo, you will not be satisfied until you've achieved the recognition and respect you feel you deserve. Part of your life path may involve the strong influence you have on your family, and you may create a legacy that they are proud to honor. In your career endeavors, you function best in positions of power and leadership, although you are quite capable of allowing others to take their turn in the spotlight. You may enjoy a career in performing arts, education, politics, or business.

The Sun rules the MC and is in Virgo: The influence of your Virgo Sun stimulates a need to follow a path that will allow you to utilize your analytical abilities and powers of discernment. Raising a family may be one of your greatest joys, and you can be a supportive and understanding mother. In your choice of career, you may be an exceptional educator, and will enjoy a career that allows you to continue learning. You may also choose designing, health care, writing, or editing, or prefer to work in supportive roles in business. If you have your own business, you will enjoy catering to those with discriminating taste, and may promote quality material and workmanship.

The Sun rules the MC and is in Libra: With your Libra Sun influencing your Midheaven, your need for harmony and justice prevails in your choice of career. If you do not work outside the home, you'll still be active in the social activities of your community since once your good taste and artistic sensibilities are discovered, no one will leave you alone! Career endeavors that allow you to employ your adept abilities in dealing with others are good choices—whether in the world of business, politics, or personal service. You have to work on dealing with competitive situations, although when push comes to shove, you can hold your own if your reputation is at stake. You add a touch of class to any career you pursue.

The Sun rules the MC and is in Scorpio: Through your Scorpio Sun you may be most driven to pursue a path that relies on your creativity. As a catalyst for change, regardless of the actual career you pursue, you may find that you're always in the midst of situations (or people) that are under construction or renovation. A career in the healing arts may be quite rewarding, and if you're involved in creative artistry of some sort, you may also discover that your work has a transformational effect on others. Business, investigative research, and psychology also offer you a place to let your light shine.

The Sun rules the MC and is in Sagittarius: With your Sun in Sagittarius, you may be drawn to a career that allows you to expand your mind and strengthen your opportunities. Not only is the field of education a good choice, but you may also be a capable saleswoman, writer, or journalist. The travel industry, publishing, advertising, and promotional work are also excellent choices.

The Sun rules the MC and is in Capricorn: The influence of your Sun in Capricorn adds a heightened business sense to your personality, and you may love the idea of cultivating a career path. As a teacher, school administrator, business executive, administrative assistant, merchant, or accountant, you can outdistance the competition. Positions that allow you to be in control will be best, although you can follow orders. You'd just prefer to give them.

The Sun rules the MC and is in Aquarius: With your Sun in Aquarius, you'll enjoy a career path that is uniquely your own. You may be quite comfortable outside the realm of traditional careers, or forging into territory that other women have been denied. Scientific fields can be exciting, as can computer technology, engineering, aerospace, astrology, writing, or humanitarian service. If you're interested in politics, you may fare best as an independent!

The Sun rules the MC and is in Pisces: With your Sun in Pisces, you feel a little uncomfortable if you realize that gaining recognition at work means compromising your privacy. To avoid this conflict, you need to learn to set some boundaries between your public and personal lives. You'll feel best in a career that relies on your creative and imaginative self-expression. Whether you choose something that involves the arts (fine arts, music, dance, theater), the film industry, beauty industry, or public service—your influence can make a difference in the quality of life.

The Moon as Ruler of the MC

The Moon rules the MC and is in Aries: Your Aries Moon drives you toward actualizing your independence and autonomy through developing a career path. You can be effective in leadership roles at home and in your community, although you appreciate team efforts in which everyone works toward a common goal.

The Moon rules the MC and is in Taurus: Your Taurus Moon influences you to make choices that will serve your need to be stable, and if you follow a career path, you will be most comfortable in a situation that appeals to your values. Your sense of structure may be useful in the building or furniture industries, but you also have a keen business sense, and might enjoy retail sales.

The Moon rules the MC and is in Gemini: The influence of your Gemini Moon may prompt you to juggle several things at once in your efforts to fulfill your need for personal actualization. You may feel an urging to share your ideas and convictions, and to build bridges of communication between others. An interest in children's issues and education may also influence your career choices.

The Moon rules the MC and is in Cancer: With your Moon and Midheaven both in Cancer, you may put mothering on the top of your priority list. In the outside world, women's issues take a high priority, and your ability to understand and make a connection with the collective is quite an impressive asset if you're working in the fields of broadcasting, politics, community service, or human relations.

The Moon rules the MC and is in Leo: The need for recognition you feel through your Leo Moon is likely to prompt you to seek a career that allows you to shine. Whether you're running your own business or working for the government or a large corporation, you need opportunities to express your talents and to be acknowledged for them.

The Moon rules the MC and is in Virgo: With your Moon in Virgo, your need for order can be useful in many careers. You may like taking on supportive roles, and can be an asset to any company or situation that requires high-quality effort and good productivity. Your affinity for teaching can also open many doors, in both education and industry, since you can be an excellent trainer.

The Moon rules the MC and is in Libra: The influence of your Libra Moon adds a powerful need to connect to others, and you may be especially adept at situations that call for human relations skills and good taste! Working in cooperative ventures or partnerships can be quite satisfying.

The Moon rules the MC and is in Scorpio: The influence of your Scorpio Moon may encourage you to take on roles that keep you out of the spotlight. A career that allows you to support and provide healing comfort can be especially rewarding.

The Moon rules the MC and is in Sagittarius: The influence of your Moon in Sagittarius is likely to stimulate your desire to get out into the world. You may enjoy a career as a teacher, journalist, or minister; but you may also find that you are adept at diplomatic relations.

The Moon rules the MC and is in Capricorn: The influence of your Capricorn Moon may stimulate a greater desire to create a career, but you may also feel that your first obligation is to your family. If you have your own business, it's likely to have a family atmosphere, although you need to watch a tendency to take on most of the responsibility. You might prefer to work from your home, but if you make this choice, keep your office doors closed when you're not "open."

The Moon rules the MC and is in Aquarius: With your Moon in Aquarius, you may feel that self-actualization through your career is highly important. Your first requirement will be work that gives you room to move and to do things in your own way. Following a rigid pattern will not feel harmonious, although you can sometimes get stuck in a rut.

The Moon rules the MC and is in Pisces: The influence of your Pisces Moon stimulates you to withdraw from the public eye, or to choose a career that affords you some anonymity. You'll enjoy exploring a life path filled with creative, imaginative options, and which is spiritually inspiring. You are drawn to the healing arts or to situations that allow you to use your psychic sensibilities.

Mercury as Ruler of the MC

Mercury rules the MC and is in Aries: With Mercury in Aries, your enthusiasm for ideas is strong, and your quick wit and sharp mind can be valuable assets. You may be a first class public speaker, saleswoman, or writer, with an endless source of exciting concepts. Concentration, however, is not your strong suit, so work that requires repetitive thinking, like accounting, might be frustrating.

Mercury rules the MC and is in Taurus: With Mercury in Taurus, you might feel better applying your mental energy to business, the arts, or environmental issues. You need a career that allows you to grow through your experience, and you will do very well in situations that provide you with a mentor.

Mercury rules the MC and is in Gemini: With Mercury in Gemini, your need for diversity in your career is amplified. Your restless mentality functions beautifully in situations that require you to juggle several things at once, but you can become overwhelmed if you have too many irons in the fire. Your communication and teaching abilities are strengthened, and careers in the transportation, communication, or computer industry are right up your alley.

Mercury rules the MC and is in Cancer: With Mercury in Cancer, you may prefer a career path that gives you a chance to deal with emotional issues. Counseling and teaching can be excellent outlets for your sympathetic mind; but you can also be effective in politics, businesses that cater to women, and the food industry.

Mercury rules the MC and is in Leo: With Mercury in Leo, you can be an especially effective communicator, and may have excellent success using your communicative abilities. Your voice may be one of your trademarks, and your dramatic manner of expressing your ideas may lead you to a career in the performing arts. In the business world, you can be a top-notch CEO.

Mercury rules the MC and is in Virgo: With Mercury in Virgo, your attention to details can be advantageous to your career development. Teaching and writing may be your top choices, but you may also have a head for medicine. Your skills in design can also open doors for you in many arenas.

Mercury rules the MC and is in Libra: With Mercury in Libra, your ability to make connections with others is strengthened, and a life path that allows you to build bridges between people can be fulfilling. Your diplomatic abilities stimulate your desire to work in public relations, counseling, or business. You may also be a gifted writer, and have an easy understanding of law and human relations.

Mercury rules the MC and is in Scorpio: Your penetrating awareness with Mercury in Scorpio can be applied to many areas of career choice, but you may enjoy a career path that allows you to probe into mysteries. Medicine, research, and psychology can be good choices, and if you write, you may lean toward material that is mysterious, metaphysical, and suspenseful.

Mercury rules the MC and is in Sagittarius: With Mercury in Sagittarius, your enthusiastic and confident manner of communicating can open many doors along your life path. You can become an inspiring teacher, but may also enjoy a career in the travel industry, sales, journalism, or broadcasting. You need a career that allows you to cultivate your perceptive abilities.

Mercury rules the MC and is in Capricorn: With Mercury in Capricorn, your powers of concentration work to your benefit in your career. In the world of business, your attention to detail and solid planning make a difference. You may love teaching and guiding others, and can be quite at home in the field of education and educational planning.

Mercury rules the MC and is in Aquarius: Your mental resourcefulness is quite beneficial in developing your career with Mercury in Aquarius. Public speaking, writing, astrology, meteorology, computer science, engineering, the aerospace industry, human relations, and higher education are excellent options.

Mercury rules the MC and is in Pisces: With Mercury in Pisces, you need a life path that allows you to use your poetic and mystical way of thinking. You'll enjoy a career path that strengthens the development of your creativity, and you may have a special affinity for the music or film industries. You may also enjoy work in the healing arts or the computer industry.

Venus as Ruler of the MC

Venus rules the MC and is in Aries: With Venus in Aries, your tastes in career may lend themselves beautifully to retail sales, fashion design, marketing, or merchandising. You are excellent in situations that cater to individual taste.

Venus rules the MC and is in Taurus: With Venus in Taurus, your appreciation for natural beauty may lead you to work in the landscaping or floral industry, forestry, or environmental management. If you're a connoisseur of the arts or music, or a performer, you may also have success in these endeavors.

Venus rules the MC and is in Gemini: With Venus in Gemini, your cosmopolitan air and love of ideas may prompt you to pursue a career in the communication industry, to work in or own a bookstore or publishing house, to teach, or write, or work in the broadcasting industry. You're a woman of many interests and talents, and your versatility can open many doors.

Venus rules the MC and is in Cancer: With Venus in Cancer, your love of comfort influences your career choices. You may have an excellent ability to work with other women, and may experience success in endeavors that cater to women's needs and domestic issues. You may also do quite well in politics, real estate, the food industry, social service, or counseling.

Venus rules the MC and is in Leo: With Venus in Leo, your flair for the dramatic influences your career choices and your success. You need to be appreciated, and can perform well in careers that allow you to be in the spotlight (at least sometimes!), but you can also be an exceptional director, manager, or creative consultant.

Venus rules the MC and is in Virgo: With Venus in Virgo, your attention to detail needs to be employed in your career, too. You have an excellent sense of quality, and may enjoy a career in design, planning, teaching, medicine, or nursing.

Venus rules the MC and is in Libra: With Venus in Libra, your refined tastes add a boost to your career, and you can be quite successful in fields that require your eye for quality. The arts offer a wide range of options, but you may also enjoy public or diplomatic relations, retail sales, or interior design.

Venus rules the MC and is in Scorpio: With Venus in Scorpio, you may be an adept and expressive artist, writer, or musician, or may have a deep appreciation for these areas, which can lead you to a career promoting or preserving them. You may also be drawn to the healing professions.

Venus rules the MC and is in Sagittarius: With Venus in Sagittarius, your love of the wide-open spaces, adventure, and freedom can prompt you to pursue a career in education, the travel industry, diplomatic relations, or sales. You'll need room to move if you're going to succeed.

Venus rules the MC and is in Capricorn: With Venus in Capricorn, your good business sense is strengthened, and you can be quite successful in fields that involve money and finance. Teaching and training others can be satisfying.

Venus rules the MC and is in Aquarius: With Venus in Aquarius, your love of the unusual needs to be expressed through your career. You may also enjoy working in innovative fields that allow you to show your ingenuity, and you may succeed in endeavors that involve others. Projects or areas that target humanitarian issues can be a positive outlet.

Venus rules the MC and is in Pisces: With Venus in Pisces, you may have excellent success in careers that allow you to use your creative imagination and sense of artistry. You may also be drawn into healing and helping professions.

Mars as Ruler of the MC

Mars rules the MC and is in Aries: Since you have Mars and your Midheaven both in Aries, you may have your eye on the prize, but you can fail to notice the effect your actions and choices have on others around you. By opening your awareness just a little, you'll be more likely to include the needs and feelings of others, and may even generate their support for your efforts. You may enjoy a job that requires physical activity, and you can be excellent in sales.

Mars rules the MC and is in Taurus: Since your Mars is in Taurus, you may not be as gung-ho about getting to the top, but you can plot a sure and certain path toward getting there. Sometimes you may need a little motivation to get you moving, and setting goals that mean something will help. You'll perform best in a career that allows you to exercise your good business sense and eye for quality.

Mars rules the MC and is in Gemini: Since you have Mars in Gemini, you need to be careful about your tendency to scatter your energy on the job. Getting too many things going at once can leave you feeling that you'll never accomplish anything. You can be a very assertive communicator in your career. You'll fare nicely in sales positions and may do well in public relations.

Mars rules the MC and is in Cancer: Since you have Mars in Cancer, you may take a more indirect approach to your targeted success. You may also be quite good at maneuvering through tight situations. Political action, public relations, counseling, and work that targets the home front (including real estate) can be good outlets.

Mars rules the MC and is in Leo: With Mars in Leo, you not only have a drive to achieve, but your need to be recognized for your efforts increases. You're not likely to allow the idea that you're a woman to be the least bit intimidating. You're well suited for positions of leadership, and can be an exceptional executive, director, coach, or creative consultant.

Mars rules the MC and is in Virgo: With Mars in Virgo, you can be precise in targeting your aims. When you go into a career situation with a game plan, there's little that can stop you from putting that plan into motion. You can be very organized, and may enjoy work in the medical fields, teaching, writing, drafting, or in fields that require excellent manual dexterity.

Mars rules the MC and is in Libra: With Mars in Libra, you try to appear well-mannered even when you feel like biting off the head of the person who offended you or blocked your opportunities to get ahead. You can be quite successful, but only if you learn to stand up for yourself. There's no need to sink to the level of those you find distasteful. You'll enjoy working in diplomatic relations, legal fields, retail outlets, interior design, museums or galleries, or fields that support the arts.

Mars rules the MC and is in Scorpio: Your Scorpio Mars adds an amazing ability to accomplish your need for recognition by taking charge. You need situations in your work that allow you to probe the depths, and will fare better when given ample room to work at your own pace. You perform well in medical fields, research, counseling, renovation, or restoration, and can be an excellent metaphysician.

Mars rules the MC and is in Sagittarius: With Mars in Sagittarius, you may not like having to wait around for things to get better, and you have little patience for a career situation that offers little compensation for your efforts. Your enthusiastic energy makes you very well suited to work in politics, sales, teaching, coaching, and motivational endeavors.

Mars rules the MC and is in Capricorn: With Mars in Capricorn, you can be determined about getting to the top in your career, and you need to target a career situation that will allow you to reach a position of excellence and self-control. You may be an exceptional businesswoman, and can also benefit from directing your efforts toward education, politics, banking, conservation, or city planning.

Mars rules the MC and is in Aquarius: With Mars in Aquarius, you will prefer to follow a career path that allows plenty of room for you to do things your way. You may be most excited about a career that targets innovation and ingenuity, and which you find mentally challenging.

Mars rules the MC and is in Pisces: With Mars in Pisces, you may be less openly assertive in your career drive, and although you may not appear ambitious, when you have your hopes set on something, you have an exceptional ability to get there. Your resilience can be helpful, but you have to be very careful about letting other people take advantage of you. Work that allows you to reach out and make a difference in the world will be most satisfying.

Jupiter as Ruler of the MC

Jupiter rules the MC and is in Aries: With Jupiter in Aries, your optimism and courage in regard to your career are enhanced. A brilliant enthusiasm gives you an edge and can open the doors to many opportunities. You may be inspired to work in fields related to recreation or sports, and can be a real asset in sales and fund-raising.

Jupiter rules the MC and is in Taurus: With Jupiter in Taurus, you know how to make your resources stretch, and you may have a knack for finding ways to use materials. This not only stretches your budget further, but may put you in the running for Queen of Recycling! Your conservatism idealism may lead you to follow a career that has practical value.

Jupiter rules the MC and is in Gemini: With Jupiter in Gemini, your interest in education is enhanced, and you may feel especially motivated to work in fields that involve youth. You may also be interested in travel, communication, and technological fields.

Jupiter rules the MC and is in Cancer: With Jupiter in Cancer, your ability to work with the public is strengthened, and others may be drawn to your caring attitude. You may find that the real estate industry offers several options, but you can also be adept at fields that appeal to the collective, like advertising.

Jupiter rules the MC and is in Leo: With Jupiter in Leo, your need to impress others plays a part in your career choices, and it's important that you feel proud of your life path. This influence also adds to your executive abilities, as long as you know how to temper your occasional bouts of rash judgment.

Jupiter rules the MC and is in Virgo: With Jupiter in Virgo, you are drawn to fields that require investigation and an eye for detail, but you must avoid becoming overly critical if your expectations are not met. Taking a supportive role in your career may afford great opportunity, but you may have to navigate beyond your occasional feelings of unworthiness if you are to experience a true sense of prosperity.

Jupiter rules the MC and is in Libra: With Jupiter in Libra, you may be especially successful in the legal profession, but can also have great influence as an artist or supporting the arts. Your outgoing nature can be an asset in almost any profession, and will definitely strengthen your rise up the ladder in business or industry.

Jupiter rules the MC and is in Scorpio: With Jupiter in Scorpio, you enjoy working in investigative fields, like medicine, police work, chemistry, or engineering. You may also be especially fascinated by metaphysics, and can develop your skills in this area either in a professional sense or as an adjunct to your life path in general.

Jupiter rules the MC and is in Sagittarius: Since you have Jupiter and your Midheaven both in Sagittarius, your ability to enjoy a truly satisfying experience through your career pursuits is strengthened. You see that your life path is more focused around experiencing the true adventure and exploration of possibilities, and you can enjoy exceptional success when you're following your intuitive voice. This position may add to your desire to travel, learn, enjoy nature, and take chances!

Jupiter rules the MC and is in Capricorn: Since you have Jupiter in Capricorn, you will benefit most from a life path that is built around well-defined goals. In order to experience true abundance and a sense of prosperity through your career endeavors, you need to make the best use of all your resources and avoid a tendency to hold back out of fear. This influence may stimulate your desire to work in education or business.

Jupiter rules the MC and is in Aquarius: With Jupiter in Aquarius, you may become an exceptional human relations expert, and can excel in fields that require good judgment assessing and directing others. As a teacher, you look for the genius in every student, and may have a very original approach to your methods. You may also be interested in educational, industrial, and political reform and innovation.

Jupiter rules the MC and is in Pisces: Your Jupiter in Pisces stimulates a need to reach out to others through your career. Work that benefits only you as an individual may seem hollow and useless. Your ability to work with groups may be excellent, and work behind the scenes can be rather fulfilling.

Saturn as Ruler of the MC

Saturn rules the MC and is in Aries: With Saturn in Aries, you may be uncomfortable dealing with authority, and may need to learn how to be assertive. You may prefer a career path that requires mental and physical activity, and where you can utilize your strong reasoning capacities.

Saturn rules the MC and is in Taurus: You may have a desire to run or own your own business with Saturn in Taurus, since being in charge of resources is right up your alley. It's easy to get caught in the trap of making money as the reason for working, when you really need to experience an enhanced sense of personal worth through your career endeavors. Your fine sense of structure and design may lend itself well in the building and home furnishings industries. You're also well-suited to run the business end of a professional practice or artistic venture, and may be the perfect executive director for your community orchestra or arts programs.

Saturn rules the MC and is in Gemini: With Saturn in Gemini, you may become an exceptional teacher, since your mental discipline and ability to build a bridge to understanding can be easily developed. You may also be drawn to the communication industries, including (but not limited to) writing, publishing, broadcasting, or transportation. Your mental attitudes have a lot to do with your sense of personal fulfillment.

Saturn rules the MC and is in Cancer: With Saturn in Cancer, you may direct your career or professional efforts into arenas that influence home and family life. You may have a cunning business sense, but need to avoid a tendency to become too emotionally involved in your business ventures. Your interest in things that have stood the test of time may lead to work with antiques, restoration, or collectibles.

Saturn rules the MC and is in Leo: With Saturn in Leo, you can be strong-willed in your efforts to fulfill your personal aims. You'll perform well in a career that requires intellectual vitality, and you can become an exceptional teacher once you learn to listen to the needs of your students! You may also enjoy the entertainment business, and have the temperament for running your own business establishment.

Saturn rules the MC and is in Virgo: With Saturn in Virgo, you can become a workaholic, since you may find it difficult to rest until the job is done to your high standards. It's very important that you choose a life path that leads to a sense of personal growth and allows you to continue to learn. For this reason, you may enjoy education, working in the health care professions, or training others.

Saturn rules the MC and is in Libra: With Saturn in Libra, you feel responsible for others, and see your career path as an opportunity to do something for someone other than yourself. Cooperative ventures can be rewarding, especially if each person involved is taking responsibility for themselves and utilizing their talents effectively. You may target a career that allows you to act as an intermediary or consultant.

Saturn rules the MC and is in Scorpio: Your Saturn in Scorpio shows a need for life work that brings change and healing into your life. You may be especially suited to work in the insurance, banking, or financial industries, but can have an interest in healing and metaphysics, too. You have very strong feelings about people and situations, and may find it difficult to work with or around anyone for whom you have negative feelings.

Saturn rules the MC and is in Sagittarius: With Saturn in Sagittarius, you have strong academic or spiritual goals and can be successful targeting a profession that allows you to fulfill these aims. You may have some trouble maintaining your focus, and if you take on more responsibilities than you can handle, you will undermine your own success. Dealing with a fear of success may be one of your great challenges!

Saturn rules the MC and is in Capricorn: Since Saturn and your Midheaven are both in Capricorn, you may feel strongly compelled to pursue a professional career. You can perform in positions of responsibility and authority with great success, although you may need to lighten up a little. Taking your work too seriously can take all the fun out of reaching your goals! You may be the quintessential teacher, and can gain exceptional satisfaction when one of your brood rises to the top. You can also work quite effectively in any hierarchy (preferably at the top).

Saturn rules the MC and is in Aquarius: With Saturn in Aquarius, you may have lofty goals for your career. You need a life path that integrates old and new—a place to bring innovation and change into existing circumstances. You may choose a career that is out of the ordinary, and may prefer working alone, although you can probably deal with hierarchies if you must. Scientific fields, industry, invention, writing, broadcasting, meteorology—all may be fulfilling. You may also "invent" your job. In fact, it's probably better if you do!

Saturn rules the MC and is in Pisces: With Saturn in Pisces, you may lack the motivation necessary to follow through with your aims; but if you have a target that will accomplish that sense of right-livelihood and make a difference in your quality of life, you can be successful. Work within an institutional setting, in healing professions, a nonprofit organization, or charitable endeavor may be appealing. You may also become successful in more artistic fields, like dance, movies, art, or music.

Uranus as Ruler of the MC

Uranus rules the MC and is in Aries: With Uranus in Aries, you have a strong desire to forge into new territory through your career, and you may be willing to take risks in your career path. You may also be influential in opening doors through your own efforts, which allows others to follow in your footsteps.

Uranus rules the MC and is in Taurus: With Uranus in Taurus, you may use your innovative ideas in a more practical circumstance. You're great at figuring out unique ways to make the best of the resources at hand to get the job done.

Uranus rules the MC and is in Gemini: With Uranus in Gemini, the mental aspect of your career path is extremely enhanced. You may also find greater opportunity working in the communicative end of technology, and you may enjoy work that allows you to use unusual methods of communicating.

Uranus rules the MC and is in Cancer: Through the influence of Uranus in Cancer you are adept at working in fields that serve women and families. Your influence in women's issues may be one of your greatest accomplishments, and whether or not you are in the forefront of political actions, you can forge new pathways.

Uranus rules the MC and is in Leo: Uranus in Leo adds a need to gain recognition for your unique abilities in your career. You need to shine in your work, and may do well in broadcasting, the entertainment industry, teaching, and positions of leadership. You just won't do it the same way you learned about in school.

Uranus rules the MC and is in Virgo: The influence of Uranus in Virgo adds an awareness of the need for improvement, which you are likely to direct toward your career. You may be the perfect woman to make innovative changes that improve efficiency, and you have an excellent ability to employ technology to aid and enhance your opportunities. You may be interested in alternative methods for solving problems, especially in the fields of health and education.

Uranus rules the MC and is in Libra: With Uranus in Libra, you may prefer to make changes that will improve the conditions in your work environment. You may also be insightful about human relations, and can benefit from working in fields that require innovative communication or public relations techniques, or you may be an innovative attorney or judge.

Uranus rules the MC and is in Scorpio: With Uranus in Scorpio, you may not be totally open about expressing your innovative ideas, although you do have them. You can be an excellent researcher or investigator since you can blend your intuitive and rational processes in your learning and investigation.

Uranus rules the MC and is in Sagittarius: With Uranus in Sagittarius, you're a trail blazer. You may make headway in the fields of education, politics, publishing, the law, and religion. You also prefer to work independently and are likely to resent being too heavily supervised.

Uranus rules the MC and is in Capricorn: With Uranus in Capricorn, you'll apply your ingenuity in ways that have a practical outcome. Your approach to business is best suited to circumstances that need innovation in order to grow.

Uranus rules the MC and is in Aquarius: With Uranus and your Midheaven both in Aquarius, you can be a leader and innovator in scientific and technical fields. You may also be involved in developing leading-edge changes in education, business, government, or industry. It's important that you have ample room to exercise your ingenuity in your profession.

Uranus rules the MC and is in Pisces: With Uranus in Pisces, you may prefer to target humanitarian projects and are well-suited for independent work in nonprofit companies and organizations. Your ideal of true humanitarian endeavors may sometimes run into blocks in the "real world," but if you feel strongly about something, you're still likely to give it a try.

Neptune as Ruler of the MC

Neptune rules the MC and is in Cancer: With Neptune in Cancer, you have probably retired from your "formal" work, but may still feel a need to reach out to the world in some way. Providing a true sense of nurturing and support to those around you can enhance the lives of others while strengthening your sense of self-worth. You may need to learn that it is not necessary to sacrifice your own needs all of the time, even though it is difficult to draw the line when you care.

Neptune rules the MC and is in Leo: With Neptune in Leo, you have reached a stage in your life that allows you to retire from caring for others and to focus more on fulfilling some of your personal dreams. It is through love that you have always experienced the greatest satisfaction, and by focusing on the heart of divine love, which guides and protects you, you are inspired to reach new horizons in your sense of fulfillment and happiness. Your energy and ideas can inspire others, and you may become the link between what has gone before and what is yet to come.

Neptune rules the MC and is in Virgo: With Neptune in Virgo, you may be thinking that you should be planning retirement instead of reflecting about your vocation, but it is unlikely that you will ever fully retire. You love the feeling of accomplishing and producing something, and when you do cease to work in a more formal sense, you'll probably have so many projects to complete that your days will still be full! You can change your life by creating a different mental attitude, and by turning your attention to detail toward visualizing a renewed life, you can see profound changes. You may also have a special sensibility to the physical body, and if you work in the healing arts, you may be especially effective in helping others transcend and heal.

Neptune rules the MC and is in Libra: With Neptune in Libra, you may be driven by your desire to make the world a more beautiful and peaceful place through your vocation. Career choices that utilize the arts, music, media, photography, psychology, or the law may be the easiest routes to satisfy your yearnings. However, as long as you're working in situations that allow you to fulfill your ideals in harmony with others, you will feel satisfied.

Neptune rules the MC and is in Scorpio: With Neptune in Scorpio, you may feel especially drawn to life work that brings true healing and transformational change. The outlets for your need to effect changes may span a wide range of possibilities, but the effect is universal. From medicine to social work to restoring property or discovering the healing powers of herbs—you are a medicine woman in the strongest sense of the term. Utilizing your psychic and intuitive sensibilities will also be necessary and can be quite natural.

Neptune rules the MC and is in Sagittarius: With Neptune in Sagittarius, your intuitive sensibilities are always working, and by listening to your inner voice, you've probably discovered your life path already. Your sense of universal justice may prompt you to pursue a career in law, teaching, religion, or related fields.

Regardless of your vocational choices, your goal is to send a message to the world through your actions and deeds.

Neptune rules the MC and is in Capricorn: With Neptune in Capricorn, you are just now entering the search for your calling, and may quickly discover that surrendering to your inner voice is the best way to achieve clarity about your career path. Your efforts in your career may involve building a new foundation that will sustain and inspire future generations, and you can accomplish this through governmental, business, and educational endeavors. But above all this, spiritual responsibility is necessary if you are to be successful.

Pluto as Ruler of the MC

Pluto rules the MC and is in Gemini: With Pluto in Gemini, your interests in change have been primarily focused on creating opportunities to further education, and on the development of the mind. You may try to understand the nature of power, but have discovered that the true power in your own life arises from the way you think. Your life path is centered around a need to bring mind, spirit, and body into harmony with the needs of your soul, and the work you have done is likely to reflect that.

Pluto rules the MC and is in Cancer: The influence of Pluto in Cancer adds a powerful drive to achieve change that will have a transformational effect on your sense of security. Whether you're involved in career pursuits or family affairs, you may be the one others look to for solving problems or getting to the heart of the issues. In career endeavors, you can be instrumental in areas that influence women and families, and you may also have an excellent grasp of psychological dynamics.

Pluto rules the MC and is in Leo: With Pluto in Leo, you are not likely to take a back seat to anyone in career matters, and you can be influential in eliminating barriers that have prevented women from achieving success in the workplace. In your family, your opinions and actions have probably created a bit of a stir, and you may feel somewhat removed from many of the old influences that shaped your life as a child. Your efforts to reform the nature of your personal relationships may extend into the workplace, where you may still meet with power struggles from time to time.

Pluto rules the MC and is in Virgo: With Pluto in Virgo, your drive to achieve a sense of self-fulfillment may not have surfaced until after age thirty. Prior to that time, you may have been facing some self-destructive tendencies that have their roots in grappling with relationship issues or uncovering your true values. Your influence in the realms of education, psychology research, medicine, politics, and community can be quite marked.

Pluto rules the MC and is in Libra: With Pluto in Libra, your drive to achieve a sense of equality and fairness in your career may be prominent. Your need to break down the barriers between men and women plays a part in your career success. You may also have a strong drive to reform the legal and educational systems, and your efforts in these areas can be effective.

Pluto rules the MC and is in Scorpio: With both your Midheaven and Pluto in Scorpio, you may feel a powerful calling to a career that is focused on bringing about deep-level changes in the world around you. Whether you choose the healing arts (including psychology and alternative medicine), business, the computer industry, or science—your influence can be one of true restoration and healing.

The Importance of the 6th House in Work and Career

The process of work itself is usually seen through the 6th House in your chart. Through this facet of yourself, you express your approach and attitudes about working. Your ability to cooperate with others is also indicated here. This house is related to your physical health, and it's no surprise that you might hear the complaint (or feel it yourself), "I'm sick of my job," when things aren't going well at work. Instead of feeling thrown off balance by the tasks required to get through life, there are ways to use this part of your time and energy to strengthen your life and get what you want from it!

The Sign on 6th House and Your Job

Aries on the 6th: With Aries on your 6th House, you function much better in work situations that allow you to work on your own without a great deal of supervision or interference. You may enjoy a job that is somewhat physically active, although you may just save your physical energy for the office softball team or weekend marathon. You have strong levels of mental creativity, and can benefit from a job that presents intellectual challenge and interest. It's easy to drive or push yourself in your work, so try to remember that before you reach exhaustion! The energy of Mars has a strong impact on your approach to work, and can indicate a tendency to become involved in disputes in the workplace. If you are in a position of authority, it is important to become aware of the way you treat others. You can be an exceptional leader, but may be somewhat harsh or abrasive when you're impatient.

Taurus on the 6th: You can be a tireless worker with Taurus on your 6th House, although you love the feeling of time off! It's important that you gain pleasure from your job, since the rulership of Venus here shows a strong need for your work to reflect your true values. You work best in situations that allow you to move at your own pace, and you can be somewhat stubborn in your attitudes toward co-workers. If you don't like them, they may not get a second chance with you. You can be a little overbearing and bossy, and need to watch your own reactions when faced with orders from your superiors. Working in endeavors that are creative is most satisfying.

Gemini on the 6th: You enjoy and look forward to work that stimulates your mind with Gemini ruling your 6th House. You have good manual dexterity, and can be adept at working with your hands, writing, and communicating. In fact, your people skills may give you the edge you need to achieve success. You have great versatility and will perform best in jobs that allow you to exercise it. Mercury's influence in this area adds a high capacity for learning, interaction, and diplomacy.

Cancer on the 6th: Your feelings about your work have a direct influence on your performance with Cancer ruling your 6th House. It's crucial that you listen to your intuitive self when choosing a job, and if it does not feel right, it's probably not right for you! When you're hard at work, you'll also find your intuition in high gear, and you can be gifted at blending your intuitive and rational processes to help strengthen your productivity and insight. With the Moon's energy connected to this house, you enjoy working with women or in fields that concern women and families. You may also find that care-taking plays an important role in your choice of jobs.

Leo on the 6th: You put your heart into your work with Leo ruling your 6th House. Because your performance on the job is important to you, you need to focus on jobs that are especially meaningful and where you feel you can make a difference. Your idealism and loyalty show in your connections to those with whom you work, and you are a strong leader, even though your manner may be somewhat reserved. With the energy of your Sun playing a powerful role in this area, you may find that you identify strongly with your job. Finding an occupation in which you have pride will not only feel better, but will assure that you'll perform at your peak capacity.

Virgo on the 6th: Virgo's influence on your 6th House brings your eye for detail into your work. You may enjoy working in technical or mechanical areas, including scientific or medical research, and you can be very helpful to your co-workers as long as they're pulling their own weight. Your work environment needs to be orderly, clean, and well-organized, although you probably have a drawer somewhere that is full of all the miscellaneous stuff you throw into it when you're in a hurry. Work in the health care field, service industries, or education may be rewarding. Mercury's influence in this area adds a need for a job that is interesting, mentally challenging, and that will employ your analytical abilities. Through this energy, you may also be especially adept at working with your hands.

Libra on the 6th: Libra on the cusp of your 6th House indicates that you need to work in an environment that is serene and pleasant. Your productivity can be affected if you work in a hostile environment. However, if conflicts arise, you may be the peacemaker. With Venus ruling this house, you may enjoy working with others, and you can be helpful and supportive, especially toward people you really like. You might enjoy working in a field that allows you to use your sense of fair play, like the law, or you might be successful in the beauty industry, interior design and decorating, or fashion design.

Scorpio on the 6th: Scorpio's impact on your 6th House strengthens your interest in scientific areas and adds an ability to excel at research and investigation. You appreciate a work environment that allows you to operate somewhat independently and provides some privacy. You may not always want to share your insights or information until you're sure that you're satisfied, and you can be quite protective of any projects you're developing. With Pluto's energy influencing this area, you may also be satisfied in fields like psychology or metaphysics, and fascinated by the processes of transformation such as evolution, restoration, ecology, and healing.

Sagittarius on the 6th: Sagittarius on the cusp of your 6th House stimulates a need for diversity and activity in your work. If you work in sales or the travel industry, you might perform best when you can get up and go some of the time. You might not even mind commuting to your job! You prefer to operate independently whenever possible, and will not perform at your peak when you feel penned in. Jupiter's energy influences this area, adding a need for a sense of play and adventure through your work. You'll appreciate working for and with others who are ethical in their business practices.

Capricorn on the 6th: One of the reasons you make such a powerful impression on people is because you usually go into situations prepared. Capricorn's influence on your 6th House indicates that you do not mind hard work when it will get you somewhere. You may demand a great deal from yourself, and if you're in positions of management, can demand a lot from others, too. You may look for ways to take advantage of the talents of others, and may be the mistress of utilizing resources, like technology, to make your job easier. Saturn's rulership of this house adds the energy of responsibility to your work ethic and shows that in order to achieve the success you desire you will have to put forth the necessary discipline. You might work well in hierarchical situations, but will prefer to be near the top of the ladder.

Aquarius on the 6th: You know how you like to do things with Aquarius influencing your 6th House. You may enjoy working in fields that allow you to use the latest technological developments to be the most proficient in your work. Working for yourself may also be high on your priority list, although you can work for others as long as you have some freedom to operate the way you wish. You can be quite innovative in your approach to your job, and may make changes or improvements that are considered to be leading-edge. With the energy of Uranus stimulating this area, you need to remain open to new changes in your work.

Pisces on the 6th: You may feel that your work needs to mean something with Pisces ruling your 6th House. Your efforts in your job may sometimes be a little overboard since you have a tendency to put the demands and needs of others first. This may stem from your need for a peaceful work environment. You may use your creative and imaginative sensibilities on the job, and can enjoy work that brings beauty, serenity, and magic into the world around you. Neptune's energy plays an important role in your approach to your job, and may stimulate an urge to become involved in charitable efforts or to work in fields that involve rescue and help.

Planets in the 6th House

Sun in the 6th: With your Sun in the 6th House, you will grow most productively in situations that give you a chance to do something for others. This may not always be easy, since you really want to work as a means to gain recognition for yourself. Certainly, it's important to work in fields that allow you to utilize your talents and skills, and that will give you a sense of personal satisfaction, but you may not feel fully satisfied with work that is just for personal gain. This is the area of your chart that is centered on service to others, and if you put your vital energies into something that makes a difference for someone else, you'll feel much more in harmony with yourself. From the eastern philosophical point of view, this house represents your dharma—your work in the world. This is the work you do for your soul and spirit to grow. When that's happening, you prosper on every level! You can still shine, and when you're putting your heart into your work, you're likely to glow. Your work environment should be healthy, since you respond strongly to poor environmental conditions. It's also important to remember to stop working some of the time and take time for recreation, exercise, and play in order to maintain your vitality. Reflect on the qualities associated with the Sun in your chart to find the particular areas that will be most natural, and then direct those qualities into a field of service.

Moon in the 6th: The energy of your Moon in the 6th House brings your nurturing abilities into the field of work and service. Those areas traditionally associated with nurturing, like the restaurant or grocery business, can be excellent options. But you may also be drawn to work as a counselor, social worker, nurse, or in fields such as child care, elementary school education, or domestic service. Learning how to keep your emotional boundaries concerning your job is important. If you're too emotionally sensitive to those in your care on the job, and don't know where to draw the line, you can compromise the quality of your work. You might bring your problems home, which is okay if you have a positive way to release them, but if you're projecting your worries, concerns, or difficulties on the job into your personal life, you can create a new set of complications. However, you must always be honest with yourself about your feelings concerning your work—even those everyday chores. Your emotions have a powerful impact on your health, which, in turn, impacts your ability to perform your job to the best of your ability.

Mercury in the 6th: When you're mentally involved in your work, your life seems to run much more smoothly. Mercury's energy in your 6th House indicates a need to work in jobs that require you to reason, communicate, and develop your mind. You'll function best in a job that has some diversity, and you may also enjoy connecting with other people through your work. Whether you're employed as a teacher, in public relations, writing, broadcasting, selling, or settling disputes, your ability to create a viable connection between people and their ideas can be valuable. You may also feel good working with your hands, and may have a very powerful sense of touch.

Venus in the 6th: Through the energy of Venus in your 6th House you can be strongly stimulated to work in areas that require artistic sensibility, and you may be most interested in work in the arts, music, or creative arenas. Whatever your talents, you'll benefit most from a job that allows you to use and further develop them. Your tastes and values play an important role in determining your work choices, and you will be more productive when you know you're fairly compensated for your efforts. You'll be most effective in a work environment that appeals to your sense of beauty. If faced with stale or drab conditions at work, you may be the first to add something tasteful, charming, or interesting to your surroundings. Work in retail sales, the entertainment industry, fashion, interior design, or similar areas can be gratifying, but the key to finding a job that works is whether or not you really do like it. After all, the energy of Venus speaks of what you truly love and appreciate.

Mars in the 6th: You're happiest when you're putting a lot of energy into your work. Mars in your 6th House adds a powerful stimulus to your need to be active on the job. Fields that require some type of action will be most rewarding. If you're in business, you'll do best if you're on the go or if you're dealing with some form of competition to provide a challenge. In industry, you'll enjoy a job that keeps you busy, and you may like working around metals. You might also be drawn to work as a physical therapist, gym teacher, aerobics instructor, coach, massage therapist, or chiropractor. If you're a physician, you might prefer surgery to the diagnostic forms of medicine. As a counselor, you will be most drawn to therapies that utilize movement to open energy. In music, you would be happiest as a percussionist. Action, energy, and assertiveness are ingredients that will help you feel most satisfied with your work.

Jupiter in the 6th: Work that provides an opportunity to travel, enhance your mind, and feed your spirit is most appealing and satisfying. Jupiter's energy in your 6th House brings a high level of confidence and good humor that is always appreciated on the job. You may be perfectly suited for work in academia, whether in the role of teacher or professor, administrator, or board member. Work in diplomatic relations, sales, promotion, fund-raising, and fields that are related to religion, publishing, and travel are all excellent choices. Environmental and nature-related fields may also be good choices, and you may have a special affinity for animals, which can be translated into your job. Whatever your choices, you need to feel that there's ample room for growth, expansion, and a positive future.

Saturn in the 6th: Your attitudes toward your work are very important, and with Saturn in your 6th House, your need to exercise true responsibility on the job is critical. You have a tendency to demand too much of yourself and others, and although it is necessary to take your work seriously, learning when to pull back a little and relieve the stress will make a big difference in the level of satisfaction you gain from the experience. If you feel that you seem to attract only situations that require you to work hard so that somebody else benefits, the first step toward changing it is to find a way to experience your own rewards. In truth, applied effort, discipline, and good judgment can be your keys to success, but overworking or staying in menial positions because you don't know how to get out of them will never produce the results you dream of achieving. You can be very successful in business when you use your sense of positive restraint in balance with the need to reach out from time to time. Jobs that require a good sense of planning, an eye for workmanship, and an awareness of structure and design can be both satisfying and rewarding. Teaching may also be an excellent outlet for your abilities. You may need to increase your own education in order to improve your job opportunities.

Uranus in the 6th: The energy of Uranus in your 6th House signifies your need to work in fields that will provide opportunities to exercise your independence and originality. You may find working in scientific, technological, or computer-related areas exciting and positively challenging, but you're also fascinated by alternative possibilities in any field. In health care, your leaning toward unconventional methods may prompt you to work in these areas. Whatever your talents and skills, your approach to using them is likely to involve something innovative. You'll also appreciate working in situations that provide ample freedom and that allow you to tackle a job in your own way. If you're stuck in a dead-end or unfair circumstance, you are likely to rebel, and may even be responsible for breaking rules that, from your viewpoint, have no other purpose than to perpetuate an outworn system.

Neptune in the 6th: Neptune's energy in your 6th House provides a need to use your imagination in your work. You may also feel more satisfied when you're working in a field that allows you to reach out and make a difference in the lives of others. In many respects, your best approach to work may be as a "rescuer," although rescuing in the healthiest possible manner is important if you are to avoid becoming a martyr! Work in charitable or nonprofit organizations may be suitable. You may also have a special feeling for animals or the environment, and may enjoy working on their behalf. This influence can undermine strong ambition, but what you lose in ambitious desires, you gain in compassionate understanding. There may be other factors in your chart that strengthen ambition, however.

Pluto in the 6th: With Pluto's energy focused in your 6th House, your work can be a phenomenal source for regeneration. You may be drawn into jobs in the health care fields, including mental health, that will allow you to experience the power of healing more directly. You may also be interested in employing your restorational energies in environmental areas or with animals, or you may be quite adept at refurbishing historic homes, monuments, or furniture. Your work needs to provide an outlet for you to bring about change, rehabilitation, and revitalization, and as long as that's happening, you'll be content. If you feel stagnant, abused, or resentful, your work can be a source of great agony.

Expressions of Creativity and Establishing Your Identity in the World

As a woman, you are innately creative. Although you may not consider yourself an artist, your creative spirit and drive are the mechanisms through which you shape your own life. Creative self-expression is seen strongly in the 5th House of your chart, and by incorporating these elements into your career, you will gain greater satisfaction from your work. If you have the time to concentrate on more recreational forms of creativity, this is the part of your chart that indicates what brings you pleasure. Life itself can certainly be a pleasurable experience—all the time, not just on holidays!

The Sign on the 5th House and Creative Self-Expression

Aries on the 5th: Aries' influence on your 5th House ignites your creative spirit, stimulating a powerful urge to have a life filled with fun and excitement. By incorporating these needs into your life, you increase your productivity. You may be most successful when you have ample room to play, and if your work allows you to use your creativity, then it, too, can become more creative and rewarding. You prefer to keep work and play somewhat separated—it may make playtime more valuable! However, your vitality is strengthened when your creative spirit is humming. You're likely to have all kinds of recreational outlets, something for each season of the year. In whatever you do artistically or creatively, it will carry your special mark. With Mars ruling this house, you may enjoy a few challenges. You might even find that taking time off to get involved in your company or community sports teams or recreational activities can add an excellent dimension to your life.

Taurus on the 5th: Taurus' influence on your 5th House brings a love of the good life. Your enjoyment of the arts, theater, fine dining, and comfort can actually inspire your own creativity, not to mention filling your senses! Creative outlets that allow you to get your hands into something may feel best, since just watching may never be quite enough. You may have a special knack for sculpting, pottery, carving, gardening, wood-working, flower-arranging, or related areas. You may even enjoy building houses, doing landscaping, or other grand-scale projects. It's also possible that you are recognized for your voice, which you can use effectively in either singing or speaking. Venus influences your 5th House, adding a need to extend your creativity into areas that truly fill your heart.

Gemini on the 5th: Gemini's qualities in your 5th House bring your need for variety into the world of your own creativity and personal artistry. You have many talents, and may find it difficult to focus on just one at a time. This multifaceted approach to your creativity can be rewarding, as long as you don't feel that you're too scattered. You may love playful activities that require excellent manual dexterity or mental gymnastics. Whether you're playing an instrument, writing, juggling, or enjoying others who excel in these or similar areas—such experiences heighten your spirits. A good conversation can also inspire your creativity, as can travel. Mercury's influence is strong here, adding a mental dimension to your creativity. For recreation, you may prefer to do different things according to your mood and inclination instead of the same thing all of the time. Some of these activities may be geared toward children (your own or others'), and you may be adept at understanding and communicating with kids of all ages. After all, when you play, you may hear the little girl inside you giggling in delight. She's never too far away!

Cancer on the 5th: Cancer's influence on your 5th House adds a love of playful and creative outlets that stimulate your emotions and fill your soul. You may have a special affinity for music and dancing, and may relish the idea of surrendering to a warm embrace and dancing into the long hours of a romantic evening. You may also enjoy cooking, gardening, and putting some of your creative energy into building your nest. Spending time with your family may be the source of great pleasure, and you will always feel good about giving gifts that come from your heart. That time you spend with your kids curled in your arms reading bedtime stories or singing lullabies may be your greatest inspiration. With the Moon's influence extending into your creative expression, you may also gain special enjoyment from creativity that provides support and encouragement to others. Giving something you've made may be one of your trademarks.

Leo on the 5th: Leo's influence on your 5th House adds a powerful drive to experience as much fun from life as possible. You need lots of room and time to play, and ample opportunities to exercise your flair for the dramatic. Whether you're watching or starring in a performance, you love entertainment. From theater to sports, you enjoy activities that allow the human spirit to triumph. Your own creative self-expression may take many forms, and you may need occasional recognition for your efforts. Standing in the spotlight has its own rewards, and one of them is the inspiration it brings for future creative efforts! Your Sun is connected to this house, and by understanding your ego drives, you'll gain insight into your best creative avenues.

Virgo on the 5th: Virgo's influence on your 5th House shows that you approach creativity and play in a rather matter-of-fact manner. You're happiest when you're producing something, and may feel most satisfied when you've put your best efforts into whatever you're doing. Regardless of your choices, you'll work diligently toward the best possible mastery of your talents and skills. You may have strong manual dexterity skills, and can be adept as a writer, teacher, or musician. Whatever your artistry, your precision and attention to detail will set you aside from everyone else. Mercury's association with this house adds a mental dimension to whatever creative avenues you pursue. It also indicates that you may find special enjoyment from recreation that is mentally stimulating.

Libra on the 5th: Libra's influence on your 5th House indicates a love of beautiful things, talented people, and gorgeous places. The peace you experience in the midst of beautiful surroundings can provide the inspiration you need to get through a difficult day. Your enjoyment of the arts can be an integral part of your life, and taking advantage of the cultural experiences in your city or area may be among your favorite pastimes. You may also be quite talented yourself, and having the time to paint, write, or design is more than just time out. These things may become the driving force behind your life. Venus' energy plays a special role in this area, indicating that you need to be involved in creative pursuits that reflect your values and personal tastes.

Scorpio on the 5th: Scorpio's influence on your 5th House adds a need for passion as part of your play time. Your need for creativity is very strong, and whether you're preparing dinner for your family, working on an oil painting, or delving into a research project—you put yourself into these things on a very deep level. You may prefer to keep your "personal" projects hidden from public scrutiny, although those who are closest to you can become privy to your current work of art. Since you may have a lot invested at an emotional level in your creativity, you don't enjoy the interference that sometimes arises from others. Recreational activities that are somewhat challenging may be inspiring, and you may enjoy spending time doing things like whitewater rafting, scuba diving, or going deep into the forest. You may also enjoy getting away to a secluded retreat or health spa, just to give yourself time to rejuvenate. The energy of Pluto is associated with your 5th House, indicating the importance of creativity and recreation as true healing elements in your life.

Sagittarius on the 5th: Sagittarius' influence on your 5th House adds a need for adventure in your approach to play, creativity, and recreation. Your creativity is inspired when you have time to travel, explore the world, interact with people from different backgrounds, attend workshops or classes, or read. You may love getting into nature, and may find that adding a dimension of reaching into unexplored territory is an excellent source of personal regeneration. A little competition can also spur you to reach into your own creative soul and express dimensions of yourself you might otherwise leave unattended. With Jupiter ruling your 5th House, you may feel most inspired by situations that open all the fences and allow you to explore freely and independently.

Capricorn on the 5th: Capricorn's influence on your 5th House adds a practical approach to your creativity. You may prefer to follow creative avenues that allow you to grow in your expertise, and you're also likely to respond beautifully to good teachers guiding you along the way. However, if your talents or artistry are too strongly criticized, or if they do not meet with your own critical expectations, you may suspend your interest. What you may need to learn is that play is not always something that should be measured, and some of the things you enjoyed doing as a child may still be important to you. Take the example of music. Perhaps you studied an instrument when you were a girl, but with all the things you have to do now that you're a "responsible" woman, you don't have time for it. Think about it: if you enjoyed it, you may need to shake off the dust and play for the pure experience of playing! If your work involves employing your creativity or artistry (which it likely does), you may also need to learn how to just stop working and relax. You probably have a great appreciation for the artistry and ability of others, so quiet your critical remarks and enjoy them some of the time! Saturn's influence in this area indicates that you may be somewhat restrained in your self-expression, but with practice and discipline, you can excel.

Aquarius on the 5th: Aquarius' influence on your 5th House adds a need for experiences that are out of the ordinary in the realm of creativity and recreation. You may totally enjoy one-of-a-kind experiences, and probably have an appreciation for originality in art and music. Your interests may also lean toward the experimental, and you may find some of the things advancing technology has to offer to be quite enjoyable. If you allow yourself to indulge your own artistic abilities, you will find that you are innovative, with a flair for unusual elements in your self-expression. With Uranus' energy influencing this house, your creative originality is enhanced. You may be a gifted artist, designer, writer, or musician. When you get away from it all, you really like to get away! Air travel may be a lot of fun, and if you're feeling stuck creatively, you may discover that you feel inspired and free when you're 30,000 feet above the earth!

Pisces on the 5th: Pisces' influence on your 5th House adds an amazing imaginative quality to your creative sensibilities. You may be so sensitive when you're in the midst of doing something creative that what you create reflects the energy of everything around you. Regardless of your choice of self-expression, you may be especially gifted. When you take time to relax and play, you prefer something that transports you to another dimension. An enthralling movie, intriguing novel, stage production, or concert can all be wonderful, but you also enjoy retreating from the world entirely from time to time to a secret place that allows you to indulge your fantasies and completely let go. The energy of Neptune is associated with your 5th House, bringing an element of compassion to your creative expression.

Planets in the 5th House and Creativity

Sun in the 5th: The Sun's energy in your 5th House brings a powerful emphasis to your creative self-expression, and to your need for play. You may have a lot invested in your personal artistry, and even if you don't think of yourself as an artist, when you think about it, you are creating your own life. Now, that's a work of art! You may have a special affinity for children, and can be quite influential in arenas that support the creativity of children. This position also adds a flair for the dramatic, and you may be known for your sense of style. Your ability to direct and inspire others is also strengthened.

Moon in the 5th: With your Moon's energy in your 5th House, you have a soul-level need for creative expression. If you have children, you may feel that much of your creativity is absorbed by their needs and activities, although this can be exceptionally rewarding and satisfying, especially if your focus is on your children's needs to become fully self-expressive as individuals. You may also be drawn to work or experiences that focus on the needs of women, children, and families, and you can utilize your own creative sensibilities to make a significant difference in these areas. You may be poetic and enjoy doing things that illustrate your deep feelings.

Mercury in the 5th: Mercury's energy in your 5th House stimulates strong communicative talents. From public speaking, to writing, broadcasting, journalism, or public relations—you have a special knack for getting your point across. Your mind may drift frequently into matters of the heart, and creative avenues that allow you to express these thoughts can be both revealing and fulfilling. You may also excel in expressions that require good manual dexterity, like playing an instrument, drawing, or drafting.

Venus in the 5th: With the energy of Venus in your 5th House, your artistic sensibilities are best expressed through a creative venue. The arts are especially important in your personal development, and are likely to provide fortunate opportunities for you as well. You may enjoy sharing your talents with young people and guiding them to open to their own creativity and appreciation for the arts.

Mars in the 5th: The driving force of Mars in your 5th House adds a powerful dimension to your creative self-expression. Creative avenues that utilize your physical energy can be rewarding—from dancing to athletics. In the arts, you may be more drawn to working with metals or sculpting. You may be somewhat competitive in your creativity, and may find that some type of challenge really gets your energy going and heightens your creative output.

Jupiter in the 5th: Jupiter's energy in your 5th House adds greater emphasis to your need for creative self-expression, and to your desire to enjoy life. You may have several areas of talent or expertise, and need to find a way to utilize as many dimensions of your creativity as you can. Travel and education may inspire your imagination. One thing is sure, though: you're rarely without inspiration. If for some reason you think you are, try breaking up your routine temporarily. The change of pace and new perspective can ignite all sorts of possibilities!

Saturn in the 5th: Saturn's energy in your 5th House requires that your approach to creative self-expression be focused and disciplined. You gain more pleasure from teaching or training others to develop their own talents then you do from showing your own. This energy can also be inhibiting to your creativity, whether that inhibition is psychological or circumstantial. When you feel creatively blocked, it is imperative to discover the reason the block is there in the first place. If you do not trust yourself or your abilities, you have the choice to improve through focused effort on the things you do well. If there are circumstances that seem to prohibit your ability to show your creativity, you may discover that it is through hard work that you rise above those inhibitions and create a different life situation for yourself.

Uranus in the 5th: With Uranus in your 5th House, you're an innovative artiste! You express your individuality through your artistry, and may be a trendsetter in your field of expertise. Your inventiveness and experimental attitudes can be expressed in almost any field of endeavor, and you'll be happiest when you are able to incorporate your special flair for the rare and unusual into your self-expression. If you have children, they may be independent and have their own unusual personalities that require your patient encouragement to develop to their ultimate potential. You may have an affinity for dealing with teens and kids with special needs.

Neptune in the 5th: You're fortunate to have Neptune in your 5th House. This imaginative energy adds a special touch to your creative power and heightens your artistic sensibilities. Music, dancing, or the arts may be an important part of your life, and you may love drama and the theater. You may also have an excellent eye for photography or cinematography.

Pluto in the 5th: Pluto's energy in your 5th House brings an intensity to your creative expression. You may have a special ability to take apparently useless or outworn things, people, or circumstances and bring them into a new life. When you're involved in an artistic project or idea, you can become totally absorbed, and may produce the best results when you're left undisturbed to follow your muse.

The Sun's Energy and Your Creative Drive

One of the most powerful creative drives in your chart is your Sun. Since this is the energy that can drive you to be noticed, learning to cultivate this aspect of yourself in a positive manner can amplify your success in life. Remember, this is the part of you that may be most easily noticed by others, and if you develop the most promising qualities associated with your Sun, it can open the doors to success throughout your lifetime.

The Sun's Sign and Your Profession

Sun in Aries: Your drive to reach the realization of your passion can be immense with your Sun in Aries. Learning the best ways to assert yourself without becoming too brash can make a significant difference in the responses you receive, and can directly affect your success. Since your high level of mental creativity needs ample outlets, you can feel impatient about the time it takes to make things happen, but as long as you're moving and something is happening, you can keep driving toward your goals.

Sun in Taurus: There's certainly no problem with your desires, since your Taurus Sun qualities help you create a long wish list. Maintaining your focus is one of the tricks you learned long ago, and when you really want something, there may be no end to your patience. The problem can revolve around determining your priorities and learning the difference between what you need and what you want. Sometimes your stubborn attitudes and refusal to change can interfere with the realization of your needs. In many ways, your success depends on knowing when to hang on and when to loosen your grasp—at least a little!

Sun in Gemini: To experience a real feeling of success, you may feel that you have to learn something from the experience. You are multi-talented with your Sun in Gemini, and may even change your career direction in order to experience a new range of possibilities. Sometimes it may seem that you're living at least two lifetimes at once. Or you may find that you're living a dual life, juggling a mixed list of priorities in your many roles. Although this keeps things interesting, you've probably found that you are happier when the juggling act involves keeping fewer things in the air at once.

Sun in Cancer: Regardless of your priorities, you will feel successful only when you've created a sense of security with your Sun in Cancer. Defining this security is a very personal thing, and you must be happy with your own definition. Your work, your roles within your family, and your creativity all depend on your sensitivity in this regard since when you're insecure, you hang on tenaciously to everybody and everything. When you're feeling stabilized, you don't even over-water the plants!

Sun in Leo: Well, admit it, sometimes it's just fun to show off with your Sun in Leo. You may even be quite low-key and gracious about giving others the spotlight. But you know that when you're shining in all your glory, the light can be blinding for a moment, and then, well, you're just gorgeous! To feel a true sense of success, you may need that few moments of fame and glory; and if you're doing it right, the Universe may even grant you more!

Sun in Virgo: You probably already have the reputation of doing things well with your Sun in Virgo, but you're after more than competency. You have some unwritten set of criteria that are akin to divine perfection, which you'd love to achieve somewhere in your life. Learning that successes come in all sizes, and becoming happy with some of the small successes, can prepare you when the big success arrives. If you're not ready for it, you may feel like shrinking away under the internal pressure you feel over that tiny mistake you made that is driving you nuts. Chances are, it's insignificant, and you'll learn from it, so let it go and just say, "thank you very much."

Sun in Libra: You may think you don't care much about success as long as it looks good on you, but you know that your Libra Sun is really driving you to reach a stage of getting things right and having life fit your set of specifications. Finding success through your associations with others may seem to be the easy way out, and you may keep trying to change them to fit your desires until you realize that you really are working on changing yourself. So look in the mirror and start over. What do you want to see reflected back at you? See that confident smile? That's the look of success. The rest should be easy.

Sun in Scorpio: Even though you can be somewhat enigmatic with the Sun in Scorpio, you are also driven to attain the realization of your desires. For anything to be successful in your life, it must be personally meaningful to you, and you must have a strong feeling about it. You simply do not care to waste your energy. But you have to know when to back off, because with your intensity, you can set the world on fire. Be gentle. Just remember that after all, as long as you know how to function in a crisis, there's no problem.

Sun in Sagittarius: With your Sagittarius Sun, you're probably pretty intelligent, enjoy learning, and have an adventurous drive; but you may be afraid of success. It's that unknown question about where to aim. If you aim for your high ideals, you could possibly fall short, so you might compromise for something else, just because it's quickly reachable. Then what's that yearning in your heart? Could it be the desire for something more!? There is your drive to succeed, and it's the adventure itself that gives you the feeling that makes the light in your eyes. After all, when you do reach that pinnacle, you'll just aim for something new!

Sun in Capricorn: Achieving success is very important to you since your Capricorn Sun may never rest until you've reached the pinnacle you desire. The measure of your success is the question: how do you know if you've made the right choices? One of the primary keys can be answered by determining whom you are trying to please or satisfy through your actions and goals. If the answer is you, then success can, indeed, be sweet. If it is someone else, you may never know for sure.

Sun in Aquarius: Even though you may have found your differences from others painful when you were a young girl, you've probably discovered that it is your uniqueness that provides the impetus to achieving true success. Your Aquarius Sun adds a drive to attain a clear perception about yourself, and your need to make a difference in the world can give you cause to aim for something out of the ordinary. Your real goal may be to transcend the bounds of mere mortality and achieve something that will open a new pathway. Although this functions primarily at a spiritual level, it does have its implications on the physical plane. In your family, you are the one who breaks the patterns. On the job, you are the one whose vision and insight inspire new direction.

Sun in Pisces: You really don't have to save the world in order to be a success, but with your Sun in Pisces, you may at least try to save a part of it in some way. Your deeper goals may have a more spiritual basis, like achieving a sense of oneness with life. You may never feel satisfied with everyday successes until you feel connected on the inner level. There is always plenty to do in the world, and sometimes you'll feel wonderful when you've created something that makes a difference. The real success occurs when your perspective changes and you see yourself and others through the eyes of true forgiveness and compassion.

Allowing Your Individuality to Emerge: Tapping Uranian Energy

Your individuality is expressed through many different energies in your chart, but the energy that is most closely associated with the unique and individualistic part of yourself is Uranus. Through Uranian energy, you display your ingenuity and make the breakthroughs that allow you to move into new experiences. Uranus also prompts your rebellious nature, and the placement of this energy in your chart shows where you are staging your own personal revolution. It is here that you need to break away from convention and allow yourself to experiment with the promptings of your intuitive insights.

Uranus in the Signs and Career

Uranus in Aries: With Uranus in Aries, you may be a trendsetter, breaking into new territory in the world. Since this influence lasted from 1928 to 1935, many of the things that have been important to you as an individual have also been important to those born during this period. Your shared vision as a collective has been connected to a need to bring women into a true experience of autonomy and personal power. The areas where you have broken ground for your own personal autonomy are shown by the house where Uranus resides in your chart.

Uranus in Taurus: With Uranus in Taurus, your primary focus for change has revolved around a need to establish values that are meaningful in the context of your own life experience. Along with other women born from 1935 to 1942, you have discovered the importance of making the most of your resources. Your shared insights with other women born with Uranus in Taurus have been connected to environmental and financial issues, and you may still feel that you are fighting for true value for women in society. The areas where you have broken ground for your own self-actualization and establishment of personal worth are shown by the house where Uranus resides in your chart.

Uranus in Gemini: With Uranus in Gemini, you were born into a life of awakened ideas and fast-paced learning. Along with other women born from 1941 to 1949, your revolution was fought with words and ideas on the battleground of educational opportunity. Your shared insights with other women who have Uranus in Gemini have been connected to educational reform, improved communication, and more effective connections between the people of the world. The areas where you have broken ground for your own awakening in consciousness are shown by the house where Uranus resides in your chart.

Uranus in Cancer: With Uranus in Cancer, you were born into a life of society's revolution within the family and have experienced the development of new insights into emotional needs. Along with other women born from 1948 to 1956, your revolution was fought in the kitchen over matters of reproduction, and at family reunions. You've changed the roles women play and the expectations of women in the world, consequently bringing an evolution in family relationships and within society itself: an evolutionary change that is continuing in its effects. Your shared insights have included a world where girls and women have the same opportunities as boys and men. To understand where you are creating this revolution within your own life, look to the house in which Uranus resides in your chart.

Uranus in Leo: You have Uranus in Leo and are integrating the importance of individual accomplishment and achievement in your life. Along with other women born from 1955 to 1962, you've broken down many barriers women have faced in their struggle for recognition as accomplished and capable individuals. Your revolution was staged within the context of career and relationships, and continues in its effect upon society. The insights you share with other women with Uranus in

Leo include the importance of establishing places for leaders who possess the courage to create change. To understand where you are creating this revolution in your own life, look to the house in which Uranus resides in your chart.

Uranus in Virgo: Uranus in Virgo stirs your need for awakening in regard to issues that affect the quality of your life. Along with other women born from 1961 to 1969, you've grown up with an awareness of the importance of the connection between mind and body. You feel the need to use your analytical mind to bring about revolutionary change. Your revolution is being staged within the context of health, science, discrimination, and prejudicial attitudes, and will continue in its effect upon society for quite some time to come. The insights you share with other women with Uranus in Virgo are connected to the importance of individual awareness in achieving a truly functional society. You've broken ground in your own ability to see clearly where you need to bring about revolutionary changes in your own life in the areas signified by the house in which Uranus resides in your chart.

Uranus in Libra: You have Uranus in Libra, strengthening your need to experience breakthroughs in the realm of relationships. Along with other women born from 1968 to 1975, you've witnessed major changes in personal relationships and their effects upon the whole of society. These changes have extended into the realm of the law and politics, and have a profound effect upon artistic expression. Your revolution is being fought within these realms, and those with Uranus in Libra will incite the changes in the law that have a major effect upon lifestyle and relationship choices. The areas in your own life where you've broken ground in your desire to achieve an awareness of true harmony and beauty are signified by the house in which Uranus resides in your chart.

Uranus in Scorpio: You have Uranus in Scorpio, bringing about a revolution in your consciousness in regard to matters of healing, psychology, birth, death, and human sexuality. Along with other women born from 1974 to 1981, you will be responsible for awakened attitudes in regard to these matters within society. If your career choices center around the health care profession or scientific fields, your methods and approaches can bring a new understanding in these areas. Along with others born with Uranus in Scorpio, you will be part of the revolution concerning women's choices in health matters, including birth and abortion. You may also confront society's needs to allow for greater privacy in decisions regarding birth and death. In your personal life, it is crucial that you allow your intuitive self to guide you when facing health-related issues, and that you try a wide variety of approaches to achieving optimal health. The areas in your life where you break ground in regard to your deeply held convictions concerning freedom of expression are shown by the house in which Uranus resides in your chart.

Uranus in Sagittarius: You have Uranus in Sagittarius, stimulating a revolution in your consciousness concerning matters of religion, spirituality, and the law. Along with other women born from 1981 to 1988, you may initiate changes that have a broad effect upon higher education and religious practices. As a collective, you and others born with Uranus in Sagittarius may create revolutionary changes that directly affect women's spirituality. In society, you may become more assertive in establishing women as political and religious leaders. Your revolution will be fought against attitudes that are counterproductive to truth and wisdom. On a personal level, your own ground-breaking experiences in heightened awareness and the achievement of wisdom are shown by the house in which Uranus resides in your chart.

Uranus in Capricorn: You have Uranus in Capricorn, igniting a revolution in your relationship to authority and the established order. This revolution takes shape in board rooms, houses of government, and banks, and affects society through chosen (or self-appointed!) leaders, teachers, and law enforcement agencies. If you are among the older generation of women with Uranus in Capricorn, born from 1904 to 1912, you have been part of the evolution that has seen women rise into positions of authority. If you are among the new generation of women with Uranus in Capricorn, born from 1988 to 1995, you will rise to power in a world where women are expected to take positions of leadership and authority. Your own attitudes toward authority are crucial if you are to be successful. You may feel that it is important to completely change the system, yet there may be a part of you that resists those changes. The best place to start is by learning about the system itself and then making changes that allow society and her systems to grow positively into the next millennium. The area in which you must address your own conflicts and need to create change is represented by the house in which Uranus is found in your chart.

Uranus in Aquarius: You have Uranus in Aquarius, and are a woman who has seen exceptional changes. You may be delighted by many of these changes, and may remember the times in your youth when your mind whirred while thinking about how phenomenal the future could be. That same wonder continues throughout your life, and your manner of exercising your autonomy and individuality will always serve as an inspiration for others who follow in your footsteps. Along with other women born from 1912 to 1919, you have learned the importance of collective cooperation in bringing about change. You've seen what can happen when destruction is the goal, and will continue to shed light on the importance of developing true humanity among the people of the earth. The area in which you experience your greatest awakening and insights is represented by the house in which Uranus is found in your chart.

If you are among the new generation of women with Uranus in Aquarius, born from 1996 to 2002, your ascent to influence and power will occur at a time in human history when the effects of technologies and advancements developed during the twentieth century will be apparent. The call to your generation includes an exceptional challenge in the realm of human rights, and it is entirely possible that women's roles will have changed so significantly as to alter the basic framework of society. Your vision, along with the vision and insights of your sisters and brothers on the planet, must extend far into the future, and your ability to reach beyond the limitations of an old paradigm, while creating an innovative and humanitarian platform, can shape human destiny for centuries to come.

Uranus in Pisces: You have Uranus in Pisces, an influence that can enhance your intuitive flow and psychic impressionability. Your personal revolution occurs in the realm of spirituality and compassion, and you may feel that it is important that your life shows the effects of your outreach and caring. Along with other women born from 1919 to 1927, you've fought a revolution centered on a need for a devotion to higher principles. Your religious beliefs and ideals have played an important role in all your life decisions, and those ideals grow more powerful when you realize the light of truth that is found within all doctrines: the importance of love. The area in your life where you experience the most profound release and transcendence is represented by the house in which Uranus is found in your chart.

Uranus in the Houses: Your Spark of Ingenuity Shining Through

Uranus in the 1st: With Uranian energy in your 1st House, you'll enjoy an occupation that allows your uniqueness to shine. You're not especially suited to the three-piece business suit and heels—you're more the "I designed it myself" woman, and need to work in a field that allows you to express your identity with few reservations. You also prefer to work on your own rather than for someone else, although if you do work for a company or the government, you'll be okay if your job gives you room for individual motivation and accomplishment, and little supervision.

Uranus in the 2nd: The independent drive of Uranus in your 2nd House may add special abilities to your "bag of tricks," and you'll prefer to work in professions that give you lots of room to experiment and grow. Your ingenuity and trend-setting ability are among your best resources, so remember that when you're trying to look at what others have done: you may be best when inventing on the spot and setting your own trends! Capitalizing on your special talents and making use of what sets you apart from the rest of the world will also improve your self-esteem.

Uranus in the 3rd: The spark of Uranian energy in your 3rd House suggests that your unique ideas and special communicative abilities can be utilized in your career development. You enjoy working in high-tech or scientific fields, and you have plenty of interesting ideas in other areas. A career that allows you to blend your intuitive sensibilities and logical thought processes will be especially satisfying.

Uranus in the 4th: Uranus in your 4th House brings a strong undercurrent of revolutionary energy into your life. You may actually change career paths more than once in your attempts to uncover your special calling, but the key element that is most attractive is the opportunity to break ground and establish new trends. Just try to remember that change for its own sake can be costly, although sometimes the only way to move into the new territory of personal development is to do something completely different!

Uranus in the 5th: Uranus in your 5th House was discussed previously in this chapter.

Uranus in the 6th: Uranus in your 6th House was discussed previously in this chapter.

Uranus in the 7th: The energy of Uranus in your 7th House may stimulate opportunities to work in a variety of social situations as you grow both personally and professionally. You may be involved in ground-breaking circumstances or may pioneer areas in partnership with others that develop new platforms for women, particularly in fields like law or even in the context of pure societal power. You do like your independence, and even when working with others will prefer to have ample room to do things on your own or in your unique manner.

Uranus in the 8th: With Uranian energy in your 8th House, you are drawn to work that delves into the undercurrents of life—fields like psychology, medicine, metaphysics, or human genetics. You can also be accomplished working in areas of financial concern and have very good ideas about methods to revolutionize them.

Uranus in the 9th: Uranian energy in your 9th House adds a special interest in the fields of education, travel, language, religion, and philosophy, and you may integrate your unique abilities and talents into these areas with great success. However, you're also likely to run into some resistance from those who enjoy maintaining the status quo. That's okay; it only makes you more determined to break ground and accomplish innovative change!

Uranus in the 10th: The influence of Uranus in your 10th House can have a monumental impact on your career development and work. You need to follow a path that allows you to shine as an individual, but you may also need to integrate your energy into a direction that somehow influences the evolution of the collective. Even if you choose a "traditional" career of some sort, you're very likely to accomplish its tasks in a non-traditional manner! You're an innovator, and can attract a lot of attention for your efforts. For this reason, you may be either famous or notorious, and sometimes it's not so much a matter of choice as it is circumstance!

Uranus in the 11th: With the energy of Uranus in your 11th House, you may be involved in work that serves the needs of your community. From social work, to teaching, to consulting, to city planning and beyond—you can be quite comfortable in situations that allow you to bring change into the world by working cooperatively with others who share your ideals.

Uranus in the 12th: The energy of Uranus in your 12th House indicates that you may not always show your unique talents to everyone. However, you can be effective in bringing innovative changes, even in such situations as institutions, and may be adept at working within a system to bring about alterations or modifications. You may also be a natural psychologist, whether you work in that field or not!

Chiron: Developing Your Sense of Purpose

The energy of Chiron is also a powerful factor in your outreach into the world. Through Chiron you discover both strength and vulnerability. The vulnerability represented by Chiron is, in many ways, like a doorway that allows you to penetrate a deeper level of personal mastery. This is a process of initiation not unlike that which a Shaman must endure in order to learn how to travel between the worlds. Through Chiron you learn how to travel between the world of your inner self and the world outside through achieving a sense of true purpose and wisdom. Chiron describes that part of you that is your "Medicine Woman." Honoring this part of yourself by allowing an awareness of your deeper sense of knowledge and ability to restore the natural balance is the essence of your Chiron force.

Chiron in the Signs

Chiron in Aries: You have Chiron in Aries, signifying a need to discover your true courage. Your life purpose is centered around your needs for pioneering unexplored territory, whether physical or idealistic. Your life work may involve breaking ground, cutting through barriers, or blasting through outworn attitudes. Your head and heart need to be in harmony with one another if you are to succeed in achieving this purpose.

Chiron in Taurus: You have Chiron in Taurus, signifying a need to discover the profound importance and effects of love. Your life purpose is centered around your needs for creating a world where you feel stable, and where your efforts create a haven of comfort. Consistency and resourcefulness can be your keys to achieving your personal aims. You may also feel that it is crucial to live in harmony with the earth, and you will be much more satisfied with yourself and your life if you are making the best use of all your resources and not wasting or abusing them.

Chiron in Gemini: You have Chiron in Gemini, stimulating a need for a life purpose centered on developing your mind. Your many talents extend into the areas of communication, negotiation, diplomacy, and politics. You may have a special affinity for children, and may be concerned about a creating a world in which children are happy, safe, and well-educated. Most of all, you will find the satisfaction you crave when you know that you have reached an understanding, or when your efforts have provided a sound link for the exchange of information and ideas.

Chiron in Cancer: You have Chiron in Cancer, strengthening your need for a life purpose that is centered around stimulating growth and providing a safe home and positive relationship with family. This family may extend to the family you develop at work or in your community, or can reach into the family of living things. Your talents may rest within your understanding of the way support systems operate, and you may be a natural therapist. You may not find the inner peace you hope to achieve until you've built a safe nest for yourself and those you love.

Chiron in Leo: You have Chiron in Leo, bringing your focus to the need for a life purpose that is centered on experiencing a true connection to creative power. This power can be directed into many arenas, but may be most effective when you have a position of leadership or authority. You shine and feel alive when you're providing entertainment, sources of recreation, venues for personal achievement, encouragement for personal development, or insights into the nature of love.

Chiron in Virgo: You have Chiron in Virgo, stimulating a need to discover a life purpose that centers around making improvements and creating healthy environments. You have insights into wellness, health care, and physical health; but you are also drawn to experiences that are centered around education, service, or the achievement of excellence. When you're concentrating on the important details of any task, and when your thoughts are pure, you feel a sense of peace and clarity.

Chiron in Libra: You have Chiron in Libra, creating a need to fill your life with a true sense of objectivity. You may need relationships with others to achieve this end since relationships provide feedback and may be the agent for real change in your life. Your personal artistry may provide the avenues through which you achieve your life purpose, and your ability to see both sides of an issue may place you in the midst of the conflicts that help you resolve your own internal turmoil.

Chiron in Scorpio: You have Chiron in Scorpio, strengthening your need to experience a life that is centered on transformation and healing. Your life purpose revolves around bringing healing into your own life, but also extends to a need to heal others. Whether you work directly in the health care professions is not important. A touch can heal, your words can stimulate harmony, your smile can bring transformation. Learning about your own sexuality and experiencing the alchemy that arises from achieving a true bonding through the exchange of loving passion may bring amazing healing into your own life. You must also address issues that revolve around birth and death, and may find that part of your life purpose is coming to grips with your deeper understanding of absolute transformation.

Chiron in Sagittarius: You have Chiron in Sagittarius, strengthening your desire to achieve a life purpose centered on accomplishing understanding and embracing truth. Your fascination with culture, religion, and education may be expressions of this deeper need. Even if your career does not lead you into these areas, many of your life experiences are likely to be connected to your search for truth and your need for understanding. Although education may be part of your life purpose, your real wisdom is likely to be developed through your life experiences. It is from this perspective that your ability to teach and guide others will be most positive.

Chiron in Capricorn: You have Chiron in Capricorn, adding a need to accomplish a life purpose that is based on achieving a true sense of success. These successes can be in any area, and are not always related to career. Supporting a child as a patient mother or teacher, providing resources when something needs to be built in your community, or lending a helping hand can all be part of this. On a personal level, you need to establish goals and find ways to realize them. Sometimes the goal may be just getting through the day. On a larger scale, you are also learning about positive self-control. It is here that you will experience the greatest satisfaction when you've found the best ways to direct your own energy toward accomplishing something that is meaningful to you.

Chiron in Aquarius: You have Chiron in Aquarius, drawing your life purpose into the arena of human development and expansion of consciousness. You may be strongly aware that your own evolution and growth have an impact on the evolution of humanity as a whole, and the choices you make in your life that are centered around rising above the ordinary may allow you to do just that. You cannot fall into the trap of elitist thinking or you will experience a deep wounding that lasts until you abandon such ideas.

Chiron in Pisces: You have Chiron in Pisces, pulling you toward a need for a life purpose that revolves around developing your spirituality and strengthening your capacity for compassion. Whatever you're doing, your sensibilities about what's happening on an inner level enhance your attunement to the person or situation. If you're working in the capacity of healer, you may be most noted for your caring and gentleness. You can extend your compassionate outreach in any field, however. Those areas that require you to utilize your imagination and talents will be the most rewarding.

Chiron in the Houses

Chiron in the 1st: With Chiron in your 1st House, you need to be especially aware of the way you present yourself to the world since your manner and attitudes can make all the difference in the opportunities you experience for growth or advancement. Self-awareness is crucial to your personal development; selfishness can be wounding.

Chiron in the 2nd: With Chiron in the 2nd House, you need to be attentive to the manner in which you utilize your resources. Time, money, and energy are all precious, and if you're wasting these resources, you may experience a direct effect that inhibits your ability to accomplish your purpose or aims.

Chiron in the 3rd: With Chiron in your 3rd House, your words and manner of communicating have a significant impact on your ability to accomplish your purpose and aims. Learning about the power of mind is one of your primary lessons, and directing your thoughts toward positive, uplifting possibilities will open many more doors than worrying or complaining.

Chiron in the 4th: With Chiron in your 4th House, the impact of your family ties is very important. Your yearning for a deep connection to family may not be fulfilled until you find your own security and create your own family. Weaving your own heritage and family traditions into your life experience can be both healing and stabilizing. Trying to completely abandon them will only leave you feeling disconnected from yourself.

Chiron in the 5th: With Chiron in your 5th House, you're finding ways to use your creativity and self-confidence to help you achieve your life purpose. Right use of your talents and abilities is crucial to your growth and plays a powerful role in the realization of your true self.

Chiron in the 6th: With Chiron in your 6th House, you're learning how to work cooperatively with others. You may have a special need to attend to health matters, and your consciousness in this regard can be one of your greatest challenges. Self-improvement is your key to fulfilling your life purpose.

Chiron in the 7th: With Chiron in your 7th House, a significant element in achieving your life purpose revolves around your connection to human society. Your personal relationships, especially partnerships, are part of this experience. You may also find that developing a real sense of objectivity about your own talents and abilities allows you to move further along the path toward experiencing a truly purposeful life.

Chiron in the 8th: With Chiron in your 8th House, you're learning that everything in life is not what is seems to be on the surface. To find your real sense of purpose, you have to dig deep within yourself, and you may have to abandon some of your old attachments in order to move ahead into a life that is truly satisfying and feels complete. Your issues with inheritance, taxes, and dying are all crucial to rising above your limitations.

Chiron in the 9th: With Chiron in your 9th House, you're searching for answers to all the ultimate questions as part of your quest to discover your life purpose. You may feel a strong urge to travel, desire to learn, and yearning to find the teacher whose wisdom will inspire you to find truth. In essence, all these things are inside you, and the travel and learning you may need most to experience will happen on the inner planes. Doing it physically is okay too. It's good practice.

Chiron in the 10th: With Chiron in your 10th House, you may feel that establishing yourself in a career is the key to finding your life purpose. This is okay, as long as your career seems to fill needs that include, and are beyond, those of the physical plane. Taking on positions of authority and leadership may be your link to your life purpose.

Chiron in the 11th: With Chiron in your 11th House, your life purpose is centered around achieving a true sense of hope and confidence for today and the future. Your satisfaction with yourself may require that you become more unconditional in your approach to others and toward yourself. Opening to a love that knows no boundaries is your key to finding your real purpose in life.

Chiron in the 12th: With Chiron in your 12th House, you'll discover that your life purpose is centered around the things you do for the collective. Whether you're giving some of your time and energy to charitable causes, working in public institutions, or concentrating on world peace during your meditations, you need to reach out with your energy into the part of yourself that connects to all that is.

～

CHAPTER NINE

OPENING YOUR HEART

*A*h, Love . . . . Songs, poems, novels, fairy tales, movies all extol the power and pleasure of love—and for good reason: love is the food of life! There are many opportunities to love—in fact, a love affair with life is not a bad idea—but you also need to "grow" love by sharing it, and therein is the seed of all relationships.

The planetary energies that are most usually associated with the expression and feelings of love are Venus and Neptune. Venusian energy radiates directly from your heart, from the center of yourself, where love resides deep within. Loving is an inner experience. The more you open to the love you hold within yourself, the more it grows. Your feelings of worthiness are represented by Venus, and as you grow to understand and appreciate your own value as a woman, it becomes easier to allow love's energy to flow through your life. Neptunian energy is Divine compassionate love—the love that does not judge and readily forgives. Neptune is the realm of romance, mysticism, and heavenly perfection. Truly transcendent Neptunian love arises when you have healthy boundaries of your own, otherwise you can become a victim of your own illusions!

In love relationships we usually think of love affairs, marriage, and family as the primary extensions of love. Regarding love affairs and marriage, I have written this material with the concept of heterosexual relationships, realizing and accepting that there are many lifestyles and choices that do not fall within this framework. Although there are some astrological indicators that a woman might seek an alternative or non-traditional relationship, sexual preference is not easily determined from the astrological chart alone. For those whose relationships are same sex, some references to a "man" may more comfortably be replaced with "partner" or "lover." However, in some instances, it is important to understand that certain planetary placements or aspects do affect male-female connections, regardless of sexual preference, and some have nothing to do with sexual dynamics! Also, in many instances, there is a need for balance indicated, with one partner playing the assertive and the other partner playing a more submissive role; gender may not be a factor.

Astrologically speaking, there are several places in the chart to look for love. The houses, which represent the different facets of your life, also extend to the different relationships you experience. The areas in your chart that deal with experiences and expressions of love will be examined later in this chapter. First, let's look at the energies of love.

Venus: The Energy of the Heart

The sign that influences Venus, and the planetary aspects to and from Venus, have a lot to say about the way you love. First, we'll look at the expression of Venus through the signs to understand the core quality of loving and the nature of your heart space. Then, to further explore opening your heart, study the aspects to and from Venus.

Venus in the Signs and Opening Your Heart

Venus in Aries: Love is your inspiration with Venus in Aries. Although you may not like to feel trapped by maudlin, sticky situations, you are a romantic and relish the game of love. The pursuit of the lover of your dreams inspires highly creative ideas and flashes of insight, and can be a lot of fun, too. You can be a tempting flirt, and even when you're involved in a committed relationship, may feel excited by the idea of arousing another's interest. To sustain love, you need to know that the passion is still alive in a relationship. The love that you hold deep in your heart stirs your sense of faith and hope, and you an enjoy open, passionate exchange of emotions in your close relationships as a means of keeping the flame of love burning brightly. Sometimes you wonder if your feelings have changed, when a relationship becomes everyday; but the truth of the matter is that love has its ups and downs, and sometimes just needs to be there, warming your heart, instead of always burning up the sheets! You have the courage to sustain love by keeping it alive, and are not likely to allow a relationship to simply wither away. If you have your way, there will always be a burning ember of desire.

Venus in Taurus: For you, love is meant to last forever. Venus in Taurus is about sustaining love, growing it, prospering on every level because the sweet presence of love adds the beauty, comfort, and strength you need to carry on. In many respects, love forms the foundation of your life and acts as the glue that holds you together. This love does not have to come from the outside or from a man, and your own creative expression and outreach to those in your care help you build a powerful bond. Somehow, though, life seems so much more complete when you're safe in the arms of the man you love. It's like a dividend. The love you hold within your heart is solid and sustaining, and once you've opened your heart to another, it's unlikely that your feelings will change; unless something drastic happens, and then, if you are hurt by the experience of loving, you can be an unrelenting thorn in the side of the one who has hurt you. Letting go is definitely not your strong suit! It's important to remember that your inner beauty and love for yourself can grow only when you are giving of yourself, and that if you've locked your feelings away, your life can become stagnant. So finding ways to let go and move on may be worth the effort after all. Place your faith in love itself, and let that energy guide and protect you.

Venus in Gemini: Love is one of the purest forms of delight for you. Through the energy of Venus in Gemini you may feel like the eternal child of wonder when your heart is filled with love. Love gives you the faith in yourself that allows you to pursue new directions, and your ability to express your feelings and talk about your needs can help to sustain love in your life. You like to demonstrate your love by keeping the connection strong, and one of the best ways is to keep the lines of communication open. When you feel the contact from the mind to the heart is strong and powerful, you trust love. Sometimes something as simple as a card or phone call is enough to ignite the flames of love. When that sense of connection is broken, you may not trust that the love is still there. It is important for you to build relationships that nourish open communication and help you develop a real understanding. A partner who shares your love of ideas, travel, or social contact will be most enjoyable. Your heart will stay open more fully when you are in an environment that allows you to express yourself, and where you can pursue your own interests without fear of undermining the relationship.

Venus in Cancer: Immersing yourself in love, surrounded by a warm embrace and tender caress, lets you sink into the feeling that life is truly worthwhile. With Venus in Cancer, you love deeply and experience love as a process that involves growth, change, and continuity. When you love someone, it's natural for you to fall into the role of caretaker, since for you, nurturing is a natural part of loving. Sometimes, though, you can express your love in a manner that feels a bit claustrophobic, and, to avoid creating alienation, you need to pay attention when your husband, lover, or even your kids seem to need a little more personal space (or room to make their own mistakes!). You're sensitive and can be easily hurt, especially if you've jumped into a romantic situation too soon. Learning how to fulfill more of your own needs is crucial since you can project a feeling of neediness, which may not be the best basis for a relationship. Allowing yourself to have what you want and need from life may be difficult at first, but it is the crucial ingredient in experiencing a fuller, more rewarding experience of love. You open your heart more fully when you feel safe and secure, and love more deeply when you're focused on creating your perfect love nest.

Venus in Leo: Love is a primary focus of your life with Venus in Leo. The experience of falling in love, surrendering to passionate romance, opening to the feeling that you are the most important part of someone's life is the stuff your dreams are made of. But stop for a moment and look in the mirror. If the truth is told, you are a very important part of your own life, right? And that's okay, as long as your self-awareness is not pure selfishness! For love to grow in your heart, it has to involve mutual respect, trust, and loyalty. If those features are lost or diminished, you may feel the flame of love is beginning to die. You really do have a big heart, and it feels wonderful when you can do something special for those you love and admire. Sometimes, giving is the way you fill your own heart with love, although you adore it when someone pampers you. Love is the place where you shine the brightest, and when your heart is open to love, you feel alive. Letting go is difficult for you, and if a love relationship ends, you may still carry a torch for that man forever; but it's to your advantage to know when to let go and move on, since if you're still stuck in the past, you can miss something pretty spectacular in the here and now!

Venus in Virgo: Sometimes you feel that you are not worthy of the love you need with Venus in Virgo. This feeling stems from the yardstick you use to measure your own perfection. Who says you have to be perfect in order to be lovable? You can place the same restraints on yourself by feeling that you can love someone only if they meet your detailed list of criteria. All these fancy restrictions may just be your way of assuring that you won't be hurt, because the thought that someone you care about might reject you is almost unbearable. So let's start from square one. You need love, and when you love, you love deeply. You love most easily when you have reached a real understanding and know that you are truly accepted for who you are. You don't have to get that tummy tuck in order to be lovable after all! To keep your heart open, you need to remind yourself that you are whole, perfect, and loving. To sustain love, you strive to make life wonderful; that's good. Trouble arises when you start trying to fix somebody because you love them. Oops! Instant opportunity for pain! So before you pull out your doctor kit, think about the situation first. Maybe you, or your sweetheart, are perfect as you are. Imagine that!

Venus in Libra: Thoughts of love have always filled much of your time. The influence of Venus in Libra stimulates a sense that you are more viable and worthy if someone loves you. Okay then, go look in the mirror again. There you are. When you love yourself (even without make-up), your heart opens more readily, and the love you give to others is more alive. If you do not really love yourself, and just know you'll feel better when someone else loves you, you'll never find what you're seeking from love. You need to know the pure beauty of your own heart, and to love another, look for their real beauty. Whether you see this through the way he laughs, the tone of his voice, or the feel of his embrace, the color, light, and magic you feel are the result of finding the beauty of love. Your life may seem more complete if you have a partner who shares your life experiences, and you'll be happiest in a relationship with a partner who believes in and practices equality, but to know that sense of equality, you must value yourself, and there you are again, full circle, facing yourself. You, too, must offer the same equality, respect, and sense of fairness you demand from those you love. After that, the rest is pure delight.

Venus in Scorpio: Love is a total experience for you with Venus in Scorpio. You need to know the absolute depths of loving, and your life will prosper on every level when you feel fully immersed in the experience of true love. You do not easily give your heart, and once you do surrender it, may never change your feelings. That does not mean that you can love only once, but you may believe that's the case when you're deeply in love. You can become addicted to love! There are many forms of love, which you know, and the real bond—the magical alchemy of connecting to someone through heart and soul—is what you seek from romantic love. You can weave a magical spell, and may be quite sensual and charismatic in your approach to loving. For excitement in love, you enjoy a bit of mystery and intrigue, and may play a few power games just to get your energy going. (That does not equal abuse, by the way.) If a relationship changes, you may have to change in order to keep the love alive, since wanting things to stay the same all the time can lead to extreme stagnation. If you're hurt by loving, you may close your heart just to avoid feeling that kind of pain again. You have to ask yourself if it's worthwhile to keep those doors so firmly shut. After all, you may be closing yourself out, too.

Venus in Sagittarius: Your Sagittarian Venus adds a desire for ultimate experiences through love. Your expectations of love are high, and through loving, you affirm your faith in life itself. Although you heard about Prince Charming when you were a little girl, you probably felt that you could ride a horse just as easily as he, and may have wondered how Sleeping Beauty could ever have just slept through so much of her life. Those fairy tales are not your vision of love. You envision a love filled with adventure, excitement, and fun. When you love, you laugh and smile a lot. It's the juicy stuff of love that adds a real sweetness to your life. The passion of the moment can sometimes carry you away, and you have a tendency to jump into emotional situations before you think about the consequences. Learning to make choices that will allow growth, maturity, and time to work to your advantage is not always easy. You're driven by, "I want it now!" As you've matured, you've found that a love that invites honesty, truth, and understanding is the most fulfilling, although you've got to share a sense of humor or you may lose interest.

Venus in Capricorn: Your Venus in Capricorn operates in a very cautious manner when it comes to matters of the heart. You prefer a quiet, slow, and safe approach to intimacy. You need to know that love lasts through all time, although you first have to prove to yourself that you are worthy of a timeless love. Just remember that nobody else can give you the love you need until you know how to find it within yourself first. Although working hard or establishing financial success adds to your sense of stability, they may never be quite enough to fill your heart. Money matters are important in your relationships, and you will be happier in a relationship that provides a strong financial base, but choosing a partner simply for financial stability will rarely be completely satisfying. Once you've given your heart, you're unlikely to turn away. One thing to keep in mind: love has a direction all its own, and it sometimes just does not make sense. As you allow love to grow, and develop trust in yourself and those you love, you will experience a truly worthwhile existence.

Venus in Aquarius: You have a deep desire to know a true sense of unconditional love with Venus in Aquarius. This begins by developing self-acceptance and eliminating excessive judgment or prejudice toward others. To open your heart to love, you begin by creating a friendship, and to sustain love, you need to know that you are always true friends. You may find it difficult to relate to a man who needs a mommy, since you need a partner who can be your equal. However, you can be tender and loving, and may show your love most clearly when you help to foster and stimulate the hopes and dreams of those who share your life. You are usually clear about how you feel toward someone, although you may need to work toward developing an understanding of those who are more emotional than you. You approach love in a "non-traditional" fashion, and are capable of sustaining a relationship only if you feel that you are free to be yourself. By finding the flame of love within your own heart and reaching out toward others without asking anything in return, your life will undergo amazing changes.

Venus in Pisces: With Venus in Pisces, you are driven to find love through experiencing a true sense of compassion. This begins by surrendering to your inner self and devoting your life to an existence that incorporates your spirituality. In matters of the heart, you dream of the perfect love, which will carry you away from your ordinary existence and transport you into ecstasy, but finding that love through your connection to another person may not be easy. It may seem okay for a while, and then, when the sparkle fades and reality sets in, you feel that you've fallen victim to your own impossible illusions. Don't lose heart: your aim is fine, as long as you can translate it into human terms! That transcendent love comes most easily when you're in the midst of your creative expression; within the context of a relationship, it emerges when you share your dreams and fantasies and put your energy into making some of those dreams real. You have a huge tendency toward codependent and addictive relationships, and can be easily tempted to give up your own needs in favor of fulfilling the needs of another. In a true loving relationship, each persons' needs are important. Sacrificing yourself may only lead you to a feeling of exhaustion.

Venus Aspects and Loving

Aspects with the Sun

Sun conjunct Venus: With your Sun and Venus conjunct, you can love warmly and openly. However, you may be a little self-involved when it comes to matters of the heart, and may feel that just because you feel strongly about someone that they must, in turn, feel the same way about you. You're probably charismatic enough to have a powerful influence on the feelings and opinions of others, but you really do want a love that is based on honest sharing between both partners. To have this, you have to be just as attentive to the needs of the other as you are to your own.

Sun semisextile Venus: The semisextile connection between your Sun and Venus adds a positive measure of charm to your personality, and may enhance your ability to express your feelings of attraction. You can send just the right subtle signals when you're interested in someone, but have to be careful about assuming the outcome.

Sun semisquare Venus: You can be a bit frustrated by your love experiences with your Sun in semisquare aspect to Venus. Part of the problem resides in your impatience. When you have a strong attraction to someone, you want resolution about the outcome immediately. If you can work toward maintaining a bit more objectivity when your heart begins to open to a loving relationship, you'll be more satisfied with the end results.

Aspects with the Moon

Moon conjunct Venus: Heightened sensuality accompanies the impact of your Moon's energy in conjunction to Venus. You may need more hugs, kisses, and tender touches, and are likely to expect a show of affection as a reasonable part of your intimate relationships. It's difficult for you to nurture love if you have to stay at arm's length! You may find conflict very uncomfortable, but can bring a soothing effect to difficult situations if you watch your timing.

Moon semisextile Venus: The semisextile aspect between your Moon and Venus adds an easy flow between the energy of your deepest needs and your ability to express them. Although you may not always talk about what you need, you can express your emotions in such a way that makes it easy for others to know how you feel. Just try to remember that some men are not the best readers of subtle signals—sometimes you just have to be more direct if you are to feel satisfied!

Moon semisquare Venus: With your Moon and Venus in semisquare aspect, you struggle between meeting your needs and fulfilling your wants. You are attracted to men for all the wrong reasons, which can ultimately result in feeling that your needs are not met. One safeguard that will help you create more fulfilling relationships is to maintain an awareness of your feelings when you're in a vulnerable state. Give yourself time to heal, make the effort to achieve closure when relationships end, and watch your own motivations when you are entering relationships.

Moon sextile Venus: Harmonious relationships can be easier to create with the help of your Moon in sextile aspect to Venus, but you still have to put effort into your close ties if you are to experience the best from them. It's easy for you to compliment those you care about, and giving of yourself feels good. Your own self-esteem is strong enough to allow you to gracefully accept compliments, gifts, and loving gestures from others, too. Expressing your feelings comes easily, and this alone can enhance your ability to attain true intimacy with someone you love.

Moon square Venus: You may wonder why you always seem to have to give more than you receive in love relationships with your Moon in square aspect to Venus. This frustration probably has its roots in your soul's history, and until you can allow love to flow openly from your heart, you may feel that the books are not balanced. Disappointments in love have wounded you in the past, so you have a little sensitivity as a result. Your initial reaction when you feel your heart opening may be to guard yourself since you don't want to repeat the pain of disappointment. The only way to change this is to learn how to fill your own heart with joy and love through the pure experience of love itself. Love without expectation. Love just to love. Begin by loving yourself and knowing that you deserve the kind of love that brings mutual tenderness, respect, and comfort.

Moon trine Venus: Your experiences of love can be self-affirming with your Moon in trine aspect to Venus. Maintaining a sense of inner harmony is easy for you because you are likely to honor your own values and feel comfortable with the choices you make in matters of the heart. Giving love by giving of yourself fills you on many levels and can bring wonderful rewards into your life.

Moon quincunx Venus: Love relationships can keep you a little off balance with your Moon in quincunx aspect to Venus. You may find that you are frequently attracted to someone who is not easily attainable, or that your timing seems to be a bit wrong. You may not trust your own judgment in matters of the heart, and it is easy to try to fill your own needs through someone else instead of filling them yourself, but every time you go too far, the Universe seems to slap you, just to get your attention. Eventually, you do get the point, and as a result, you become adept at handling affairs of the heart. You may always find that there is a tendency to get yourself into a bit of trouble, especially when you are feeling needy, ignored, or lonely. If you can identify the source of your yearnings, you'll be much more successful at really satisfying them!

Moon opposition Venus: Your need to learn about true cooperation in loving relationships is underscored through the influence of your Moon in opposition to Venus. It can be difficult to know exactly how much you are supposed to give, and when it is your turn to receive. The only solution is to maintain a clear awareness of your feelings, and to ask the same of your husband or lover. Part two is sharing that awareness and striving to create a real harmony between your needs and feelings for one another. Too much selfishness on either part will result in withdrawal and undermine trust. You are a lovable woman, and may have to convince yourself that your needs deserve just as much attention as those of others.

Aspects with Mercury

Mercury conjunct Venus: Talking about your feelings can enhance your love relationships, and it's easy for you to express your feelings with Mercury conjunct Venus. You may be most attracted to someone whose sense of refinement is well-developed, and may find it much easier to open your heart to a man who appreciates your ideas and enjoys open communication.

Mercury semisextile Venus: With Mercury and Venus in semisextile, you're more at east in relationships that allow an openness between partners—where you both share your thoughts and feelings. Although you're not always comfortable initiating these expressions, if you feel that something is missing in your close connections, ask yourself if you really feel that you are understood. Your need is to bridge the gap between head and heart, and make them work harmoniously together.

Mercury semisquare Venus: With Mercury in semisquare aspect to Venus, you have trouble clearly communicating your feelings. Sometimes it's just a matter of semantics. You can also send mixed messages, and may attract men who do the same thing. Clarification can be achieved by first reflecting on what you really want to say, and then making sure that you are understood. Intent is not always enough!

Mercury sextile Venus: Your outgoing nature can be quite attractive with Mercury in sextile aspect to Venus. You enjoy relationships with others who share your particular talents or artistic leanings. You appreciate a man who has good taste, or at least shows respect for your own! Communication remains an important quality in your relationships throughout your life.

Aspects with Mars

Venus conjunct Mars: Your sensual and sexual drives are enhanced through the conjunction between Venus and Mars. This quality adds a powerful magnetism to your personality, and you may find that you are forever embroiled in the game of love. It is crucial that you maintain awareness of the signals you project, since you can attract interest or attention when you don't intend to do so. A healthy sexual relationship is an integral part of any love relationship if you are to maintain your interest and experience the energy you desire from the process of intimacy. As time moves along, you may discover that the sensual side of your relationship is not always just sexual. You will always require passion from yourself, and will feel most open to expressing love when you feel passionately about your partner.

Venus semisextile Mars: The game of flirtation and attraction can be a great deal of fun with your Venus in semisextile to Mars. You may find that the steps between your initial attraction and close personal encounter add a significant boost to your love life, and that these are the experiences you recall fondly over the years. You may be adept at sending the right signals when you're interested in a man, but sometimes you miss the signals you receive in return if they are too subtle. Innuendo can be intriguing, but sometimes a good old-fashioned hug is just what you need.

Venus semisquare Mars: You have some conflict between your passions and emotions with Venus in semisquare aspect to Mars. Part of the problem arises when your interest in and attraction to someone is heating up and you are not quite ready for action. Despite your efforts to appear somewhat demure, your eagerness to experience contact can override your best judgment, and you tend to jump in too quickly. This can leave you feeling unduly exposed emotionally. If you are hurt, you can become somewhat punitive in your actions and attitudes, which can undermine your ability to resolve conflict or turmoil in your relationships. Establishing an emotional pace that allows you to feel less exposed will resolve many of the potential problems that can arise from this influence.

Venus sextile Mars: Your ability to attract relationships that are good for you is strengthened through the sextile between your Venus and Mars energies. Your timing is also good, in the sense that you are likely to honor your own vulnerabilities and have a sensitivity to the same in the men you attract, allowing a relationship to move toward intimacy at a pace that feels comfortable. These energies also support your confidence in yourself as a woman and lessen your need to compete with the men in your life.

Venus square Mars: Conflicts in relationships may be more the norm for you than peace and harmony with Venus and Mars in square aspect to one another. You enjoy a relationship that is filled with passion and excitement, but it may take a while before you learn to discriminate between painful and positive forms of conflict. Beneath the surface, you feel a bit competitive with the men in your life. If you can find some manner of open competition with your lover or husband, whether through sports or games, it will help to diffuse some of the potential disagreements you encounter in your relationships. Dealing with your own feelings of anger is also crucial, or you may find that you continually attract angry or violent men into your life. Once you learn that you do not need to suffer in order to prove your worthiness for love, the entire nature of your relationships will change.

Venus trine Mars: When you're sure of what you want from a love relationship, it's reasonably easy to achieve it with your Venus and Mars in trine aspect. Your good fortune in love may seem uncanny at times, and learning to show your appreciation for the positive things you enjoy through your love relationships will assure that this productive cycle will continue. Your kindness and tenderness are easily expressed through your actions and attitudes, and will attract the same from others. You may be demonstrative in intimate relationships, and can enjoy a satisfying sexual and emotional bond with your partner.

Venus quincunx Mars: The problem with your relationship history may reside more in your timing than anything else with Venus in quincunx to Mars. Knowing when to be assertive, when to wait, and when to surrender to passion is not easy. To become aware of your own internal rhythm, tune in to the feelings you have in response to your actions in relationships. A little nervousness may be normal, but feeling totally petrified may tell you that you are not yet ready to jump into intimacy. Learning to be aware of the signals you receive from your partner is also difficult, but is necessary if you are to achieve a sense of harmony.

Venus opposition Mars: You are a very passionate woman. The opposition between the energies of Venus and Mars stimulates a strong level of desire. When you want to be close, there's little that can stop you. You can sometimes be extremely aggressive, and need to allow space in your intimate relationships to take the lead. But you also enjoy being pursued; the only problem is that you don't like waiting for satisfaction! Therefore, you need a man who knows what he wants and who will honor your own autonomy at the same time. It's an interesting challenge, but can be exciting in the right circumstances. In the wrong situation, though, you can attract disruptive, angry, or difficult men. Bringing your Venusian qualities into play involves maintaining an awareness of the need for love and harmony in the midst of passion, and by doing so, you'll attract relationships that portray the best of both worlds.

Aspects to Jupiter

Venus conjunct Jupiter: Your generous and gracious nature, stimulated by the energy of Venus in conjunction with Jupiter, can attract good fortune through your love relationships. It's no accident: you draw positive situations because you create them! When your heart is open, there's nothing you would refuse the one you love. Allowing the flow of love to fill your life with joy increases your ability to give of yourself and your energy. It is tempting to be too indulgent, however, so remember that before you go out to shop for a birthday gift for the one you love! Your intimate relationships are most meaningful when you share ideals, beliefs, or philosophies with your lover or husband, and striving to accomplish a shared vision will add a special spark to the energy of love.

Venus semisextile Jupiter: Sometimes you jump right into relationships before you've had a chance to think about consequences. With Venus and Jupiter in semisextile aspect to one another, you are enthusiastic when you're in love; but if you rush in to situations, you may find yourself back-pedaling rather quickly if you feel overcome by the circumstance (or person). You're one woman who can benefit from counting to ten (okay, five!) before you take the leap.

Venus semisquare Jupiter: When you're in love, you like to give a lot to your lover. The problem with Venus in semisquare to Jupiter is knowing where the limits need to be! Sometimes, especially if you're feeling a little needy, you can be overindulgent toward your lover. If it becomes a habit, you can expend too much energy trying to please and may lose track of what your real feelings and needs are within your close relationships.

Venus sextile Jupiter: With Venus and Jupiter in sextile aspect, you need love relationships that fulfill your highest ideals. Sharing similar religious or philosophical beliefs with your lover or husband will strengthen your ability to love fully and completely. You may also find that a partner who enjoys travel and cultural events will stimulate the opening of your heart. For your love relationship to prosper, it needs to be inclusive. Social, family, and community ties are important to you, and you'll appreciate a partner who shares your priorities.

Venus square Jupiter: Not that you are interested in a man only for his money, but it's definitely a consideration with Venus square Jupiter. Just looking for a Mr. Right who has the bucks is never quite enough, and you know it. So you love wonderful things and have expensive tastes, but if money becomes the real drive, you may have all the stuff and little of the real satisfaction. However, if you fail to take finances into account when making a commitment in your relationships, you'll do yourself a disservice. Just knowing where to put money on the priority list is the problem! Being honest with yourself is where you start, and taking that honesty into your relationship is the next step.

Venus trine Jupiter: When you're in love you like to share everything with your lover. With Venus trine Jupiter, there's a feeling that you have no limits, and a need to experience love as ever-growing and expanding. Love generates more love; and so it is. You'll be happiest with a partner whose philosophies, beliefs, and ideals support your own, and may find that sharing your hopes and dreams for a better life inspires you to remain ever in love with each other.

Venus quincunx Jupiter: You have great expectations of love with Venus in quincunx aspect to Jupiter. Those expectations include how you think you'll feel about yourself and your life when you know somebody really loves you. But you've probably already run into trouble: nothing ever changes until you feel good about yourself! By channeling this energy toward opening to your own vision and allowing yourself to create that vision, you've begun. The fine-tuning involves connecting that vision to your deeper needs, and to the knowledge that love never fails. It is always there, burning brightly in your heart.

Venus opposition Jupiter: When you're in love there's no end to your confidence and hope. With Venus in opposition to Jupiter, being in love is probably near the top of your list of great life experiences. That's a good thing, but loving continues far beyond the "in love" stage. If you set "falling in love" as your horizon, you may never know how much further you can go. If you see falling in love as the opening of a vast doorway to your heart, then the journey of loving is never ending. The other part of the puzzle involves opening your heart to your true feelings and needs, and allowing love to grow within you. By seeing love as an outside object— a man, for example—you'll always feel frustrated. Building the bridge between your heart and the heart of your lover assures that you'll discover a new horizon of possibilities together.

Aspects to Saturn

Venus conjunct Saturn: With the energies of Venus and Saturn in conjunction to one another, you can be too self-restraining in your expression of love and affection. You may feel that you need assurances before you open your heart, and if you're waiting for a guarantee, you may never experience the true love you need. In all your attempts to keep your heart protected, you can shut the door so tightly that you cannot allow the love you have inside yourself to flow freely. Learning to give of yourself in ways that feel good is the beginning to establishing a real sense of happiness, but making a list of requirements (even if it is subconscious) may result in feeling that love is always like the carrot on the stick: a lot of promise, but little result. There is a difference between extreme judgment and supportive critique! Begin by supporting the positive attributes you possess within yourself, and allow yourself to share those talents and abilities without feeling that you have to get something for them. The rewards will be forthcoming, but more importantly, you'll feel the love in your heart taking wing.

Venus semisextile Saturn: With Venus in semisextile aspect to Saturn, you're probably interested in the idea of commitment before you completely give your heart away. First of all, once you give the love in your heart, it does *not* disappear! And secondly, the real commitment you're making is the one you make to yourself. Discovering that you are the one who generates the love you feel, and that you are the one who controls how much of that love you give to others, can lead you to become more self-assured in your relationships. Love readily replenishes itself the more it is shared. Most importantly, the real magic is that when you truly open your heart to love, the love itself streams into an eternal process. Now, that's a commitment!

Venus semisquare Saturn: All the romantic rambling you've heard about love has probably gotten on your nerves. With Venus in semisquare aspect to Saturn, you require proof of the reality of love. Of course, the fact that love is not tangible is the first problem. Sure, there are a few tangible things that help to confirm that somebody cares, but you just can't get your hands on love itself. You have to feel it, and that means you have to trust yourself. It's okay to test the trust you have within a relationship. It's probably even necessary, but in the interim, you have the experience of loving and allowing someone to get close to you. That is the tangible reality.

Yet beyond the physical plane is something more, with a value that can be measured only in terms of how much you've opened your heart and listened to the melody of love. You may feel only disappointment if you become too selfish, since the love that vibrantly began will seem to wither. Staying open, allowing the flow—in and out, giving and receiving—will help to remove the blocks and encourage love to grow.

Venus sextile Saturn: When you love, you love deeply and with commitment. The energies of Venus and Saturn in sextile to one another stimulate a need to experience continuity and growth through love. You may even discover that sometimes you have to sacrifice something you want in order to fulfill a higher need, and when you do, love grows even more fully. You are willing to pay the price for a love that lasts, since you know how precious it is. The beauty you feel within your heart through sustaining love radiates through every part of your life.

Venus square Saturn: Loving is not always easy for you with Venus in square aspect to Saturn. Somewhere, deep in your heart, you feel that you do not really deserve love. That's for someone much more beautiful and perfect than you feel you are. You have one remedy for this problem: stop it! Use that Saturn energy to establish a new foundation for love, and begin by learning the difference between selfish, fear-driven love and generous, compassionate love. Just because you were hurt somewhere along the line, you do not have to continue the process of pain and suffering. Opening the doors to your heart will not be easy. It's like a cosmic test. You may be disappointed yet again; and the test is to find if you will still allow the energy of love to flow, even in the midst of endings or loss. Insisting on guarantees will never work, yet making a commitment to loving relationships that allow growth and opportunity will surprise you. This is your great challenge, and it will resonate through everything you do.

Venus trine Saturn: You are reliable in your love relationships with Venus in trine aspect to Saturn. You believe in a love that endures, and will grow best in relationships that provide an opportunity for mutual trust and support. Patience with your own mere humanity adds a sense of practical humility, and reflects in your attitudes of helpful acceptance toward others. You're willing to put effort into your relationships instead of just expecting that they arrive ready-made. Opening your heart is easy when you trust yourself, and developing that sense of self-acceptance is one of the key ingredients toward experiencing the kind of relationship that can stand the test of time. For you, love is the great teacher, and you are the willing student.

Venus quincunx Saturn: Sometimes, loving is a series of frustrations. The stimulus of Venus in quincunx to Saturn provides a sense of disappointment through love, especially if you've gotten into situations that were counterproductive to your growth. In essence, you're here to learn about the difference between healthy and destructive loving. Once you've gotten the feel and taste of a healthy connection, you can repeat the process. The first contact is between your ego and your inner self in a mutually supportive link. When you remain connected to the little gyroscope in the center of your heart that sings when you're in a situation that allows love to flow, all is well, but when you try to pretend that the gyroscope does not work or that the song does not matter, you feel the pain. It's like Pavlov's dog: you're training yourself to know the difference. Just remember who is running the experiment. It's not the guy you love. It's you.

Venus opposition Saturn: Love can be a test with Venus in opposition to Saturn. It's a test of your ability to remain open, even when your heart is broken. It's a test of your faith in the experience of love itself as a pure quality. It's a test of your own sense of worthiness. You may think you've just run into bad luck or bad choices if you've had disappointments in love, but the real obstacle is your fear. You can overcome this obstacle by really loving yourself and developing a sense of acceptance toward others. Learning to give without expectation is another key element that will allow you to change your experience of love, but it's a more difficult test.

Aspects to Uranus

Venus conjunct Uranus: Your independent nature strongly influences the way you open to love with Venus in conjunction to Uranus. Philosophically, you agree that unconditional love is your goal, but your experience tells you that you have a few conditions. One of them is to have a love that can withstand change. Life itself provides many of those changes, and you've already learned about the disruptions that can occur when the unexpected arrives on your doorstep. For you, relationships are only part of the picture of love. As a result, you feel close to your lover for a while, but when you're involved in something else, you seem to drift away. A relationship that allows room for individual autonomy is also necessary (and that means you may have to give the same thing to him). If you feel that you tend to attract flaky guys or men who are unattainable, turn around and look in the mirror. Exactly how emotionally available are you? Maybe you really don't want a single relationship to be the primary focus in your life. If that's the truth, then accept it and be honest about it. If not, surrender to your need to be close, at least in the here and now. You may discover that you like it, and that you're really not giving up your freedom after all!

Venus semisextile Uranus: You're attracted to relationships that are out of the ordinary with Venus in semisextile to Uranus. Maintaining your autonomy is paramount, and you have such a strong need for independence that you're willing to function without a sense of commitment—for a while, at least. What you really need is a situation that allows you to keep your options open, and that can be created within the context of responsible, committed relationship—but on terms that fit your individual needs. The standard contract—love, honor, and obey—is not your style, particularly the "obey" part. What you're seeking is a love of free expression and unrestrained possibilities. That is something you'll promise, because it is something you can deliver!

Venus semisquare Uranus: The thrill of loving is a pure elixir of life for you with Venus in semisquare aspect to Uranus. You are a little experimental in your attitudes toward relationships, and you love more readily when you feel unrestrained. Sometimes you're difficult to reach on an emotional level, especially if you're on one of your independent jags. They surface occasionally, and can be disruptive in a relationship that demands the same thing all the time. If you are to have a successful relationship, you need lots of room to be yourself, to explore your options in the world, and to feel unfettered. The problem is that you may feel this means you cannot tie yourself to one person, at least for very long. After all, what would happen if you missed something?! You may need to review your attitudes toward commitment and consider the possibility of loving freely without conditions and expectations. That's a commitment in itself, and requires great diligence to accomplish successfully.

Venus sextile Uranus: Your originality and ingenuity are quite attractive with Venus in sextile aspect to Uranus. It's easier for you to open your heart to someone who is as autonomous and self-sufficient as you. In the process, you find that you cherish the friendships you create more than the passionate bedroom encounters. However, there's nothing wrong with either. It's likely that if you end a relationship with a lover, you will become friends, and it is at this level that you may experience the most profound sense of unconditional love. You can incorporate that feeling into your intimate relationships, too, but it requires a partner who will not feel threatened by your autonomy and occasional emotional distance. You're quite willing to flow with changes, and probably even create a few just to keep your energy moving.

For your relationship to be successful in the long term, it must be open, allow room for individuality, and encourage free thinking on the part of both partners.

Venus square Uranus: Sometimes you just need to make changes with Venus square Uranus. You do not easily tolerate restrictions in relationships, and if you're in a circumstance that is too inhibiting, you will rebel against it. You also tend to be most attracted to men (and women) who are emotionally detached or unavailable in some way (married, living in another country, aliens from other planets, etc.), and until you realize that this happens when you really don't want to be tied down, it will continue. Okay, so maybe they're not aliens, but they can certainly seem that way when you try to get into a really intimate situation. Your own needs for intimacy can seem quite alien to you, and if you are to incorporate them into your life, you first need to recognize that you are not interested in repeating patterns women have repeated for centuries. You will have a relationship your way or not at all. Before you can experience a truly satisfying level of intimacy, you need to come to grips with your deeper emotional needs instead of just seeking thrills. You are a truly unique woman who needs a truly unique kind of love. Your mission, should you choose to accept it, is to find out about the true nature of love.

Venus trine Uranus: With Venus and Uranus in trine aspect to one another, you possess an unusually magnetic and attractive quality. You can love with abandon and enjoy the pure pleasure of sensuality. Loving can be purely thrilling, and the high energy you experience when you're in love can alter your entire life. You prefer relationships that allow ample freedom, and will strive to offer the same liberties to your partner as you demand for yourself. Non-traditional relationship styles may be appealing, and you are capable of creating a truly unique experience of love.

Venus quincunx Uranus: You enjoy relationships that are full of surprises, until the surprises leave you in a lurch, unprepared for the unexpected. With Venus in quincunx to Uranus, you are likely to send mixed signals about your emotional availability (probably because you vacillate in regard to whether or not you really want to get involved). This can result in a series of frustrating, albeit interesting, relationships. You attract men who seem to be great in the playful part of relationships, but when they have to deal with commitment or responsibility, immediately disappear. Your own emotional changeability can be confusing to someone who wants a predictable woman. Sorting through your priorities in a love relationship involves staying closely connected to the here and now, since your life circumstances are subject to change. Incorporating this need for growth, change, and openness into your relationships will ultimately save a lot of heartache. You have the right to demand accountability from your partners, but you must be willing to come forth on your own, too.

Venus opposition Uranus: So, you want a relationship that offers absolute freedom. Okay. Can you give the same thing in return? With Venus in opposition to Uranus, you are very likely to resist anything that looks like commitment, especially if it is restraining. Your own rebellion can create disruption and change in your close relationships, and you wonder why you seem to attract men who never want to grow up. You love unusual people, adore your friends (although you may not have seen them for decades!), and attract unique situations. The thrill of being in love is wonderful for you, but you lose interest when that intensity is not retained. When you stop and think about it, maintaining such a high level of intensity might result in spontaneous combustion! That's why the course of love has its twists and turns. It does not mean that love no longer exists when your feelings change. Love has just evolved. If you are to evolve with it, you will learn to flow with the current of change. Those relationships that allow ample room for personal evolution, individual autonomy, and true equality can work for you and for the ones you love.

Aspects to Neptune

Venus conjunct Neptune: Love is the force that shapes and sustains your life with Venus conjunct Neptune. Your romantic nature inspires you to believe in the ultimate possibilities of love, and you may have very definitive fantasies about loving. When you're in love, your compassion knows no bounds. You feel that you could sacrifice anything for the man you love, and sometimes do. Yearning for a soul mate, you expect the same high ideals from your partner, although you may not always find them. Your emotional boundaries are flexible, which allows you to feel what others are feeling, but that can also be confusing when you're trying to determine what's going on with you individually. You may not always feel confident taking the initiative in love, and may spend more time fantasizing about possibilities than you spend acting on your desires. You need a love that honors your spirituality and sensitivity, and you need to safeguard against falling into situations that abuse your kindhearted care and concern.

Venus semisextile Neptune: You feel that love is your opportunity to transcend the ordinary with Venus in semisextile to Neptune. A partner who shares your desires to make the world a better place and whose emotional sensitivity allows you to share your soul is your ideal. However, you may also attract men who need to be rescued in some way, and you must be aware of your tendency to sacrifice your own needs in favor of another's. In some situations this is necessary, but it is not a requirement that you give up your own needs on a permanent basis! You need a love that is both physical and spiritual, and may discover that blending these qualities allows you to manifest the stuff that dreams are made of.

Venus semisquare Neptune: You have too many illusions about love with Venus in semisquare aspect to Neptune. Believing that finding the right partner will turn your life around can be going too far, since in essence, you must surrender to the perfect power of love that resides within your own heart before you can attract the type of lover you need. You can be very vulnerable when you open your heart, and need to allow ample time to discover the real nature of those you are learning to love before you make long-term commitments. Your tendency is to see what you desire to see, and to reflect your own beauty and power onto the one you love. Once you can assimilate the true compassion and caring you feel deep within yourself and project the same with clarity and confidence, you will attract a lover whose purity of spirit compliments your own. You must become love in order to have it.

Venus sextile Neptune: When you love, you love deeply and completely. With Venus in sextile aspect to Neptune, you have the capability of surrendering totally to the essence of love. Your gentle, caring manner attracts a partner who will desire to love and protect you. You know when you've found your true love because something deep inside you opens up and transports you. Although you have some tendency to hold unrealistic expectations of those you love, you do it in such a caring manner that they may surprise everyone else but you by their accomplishment of apparently miraculous change. You know when it's time to forgive and move on, which allows you to remain open to feelings of joy, even in the midst of change. Your devotion to high ideals also plays a part in your love relationships, and you are capable of sustaining a love that originates at a very powerful level and will last through eternity.

Venus square Neptune: In square aspect to Neptune, your Venusian expression takes on an otherwordly quality. Your yearning may be for that perfect lover whose spirituality, passion, purity of spirit, and drive all stem from the highest possible level. Loving in such a manner would seem to remove you from the bondage of ordinary life and transport you into true bliss. Although this seems possible in fairy tales or movies, it's really difficult to find those elements in another human being. You may also operate under the illusion that you must first sacrifice yourself before you are worthy of love. It's all too easy to project unrealistic feelings onto your lover, and it is just as tempting to try to alter yourself to please a man so that he will love you. Whether those alterations are in your behavior, your appearance, or your attitudes, if you submerge your real self beneath the illusions of what you feel will make you more lovable, you're selling out. If you want to experience the ecstasy you dream about, you'll surrender to a love that honors your real needs, and learn to avoid situations where you become addicted, co-dependent, victimized, or abused. Forgiving the shortcomings of the man you love is one thing; allowing him to deceive or victimize you is another! Know when and how to give help, but be careful of emotional rescue ventures!

Venus trine Neptune: Your romantic nature is enhanced by the influence of Venus in trine aspect to Neptune. When you're in love, you create at atmosphere of magical possibilities that transports you into another dimension. Love can be a purely transcendent experience for you, since you are capable of opening your heart to a true feeling of compassion. Your gentility, creativity, and artistry can be especially attractive, and when you're involved in a loving relationship, you are comfortable sharing the secrets of your heart. Allowing love to flow as you follow its course is natural for you, and you will be happiest in relationships that support your sense of divine harmony. Forgiveness and acceptance keep the energy of love flowing freely.

Venus quincunx Neptune: You definitely have your dreams and hopes about love, although it may seem that reality leaves you with the short straw much of the time. The influence of Venus in quincunx to Neptune yields an energy of confusion in matters of the heart, and may lead to some disappointment in love. It's not really love that disappoints you as much as it is your experience of loving. You tend to project what you want to see onto your lover, especially in the early stages of a relationship when what you're feeling is the energy that is triggered inside yourself. You've let go of the barriers to your heart. By allowing a little time for the dust to settle, you can begin to filter the reality of the person you love into the picture. Although you may have thought you wanted one thing, you may discover that your deeper needs have led you to something quite different. When you begin to think of this as serendipity rather than a curse, the whole picture of your love life will begin to change.

Venus opposition Neptune: Your projections about your lover or partner frequently overshadow the real person with Venus in opposition to Neptune. Even though you may not want to admit it, you are more likely to see only what you want to see when you're in love. That feeling of being transported into another world when you're in love is actually quite accurate, but it's not the guy who's gotten you there all by himself—it's the stimulated energy inside you that allows you to soar! It's not easy to separate your dream lover from the real person standing before you. You may always project some of your own power and tenderness onto the man you love; but as long as you can allow the reality of the person to emerge into your field of vision, you stand a chance of having a relationship that can truly serve both your needs. Otherwise, you may fall into the trap of delusion, deception, or emotional abuse. Just because he's the most gorgeous man you've ever seen, it may not necessarily follow that he is what you really need—or that he's *real* for that matter! In all your attempts to become as beautiful as possible, just to make sure that the right man will be attracted to you, you can lose yourself. You really do not have to sacrifice yourself to know love, but when your heart is filled with love, you're willing to drop all your boundaries and merge completely. There's a difference between a soul connection and codependency or emotional addiction. It's drawing the line that's difficult. By allowing for periods of privacy and contemplation, you can maintain your connection to your own inner self, which will allow you to keep your emotional boundaries reasonably intact.

Aspects to Pluto

Venus conjunct Pluto: You love with intensity and can experience absolute transformation through loving with the energy of Venus in conjunction to Pluto. For you, loving is the ultimate healer, and you seek relationships that allow you to open to your true power. Just dabbling in a relationship is rarely enough; you prefer to immerse yourself in the experience of loving, totally. Your refusal to compromise concerning your needs requires that you find a special relationship that is based on healthy, honest interaction and support. You can become obsessive in your relationships, and need to learn to back away from your intense involvement from time to time, just to get a different perspective. Enhanced sensuality is part of your expression of love, and you may find that you need a relationship that allows you to explore your sexual needs as fully as possible. Although you may not be open with just anyone about your deeper needs, your lover probably knows many of your secrets. For this reason, it is crucial that you choose your relationships wisely, basing them on mutual trust and honesty. You are seeking a love that can bond you with your partner on as many levels as possible.

Venus semisextile Pluto: Love is like a key that opens the doorway to the depths of your consciousness. The influence of Venus in semisextile to Pluto brings the opportunity to experience personal regeneration through love. You may not always find it easy to open your heart, since you need such a powerful experience of love, and it's probably better to approach love gradually instead of just diving in heart first. Since you're likely to experience more than one important love relationship in your life, you may discover that love has many features. You may run into your own resistance more than once in the course of experiencing love, especially if you feel that you might lose a part of yourself in the process. When you do find another whose heart welcomes your own, you can love deeply and passionately.

Venus semisquare Pluto: Loving is not always easy for you with Venus in semisquare aspect to Pluto. Your own insecurities that stem from previous disappointments or hurts can block your ability to open your heart. Reasonable caution makes sense, but closing your heart hurts you on many different levels. You are capable of rising above these old wounds, and may discover that the process has made you stronger. Learning to trust your own ability to love strengthens your lovability! Instead of always feeling hungry for love, allow yourself to create a feast by plowing through those barriers, finding the key to your heart and opening the door. Love is an ever-changing experience; it does not stay the same. The same is true of you.

Venus sextile Pluto: You can feel the power of love with Venus in sextile aspect to Pluto. Relationships that stimulate your growth and strengthen your sense of wholeness are an integral part of your life, and your influence in the lives of others can be quite positive. With an awareness of the ever-changing nature of love, you can embrace the process of true alchemy through loving. Each time you open your heart to love, you experience a new level of personal transformation. Since your deep desire is for a love that connects at your core level, you are more likely to experience intimacy as a positive process and welcome the removal of personal barriers. You may still be a little guarded, especially when you run into your vulnerabilities, and at this level, you have a few simple levels of protection. You do not feel the need to maintain strong barriers between yourself and those you love. Letting go of the past is a continual process for you as you move through the different stages of your life, and you are capable of handling endings with a sense of grace and acceptance. Knowing when to let go and move on is one of your best attributes.

Venus square Pluto: You may find it difficult to trust that love will bring positive changes into your life with Venus in square aspect to Pluto. It's likely that you've been deeply wounded through love, and as a result, you have erected some amazing barriers to protect your vulnerability. If you've had experiences that have felt too possessive, either from your side or your lover's, you've realized that loving is very different from owning someone. You also struggle with the feeling that you are not worthy of love. Whether or not you feel you are beautiful, you may still undergo a series of alterations to improve or change your appearance in order to become more acceptable. If you are making these changes for reasons that are positive, healing, and supportive, then move forward, but if you're tempted to re-shape yourself in order to appeal to someone else or to an external set of ideals, think again. The real changes need to occur on an inner level. You need to be able to look in the mirror, gaze into your own eyes, and see love. If you can't see it, how can anyone else find it? Somewhere, deep in your heart, is the essence of real love. You already possess it, and nobody can take it from you. You can hide it from yourself and everyone else, but it calls to you, needing your touch and embrace. It is only through allowing love to work its magic in your life that you will know true healing, and all you have to do is to create space for it to happen without trying to control it.

Venus trine Pluto: Your need to find a lover whose embrace will transform your life stems from the energies of Venus in trine aspect to Pluto. You are capable of creating a love that brings rejuvenation, hope, and power into your own life and into the lives of those you love. Although you love with great intensity, you can allow your lover the space he needs, and can give yourself the same. You know that love continues beyond the physical plane, and when you give your heart, you extend energy that lasts into eternity. There is room in your heart for love on many different levels, and you have the capability of building a true bond of trust, understanding, and deep caring with those who know your heart.

Venus quincunx Pluto: The road to the kind of love you need is a little rocky with Venus in quincunx aspect to Pluto. You've probably had a broad spectrum of experiences through loving, some of which have brought you to the heights of ecstasy, others to the cliffs of despair. It's all part of love—the twists and turns, the passions and betrayals, the new life and endings. You may even be an expert in relationships since you've seen so many facets of love. That is unless you've given up and decided that love just isn't worth the trouble. Deep in your heart, you know that's not true. You've felt what it's like to be renewed through love. All you have to do is remember the part of yourself that is strong enough to make it through any test, and call on her to help you. Developing a real sense of trust in your deep feelings about people is an excellent beginning toward changing the way love works in your life. Instead of just jumping in when the passion is overwhelming, you're at least learning to take a deep breath first! Who knows, you might even become a champion swimmer!

Venus opposition Pluto: With Venus in opposition to Pluto, you must confront a lot of negative feelings in order to get to the essence of love. You have to get beyond mistrust, shame, disappointment, fears of abandonment, and the ghosts of the past before you are truly transformed by the experience of loving. Opening your heart is not easy. You may even think you've lost the key, until one day you realize that it's been there in your hands all along. You've always had a deep yearning to love and be loved, fully and completely. The problem lies in finding the right partner, which is true for every woman. For you, some of the old wounds, beliefs, or fears may be buried so deeply that you feel too vulnerable. Love is not there to hurt or harm. Love exists to heal and transport you. There is a condition, though: real love harmonizes with your needs. It begins when you can confront yourself with the realization that you deserve the love you need. Once you fully integrate this feeling into your heart, the love will work like a beacon to attract that special and unusual person who can sense those needs, truly and honestly. You also have to get beyond your own tendency to attract severely wounded individuals who do not want to be healed. When both of you are focused on transformation, it's a different story.

Neptune: The Love of Divine Compassion

Neptune's energy stirs your imagination. Through Neptune you fall in love with love itself. By allowing Neptune's energy to flow through your life, you allow yourself to reach beyond your personal needs into the collective and love humankind and all life. Neptunian love is spiritual in its origins; but since Neptune doesn't know much about boundaries, there can be problems when you try to translate this form of loving into the human experience. Neptune dissolves boundaries, and when you are spiritually bonded with another, you discover that the love you feel for one another transcends the boundaries of yourself. To experience the most from Neptunian love, you must learn to surrender to your Higher Self and to let go of your need to be in control. Let love flow. To avoid the problems that arise with Neptune, you must also know your inner self or you can fall into the traps of addictive relationships, co-dependent issues, and destructive abuse. Reflect on the meaning of Neptune in your chart. It is your key to compassion—for yourself and for others.

Neptune in the Signs and Ideal Love

Neptune in Cancer: As one of the generation of women born with Neptune in Cancer, you have a very special tie to your family. You hold the belief that intimate relationships are a necessary part of the continuity of family, and you have a strong sentimentality about the idea of the traditional family. When you open your heart and embrace another through love and care, they become part of your sense of family. It is important that you share similar beliefs and ideals with your life mate, since this may be the primary tie that binds you together. Developing a true understanding of the spiritual essence and focusing on this energy as the "glue" in your relationships, you can indeed become an expression of divine tenderness and support. These are the teachings you pass on to the generations that follow you.

Neptune in Leo: As one of the generation of women born with Neptune in Leo, your belief that the energy of God as an energy of Pure Love is at the core of your own ability to love another fully and completely. You are capable of sustaining love, and may be driven by the ideal that love is the ultimate healer. When you surrender your own will to that of divine love, your heart opens and allows acceptance, forgiveness, and understanding. You may hold the belief that men should be the head of the household and take care of the family, but you have also struggled with the fact that this is not always the case. The contrast between the reality and the ideal has lead you to discover your own individual power, which, when blended with that of your partner, can be even more effective if you are each driven by a common sense of love and compassion. Most importantly, the experience of this energy allows you to accept your own power as an individual woman who has played the integral role of focus and power for many years. It's time that you appreciate yourself and allow regular contact with your divine essence, which is there to recharge and revitalize you whenever you need it.

Neptune in Virgo: As one of the generation of women born with Neptune in Virgo, you are working toward a sense of spiritual perfection. This influences every aspect of your life, especially your relationships, and relationships that distort your sense of divine harmony may be especially difficult for you to tolerate. You also have a kind of addiction to perfection that makes it almost impossible to feel that you really deserve the love you need. When you realize that everything is perfect, including you, loving gets easier because self-acceptance is easier. This is especially critical at this time in your life when you are facing the process of aging. After all, you've had a kind of fascination with youthful vitality. You can still radiate that energy regardless of your chronological age, and may finally be willing to deal directly with the perfection of each stage of your life. In your relationships, you will be challenged to release dysfunctionality and face your real needs. These include a life of truly simple pleasures, unencumbered by external pressures that get in the way of just enjoying the company of those you love.

Neptune in Libra: As one of the generation of women born with Neptune in Libra, you have been inundated with endless images, stories, and myths about true love and romance. You've dreamt of the perfect marriage, and may have believed that you would, indeed, be rescued by that perfect prince. As you've grown up, you've found that the prince may not only be late, he may not arrive at all! Hope springs eternal, however, and thanks to open discussion about relationship, you've also learned about addiction, codependency, and dysfunctionality, and found some ways to get out of these patterns and traps. Rule number one: Create your own dream by understanding yourself and your needs. From that point, you begin to separate from the trap of the collective still searching for the perfect other, and from the beacon of your own soul, you send out a light that attracts someone who may, indeed, fit your needs quite nicely after all.

Neptune in Scorpio: As one of the generation of women born with Neptune in Scorpio, you are seeking relationships that involve total connection. When you finally open your heart to love in an intimate relationship, you need to feel that you can create a true bond with your lover and mate. Halfway connections don't cut it, and if you're the one resisting, it's crucial that you discover the root of your fears or blocks. Your experience of compassionate love involves surrender to the processes of transformation, and that transformation may involve getting to the core of why you need intimacy in your life. Sexuality is certainly a part of the drive, but it is not for pure pleasure alone, nor is it for simple regeneration of the species. There is a link of energy formed during the process of intimacy that leads to the alchemy of loving, and it is that link that you are learning to understand more fully.

Neptune in Sagittarius: As one of the generation of women born with Neptune in Sagittarius, you may be intimately involved in reshaping the definition of marriage. Laws that reflect the true nature of loving and making commitments may be difficult to initiate, but are important parts of your task as a collective during this lifetime. On a personal level, you may find that your primary drive in relationships involves finding a partner who shares your quest for truth and understanding. To open your heart to real compassion, you need to feel a sense of trust that originates from your common ideals and values. Once your vision is focused with that of your partner, you can create amazing changes that will form the basis of the teachings you pass on to your children and future generations.

Neptune in Capricorn: As one of the generation of women born with Neptune in Capricorn, you may be most comfortable in relationships based on values that have been proven over time. This does not mean that you will have to follow the same patterns your grandparents followed, but that, instead, you can create new avenues based on the lessons learned from past experience. You may be tempted to try to put all relationships into categories, but you are likely to find that they simply do not fit since some relationships cross a few of the lines! But what you can accomplish successfully is a return of personal responsibility to intimate relationships within the structure of the family. Perhaps you can create a non-dysfunctional family process, which allows mutual support for all concerned and utilizes the power of each individual to create an integrated whole that is virtually invulnerable.

Neptune's Aspects: Sensitivity to Inner Light

Aspects with the Sun

Sun conjunct Neptune: With your Sun and Neptune conjunct, you need to be aware of a tendency to attract men who are perfect for your projections. You see only what you wish to see, and can be especially dazzled by a man who seems to embody your ideals. Before you make a commitment, take time to discover the person behind the mask you've projected onto him. Once you learn to accept your own needs for individual expression, you may not need a man to express the power side of your personality. You will appreciate, instead, a man who understands and honors your sensitive tenderness and supports your autonomy.

Sun semisquare Neptune: Since your Sun and Neptune are in a semisquare aspect, you may have trouble seeing men as they are. Your dream of the perfect man has probably met defeat more than once when you've awakened to realize that there is no such animal, but you can still fall into the trap of seeing only the illusion and failing to realize the real person. Once you have a stronger sense of yourself as a whole person, you will not be tempted to project so much of yourself onto the men in your life.

Sun sextile Neptune: The influence of your Sun in sextile aspect to Neptune indicates that you need a relationship that embodies many qualities, ranging from physical to emotional to spiritual connections. Integrating the spiritual essence of yourself into your relationships is easy when you have a partner who respects and supports you as a whole woman. You are most drawn to a man whose spirituality is a powerful part of his life.

Sun square Neptune: With your Sun in square aspect to Neptune, you have a history of rescuing men who don't really appreciate or acknowledge your sacrifice. If you're sacrificing your own dreams and needs so that the man in your life can have his, you're in trouble! If you're making excuses to yourself because your man drinks too much, uses drugs, is not available for the kids, runs around on you—whatever they are—you have lost yourself to an illusion. By learning to set reasonable boundaries and to identify the situations you can and cannot support, your life will change. Your ability to love fully will change, but if you stay stuck in the same old dependencies, your life will be more like a nightmare than a wonderful dream.

Sun trine Neptune: The image of the perfect man can be rather realistic with your Sun in trine aspect to Neptune. You certainly have your hopes for what you want, but you also allow room for mere humanity. After all, if you share a vision with the man you love, and you can use your combined energies to create that vision, life can be a wonderful experience. You may even decide that you are perfectly comfortable without a committed relationship, but there are other factors that relate to these needs.

Sun quincunx Neptune: What you read in the romance novels and see in the movies inspire you to believe that love can, indeed, conquer all—and it can, but in real life, you may still be confronted by men who leave their underwear in the middle of the floor, who can't figure out how to handle money, or who just have no sense of taste. That's okay, you can handle it as long as there is honesty, trust, and communication. You need a relationship that allows room and time for the spiritual side of life, and in which there is a real support. The other things are just adjusting to life, and you're quite good at that.

Sun opposition Neptune: You never feel satisfied with any man who shares your life with your Sun in opposition to Neptune. That is, at least, until you release the man you love from the illusion of perfection he must meet before you can accept him. Strangely enough, this all goes back to seeing yourself clearly and accepting yourself as you are. You must learn to create positive boundaries between yourself and those who share your heart because you are so sensitive that you will respond emotionally to their feelings as though they were your own. If you fall into patterns of codependency and dysfunctionality, that's okay as long as you are working to get beyond the traps involved, but if you're in denial about the truth of your relationships, you have much more work to do.

Aspects with the Moon

Moon conjunct Neptune: Since your Moon and Neptune are conjunct, it is sometimes difficult to separate your real feelings from those you imagine or dream about. Introspection, meditation, and contemplation can help you sort through the differences between what is real and what is not, especially when it comes to finding a man to share your life. Your tender, caring nature may draw men into your life who need compassion and understanding, and it's good to give it, but not to the point of your own exhaustion. It is crucial to set reasonable emotional boundaries in your close relationships to avoid exhausting yourself.

Moon semisquare Neptune: Since your Moon and Neptune are in a semisquare aspect, you may find it difficult to maintain your emotional boundaries. There can also be some frustration between the reality of what you are experiencing in your personal relationships and what you dream of experiencing. In order to bring your dreams into reality, it is crucial that you spend time each day connecting with the innermost parts of yourself. Allowing time for inner reflection will make it easier to capture the truly imaginative possibilities of sharing your life with another. When you're involved in the everyday elements of your relationship, try to be aware of the times when you need to step aside and allow others to have their own space. You also need to define your needs and expectations more clearly in order to avoid disappointment when you feel slighted or misunderstood.

Moon sextile Neptune: Since your Moon and Neptune are in sextile aspect, you can easily open your heart to express compassionate understanding, caring, and tenderness. In any relationship, these extensions of yourself can be rewarding for all concerned. You can also allow the man you love to support you emotionally, and if you feel you need a little more attention, just ask. How could he refuse?

Moon square Neptune: Setting emotional boundaries is not easy for you with your Moon in square aspect to Neptune, and you may find that you are continually giving of yourself and asking nothing in return. Oh, but you dream about it; and you need support, strength, and love from the man you adore. There are different ways to express these needs, and therein is the variation in the possibilities of receiving. If you're whining, complaining, or suffering, you may be ignored, and you don't have to be sick to gain support, either. There are healthy ways to ask, but if you're in an unhealthy situation, it's difficult to get the answer you need. If you're feeling victimized, take the first step of deciding that you no longer want or need to be the victim. A lot will change after that!

Moon trine Neptune: With your Moon and Neptune in trine aspect, you may find it easy to trust your feelings when you're opening to love. Your sixth sense about other people is usually clear, and when you've found the right partner for your needs, you know. You still have to watch a tendency to be too emotionally sensitive, but it's not usually a difficult problem.

Moon quincunx Neptune: When the Moon and Neptune are in quincunx aspect to one another, you can have trouble seeing things as they are. That includes people, and if someone appeals to your need to rescue, you may jump right in—even if your life is running on a different course. Keeping a close connection to your inner self is imperative or you run the risk of confusing compassion with martyrdom.

Moon opposition Neptune: With your Moon and Neptune in opposition, you have a strong need to find your soul mate. The sense that you are not complete until you've merged with your perfect partner may drive you into relationships that are a far cry from your real needs, until you've made some changes within yourself. If you're too needy in your relationships, you will lose a part of your self esteem. Nobody else has the other half of your soul—it's there in the center of your being. There may be a partner who can help shed light on that aspect of yourself, and this can be a healthy connection if you are both honest about the realities of each of your lives.

Aspects to Mercury

Mercury conjunct Neptune: With the energy of Mercury and Neptune in conjunction, you'll wax poetic when you're in love. Even if you've never seemed to be lyrical, when you're in love you may find yourself humming love songs or doodling love poems while sitting in reverie at your desk. You adore hearing the whisper of magical words and feel rather complimented when your sweetheart names your special song. You lose your boundaries when a man writes the most beautiful words about you, composes a song inspired by you, or dedicates his artistic outpouring to you. Even if it's never happened (yet), you can still dream, right?

Mercury semisquare Neptune: You may dream about a perfect love and can be strongly influenced by those overly idealistic images in stories, movies, magazines, or on television. With Mercury semisquare to Neptune, it's important that you learn the difference between what you wish you were hearing and what is actually being said. You'll leave yourself open to disappointment if you hear just those things you want to hear, instead of listening to the whole story.

Mercury sextile Neptune: Beautiful words, poetic ideas, and spiritual quests are all part of your fantasies of love with Mercury in sextile aspect to Neptune. If you put your energy and focus into creating the manifestation of these ideals, you may actually see some of those dreams become real. You'll adore a man who is spirituality genuine and whose ability to show compassion is part of the core of his being, because that is a reflection of a true part of yourself.

Mercury square Neptune: The difference between fantasy and reality concerning the nature of love is sometimes difficult to determine with the energy of Mercury in square aspect to Neptune. You may be prone to "selective hearing," listening to the things that fit your fantasy of what you want to experience and ignoring those things that would shatter your fantasies. This type of thinking is a form of denial, and you may also have some tendencies toward codependency in your relationships. Take a look in the mirror every morning and remind yourself what you know and how you think and feel about things. Don't let yourself be swayed by someone else who seems to know more than you do. Who knows you better than you know yourself?

Mercury trine Neptune: Since you have Mercury in trine aspect to Neptune, you're the perfect candidate for creating wonderful representations of love and compassion through your words. Your lyrical abilities can extend to the way you talk, and your mannerisms are fascinating. You actually attract more men than you realize, since you spend some time in your own inner world. It is that quality at work when you finally let go and share your life and fantasies with someone you adore. Promise yourself to always make time to get away with your lover so your dreams have a safe place to overtake your life—for at least a little while.

Mercury quincunx Neptune: Sometimes making the adjustment between your wishes and the reality of your life can be rather frustrating. With Mercury and Neptune in quincunx aspect, you can "accidentally" leave the wrong impression by projecting double-messages—saying one thing and doing another. In some ways, this is a form of self protection; but always keeping him guessing is not the best way to build trust in a close relationship.

Mercury opposition Neptune: The ideals of love versus the logical facts of life can sometimes leave a huge gap. With Mercury in opposition to Neptune, you definitely have your fantasies about what it means to have the perfect connection to a partner. Your problems arise when you get into the vague zone and fail to clarify what you need, what you feel, or what you really meant to say. There's a time and place for magical thinking, but if you really want a commitment, you may have to come down to earth for a few minutes if you want it to stick!

Aspects with Mars

Mars conjunct Neptune: With your Mars and Neptune in conjunction, you project a powerful illusion about the nature of your perfect man. You may think you want a man who embodies all the traits you dream about, but discover instead that you attract men who are never what they seemed to be in the beginning. The problem may be in what you project onto the men who capture your heart. If you see only the illusion of perfection, you are already in trouble, since if anyone is still in human form, chances are they are not perfect! You are a very sensitive woman who desires a sensitive man, and that's wonderful as long as the sensitivity does not extend to behaviors that are deceptive or abusive. If you've felt victimized, it's crucial that you discover your own role in the victimization so that you can change your patterns. Learn to say "No."

Mars semisquare Neptune: With Mars in semisquare aspect to Neptune, you may attract men who are dishonest with you. That dishonesty can range from minimal to extreme, and depends to a great extent on your ability to be honest with yourself about what you want from a man. To avoid falling into disillusion in your relationships, allow ample time to discover your real feelings and motivations before you become deeply involved. If you've already jumped into a situation that leaves you barely treading water, do what you can to extract yourself before you are exhausted. Act upon your hopes and dreams, but always remember your humanity and the humanity of others in the process.

Mars sextile Neptune: You can be relatively clear about the true nature of the men you attract with Mars in sextile aspect to Neptune. While you can support and admire a man for his dreams and ideals, you can also see the reality of the present moment. By working together with the ingredients you possess in the relationship, you may very well manifest those dreams. You may also be clear about your own dreams that need the support and understanding of the man you love. This mutuality can be shared on many levels, and can build a powerful bond that helps to sustain you when reality is harsh.

Mars square Neptune: You can have great difficulty in relationship with men due to your unrealistic expectations and projections with Mars in square aspect to Neptune.

You may be very strongly attracted to a man on one level, only to discover that he is not at all what you thought. You may discover someone you like at the core of his being, but you may also find that you cannot deal with him at all. This tendency to be disillusioned by men stems from your inability to assert yourself in a clear and straightforward manner. It's hard to pursue your desires when you're not sure what they are! Spend some time listening to your inner voice. Explore your own sexuality. Examine the differences between your dream lover and the men you attract. Somewhere in the core of your being is the magnet that will attract someone different, but it requires a lot of work to get out of your old patterns.

Mars trine Neptune: With Mars and Neptune in trine aspect to one another, your experiences with men help to sustain your faith in healthy relationships. Although you have your ideals, you also assert yourself when you need to pursue something different beyond your relationship. For example, if you need to feel satisfied through a career, you can do that without threatening the integrity of a supportive relationship. You will grow most fully in a relationship that sustains you on multiple levels—physical, emotional, and spiritual.

Mars quincunx Neptune: With Mars and Neptune in quincunx aspect, you may have had a series of relationships that have led to disappointment or disillusionment. You believe that men cannot be trusted, or that they can be trusted only to a certain level. The fact of the matter may be that you do not trust yourself or your judgment concerning men because of your experiences. Learning from your past can be helpful, but to break any patterns that have been codependent, addictive, or abusive, you first have to decide that you don't need that old garbage any longer. Forgive yourself. Forgive your past. Begin anew with your eyes open, your senses sharpened, and your will pliable to the truth and only the truth.

Mars opposition Neptune: With Mars in opposition to Neptune, it's difficult to see the men in your life as they are. Your projections can totally overwhelm the reality of a situation until you become fully disillusioned and wonder what happened. To avoid falling so far from your dreams and hopes, it is crucial that you allow ample time to explore relationships before you make commitments. Any dishonesty you hold within your own heart will more than likely be expressed by inappropriate, deceptive, or abusive men. Although you may have to sacrifice something in order to have the kind of relationship you need, there is never a need to totally sacrifice yourself.

Aspects with Jupiter

Jupiter conjunct Neptune: Jupiter and Neptune conjunct signify your need for intimate relationships based on high principles. You need a partner whose values and morals echo your own, and you will feel uncomfortable in any relationship that compromises your own sense of what is right.

Jupiter semisquare Neptune: Through the semisquare connection between Jupiter and Neptune, you attract relationships that cause you to take a careful look at your beliefs and ideals. If you are firm in your own ideals, the challenges will only help you confirm what you know to be true and right. If you are uncertain, the experience of relationships may offer a contrast to your early upbringing, allowing you to re-evaluate your beliefs and ideals.

Jupiter sextile Neptune: With Jupiter in sextile aspect to Neptune, you may find that you attract relationships with men whose moral and spiritual values are similar to your own. Even if your religious backgrounds differ, you can be flexible and open to the possibility of other options as long as they are based on higher truth. You need to incorporate spiritual practices into your relationship, and when you make a commitment to a relationship, will find that the spiritual focus of that commitment is a powerful source of inspiration and hope.

Jupiter square Neptune: Jupiter's square to Neptune indicates a frustration between your ideals or beliefs and the essence of Truth. On an inner level, you feel that a particular path is right, but the teachings you've learned may not echo those inner feelings. It's like the discovery of hypocrisy from someone who speaks about one truth but lives a life that does not reflect that truth. You are struggling to integrate the truth with your beliefs, and your relationships act as a catalyst that challenges you to explore those ideals further. You may also find that differences in spiritual practice are difficult to handle in your relationships.

Jupiter trine Neptune: With Jupiter in trine aspect to Neptune, you need to incorporate a sense of spirituality into your intimate relationships. It is important that you find a partner who shares your morals and beliefs, although you can be open to differences as long as you agree on principles. You may discover your perfect partner while in pursuit of your spiritual quests.

Jupiter quincunx Neptune: With Jupiter in quincunx aspect to Neptune, you need to be aware of the subtle differences between your values and ideals and those of your lover or husband. At first, these may not seem to make a difference, but they can become very important over time. Usually, these differences surface when deciding on spiritual or religious teachings for children, but they can surface when you're trying to choose a minister for a wedding. If you compromise, you may regret your choices. Your own moral and spiritual values are extremely important, and you need to be clear about them.

Jupiter opposition Neptune: With Jupiter in opposition to Neptune, you need to be very clear about your ideals and aims in relationships. It's easy to misplace your values and become devoted to someone who seems to share your ideals, but is not living a life that reflects the principles of the teachings. If you avoid the importance of spirituality within the context of your relationships, you may wake up one day to discover that there is a huge gap between you and your husband or lover.

Aspects with Saturn

Saturn conjunct Neptune: The energies of Saturn and Neptune in conjunction generate an internal conflict between material issues and spiritual concerns. You can be quite idealistic, but you're also impressionable. It's sometimes hard to see things or people as they are, and you can be easily influenced by others when it comes to determining your priorities. When you're in love, you fly into the world of fantasy and forget about your responsibilities, since it's so much more fun to feel ecstasy than it is to worry about paying the bills. When making decisions about relationships, you tend to rely more on your emotions than on practicality, which can result in disappointment in the long term. In order to have a more balanced life, you can benefit from integrating some form of meditation into your routine as a means of gaining clarity and objectivity. You also need to develop relationships with friends and counselors who can provide a different perspective. In all matters, though, it is crucial to remember that the choices are yours, and that you will be the one who has to live with them!

Saturn semisquare Neptune: You may not always trust your judgment concerning other people, since Saturn in semisquare aspect to Neptune can create a frustrating sense of uncertainty. This can be the result of past experiences that have involved deception or loss, leading to an undermining of your trust in yourself. You want to see the best in others, but have probably discovered that many people do not operate from this level. In intimate relationships, it is crucial to clarify your shared visions and hopes, since just assuming that you are on the same wavelength can lead to disappointment. It's important to avoid the tendency to isolate yourself just because you feel insecure. That isolation can add too much intensity to the insecurity. Certainly you need some privacy and time for contemplation, but you don't need to hide.

Saturn sextile Neptune: Your dreams for your future are very important, and with the help of Saturn in sextile aspect to Neptune, you are capable of manifesting them, particularly if they are in harmony with your highest needs. The relationships you want to have actually begin at an etheric level—within your dreams and hopes. You prepare yourself to become the partner you wish to be by "practicing" on an inner level and learning to stay connected to the core of your being. You can integrate this inner sensibility with the outside world easily, particularly if you dedicate some part of your life to developing links between the spiritual and material planes. You will benefit from an intimate relationship that supports your spirituality, and from a partner who shares your ideals.

Saturn square Neptune: With Saturn in a tense square aspect to Neptune, you may feel frustrated by the stark contrast between your fantasies and the realities of your life. In essence, you know that there does not have to be a gap, but when you run into trouble, you've probably gone too far to one side of the pendulum. These extremes are the result of your fears and anxieties, which block your ability to surrender when you want to let go and flow with the currents of life. If you jump into situations that are not good for you, you may feel you'll be forever stuck. What you need is perspective, and you can develop that by giving yourself a mechanism that provides some objectivity. Meditation, psychological counseling, and even therapeutic artistic expression can all help you see your life from a different viewpoint. Then your faith in yourself is more readily restored.

Saturn trine Neptune: Energized by the trine between Saturn and Neptune, you attract relationships that support your needs for self-actualization. Your ability to make choices that reflect your deepest needs is strengthened, and you are more likely to explore many different facets of a relationship before seriously committing to it. You are very capable of listening to your inner voice and directing what you feel from an inner level into your everyday life. If you are still seeking to find your life mate, begin to work on an inner level to prepare yourself fully to become the partner you need to be. Allow some time to visualize the life you wish to live, the types of things you want to accomplish individually and within a relationship. See yourself as whole, happy, and fulfilled. That energy will radiate from the core of your being and can be the perfect magnet to attract the partner you desire.

Saturn quincunx Neptune: It's sometimes aggravating when you have to fit your dreams into the world of reality. Energized by the quincunx aspect between Saturn and Neptune, you are constantly attempting to shape your life in such a way that will allow you to feel spiritually connected while still operating realistically. This can be particularly so in the realm of relationships, since your fantasies about the kind of partner you need rarely have a chance to manifest through a real man. You don't have to compromise your deeper needs, though, so remember that when you're making choices. If you really don't like the guy, it's not a problem, but if you love the man and dislike his personality, then you have a dilemma. Sometimes, the problems are simple ones, like different belief systems. If you can still make time in your life for the things that are ultimately important to you, it's likely the relationship can work; but if you have to sacrifice your spirituality, security, or safety—think again.

Saturn opposition Neptune: Your struggle to decide when you need to hang on and when you need to let go is energized by Saturn in opposition to Neptune. This can be particularly problematic in relationships because your dreams for the possibilities may not always be supported by the reality of the situation. You can go too far and spend all your time trying to support "what could be" instead of dealing with "what is." This conflict can also be seen in the manner you choose to handle your personal responsibilities, and you can vacillate between your desire to have someone take care of you and your need to care for yourself. Although you may think that life could be much nicer if your husband would do all the hard work, pay all the bills, and carry the burden of responsibility, you will probably find that you sacrifice a part of yourself in the process. That aspect of yourself is what is required to integrate your fantasies and dreams into the world of reality.

Uranus-Neptune Aspects

Uranus conjunct Neptune: You have Uranus conjunct Neptune. These two outer planets come together by conjunction about once every century and provide an influence that affects a generation of men and women. You're here to break some of the old fantasies about love and perfection and to create a new approach to spiritual ideals. These changes will, of course, affect the way you relate to others. Your parents may not understand some of your choices, particularly those that cross philosophical or religious barriers, and you may not always be at ease with others whose ideals challenge your own.

Uranus semisextile Neptune: The semisextile aspect between Uranus and Neptune happens about once each century and influences a generation. The steps your generation takes to blend religious or philosophical ideals with scientific or technological developments can have a strong impact on your lifestyle and on future generations. It's important that you know how to use compassion while moving forward into new frontiers.

Uranus semisquare Neptune: The semisquare aspect between Uranus and Neptune happens about once each century and influences an entire generation or collective group of individuals. In many ways you feel that you are among the forerunners of a new set of ideals, and you have some conflict between the beliefs and ideals (or lack of them) you were taught by your parents and those you seek for yourself.

Uranus sextile Neptune: You were born with Uranus in sextile aspect to Neptune, an aspect that occurs about once each century. As a generational influence, this aspect shows increased idealism and new approaches to religion, philosophy, and personal ideals. You will be happiest in a relationship with a man who gives you plenty of room to find and follow your own spiritual path.

Uranus square Neptune: With Uranus and Neptune in square aspect to one another, you are part of a generation filled with an uncomfortable concern for religious and spiritual ideals. You may not know whom you can trust in the worlds of politics and business, and are likely to struggle with your search for a meaningful spiritual path that is part of the framework of your life on its most intimate level. It's important that you learn ways to identify fanaticism, since you can either fall victim to others and their fanatical ideals or become too overbearing with your own. The influence of these energies can be problematic in relationships, particularly if you do not trust your inner voice and allow another to determine your needs in areas that you must discover for yourself.

Uranus trine Neptune: You were born when Uranus and Neptune were in trine aspect to one another, a cycle that influences a generation of men and women. You're among the women willing to try things that are out of the ordinary, and are part of a generation whose efforts are focused on breaking into new territory in the fields of psychology, spirituality, and consciousness. As an individual, you may feel comfortable exploring directions that would have been unthinkable to your parents and that can open new possibilities for your personal growth.

Uranus quincunx Neptune: The quincunx between Uranus and Neptune in your chart affects other women born in your generation. These generational aspects set a tone for changes in the collective, but also symbolize quests that are important to you as an individual. You may not be comfortable around others who are radically different, and extreme differences in religious beliefs or cultural backgrounds between you and a man might be very difficult for you to bridge. You probably have some curiosity about what else might be out there, but just don't like having those alien situations present inside your personal boundaries.

Uranus opposition Neptune: The opposition between Uranus and Neptune occurs only about once each century, and its influence is more generational than individual. You may try too hard to make logical sense out of things that do not fit into a logical paradigm. If you are secure in your sense of personal identity, this aspect can be a boost to creative expression and to developing ideals that alter the shape of life in the world around you.

Neptune in any aspect to Pluto: Neptune and Pluto aspects have a long-lasting effect and usually signify things that are related to historical and long-developing changes in human consciousness. Individuals do not necessarily express these energies in a well-defined manner through individual love relationships, since their influences can go on for many decades.

The 5th and 11th Houses: Giving and Receiving Love

The houses in your chart that amplify love relationships are the 5th, 7th, and 11th Houses. Through the 5th House you experience giving love. It is through this facet of yourself that you have love affairs, playful and recreational relationships, and where you produce the offspring of loving. The offspring can range from artistic endeavors to children. When dealing with relationships, this is the space that is usually occupied by loving another in an intimate sense.

The Sign on the 5th House: The Key to Your Heart

Aries on the 5th: There's little doubt when you love someone because you can be quite direct in your expression of love with Aries influencing your 5th House. You need ample freedom for your expression of love, and enjoy spontaneous bursts of passion. Playing the assertive role in relationships, at least occasionally, feels natural to you. It's easier to open your heart when you feel the spark of attraction that challenges you to take action. Those quiet, casual affairs of the heart can be interesting, but will never have the power and intensity of an exciting entanglement.

With Mars influencing this house, you will find that you are most enraptured by love experiences that are daring and full of life. You can also be a tease, and love to play taunting games that stir a bit of controversy. A fast-paced exchange of sharp wit and funny jabs may be the perfect beginning to a delightful romance. You'll enjoy love relationships that are playful, recreational, and filled with activity. You're not likely to appreciate love relationships that inhibit your freedom, and you need plenty of room to explore the territory of your heart.

Taurus on the 5th: Your sensuality takes center stage when you're in love. The influence of Taurus on your 5th House adds an earthy nature to your experience and expression of the pleasure of loving. When you open your heart, you become strongly attached, and prefer to love fully and completely. You need plenty of time and space to explore the physical side of your love relationships, and enjoy sharing quiet time in comfortable surroundings with your lover. Since Venus influences this house, you prefer to play the role of enticer in your love relationships, and can send very well-defined signals to your intended target. For you, it's safer to let the man be the pursuer, although you become impatient if he takes too long. The connections you make through opening your heart are powerful enough to sustain through time. If a love affair ends, you may have trouble letting go since you invest so much of yourself in loving. You also struggle with changes within your relationships, and need to recognize the importance of changes that stimulate growth. The experience of loving will never leave you, even if your lovers change.

Gemini on the 5th: You enjoy love affairs that stimulate an exciting meeting of the minds. Gemini's influence on your 5th House can be rather distracting when it comes to matters of the heart. Your delight in someone different can tempt you to carry on more than one relationship at a time, just to keep your life interesting. You have trouble committing to just one person, since there are many different facets of your personality that need to be satisfied through your love relationships. Mercury's influence in this house confers a clever mentality that is the nectar you use to attract the bees to your romantic hive. For a man to appeal to your heart, he will first have to get through the gates of your mind. The man whose intelligence matches his dexterity as a lover can fare quite nicely.

Cancer on the 5th: The experience of loving and opening your heart is purely magical for you with Cancer influencing your 5th House. When you're in love, your romantic heart is alive and filled with passion and desire. You relish getting close to the man you love, and thoroughly enjoy the physical pleasures of loving. Sometimes, though, just cuddling together is enough to warm your heart. When your heart is open and love is flowing, you show care, nurturing, and tenderness as part of your love expression. You need to be needed. You must safeguard against a tendency to try to absorb your lover into your life—that can be too claustrophobic. With the Moon also influencing this house, you show deep devotion to those you love—from children to lovers. Through this devotion your creativity is kindled, and you gain pure enjoyment from the experiences of making your favorite chicken soup, the best cookies ever, and those special presents for the holidays.

Leo on the 5th: You would risk everything on love with Leo ruling your 5th House. When your heart opens to love, you invest yourself fully in the process. There's no halfway—not enough power and intensity for you! You expect loyalty from those you love, and even if a love affair ends, you will be deeply wounded if you feel that your lover has said or done anything damaging toward you (although a part of you will want to know every detail). When your attention is focused on the man you love, you can be enticing, and you enjoy demonstrating your affections in very dramatic ways. However, if you do not receive the same in return, you lose interest in the relationship. Since the Sun rules your 5th House, your ego needs a bit of stroking for your heart to stay open. It's just as simple as that. You simply cannot give all of yourself to anybody, which helps you avoid some of the traps of codependency. You have to safeguard against becoming too selfish or self-centered in love relationships. Then, your heart is not really open—you just want attention!

Virgo on the 5th: Virgo's influence on your 5th House adds a practical and methodical approach to love affairs. You're not likely to open your heart unless you have a meeting of the minds. You may even have a list of the characteristics you hope to find in a lover, and may not let a number of men through the door if they fail to meet your strict criteria. This sense of discrimination can be helpful, particularly if you tend to be overly romantic. The energy of Mercury plays an important role in the way you show love. You enjoy sending special cards and letters to keep the connection strong, and might even be tempted to write poems or stories based on your experiences of love. Maintaining a mental connection with your lover will always be important, but you can also close the door to your heart by allowing feelings of imperfection or inferiority to get in your way. Take a personal inventory (that should be easy for you!), and oil those rusty hinges on the doors to your heart. Allow yourself to play a bit more. Your sensuality can be a lot of fun when you let it out.

Libra on the 5th: You have a powerful need for love relationships with Libra influencing your 5th House. The feedback and support you experience through heart-centered connections can be positively self-confirming. You probably like giving the same support to those you love, too, but you don't like having to deal with heavy responsibilities in your love relationships. You like loving to be fun, pleasurable, and comforting. All the hard stuff just does not fit with your image of the perfect love—even if it is reality. Well, you don't have to like it, but at some point, you will find that you have to deal with it! You must be careful to avoid falling into the trap of believing that the only thing that confirms your worth is the kind of love relationship you have. The influence of Venus on this house adds a strong desire to play the role of the temptress, luring the man you adore. You enjoy the game of love, even when it becomes too "gamey." When you open your heart, a level of beauty emerges that you cannot experience any other way. It is important to learn that this opening is a two-way street.

Scorpio on the 5th: The extreme passion you feel when you're in love can be absolutely addicting, with Scorpio on your 5th House. You love the touch, taste, and feel of being in love, and open your heart most easily when your sensuality is powerfully stimulated. You can be exceptionally attractive, and project a quality that is enticing to the opposite sex. You love the experience of being a woman, especially when you're in the depths of passion, allowing your power and energy to pour forth. However, your profound curiosity about sexuality prompts you to explore the physical aspect of love affairs with the mind and heart of an investigator. Since Pluto rules this house, you can be somewhat invasive and intimidating to your lovers, and need to be aware that your own intensity may be normal for you, but overwhelming to someone who's not used to it. If you're hurt by a lover, you can become vengeful; and if you feel insecure, you can be quite jealous. These feelings destroy the truly loving elements of a relationship, and it is important to be aware of your motivations and deeper feelings if you are to avoid going too far with jealousy. When a relationship ends, you end it *forever*. For you, there's no turning back. You're in or you're out, and that's it.

Sagittarius on the 5th: The feeling of opening your heart to love brings pure joy, with Sagittarius influencing your 5th House. You've experienced the transformative power of joy more than once in your life, and know that when you reach out and give of yourself to others, the energy you receive in return can be sweet indeed. You attract a wide variety of relationships over the course of your life, and may be especially interested in relationships with men whose backgrounds are different from your own. There's more adventure that way! You love to travel, and will probably enjoy sharing travel with your sweetheart (although sometimes, traveling alone makes your heart sing, too). When you fall in love, you really go for it; sometimes, you act too quickly before you've had a chance to think about what you're doing. Just because the guy is gorgeous and knocks your socks off, that does not necessarily mean it's safe to change your life for him! Jupiter's influence here adds a confidence and enthusiasm to your approach to loving; sometimes, it adds too much enthusiasm, so remember to take a deep breath and try to think before you leap from the cliffs of the heart.

Capricorn on the 5th: Sometimes you're a bit cautious about opening your heart with Capricorn influencing your 5th House. One thing is certain: you will have to take responsibility for your actions, especially those involving love affairs and children. Since you feel that sense of responsibility, you hesitate before you let yourself really open to the experience of giving love. You may also be afraid of love. It's really not love that you fear, but the possibility of losing it. What you must learn to trust is that love is eternal. Even when relationships end, the love continues on its course. Sometimes that course simply does not involve the physical presence of your lover! Saturn's influence here also tends to attract relationships that are karmic in nature: you're paying off debts of your soul by opening your heart. Resisting will not always work in these instances. Sometimes you have to go with the flow and do what you know you have to do. There's that responsibility thing: but it's a responsibility to yourself most of all. In essence, you are a very sensual and earthy woman, and you need close physical contact in your life. It's just that you sometimes cannot allow yourself to have that experience without first knowing there's a commitment. Changing the nature of the commitment to one of respect, honor, and trust is the perfect key to fully opening the door of your heart.

Aquarius on the 5th: The influence of Aquarius on your 5th House provides an unconventional approach to affairs of the heart. You can be rather experimental through your love affairs, and look for unusual options to fulfill your desires. To open your heart, you need to know that you are free to be yourself, without conditions. A love without boundaries is best for you, although that really does not mean "no strings attached." Taking an irresponsible attitude in your love relationships will leave you with a broken heart. Perhaps a safer approach, particularly in your young adulthood, is to be focused fully on the moment and enjoy it completely and honestly. If you are not ready to make a commitment, but want to allow the love you feel to flow easily, let your lover know that. You may also discover that you attract men who are emotionally distant, and that will continue to be the case until you allow yourself to be more available on an emotional level. With Uranus ruling this house, you need to develop friendships as part of your love relationships, and may find that your most enduring love occurs between yourself and those who are your dearest friends. A friend can also be a lover or life partner.

Pisces on the 5th: You long for a love that allows you to open on spiritual and emotional levels. Energized by Pisces on your 5th House, you have dreams of the lover whose purity and passion allow you to transcend beyond the ordinary into the realm of ecstasy. Opening your heart to allow love to flow is not always easy for you, though, because you do not like the feeling of vulnerability that accompanies an open heart. Letting go of your fears is a crucial part of experiencing love, and that may involve working on forgiveness toward those who have hurt you in the past. You don't have to forgive them because they deserve it, but because you need it! Neptune's influence here adds an immense capacity for the experience and expression of compassionate love, but this can happen only when you've surrendered your life to the needs of your soul instead of the needs of your ego.

Planets in the 5th House: Heart Stimulants

If you have no planetary energy in your 5th House, there is no need to be alarmed, because this does not indicate that you will be without love in your life. As you've seen above, you have definite inclinations in love relationships. To further understand what you need from a lover and how you can become more adept at giving love, study the planet associated with this house. The energies that are found in the 5th House play a particularly important role in the way you give love.

Sun in the 5th: With your Sun energizing your 5th House, you invest a great deal of energy in doing what you love. Life needs to be pleasurable and fun, and part of that is the fun of giving love to others. The manner in which you approach giving love through love affairs and in relationships with your children is important, since if you are only self-serving, your actions and energy may usurp another's needs in favor of your own desires. When you are attentive to the give and take of love relationships, you can experience exceptional joy through loving. The choice is yours.

Moon in the 5th: Your Moon in the 5th House brings a powerful need for the experience of love and loving in your life. Opening your heart fills your soul. It's like a cosmic fountain of energy that replenishes itself each time you give love. You must avoid becoming too self-serving in your love relationships, especially if you're prompted by feelings of neediness. Because you are emotionally expressive when you're in love, you are also the one who does most of the expressing, while your partner holds more inside. Watch for this tendency to be the one who acts out the emotions of your relationships because it can be exhausting in the end. Use your own emotional sensitivity to encourage the free flow of expression from those you love.

Mercury in the 5th: Mercury's energy in your 5th House adds a need for relationships that stimulate communication and open exchange of thoughts and feelings. It may be easier to talk about what you think than it is to express how you feel, but if you work on it, you'll find you can do both quite nicely. You think about love a lot, and are learning about the importance of attracting what you hold in your consciousness. The mind is the generator of the offspring of your life. Think about it.

Venus in the 5th: Venus feels good in your 5th House. This energy stimulates the expression of your feelings of love, and is helpful in opening your heart. Giving of yourself, your creativity, and your energy allows you to take love to a higher level. You are very attracted to a lover whose artistic tastes and sensibilities are compatible with your own, and you fall in love with his creativity as much as you fall in love with him. You'll appreciate a lover who acknowledges and supports your own creativity, and may lose interest if he is too self-absorbed.

Mars in the 5th: You really enjoy the game of love with Mars in the 5th House. This energy stimulates your tendency to initiate relationships, since you're the one who takes action to get things moving. Although you may enjoy taking the lead, you also like the feeling of being pursued, and have a knack for keeping the energy of the chase going in your relationships. Keeping passion alive is an important part of allowing your heart to remain open. You can be a bit selfish in your relationships, though, since you really like to do things your way. Let him drive some of the time.

Jupiter in the 5th: Jupiter's energy in your 5th House adds a dimension of adventure to your love life. You might be most fascinated by someone whose cultural or educational background is different from your own. An intelligent and thoughtful man will be extremely interesting and fascinating to you. Travel, learning, and lively discussion all spark your interest and accessibility. You'll feel much more excited about a relationship that encourages your freedom of expression, too.

Saturn in the 5th: With Saturn in the 5th House, you like to be in control of your love relationships. This can mean that you hold back, but it can also mean that you take charge and do things your way or not at all. You can be judgmental of your lovers and children, and need to watch a tendency to withhold your affections as a means of punishment. When you do that, you're only punishing yourself because you've created a dam in the flow of energy from your heart. Taking responsibility for your expressions of love is important, and if you try to foist the burden or problems onto your partner, you'll only make matters worse. If you end a relationship, be aware of your tendency to blame the other guy. If you don't deal with the problems you experience within yourself, you'll repeat the same pattern. His name and face may be different, but you feel like you're still dealing with the same old garbage.

Uranus in the 5th: The excitement and thrill of being in love can be absolutely addicting with the energy of Uranus in your 5th House. You have interest in love only when you're in those early stages. You know: you've lost your mind. You feel like you're plugged into a high voltage circuit. You've been transported into another dimension. Well, okay, that is wonderful, but it's only the beginning. If something didn't get your attention, you would never open your heart. You definitely need an unusual type of love, and will approach your loving relationships in a non-traditional manner. Yet sustaining love is not always easy for you. Unless, that is, you can keep the excitement alive, and you can do that, in your own unique way. That's why Uranus is there in your 5th House—you're learning how to re-energize the experience of loving freely, unconditionally, and without boundaries.

Neptune in the 5th: Neptune's energy in your 5th House encourages you to spend a lot of time dreaming about the perfect love. Reverie and fantasy can be healthy, and in the best situations, your intimate relationships will allow plenty of time for you to indulge in playful fantasy and high-level romance. Be alert to the possibility of falling in love with love, or with the things you wish to see in others, and try to take off your rose-colored glasses from time to time. Make time in your life for giving of yourself, whether through charitable ventures, in community service, or through your creative or artistic self-expression. Avoid the temptation of looking for a love that will rescue you from a life that does not fit your dreams.

Pluto in the 5th: Energized by Pluto, your 5th House expression of love can be totally absorbing. Those hypnotic love affairs can be rather addicting, and you can be compulsive when you're in love. When you open your heart, you feel that you expose your soul. Your secret fantasy is to bond on a soul level with your perfect mate and to be transformed in the process. This is the alchemy of love and the power of sexual bonding. Because you may need to love on such a deep level, you're not likely to open your heart to just anyone. In fact, opening your heart at all is not easy for you. A transformational experience like giving birth to a child can help you immensely. In fact, a child may be the key to your spiritual and emotional rebirth; but so can loving the right partner. Now, that's not the perfect partner. It's the man who understands your vulnerabilities, but who will support you in removing the barriers to your heart.

The 11th House: Developing Unconditional Love

It is through the 11th House that you learn about unconditional relationships, and where you open to receiving love and support from others. Here you find your friends, your supportive professional allies, and your community. Through this facet of yourself, you develop your special interests; and here you set your goals for the future. It's wonderful the way friends support your aims, provide feedback when you need objectivity, and comfort you when you're facing challenges. Your approach to friendship is also seen through this part of your chart, and planets in this house indicate the kind of energy you look for in your friendships, along with some of the issues that might arise in the process of becoming friends.

The Sign on the 11th House: How You Receive Love

Aries on the 11th: Aries on the cusp of your 11th House indicates that your friendships play a very active part in your life. Your friends provide the impetus for many of your ideas, and inspire you to take action that will assure your independence and personal autonomy. You enjoy getting together with your friends to play sports, take aerobics classes, or share a challenge of some sort. You enjoy friends who take an active, assertive approach to their own lives. However, you may not share everything with your friends, which is probably okay, since you are all rather independent-minded. Your free spirit attracts friends, both men and other women, who are comfortable with the fact that you need your independence. In opening your heart to receive love, you find that you are the one with the keys. If you're waiting for someone else to open the door to your heart, you may be sadly disappointed, since you are the one who has to initiate this process. Then, once you've done that, it's easy for others to give their love to you. With Mars ruling your 11th House, you may find that you are frequently the one who takes the first step, with friends or lovers. That may just mean that you smile first, so don't think there's anything complicated about it!

Taurus on the 11th: With Taurus on the cusp of your 11th House, you need friends who will be there for the long term. Your friendships form the rock of your emotional stability, and there is probably a special female friend who provides a strong support in your life. You can also be a supportive and loving friend, and enjoy being part of your friend's success. You may not appreciate feeling that a friend is leaving you behind while she is progressing, and it's important to talk about these feelings if they arise so that you can salvage your friendship. Sometimes you tend to hold back, just to protect yourself emotionally, and that can be a problem if you really want to clarify what's happening. Your best friendships provide comfort and strength, and require the same from you. It's not always easy for you to open your heart to receive love, and your friendships can provide the stability you need to learn how to let love, caring, and support into your life. The energy of Venus influences this area of your life, indicating that your closest friends will probably be other women. You'll also enjoy a friendship that reflects your tastes and values, and may have a good friend who is artistically gifted.

Gemini on the 11th: Gemini's influence on your 11th House shows that your friendships are forged through a meeting of the minds. When you get together with your girlfriends, you always have a lot to talk about. You probably have friends from a variety of backgrounds and with myriad interests. With your closest friends, you are drawn together because you think alike. Sometimes it may seem that you part and greet one another in mid-conversation, but that's okay. The mental link you have to one another probably keeps the connection strong enough that you don't ever really lose anything in your understanding. Mercury's energy influences your friendships by forging a bridge of understanding, and it is through developing your mental connection that you unlock the doors to your heart. You feel most supported when you know you have somebody who will listen. This is one of the best ways to allow love to flow into your life.

Cancer on the 11th: With Cancer influencing your 11th House, your friendships have a very special place in your heart. Your friends provide a special form of nurturing support, and even though you may not always be able to be with them, you always feel connected. You do need at least occasional contact, and will enjoy sitting down to a marvelous lunch or dinner with a girlfriend to talk about what's happening in your life and to learn how she's doing. In fact, getting together for lunch may be the best way to keep your friendships alive, since the influence of the Moon in your friendships is so powerful. This means that your emotional ties to your friends are based on very primary needs—the need to offer and experience care and support. You may find that it is not always easy to open your heart to receive love, since you probably feel more at ease when you're doing something for someone else. But when you do open your heart and allow that love to flow in, you *are* doing something for somebody else: you're allowing them to connect to you. You're not likely to let just anybody in—only those who feel like they're part of your soul.

Leo on the 11th: Leo's influence on your 11th House indicates that your friendships are based on strong loyalty. You appreciate friends who acknowledge your accomplishments and who support your self-expression. Sometimes, though, it's harder to give them the same attention, so avoid being too self-absorbed and give your friends a chance to show off, too! You may not intend to ignore their accomplishments, and would be the first to want to open doors for them, but intentions and actions are sometimes different. You may also have friends in positions of influence and prominence who share and compliment your own interests and actions. With the energy of your Sun stimulating this area, you love being surrounded by those who share your interests, and can be influential and inspiring to others. Opening your heart to receive love feels wonderful to you, and you truly appreciate the admiration, care, and affection that comes your way. Just try to remember to get your ego out of the way, and learn to distinguish between true friends who really care for you and those who would stroke your ego for a few favors.

Virgo on the 11th: Virgo's influence on your 11th House indicates that you prefer to limit your friendships to those that are most worthwhile. You are a good and understanding friend, although you do not appreciate wasting your time in non-productive situations. When a friend needs to sort through problems, or needs help with a job or project, you can be the best person to call, and you really enjoy helping out. You also like the feeling of giving your time to those who are less fortunate, and may be a friend to your community through your charitable efforts. You also have a special affinity for animals, and truly feel that your pets are your friends. You are comfortable taking part in efforts that protect the interests and needs of animals. With Mercury's energy influencing this area of your life, you find that your most special friendships are with men or women who truly understand you and your ideas. It's much easier to open your heart and allow love to flow in when you're clear about what it means, and that happens by first reaching an understanding in your relationships, especially friendships.

Libra on the 11th: With Libra's influence on your 11th house, you have many friends, especially in the sense of a large social circle. When you're involved in something that has meaning and value in your life, like a special interest, you discover many friends along the way. During the times you're sharing these experiences, you feel very warm, supported, and appreciated. However, you may not have very many close friends, because it's not always easy for you to open your heart and allow love to flow in at a deep level. You feel that you want to save that experience for someone special. You can also feel a little insecure, especially when you start comparing yourself to those in your circle of friends. Once you learn to avoid establishing your own worth relative to that of others, you'll find that your heart opens much more easily. You may also find your perfect mate through your friendships, and the man you marry or choose as your companion may first be a good friend. This relationship will have established your mutual appreciation and shared interests, an excellent beginning to any relationship.

Scorpio on the 11th: With Scorpio influencing your 11th House, you tend to shy away from friendships until you know you can trust someone. You spend a great deal of time observing the way a potential friend behaves, and certainly notice whether or not she can keep a secret. You're not likely to open your heart to anyone who would divulge your confidential information. You'll probably approach special interest groups or political situations with a bit of skepticism in the beginning, but if you have a strong interest or cause, once you're involved you can be extremely influential. With Pluto's energy connected to this area, you may find that more people confide in you than you confide in them. This is good if you work as a counselor or advisor, by the way. For those few special friendships you develop, you will have a deep connection and hold them in a special place in your heart. It's simply not easy for you to allow love to flow into your heart—receiving love can be a challenge. That may seem strange, but when you take a careful look, you'll find that it's much easier to give than to receive. You do want to feel support, tenderness, and care, you just don't like feeling vulnerable!

Sagittarius on the 11th: Sagittarius on the cusp of your 11th House shows that you thoroughly enjoy your friendships. You feel that you can't have too many friends, and your circle of friendships is likely to include people from diverse and interesting backgrounds. Joining with your friends to generate interest and enthusiasm in an idea or project adds fire to your soul, and you may be especially influential in organizational or political efforts. Your closest friends will share your beliefs and philosophies about life, and may even inspire you to pursue your spirituality in a more meaningful manner. However, you may not always be a reliable friend when it comes to being there all the time. You need friends who will understand your far-reaching approach to life, which requires a great deal of freedom and independence. With Jupiter's influence in this area, you can be generous with your time and energy toward your friends, and if you can open a door for someone, you will. You appreciate the generosity of others, and when you've been the recipient of affection and good will, you can open your heart and show gratitude. You may not like deeply emotional shows of affection, especially in public. The best way to open your heart to love is through laughter, especially when it's stimulated by a genuine warmth and good-natured humor.

Capricorn on the 11th: Capricorn influencing your 11th House shows that you prefer a few solid and safe friendships. Large groups of people make you uncomfortable. You may even have a special friend whom you've known all your life, or at least most of it. For you, the passage of time deepens your affection and appreciation for your friends. Because Saturn's energy influences this area, you also have friends who are older. The age differences may have been more marked when you were a young girl, and as you've matured, you may have made friends with teachers and employers. It is not always easy for you to receive love, partly because you tend to be too judgmental about whether or not you deserve it. When you've developed a sense of trust and commitment, you can open your heart and allow love to flow in. Begin by making that commitment to yourself. Remind yourself that you deserve the love you need.

Aquarius on the 11th: Aquarius on the cusp of your 11th house indicates that your friendships are based on open, unconditional acceptance. You will appreciate friends whose aims have a humanitarian focus, and who understand and embrace tolerance for all people. Certainly you have your preferences when it comes to spending your time with friends, but you are capable of connecting to people from different backgrounds as long as you can create a meeting of the minds. This usually happens through universal principles. You operate best in friendships that support and encourage your free expression as an individual, and you may also join together with groups of friends to support special interests that are designed around humanitarian principles allowing others to express their own individuality and freedom. It's easier for you to open your heart to receiving love when you feel that there are no strings attached, no conditions required. That does not mean you cannot make a commitment; it means that you need to know you are accepted for who you are before you can let love flow into your heart from another. You need to know a love without boundaries, and will find that you can even give love more readily when you've experienced unconditional acceptance from others. The energy of Uranus rules your 11th House, indicating that you invite unusual individuals into your circle of friends. You love genius in its many forms, and appreciate friends who are excited about and free in their expression of their own ingenuity.

Pisces on the 11th: Pisces on the cusp of your 11th House signifies that your friendships can have a spiritual and deep-seated emotional bond. Those who share your beliefs and ideals are readily invited into your circle, and you have lifelong friends whose history parallels your own. Compassionate understanding is the tie that binds when it comes to your friends, but you can also get into trouble if you fail to maintain your emotional boundaries with your friends. If you feel that a friend is taking unfair advantage of you, examine the part you play in that situation. You may need to clearly define when you are and are not available to them. Neptune's influence in this house adds a special psychic connection to your close friends. This energy enhances your ability to forgive your friends, too. It's probably a good idea to be very careful when you're making business agreements with friends, since it would be difficult for you to draw the line between business and friendship. If at all possible, try to avoid linking the two. Overall, it is through your friendships that you develop your most compassionate links to your heart. These relationships teach you how to open to receiving love. For you to open your heart to let love in, you first need to forgive yourself and let go of the past.

Planets in the 11th House

If there are no planets in the 11th House, the lack of planetary energy can be indicative of your ability to accomplish many of your aims on your own. There is, however, no particular meaning that is related to a lack of friends or inability to create friendships. Look to the planet that rules this house to understand the qualities you will seek in your friends and the kinds of activities you might prefer to share with them.

Sun in the 11th: The Sun's influence in your 11th House draws the support of special and influential friends. You rely on your friends to help you achieve a truly objective perspective about yourself and your goals. You also play a very powerful role in the lives of your good friends, who see your light and understanding as an important part of their own success. Since you tend to identify with your friends, it's crucial to choose friends who will be a positive influence in your life and whose aims and objectives are in harmony with your higher needs. You will definitely be known by the friends and associations you maintain.

Moon in the 11th: With the energy of your Moon in your 11th House, you probably have many acquaintances and a few very special friends. Your women friends are especially important in your life; you need their support and care, and feel that it's necessary for you to provide the same for them. You have powerful emotional ties to your friends. This energy definitely draws what you send out, and if you're feeling unsupported or that your friend has taken advantage of you, try to clarify the part you have played in that process. You're willing to flow with the changes friendships must endure, and can stay close and supportive to your good friend, regardless of her ups and downs. The wisdom of knowing that friendships have their own cycles is part of your deeper understanding of life, and you may also discover that those cycles are directly related to your own changing needs.

Mercury in the 11th: Sharing understanding and speaking the same language (figuratively) is important to you with Mercury in your 11th House. Talking with your friends is a high priority, and you go out of your way to make yourself accessible so that this link is maintained. Your friends also give you something to talk about, but you have to be careful to avoid excessive gossip! You may have friends in a broad age group, and will be likely to attract the friendship of young people throughout your life. You like the way young minds think, and since youthful ideas keep your own aims spinning, it's fun to spend time around these inquiring minds.

Venus in the 11th: You love spending time with your friends with Venus in your 11th House. This energy is likely to attract women friends and artistic individuals whose tastes and refinement are appealing to you. Through shared efforts with friends, you also strive to support and protect the arts within your community. You'll probably meet and establish your best friendships while pursuing your own artistic interests, and appreciate friends who applaud your own talents. Sometimes you can be a little lazy about doing things for your friends—it's easier when they're doing something for you; but it's hard for you to say "No" when your support is requested. It's a good idea to have a few parties that encourage camaraderie and sharing—you like playing the role of the hostess with the "mostest."

Mars in the 11th: Participating in activities with your friends can be invigorating with Mars in your 11th House. You may even rely on your friendships to motivate you, although you can be quite a motivator yourself when others are counting on your support. Your display of courage and strength attracts friends, and working together to accomplish something important can forge a powerful bond with your friends. You may have several male friends, and probably like women who are rather independent and assertive. If you're uncertain of your own power or do not stand up for yourself, you may attract "friends" whose influence can bring turmoil and disruption into your life. Also, if you've not found positive ways to deal with your anger, you may attract other people with whom you create destruction. These disrupters are not really friends in the truest sense, especially if they're always helping you get into trouble. It may be up to you to develop your Mars assertiveness powerfully enough so that you can break your ties.

Jupiter in the 11th: Jupiter's energy in your 11th House brings abundant blessings through your friendships. Together with your friends, you accomplish amazing things. If you have political leanings, this influence attracts others with whom you can send a very powerful message. Whether or not you travel (which you enjoy), you probably have friends in many different places and from different cultures. Your closest friends share your philosophy of life, and you forge your most intensive bond of friendship with someone whose devotion to truth and justice is equal to your own. It's important to avoid an attitude that prompts you to take your friends for granted. You attract wealthy or influential friends, and enjoy sharing time with friends who enjoy the good life. However, you can develop some of your acquaintances because of their social or political value, especially if your Jupiter energy shows internal conflict in your chart. Spending time with others who indulge in wasteful or excessively extravagant lifestyles may be pleasant only temporarily since overindulgence can be costly for you on many levels.

Saturn in the 11th: Saturn's energy in your 11th House draws friends who are connected to your work or profession. Although you may have many associates, your close friends are few and far between. You definitely forge friendships that will endure the test of time, especially if you take your responsibilities toward your friends seriously. Although you don't really like having to give excessive amounts of time and energy to friendships, particularly if your work or family demand much from you, your real friends will understand your priorities and support them. It's important that you communicate these priorities if you are to maintain the highest level of friendship, however. If you're tempted to use your friendships simply for your own gain, you will pay a very dear price, but this is probably not a major problem as you mature into adulthood.

Uranus in the 11th: The dynamic energy of Uranus in your 11th House attracts a broad spectrum of friendships. You can relate to almost anyone, although your closest friends are those whose aims and ideals are expressed through interests similar to your own. When you were a young girl, you probably had friends from many different backgrounds, and you may have run into some conflict with your parents over some of your more controversial friends. Now that you are a woman, you may still have unusual friends, and cherish those who are proud to be different. You may even join with them to fight for their rights or champion humanitarian causes. Although the ideal of unconditional love is easy for you to understand, you may not always feel satisfied with the give and take of friendship, and will discover a broad gap between the walk and the talk. Your quest is to incorporate a true sense of power within the context of individuality, and to bring a revolution into the world of apathy. Of course, you might prefer a revolution of ideas and change in ideologies to a revolution of guns, violence, and destruction. Therefore, it's imperative that you have some clarity about connecting with others whose aims are truly pure and motivated by positive change for the good of humanity.

Neptune in the 11th: Through the energy of Neptune in your 11th House you seek friends whose ideology and beliefs echo your own. Your closest friendships are forged when you discover your shared ideals, and you appreciate a friend whose spirituality is genuine and pure. You are determined to do things with your life that will make a difference in the quality of life for others, and are likely to find friends who are also participating in these experiences. Whether through the arts, charitable efforts, spiritual paths, humanitarian service, or public institutions, as long as the motivation is to uplift the spirit of humankind, you find very dear and special friends. You are also vulnerable when it comes to friendships, and if you choose friends indiscriminately, you can be deceived by them. You like to think the best of your friends, and give them the benefit of the doubt when they do not deserve it. Listen to your intuitive and psychic sensibilities regarding your friends. If something does not feel right, don't get involved. It's difficult to do, especially if you begin to feel guilty because you've said no, but sometimes you have to draw the line.

Pluto in the 11th: Through the energy of Pluto in your 11th House you attract friends who are involved in creating transformational change. You may not easily open to the experience of friendship, and your few good friends will understand your needs for privacy and confidentiality. Your intensity can sometimes be intimidating, and you need a friend who will embrace and support your power instead of being jealous or offended in some way. Although you do not necessarily distrust your friends, you may find that experiences and changes put their trustworthiness to the test from time to time. You have a deep appreciation for your women friends, and attract powerful women into your life. Cooperative efforts with friends can be a highly effective method for bringing about significant changes in the world around you, and your energy may be the catalyst to get these things moving. Just be sure that your motives are pure, or directed toward ends that will stimulate growth and opportunity.

The 7th House: Partners and Social Contracts

The 7th House illustrates what you're seeking from a partner. More importantly, this part of your chart tells a story about the kind of partner you really want to be. This is also the realm of social contact, and it provides information about your approach to socialization. Although marriage agreements are shown in the 7th House, planets here (or a lack of planets here) do not "promise" marriage or its lack. If your 7th House is highly activated, you may be more motivated to find a partner. In some schools of astrology, certain planets in the 7th House are said to block or prevent marriage, while others indicate the possibility of multiple marriages. Remember—it's not the planet but how you use the energy of the planet that tells the story of your partnerships (or lack thereof!).

The Sign on the 7th House: Your Approach to Partnership

Aries on the 7th: Your 7th House is ruled by Aries, indicating that you are the one who initiates partnerships. You need relationships that provide ample room for independence and autonomy, especially your own. It's important that you try to be fair-minded in this regard, and that you avoid any type of passive manipulation of your partner since it will only come back to haunt you. If you attract a man who is very strong-willed and controlling, you can learn to stand up to him. In fact, you may prefer a relationship that is active and somewhat challenging. If you do not know how to assert your own needs, you may ultimately grow to resist his control and can become belligerent instead of cooperative. You need a relationship based on equality and harmony, but with Mars ruling this house, you need to direct your own energy into making the relationship work to the benefit of both parties. Dealing with anger in a direct and forthright manner can make a big difference in the nature of your personal contentment with your marriage.

Taurus on the 7th: Your 7th House is ruled by Taurus, showing that you need a partnership that provides stability, security, and comfort. You are most attracted to a man who knows how to establish these things, and appreciate a partnership that allows you to develop your creativity and express your feelings of love. You like a quietly assuring relationship that allows room for growth and change, as long as the changes are in accordance with your own desires. Those unexpected changes and crises test your commitments, but if you deal with them openly, your commitments can be strengthened. It's important to remember that your partner does not "belong" to you, and that he does not own you, either. With Venus' energy driving your needs in this area, you also expect your partnerships to reflect a true sense of love and appreciation, although you will probably have to make a special effort to show this support much of the time instead of just taking it for granted.

Gemini on the 7th: Your 7th House is ruled by Gemini, showing that you appreciate a partnership for the opportunity to develop true understanding and clear communication. The exchange of ideas is part of the strength of your relationships, and if your marriage or partnership does not provide room for this exchange, you will quickly lose interest. You seek a mate whose interests are diverse and whose intelligence is equivalent to your own. Sharing travel, education, and social contacts can be an important ingredient in your partnership. With Mercury's energy influencing your experience of partnership, you discover that the manner in which you create and attract your relationships depends on where your own mind is focused. Your life partner's origination is in your ideas, thoughts, and visualizations. You can alter or change your experience in partnership by changing your attitudes and refocusing your thoughts, and if you're in a situation that is working well, you can bring improvements in this manner. If you've not yet found your ideal mate, work on what you're creating with your thoughts.

Cancer on the 7th: You have Cancer on your 7th House, signifying that you need a partner who will help you create a real sense of home and family. If your aims in this area are not mutually supportive, you will experience internal and external conflict. You are sensitive to the needs of your partner, although it may not always be easy for you to illustrate that sensitivity, especially if work or children demand much of your time. Sorting your priorities is crucial to the sense of success you experience in your personal relationships. With the Moon's energy influencing this area, you need to feel comforted by your mate or husband, and expect that the unwritten law of marriage involves providing this support. If your mate is not particularly demonstrative, you may be disappointed. Expressing what you really need from your partner is the best way to assure that you might actually have those needs fulfilled. You also need to encourage your partner to do the same—then there's no guess work! Although this means creating a certain level of vulnerability, it is a necessary element of achieving a real sense of connection and understanding.

Leo on the 7th: With Leo's qualities influencing your 7th House, you seek a partner who will support your ego needs, although you may not be particularly open about that desire. You also need to be proud of your mate, and will be more capable of supporting him in his efforts when he seems to be making the most of his life. Since the energy of your Sun influences this area, you can become too self-absorbed. If you have not developed a sense of yourself, you may feel that your identity is defined by your partner. It's important that you deal with your ego's needs within your relationships, and that includes your need to play roles that allow you to shine from time to time. However, it's just as important to make room for true equanimity within your partnerships.

Virgo on the 7th: With Virgo's qualities filtered through your 7th House, you need to show great discrimination in choosing your mate. Your husband or partner will come under great scrutiny throughout the course of your relationship, and you may tend to choose someone you feel you can improve in some way. Although you can be supportive and helpful, if you're trying to perfect a man, he will probably resent it unless he has solicited your assistance! You may also attract a very critical mate, and feel that you're never quite good enough for him, or that you're victimized by him in some way. The only way out of this trap is to stay clearly aware of your identities as individuals, and to avoid buying into those negative projections as the true reality of yourself and your life. But if you're just trying to please your partner all the time, you may wake up one day to find out that you don't know who you are or what you want. When you take time to reflect, you will probably discover that you've been doing for your partner what you would like to do for yourself. With Mercury's influence in this area, you can make changes in your approach to partnerships by purifying your own thoughts in regard to the roles you're playing and your needs in this area. Open communication is important. Assumptions can be stultifying.

Libra on the 7th: With Libra's qualities projected into your 7th House, you need a truly functional partnership where each individual is treated equally and contributes equally. This sounds good philosophically, but is very difficult to accomplish, and you may have to take the lead to accomplish your real aims in marriage. The first step toward a healthy partnership is mutual self-acceptance and self-awareness. With Venus' energy involved in this area, you can extend your appreciation and support to your partner most readily by sharing affection. Expecting that your mate will automatically show affection to you will probably lead to disappointment, so remember that when you're feeling unappreciated or ignored. Relationships are definitely a two-way street.

Scorpio on the 7th: Your 7th House is ruled by the sign Scorpio, indicating that you have strong emotions about marriage and partnership. Wading in the shallows of commitment is not for you; you want to know how it feels to immerse deeply and completely. The intensity of your approach can be rather daunting for others who shun the possibility of committed relationships. You may also be faced with lessons about control in relationships. Whether you or your partner have control issues, it is crucial that you approach the essence of control honestly. With Pluto ruling your 7th House, you are likely to run into power plays. These can be handled in a healthy manner by addressing issues when they arise, and by allowing ample room for autonomy of both individuals. If you are not addressing your own needs for autonomy, you may attract men whose hunger for power leads to abuse on some level. You can also abuse power yourself, so be aware of where the lines are drawn.

Sagittarius on the 7th: Since you have Sagittarius influencing your 7th House, you need lots of freedom within your partnership or marriage. Any partner who tries to hold you back will only be frustrated, so he may as well give you the independence you require or he won't have you at all. You may also attract highly independent men, and in order to have the trust and understanding required to sustain a partnership, you need to clarify what you expect from one another. You'll appreciate a man who is an excellent companion and enjoys traveling down the road of life with you, although you may each take your own personal journeys from time to time. During the periods in which you connect, you need to plan, talk, and envision your future goals and desires. Since Jupiter's energy is influential in this area, you can gain excellent support through a partnership when you're participating together in something that will allow you to feel that you're heading toward a brighter future.

Capricorn on the 7th: Through the influence of Capricorn on your 7th House you may experience some frustration in finding the right partner. Your own emotionality and neediness can attract men who are also very needy themselves, and you can be caught in emotional traps that are anxiety-producing instead of mutually supportive.

If you attract men who want to be mothered, you may at first feel that you can do it, until you confront your own need for a little comfort and support. For this reason, it is crucial that you share your needs and feelings with your partner and determine whether or not you can be mutually supportive to one another. Since Saturn drives your needs in partnerships, you can become entangled in relationships out of a sense of obligation or responsibility, and it can be difficult to extract yourself from a marriage even if it is not working. Realizing this, it is very important that you make an effort to understand your aims, obligations, and needs before you make a commitment.

Aquarius on the 7th: With the qualities of Aquarius filtered through your 7th House, you are likely to attract a partner whose needs for independence and autonomy are as strong as your own. It is imperative that you connect with a mate or husband whom you respect and who will respect you. This will occur most readily once you have developed your own self-respect and when you know how to avoid too much self-absorption. Although you may think you want complete autonomy, you really do love the idea of attentive support from a partner. With the energy of Uranus driving your approach to partnerships, you will be most successful when you develop the experience of unconditional acceptance and learn to project that toward the person who shares your life.

Pisces on the 7th: Through the qualities of Pisces on your 7th House you attract men who may not see you very clearly. It's easy for a man to project qualities of perfection onto you that only add to your feelings of imperfection (especially when you feel you're not living up to his expectations). You can also be guilty of not seeing the men in your life very clearly. You may be very attracted by a man who appears to be spiritual, artistic, or sensitive, only to discover that he is not at all what you thought. You can also attract a man who needs to be repaired—emotionally or physically—and may do your best to try to fix him, support him, or improve him. You feel that you have to sacrifice your own goals or needs so that he can realize his dreams; but these responses to being a partner border on codependency. Unless you know where to draw the line between support and martyrdom, you may end up feeling very used and abused by your mate. You can also go too far and become nagging, overly critical, and difficult when you finally lose your patience with your mate. Since the energy of Neptune drives your approach to marriage and partnerships, you are capable of creating a relationship that can be spiritually alive and awake, but it takes some work on your part. You must learn to identify the difference between deception (including self-deception) and possible dreams, and you must practice forgiveness, tolerance, and acceptance.

Planets in the 7th House: What You Can Give to Partnerships

Sun in the 7th: With your Sun, the energy of your ego self, in your 7th House, it's easy to identify who you are within the context of your partnerships. Lending your vitality to a relationship can enliven your life, but it can be a difficult trap if your approach borders on codependency. If you feel that you are not complete until you are Mrs. Somebody, it's crucial that you take the time to examine why you feel that way. Certainly, experiencing the joy of a supportive partnership can lift the burdens of life and provide a source of strength, but that's not the problem. The problems with this placement arise when you feel you cannot cope with life if you are alone. Developing your individual autonomy is more difficult with this placement, and requires that you create a true partnership between your inner self and the roles you play in the outside world. Your real self needs to shine through in all that you do. Living through the man in your life will always feel incomplete, since standing in another's shadow makes it difficult to let your own light glow brightly. If you are in a partnership, you can be the light of your husband's life in many capacities, while still functioning as an individual in your own right. It just takes more confidence, more awareness, and more self-love to accomplish.

Moon in the 7th: Your Moon resides in your 7th House, opening your soul to the hunger for a mate. If anybody yearns for the experience of a soul mate, it is you. However, finding that man can be difficult, especially if you over idealize. In essence, your soul mate is inside you, waiting for you to fully embrace her! You may give more of yourself to a partnership than many women might. You need to know the support and caring of a mate, and in order to grow emotionally, must feel that your needs are important to your partner. Feeling at home with a man has many dimensions, and the promise of creating a home with your partner is high on your list of priorities. Good questions to ask before marriage will center around home and family. Just be sure the answers are mutually supportive!

Mercury in the 7th: Mercury's placement in your 7th House indicates your need for communication within the context of working partnerships. You require a partner who not only understands you, but who is interested in your ideas. You can be a more effective partner, giving more of yourself to the relationship, when you have a meeting of the minds. Open agreements and clarification about your different roles is necessary to your personal growth. You may also find that you learn a lot from the experience of partnerships, and that you can provide excellent feedback to your husband or mate, especially when you're really listening!

Venus in the 7th: Venus energizes your 7th House with your needs for harmony, love, and pleasure expressed through your connection to your partner. You are a loving and supportive partner, and seek the same from a husband or mate. You can create a very happy marriage since you're willing to open your heart to your partner and allow love to carry you through the ups and downs of life. As a rule, you're more than happy to demonstrate your appreciation to your partner through affection, care, and compliments. If you choose to remain single, you still attract situations that provide positive support. You're likely to attract a mate whose financial support provides you with the opportunity for an easier lifestyle. It's also easier to generate financial resources in cooperation with your partner through this energy.

Mars in the 7th: Asserting yourself within your partnership can be a challenging and exciting experience, but you can also experience a great deal of frustration if you are uncomfortable with your self-assertiveness. With Mars in your 7th House, you're most attracted to men who are themselves strong, assertive, or competitive. As a result, power struggles can arise. Just trying to avoid them will do little good. You need people in your life who enjoy a challenge every now and then, and may channel much of this energy into partnerships. Finding positive outlets for your competitive edge can be fun—games, sports, or other recreational activities can smooth rough edges and still keep your juices pumping. Sometimes arguments are simply the result of pent-up hostility that could be released through some type of physical activity. Men may accuse you of trying to take charge too much of the time if you are expressing your own assertiveness. For this reason, developing techniques that allow you to assert yourself with confidence will help you get past any hostility you encounter. Just watch for reactions to help you gauge your next move, and go girl!

Jupiter in the 7th: You have high expectations of marriage and partnerships with Jupiter in your 7th House. This energy can be very beneficial to your relationships since you will approach commitments and agreements with a sense of optimism and confidence, and you enjoy expressing your generosity to your partner. Consequently, you also gain a great amount of support from your husband or mate, including financial benefits. It is important, however, that you clarify your expectations to avoid disappointments or misunderstandings. Shared philosophical and moral values are an important aspect of marriage, and you will enjoy a more fulfilling relationship if you feel that you and your mate are on the same wavelength spiritually.

Saturn in the 7th: Your motivations for getting married are important to understand with Saturn in your 7th House. Marriage may seem like a security arrangement, and can definitely provide structure and support in your life. However, if you rely on another person to generate your sense of security, you will always wonder if you're really secure. You may end up in a situation where you feel controlled or inhibited. Learning to be personally responsible as an individual and within the context of a relationship is one of your primary lessons. You do not need to marry to find someone who will care for you like a father. If you do, you may wake up one morning to discover that you are a prisoner of your own fears. However, you may prefer to marry a man who is older than you because you need a partner who has some maturity. Sometimes Saturn in the 7th House delays marriage, and in today's world, the delay is frequently a result of a woman's choice to establish herself in a career. One thing is certain: when you do make a commitment, you intend to honor it, and will expect the same from your husband or mate.

Uranus in the 7th: Your independent spirit may stir up trouble with Uranus in the 7th House. Your freedom song takes a high priority, and you have your own ideas about what a marriage should be. These ideas may run counter to societal "norms," which is okay with you, since you're a ground-breaker in this area anyway! Any vows you exchange will be unique to your situation. You need a partner who will honor your need for autonomy, and you will enjoy a relationship with a man who is comfortable with his own independence. You may attract a series of unreliable men, especially if you have not yet learned to discipline yourself when it comes to commitments. Finding that real freedom entails responsibility is one of your most challenging lessons, especially within the context of personal relationships.

Neptune in the 7th: You have vivid fantasies about marriage and partnership with Neptune in your 7th House. In your approach to finding a mate, you can deceive yourself if you're just looking on the surface, since it's easy to see only what you project onto a man instead of seeing him as he is. To avoid disappointments in marriage, you need to give yourself time to explore the differences between the fantasy of marriage and the reality of a working partnership. Although you may be capable of building a dream with your husband, you can feel like you're living in an illusion if you have no foundation or if you lack mutual understanding. You may be tempted to play the role of the martyr in your relationships, which will get you nowhere fast. There is a difference between compassionate understanding and codependent denial, and discovering that difference requires personal honesty and courage. You can create a better world with the man you love, but you must share the same vision. At some point you will have to create a strong foundation of trust and integrity to support your dreams, and from that platform, your possibility of achieving the realization of your hopes becomes more plausible.

Pluto in the 7th: Creating harmony within the realm of partnerships can be very challenging with the energy of Pluto in your 7th House. If you've developed a conscious awareness of the manner in which you handle control issues, you are familiar with your need to hold the reins of power within your relationships. Although you may not do this directly since you can be the power behind the throne, you can still be highly influential concerning the effects and outcome of marriage and partnerships. In many respects, marriage can provide the catalyst for your awakening and healing, but the wrong marriage can also be extremely wounding. If you're in a healthy relationship, each of you will be transformed by the experience of working in harmony with one another. There is also the tendency to attract abusive relationships, and you may wonder about power issues in such a context. It may be readily apparent to you that you are being abused, and you must come to grips with your role in the abuse. Once you realize that you do not need to repeat the same wounds, you are altering your life course. By transforming your own attitudes toward yourself and your mate, you can extract yourself from abusive patterns and move into an experience of healing.

∽

CHAPTER TEN

POWER ISSUES: SEX, MONEY, AND CONTROL

*P*ersonal power is an individual expression, and has different meanings for each person. As a woman in the world today, your opportunity to experience and express your personal power is largely dependent upon the manner in which you develop it. Particularly in the western world, as times have changed and the power base has gradually evolved beyond the patriarchal control of the last centuries, women are seeking to define their place in the world—collectively and individually.

Gaining influence in the world through career and financial development, you begin to understand the different levels of power. Within the family, your roles are also evolving. You are freer to express your sexual needs and desires, and you demand that you are respected as a person and not sexually abused. Everything stems from your ability to identify, embrace, and assimilate the true nature of your power as an individual woman.

Identifying Your Power Base:
Personality and the 1st House

On a personal level, you can begin to identify much about your own power by looking deeply into the meaning of your 1st House—your personality self. Earlier in this book, you read about what you project about yourself as identified by your Ascendant. Your first house further defines that projection of the Self and is an area where you carve out the way you show yourself to the world on your own terms. It is here that you shape the image others see, and this goes a long way toward determining the way you use your personal power and exert your influence in the world around you.

The Sign on the 1st House: The Way You Operate

Aries on the 1st: Through your Aries Ascendant you can express a strong level of assertiveness, but unless you develop some finesse, you may appear to be more aggressive or hostile than assertive. You operate best in situations that allow you to be active, and the aggressive side of your personality usually emerges out of frustration when things are just not moving. If you show the abrasive side of your personality, you elicit a hostile response from others, or may even alienate those you hope to impress. You blaze a trail with your independent actions and attitudes, and have the ability to muster amazing courage in the face of challenges. This is very empowering, but you'll feel even more strength when you know you've gained the admiration and respect of others who appreciate the value of your efforts. Also, developing cooperation will strengthen your leadership abilities.

Taurus on the 1st: Through your Taurus Ascendant you appear quite placid; but that's only at first glimpse. Beneath that calm demeanor is a stubborn streak that could win awards. You will stand immovable before you'll give an inch if you do not agree with something or someone, or if you do not want to make a change. If anybody pushes you too far, the raging bull side of your personality takes over, although it's uncommon. You gain power by maintaining your composure most of the time and standing firm when necessary. Your personal power grows when you establish a truly positive platform of personal security, which is based on a strong sense of self-worth. You can lose power by failing to move forward when it's time to step ahead.

Gemini on the 1st: Through your Gemini Ascendant you show the face of the eternal questioner, always eager to discover something new in the world around you. Your power emerges through your ability to communicate effectively with others, and by developing your mind and increasing your understanding you become an important link in the evolution of human thought. You are distractible, and it is the tendency to get off track that can undermine your power. Instead of developing your understanding, you wade in the shallows of simplicity, glancing across the surface and never penetrating the depths of wisdom. The power of the present moment holds many opportunities for you, especially when your mind is focused and connected to the here and now. From this point, you can create endless possibilities for your personal growth, which will be further enhanced through mental clarity and awareness of the world around you.

Cancer on the 1st: Through your Cancer Ascendant you appear caring and nurturing, and seem to be open to the needs of others. This attracts all sorts of relationships, especially from people who need to be mothered; but you may not enjoy having to take responsibility for everyone else when they need to learn how to carry their own burdens, and rather than face up to the challenge of telling them to pick up their bags and move along, you take the indirect approach, which leaves questions and confusion. When you're too indirect, you lose power. You don't want to fight or cause someone to be upset with you because you don't like the emotional fallout. You can play hide and seek forever and never get your point across.

You may also feel emotionally vulnerable and create a kind of "shell" to protect yourself from possible harm. That shell can even be physical, like excess weight or layers of clothing. These things destroy your power by inhibiting it. You have the choice of talking about your feelings, soliciting the feelings and needs of others, and creating a forum that allows those within your circle to be comfortable taking care of themselves while supporting the needs of their family—your family. Instead of creating a dysfunctional family, whether at home or at work, use your nurturing sensibilities to change the atmosphere. Become personally powerful by learning how to say good-bye when necessary, and by welcoming newcomers with a clear projection of who you are. Most of all, be aware of the manner in which you manipulate others, because you lose a lot of ground if you're always trying to maneuver everyone into position instead of recognizing where they stand and what they need in the first place.

Leo on the 1st: Through your Leo Ascendant you demonstrate a strong sense of presence. You may feel that you are powerful only when your presence is acknowledged by others, and can even be demanding in your desire for attention when you're feeling insecure. The more demanding you become, the less powerful you are. The respect and admiration you desire arises when others show their loyalty from love, not from fear. Although you may think you always operate from a pure heart, take a careful look. Have you, in your need to establish yourself, been too self-absorbed? Self-awareness and self-absorption are very different. In the instance of self-awareness, you are also sensitive to the needs and desires of others as individuals. This can be especially trying in relationships with your children. You can be such a marvelous light in their lives, and the path you've forged in the world can provide inspiration to them, but if you try to force your will too strongly without honestly assessing what they need or want for themselves, you may lose their deep trust. You demonstrate your greatest power when your actions, words, and attitudes radiate from the heart of love. Then, your self-assurance is genuine and shines brilliantly through a regal personality.

Virgo on the 1st: Through your Virgo Ascendant you project an aura of precision and discrimination. This can be very empowering, especially if your energy reflects self-confidence and self-assurance, but you're also very self-critical, and undermine your power by holding yourself back, or by going too far in understating your best qualities. There's a huge difference between understated sophistication and insecure inhibition in the way you dress, talk, or act, and adopting a sense of self-acceptance can help you establish a more competent self-projection. You may not be power-hungry, and that's okay; but if you want to accomplish the realization of your aims, you need to embrace your personal power as a positive force, use your eye for detail, and your feel for quality to your best advantage. Just watch your tendency to offer too many critical "suggestions" to everyone around you. They may not be ready for the perfection you would like to see in them, and if you try to force it on them through constant bickering or nagging, you'll quickly lose any power you've gained!

Libra on the 1st: Through your Libra Ascendant your personality takes on that unmistakable air of refined grace and good taste. Your power radiates as true beauty that is attractive and inspires a real sense of peace and harmony. In the world you are a voice for justice and fairness. This begins with a deep sense of self-worth, which is critical to your ability to allow your beauty and intelligence to shine forth.

You may question your value, or wonder if you're beautiful or smart enough, and you have an uncanny ability to compare yourself with other women. These comparisons, especially when occurring unconsciously, undermine your personal power. If you're always worried about what everyone else thinks, you lose track of what you think and feel. You also undermine your power when you spend your time trying to keep everybody happy, or when you adopt behaviors that are placating. Peace at any price is too costly, especially if it means that you give and give and never allow yourself to receive. By remaining honestly conscious of your real needs while still acknowledging the needs of others, you will establish that sense of balance in your relationships that is truly empowering to everyone.

Scorpio on the 1st: Through your Scorpio Ascendant you radiate definite charisma; but you've probably discovered that people respond to you in either a hot or cold manner, and if you wonder why, well, it's your power! Even when you're not trying to appear powerful, you radiate an intensity that is impossible to miss. Your energy stirs others, and sometimes you don't have to say or do anything. What they feel is the force that radiates through you, which is a catalyst for change. It's like a cosmic roto-rooter that brings everything up to the surface. So if someone is unstable, dishonest, or has something to hide, they may feel exposed when they are around you. If they have issues they really don't want to address, they can feel rather uncomfortable because your energy stimulates those issues. This is marvelous if you're in a situation designed to create change, like working as a healer, therapist, or renovator. Here, your innate power works like a magical elixir. You may feel somewhat vulnerable yourself, and if you've experienced emotional traumas that have lead you to mistrust others or to feel a need to protect yourself, you project a barrier. It's not visible, but it can be felt.

Your protective walls can undermine your power because they hold you back. You must work very hard to deal with your underlying issues if you are to project the purest sense of yourself and allow your healing power to radiate in a positive manner. Then, regardless of what you do, you'll see remarkable changes that cause even you to be amazed at how phenomenal life is. If you remain wounded, mistrustful, or angry, you will radiate these feelings in a very intense manner and undermine your power completely. These are not easy choices, but you must make them if you are to know the difference between having power over your own life and attracting others who will usurp, misuse, or abuse your power.

Sagittarius on the 1st: Through the qualities of Sagittarius on your Ascendant you radiate a power that stems from confidence, optimism, and a sense of adventure. These qualities attract good fortune, open opportunities, and endless possibilities. You can undermine your power by avoiding the responsibilities that accompany a real sense of freedom. Setting limits is crucial if you are to have the abundance you crave. Certainly life seems to be more fun when you are at play, and if you can arrange your life to find work you truly enjoy and surround yourself with people whose wit and wisdom keep you laughing, you will find it easier to develop your personal power. Making the choices that are related to taking the responsible route without including your need for play will be just as damaging as avoiding responsibility altogether! You cannot afford to sell out: you must follow the high road and continue your search for the ultimate life has to offer. You have to believe in yourself, and every time you make choices that undermine your sense of confidence, you need to take a look at what was motivating you. Finding the balance point is the hard part: knowing when to rush forward into the future and when to stand confidently in the present. Your principles can guide you, but you cannot force those principles on others; their beliefs and ideals may be different from your own. Yet you can inspire others to find the truth when you've managed to stumble into it yourself!

Capricorn on the 1st: Through the qualities of your Capricorn Ascendant you show a strong need to establish a sense of control in your life. You feel most powerful when you are in charge, and have the essence of "executive" or "director" or "boss" in your manner and attitudes. The problem arises in knowing the difference between control and excessive restraint. Trying to fit yourself into a mold that really does not fit will diminish your sense of personal power; you need to let your own stripes define who you are. It's wonderful when your parents, husband, or children have good feelings about who you are, and that will probably always play a part in your choices, but you have to feel good about the woman you see reflected in the mirror, too! Otherwise you'll operate from the attitude that stems from feeling controlled by others, and that can lead to a very sour disposition or depression, which are definitely not empowering. Your attitude toward the responsibilities you've taken on is a crucial factor in the way you create power. You will always attract situations that require you to be responsible, but that does not mean you have to be responsible for everyone else and their inabilities, dependencies, or problems. You can be the support when someone needs to recuperate; you can be the teacher when someone needs a guide; you can be the dominant leader when there is a lack of direction. Each of these experiences allows you to use your power in the most positive sense. Staying stuck in something you do not need, resenting the choices you have made, or hating your life situation does nothing to empower you as a woman. You can create a structure that allows you to stand tall, and from that position gain strength and experience a real sense of power.

Aquarius on the 1st: Through the qualities of Aquarius on your Ascendant your personal power is most readily expressed when you feel truly free. You like being different, and go out of your way to make sure that others know you are not cut from the same cloth as the rest of the herd. As a little girl, you may have felt isolated because you were different, but you've probably learned that your differences are what define your sense of identity, and these differences can be the basis for your personal power. You may still feel a little insecure, and if you have experienced isolation or chastisement because of your differences, you can become negatively rebellious. If you carry your rebellion into destructive avenues, you quickly lose power. Sometimes you use rebellion as a power play, and feel that if you overturn the status quo, everything will automatically change for the better. Clear motives are crucial to the outcome of your revolutionary actions, words, or thoughts. You can be an effective instigator by creating change and making breakthroughs. Aloof resistance may not be your best avenue, though. Cooperative, collective efforts may be even more effective, especially if you're ready to challenge an outworn attitude, law, or social system, and in these instances, your intelligent ideas and innovative methods can make an exceptional difference.

Pisces on the 1st: Through the qualities of your Pisces Ascendant your power arises from your compassionate and imaginative sensibilities. You can be calm in the midst of chaos when you are connected to the inner peace that flows from your soul, and you may be content to live your life in contemplative service. You have the capacity to develop an inner awareness that is exceptionally empowering because it allows you to remain connected to The Source; but you may also have dreams of a life that contrasts starkly with the reality you currently experience. You can attract situations that victimize you, and removing yourself from the position of victim can be very difficult. Using your dreams to prompt you to make positive alterations in your life strengthens you. If you are afraid to do the work necessary to realize your dreams, you lose confidence in yourself and feel that you have no power over your own life. You may fear failure, and consequently determine not to try anything. It is tempting to live vicariously through others. By developing your own artistic and compassionate sensibilities, your personal power can grow. You don't have to be the star performer or Nobel Prize winner, you simply need good avenues to allow your artistry, sensibilities, and imagination to flow, in whatever areas they manifest.

Planets in the 1st House: Personal Energizers

Sun in the 1st: With the energy of your Sun in the 1st House, you feel that you need recognition in order to be powerful. The manner in which you achieve this recognition makes all the difference between a power that is growth-producing and a power that is self-destructive. You are the perfect woman to take on leadership positions, and will grow in the process, but you always sense that you have to keep your ego in check in order to be as effective as you would like. Using your light to guide others may be much more difficult than standing alone in the spotlight. In your relationships, your need for attention or focus on yourself can be problematic, especially if you forget the needs of your husband or mate. However, you must acknowledge that some attention, and the achievement of your aims, is an important part of your life, and that you require a relationship that provides this opportunity. You also like to be in charge of situations, and can learn to assert your will in such a manner that others will be happy to follow your lead.

Moon in the 1st: You've learned that your Moon's energy in your 1st House brings a strong sense of emotionality to your personality projection, and if you or your efforts are not appreciated, your feelings are hurt. This weakens your sense of power, and may lead to emotional withdrawal on your part. You can also be totally absorbed in the feelings of the moment, altering your perspective of the big picture, which can leave you feeling weak or vulnerable. To experience the total power you need in order to be confident and trusting, it is important that you acknowledge your feelings without allowing them to overshadow your judgment. You also need good outlets for your emotional sensitivity, such as working in a profession that allows you to be supportive or understanding of others, but you have to work hard to keep your own emotional boundaries intact. Part of this will happen through maturity and self-awareness, and you may be more capable and confident about maintaining objectivity as you gain experience. You possess the energy that allows you to fully embrace the dynamics of being a whole woman, and if you can integrate your awareness of the many changes you experience through hormonal shifts, life changes, and the cycles of time into your life, you will develop an internal wisdom that is always supportive and strengthening.

Mercury in the 1st: Mercury's energy in your 1st House brings an opportunity to strengthen your personal power through enhancing your communication skills and improving your mind. Learning may be a lifelong passion for you, and others will learn to look to you for information, clarification, and understanding. If you're confident in your abilities as a communicator, you'll gain power through writing, speaking, public relations, or teaching. However, if you do not trust your communicative ability, it's a good idea to develop it, because this is one of your keys to establishing an identity that feels right. You may also be quite talkative, and can undermine your power by chattering endlessly about meaningless details or gossip, so try to be aware of the nature of what you're communicating!

Venus in the 1st: The beauty, charm, and grace established by the energy of Venus in your 1st House are empowering. You don't have to be on magazine covers to feel or be beautiful, but you do have to feel good about yourself, and if you cultivate your best qualities, you will attract exactly what you want and need from life. That's empowering! Developing your self-esteem has long-ranging benefits, and once you have the key, you may find that you attract others who want to know your secrets. This, too, can be empowering, and you may even feel better about helping others to develop their own sense of worth and importance. Cooperation and a loving nature are in your power tool kit, and although you may not think of these qualities as powerful, they are ultimately the most powerful of all.

Mars in the 1st: With Mars in your 1st House, you like to win, and prove your power through competitive or challenging ventures. Whether you're running a marathon or climbing the ladder in your profession, you like to feel that you can conquer anything. You have amazing courage, which is exceptionally empowering. In the process of meeting some of life's challenges you can be a bit abrasive, and must be aware of the way others are responding to your assertive nature if you are to avoid generating hostility. You will fight for yourself when necessary, but you can also be belligerent in a negative sense unless you're aware of the impact of your actions. Reacting spontaneously to every situation can get you into trouble and weaken your effectiveness. If you are accident-prone, part of the problem may be the result of jumping into situations without thinking, or moving too quickly for the circumstances. To be really powerful, you need to establish your independence and autonomy without creating extreme disruption or destruction in your path.

Jupiter in the 1st: Jupiter's energy in your 1st House adds confidence to your personality and is very empowering. Your humor and open-minded attitudes are attractive, and your desire to experience life as an adventure adds an optimistic quality that attracts positive fortune. You love sports and fitness activities, but you can also be self-indulgent. To establish your physical power and strength, you need to allow time in your life to build your endurance and support your physical vitality. Staying active may actually enhance your personal confidence! You are also strengthened when your life path supports your highest beliefs and ideals, but lose power if you adopt hypocritical or prejudicial attitudes.

Saturn in the 1st: Saturn's energy in your 1st House can be empowering when you learn how to deal with control issues. Taking responsibility for yourself is the most empowering thing you can do. That's different from taking care of everything and everyone, Superwoman, so remember that! You may be a little shy, especially if you feel insecure about yourself, the way you look, or your capabilities. For this reason, it's important that you carve an image that feels safe, secure, and strong. Your education and experience can be stabilizing, and if you need to get that degree before you venture out into the world, then do it! Whatever you need to accomplish to fortify your stability is very necessary for you. You can become a real sourpuss if you cling to the negative energy of Saturn, and you need to let your sense of humor and self-acceptance grow if you are to avoid showing this negativity. You may tell yourself that you're only being realistic when you see the glass as half-empty, but if you use that negative evaluation to alter your confidence, you're just being self-defeating. If you tend to feel depressed on a regular basis, talk over your feelings and concerns with your physician to determine if you need to address the physical side of depression. You may just be tired from taking on too many responsibilities, but you may also need to give yourself some biochemical support!

Uranus in the 1st: With the energy of Uranus in your 1st House, you possess a truly unique persona, and your greatest power arises when you step away from the burgeoning crowd and allow your individuality to shine forth. As a child, feeling different may have meant that you were not always included. As a woman, being different can be worn like a badge of courage and honor, once you understand how to use your uniqueness to your advantage. Finding your own style is part of expressing your power as an individual—in your manner of dress, your hair style, and even the way you speak and walk. Taking the time to discover what feels right, looks right, and expresses what you want to say about yourself will give you the reaction you want and need from the world. Now, that's a great beginning!

Neptune in the 1st: With the energy of Neptune in your 1st House, your power as an individual may be difficult to grasp at first. You may be an exceptional actress, artist, or performer—even if you're not on stage! Sometimes you may be tempted to take on a role just because it will give you some sense of identity, and your roles may begin to feel like you. Although the roles you play may be a part of who you are, there is a core element of your being that is different from those roles. Finding your core self is your task, and it is through exploring your spirituality and creativity that you will locate the keys to this aspect of yourself. You can feel invisible some of the time, and wonder why nobody seems to see you as you are. First of all, you have to become more aware of what you are projecting, and be willing to alter your self-projection as you change and grow. You must also realize that you can be especially sensitive to the projections of others, and that this can be both empowering and defeating. If the projection is accurate, it will support your sense of self, but if the projection is something that has nothing to do with who you really are, you will begin to feel lost, victimized, and confused.

Your relationships are a crucial means of learning about your personal power because they tell you what you are projecting and what others are projecting onto you. Learning about codependency and working to avoid the traps involved in codependent and addictive relationships is a major step in regaining your power and confidence. The rest of the work involves the fun part: making your dreams real. You're the only one who can do it, and you can be successful if those dreams arise from the promptings of your higher nature.

Pluto in the 1st: Pluto's energy in your 1st House brings power issues into your life at an early age. Whether you were involved in a family situation that was somewhat overwhelming or you had experiences that led to feelings of abandonment, you've probably learned to distrust others, and may even distrust yourself. You are actually quite aware of what is happening beneath the surface, but you may not let many people know you have this awareness. A sensitive person will be able to tell, and may even support your awareness, unless they have something to hide. To truly express your personal power, you first have to do some work within yourself addressing issues that stem from guilt, shame, or disappointment. If you allow these negative feelings to hang on, they undermine your power and confidence. Once you've released yourself, the healing process itself empowers you to make changes that can be awe-inspiring. You need to feel that you have control over your own life, and that there is no one who can take that power from you; but first you have to convince yourself that this is true by examining your motivations and desires. If they stem from hopeful, healing feelings, there may be little that can stop you from creating transformation and regeneration within yourself and the world around you.

Establishing Your Place in the World: The Midheaven

Another power space on your chart is your Midheaven. This point, which is usually at the top of your chart and marks the cusp of the 10th House, is like the crown and torch of the Statue of Liberty. Here are the indicators of the types of people you most admire and the clues to what you need to develop within yourself to attain unshakable self-respect. The Midheaven is signified by the letters "MC," which abbreviate the term "Medium Coeli."

The Sign on The Midheaven: Your Crown of Power

Aries on the MC: Through your Aries Midheaven you are striving to experience the power that comes when you are leading the way. Your admiration for great leaders may prompt you to find a mentor whose inspiration fosters your courage to forge your own pathways to success. Although meeting challenges can be empowering to you, disruptive outbursts or abrasive attitudes can work against your aims.

Taurus on the MC: Through your Taurus Midheaven you seek power by establishing a solid and reliable base. This includes financial success, but should not be limited to material things alone, since you feel more powerful when you know that your efforts, reputation, and position will endure the test of time. You appreciate and admire those who know how to use their talents to create success and who know how to use and build on their resources.

Gemini on the MC: Through your Gemini Midheaven you are keenly aware of the importance of developing your mind. The power of mind extends beyond the intellect, and the work you choose reflects your desire to expand your own consciousness into the realm of understanding. You admire those who are intelligent and articulate, and learn best from mentors who encourage you to pursue your interests in education and communication. If you fail to develop your capacity to link your thoughts and understanding with others in some way, you will feel less powerful. Utilizing your versatility is a major key to establishing your place in the world.

Cancer on the MC: Through your Cancer Midheaven you experience the need for the power that arises when you feel connected to a world that is safe and secure. You have a deep understanding of the power of human potential, and feel drawn to using your own influence to help foster the needs of children and stabilize the role of families. Your admiration for those in public service is strong. Whether you like it or not, you've been immensely influenced by your mother and the women in your family. You may ultimately take on a role that is akin to family matriarch within your family, from which you can wield immense power. But you may also perform well in roles that allow you to initiate new opportunities for women in the world.

Leo on the MC: Through your Leo Midheaven you have a deep fascination with achieving power, and may not rest until you feel that you've accomplished being in control of your own destiny. This can, of course, have strong implications in your career, but it extends to the way you perform in positions of influence within your personal relationships, too. Although you admire great leaders of history, you also have a deep admiration for those whose creative self-expression has opened the way to their success. The way you give and take orders makes a lot of difference in your sense of personal accomplishment, since you really do want prestige but find that it comes only when you lead and follow with equal grace.

Virgo on the MC: Through your Virgo Midheaven you feel that power arises only when you've achieved perfection, although your ideals for perfection may be astronomical. Your admiration for perfect performances by anyone, from athletes to artists, is unqualified, and you truly appreciate others who are striving to improve themselves. Despite your continual search for the ultimate, you grow into your power when you fully embrace both your strengths and your limitations. You also know the importance of cooperative efforts, and can be especially influential in situations that target improvements. Some of your greatest mentors are your teachers, and when you realize how much you appreciate your teachers for just being themselves, you find that on this level, you can also accept and empower yourself. After all, you are your own ultimate teacher!

Libra on the MC: With Libra at your Midheaven, you experience power in the form of justice and fairness, and may strive to find a career expression that allows you to work toward these ends. You admire those whose work in the law or politics affords greater opportunity to a broad range of people, and may yourself feel that your real power will manifest when you make an impact on society in some manner. You don't have to be a judge or politician to do it, either!

Scorpio on the MC: Through your Scorpio Midheaven you have a deep desire to achieve a position of power, although this does not mean that you necessarily have to gain massive recognition. You may even prefer to work behind the scenes, and can accomplish things that infiltrate society and create transformational change without ever having your name in the headlines. Your admiration for those who can get to the heart of the matter in any field is very strong, and you appreciate individuals who are willing to rise above corruption or whose efforts expose corruption. Since you may be drawn to investigate many of life's ultimate issues, you will frequently come face to face with raw power. What you do with it is up to you.

Sagittarius on the MC: Through your Sagittarius Midheaven you are drawn to the power of Truth. This can stimulate a life path centered on adventure and discovery, even if those adventures are experienced quietly in your own backyard. Some of your most powerful life experiences are likely to occur on an inner level, and your fascination with the mystics and philosophers throughout time may stem from your own experiences of rising above the ordinary into the realm of understanding. Through incorporating this awareness into your life experience, you can be more tolerant and accepting of yourself and others, but can lose power when you expect the impossible from other people or from life itself.

Capricorn on the MC: Through your Capricorn Midheaven you are drawn to power that has a strong element of structure and control. This manifests within society through government, big business, and the world of finance. It also exists in classrooms, on farms, and within families. The structures that form the basis of your own security are personal, and it is crucial that your own ambitions are tailored to goals that fit you as an individual woman. You have deep admiration for those who have shown success in their lives, and you need that same admiration for yourself. Creating a structure in your own life that allows you to grow and has room for the processes of change will allow you to experience the real power that emerges when you are stabilized. Power for you will never be complete if you are simply wielding control over the lives of others. You are much more whole when you are building character.

Aquarius on the MC: Through your Aquarius Midheaven you are well aware of the importance of a group-oriented power base. Power in numbers works only if you are affiliated with those whose views and ideals reflect and strengthen your own, however. You admire those whose efforts are dedicated to the principles of liberty and universality. Work for the collective or humanitarian service can encourage your rise to prominence and influence.

Pisces on the MC: Through your Pisces Midheaven you are drawn to the power of that which is beyond the limitation of the physical plane. Your interest in spirituality, creative artistry, serving the needs of those less fortunate, making the world a better place—all stem from this influence. Your admiration for those who go the extra mile, and for those who are devoted to improving the quality of life, inspires you. When your life is oriented in such a way as to allow time and room to explore and participate in such endeavors, you may feel more whole and alive—more powerful. The power of compassion is paramount in your life, and active compassion can be personally strengthening on many different levels.

Aspects to the MC: More Power!

Sun conjunct MC: The energy of your Sun conjunct your Midheaven adds to your need for recognition and increases your personal ambition. The manner in which you go about achieving that ambition will determine whether or not you are successful in the ultimate sense, and part of that depends on how you handle the power you gain in your life. If you are too dictatorial, or are motivated entirely by your need to be the one in the spotlight, you may end up alienating others or diminishing your influence because your ego gets in the way. You may also be tempted to live out your needs for power through the men in your life, but will discover that this never quite works for you in the long run. You have to accomplish your achievements on your own.

Sun semisextile MC: The energy of your Sun in semisextile aspect to your Midheaven strengthens your ability to accomplish your aims, especially if you are willing to take the necessary steps that will allow you to grow into your power. Some situations in your life allow you to rise to prominence with apparent suddenness, but you will know if you're prepared to handle it. You may find that political involvement is especially empowering, particularly when you use your influence to support the needs of the community.

Sun semisquare MC: With the energy of your Sun in semisquare to your Midheaven, you are strongly driven to achieve success, but may be insecure about getting there. Setting goals can be especially helpful, but you also need to understand your motivations. When you are clear about your underlying motivations, you can then determine if they really fit your needs or if you're trying to accomplish something just to please another. Once you're on track and secure in your own identity, you can be catapulted to success through focusing your will in harmony with your higher needs.

Sun sextile MC: Your Sun's sextile aspect to your Midheaven adds strength to your capacity to succeed in achieving your aims and realizing your ambitions. You need recognition for your efforts, and it is recognition that will act as a platform for future achievements and personal growth. Power for its own sake is not your issue, but accomplishing your goals in the spirit of self-fulfillment is definitely empowering!

Sun square MC: The frustration that arises from your Sun in square aspect to your Midheaven results from a deep-seated need to overcome the obstacles in your path in order to prove your power. Although some of those obstacles may be the result of life circumstances, you realize that you have a part in placing (or maintaining) many of them, especially if your attitudes about achieving your goals are stubborn or fearful. If you feel that others are standing in your way, it is important to determine if that is really the case or if you simply do not trust your own abilities. By surrendering your ego's need for control or recognition to your inner need for true personal fulfillment, you may find that your goals are clearer and within reach.

Sun trine MC: Success looks good on you. With your Sun in trine aspect to your Midheaven, you can utilize the personal power gained when you accomplish your aims to boost you further toward new goals. You may also be very comfortable using your own success to influence or facilitate the success of others.

Sun quincunx MC: The quincunx between your Sun and Midheaven illustrates a frustration between your ambitions and your perceived abilities. You may not like the idea of being in the spotlight, or you may be uncomfortable seeking the recognition you need in order to progress in the world; your talents can speak for you if you let them. This means you may have to cultivate your special talents if you wish to experience true self-fulfillment.

Sun opposition MC: With your Sun in opposition to your Midheaven, you struggle between your need for security and your ambitions. You may fear success, especially if you feel that success in the world will mean exposing yourself or your vulnerabilities; but if you work toward establishing a true sense of personal security, outside success may not feel as threatening to you.

Moon conjunct MC: The energy of your Moon in conjunction to your Midheaven draws many opportunities for success. The support and influence of other people can open a lot of doors, and your own support of others will open even more. You need to establish a level of ambition that feels comfortable, and you will be most fulfilled when you are accomplishing your aims. Your ambitions definitely have a cyclical nature, and you will be most empowered when you listen to your inner voice in this regard.

Moon semisextile MC: Your Moon's energy in semisextile to your Midheaven adds a positive level of sensitivity to your need to accomplish success. Although you may feel driven to achieve your aims, you may also feel good about allowing the changes in your life that inevitably accompany success.

Moon semisquare MC: With your Moon in semisquare aspect to your Midheaven, you need to be aware of your subconscious feelings about achieving success. If you are afraid of success or fear failure, it's important to find out why. Then you can work on your inner dragons and change your approach to accomplishing a sense of self-fulfillment.

Moon sextile MC: Your sense of security with yourself plays a valuable role in achieving your ambitions with your Moon in sextile aspect to your Midheaven. In addition, you will be most successful in the world when you feel good about what you're doing. Finding a life work that fills your soul not only supports your personal growth but touches the lives of others in a positive manner.

Moon square MC: You may feel frustrated with your roles in the world with your Moon in square aspect to your Midheaven. This is particularly true if you seem to be doing too much caretaking and accomplish little self-fulfillment. Listening to your inner needs and working to eliminate your old self-defeating subconscious messages is very important to you. If you try to ignore these subconscious motivations, you may find that you're caught up in situations that simply do not feel right.

Moon trine MC: You love the feeling of success with your Moon in trine aspect to your Midheaven, and you can be quite satisfied with successes of all types—from career to family to little leaps you make just for yourself. You can easily accept careers that have a cyclical nature, and may even welcome some of the down times for your own rejuvenation. Working in fields that support the needs of women and families may be especially empowering to you. You may also make strides that have a positive effect upon the lives of women and girls who follow after you.

Moon quincunx MC: Finding the right path in life can be a bit frustrating with your Moon in quincunx to your Midheaven. The answer may be as simple as listening to your changing needs instead of trying to keep everything constant all the time. Flexibility in your schedule may be important to your happiness in your work, but you also need to develop flexibility in your consciousness that will allow you to refocus your aims from time to time. What was important in the last decade may no longer be meaningful.

Moon opposition MC: Although you may not like the feeling of being exposed with your Moon in opposition to your Midheaven, you feel a strong need to be acknowledged for your contributions or successes. The support and recognition of your family may be first and foremost, and it's crucial to accept these levels of support as extremely valuable in your life. If you are working in the "outside" world, you may become instrumental in drawing attention to the importance of family needs within the context of the workplace.

Mercury conjunct MC: The energy of Mercury in conjunction to your Midheaven adds a strong mentality to your power base. You're more empowered when your mind is stimulated and when you have an opportunity to express your ideas. You may also be drawn to work in fields that are oriented to education, communication, or travel for these same reasons. Variety in your career activities is also strengthening, since repetitive actions may not be very mentally stimulating at all!

Mercury semisextile MC: Through the influence of Mercury in semisextile aspect to your Midheaven, you experience a need to stimulate your mind through your life path. You'll feel most empowered working in a field that is mentally creative or challenging, and you may even present concepts that bring positive or innovative changes into your work environment.

Mercury semisquare MC: Mercury in semisquare aspect to your Midheaven provides the need for mental challenges in your choice of career. You may also find that you sometimes feel ill-prepared to handle some of the tasks required of you, particularly if you are not using your own mentality to think through and accomplish the tasks at hand. Making choices that allow you to increase your understanding at a pace you can handle is the key to feeling powerful in your career.

Mercury sextile MC: Cultivating your intellectual abilities enhances your confidence and success in the world. You may also be adept at working with people, and will probably enjoy working in fields that require good people skills. Getting the education you need is an important step, and your acceptance and understanding of this approach can be especially empowering.

Mercury square MC: You will accomplish your greatest sense of success when you are mentally challenged and learning something. With Mercury in square aspect to your Midheaven, your desire to share your ideas sometimes runs into confrontation, but that only strengthens your resolve to get your point across. Developing your intellectual capacities and cultivating positive communication skills will go a long way toward helping you achieve the success you desire.

Mercury trine MC: The people you meet in your life can be very influential in help-ing you accomplish your aims. Mercury's trine aspect to your Midheaven operates through your ability to network. This is especially true if you are clear about artic-ulating what you hope to achieve and clarifying your ideas. Your communicative abilities can be a strong asset in a career.

Mercury quincunx MC: With Mercury in quincunx aspect to your Midheaven, you may have some trouble getting your ideas across in your career. This can be espe-cially true if you jump into a situation unprepared, including opportunities for spontaneity. If you've developed your "data base" by continuing to learn or improve your skills, you'll be ready for the inevitable changes and challenges asso-ciated with your work in the world.

Mercury opposition MC: Mercury's opposition to your Midheaven can underscore a sense of mistrust of your own intellectual abilities, or you may be caught in life experiences that have made it difficult to complete your education or accomplish the learning you need. Maintaining your focus on your long-range goals is impor-tant, and choosing opportunities that allow you to continue to develop your mind or enhance your skills will stimulate greater success and strengthen your sense of personal power.

Venus conjunct MC: Although you may not be driven to accomplish success for the power it brings, you can enjoy positive benefits from becoming an influential woman. Your aims are underscored by your desire to express your artistry and cre-ativity; and by cultivating your talents, you will achieve great success. You may also do quite well in the business world, since you have a good understanding of money and the value of things. Being a woman works to your advantage because you innate-ly know how to use your feminine strengths to your advantage. This aspect helps to assure that others will acknowledge the value of your efforts in your chosen field.

Venus semisextile MC: With Venus in semisextile to your Midheaven, your talents and abilities may have been obvious in your youth, although you may have made choices that seem to have altered your use of them. When you look at it, you'll real-ize that activities like those piano or dance lessons extended benefits in other areas of your life as an adult woman, even if you are not on the concert stage! Anything that develops your self-esteem improves your opportunities for success, and that is as true now as it was when you were a young girl. Your life work may involve the arts in some way, and may also extend into avenues that are particularly appealing to women. Cultivating social skills and using your grace and refinement to your advantage can strengthen your standing in the world.

Venus semisquare MC: With the energy of Venus in semisquare aspect to your Midheaven, you may feel most accomplished when your life work involves the use of your sense of artistry and refinement. If you feel that being a woman gets in the way of your success, look deeply into the issue to discover where your own insecurities reside, and go from there. If you discover pitfalls in your path to success, you can lift yourself out of them by working on your self-esteem.

Venus sextile MC: You are empowered by your own expression of artistry and feminine grace with Venus in sextile aspect to your Midheaven. Regardless of your career choices, you use the essence of being a woman to your advantage. You may enjoy a career in the arts, but can also do very well in business, since you have an excellent sense of the value of things and people.

Venus square MC: You feel challenged to bring a sense of grace and fairness into the world through your career with the influence of Venus in square aspect to your Midheaven. However, you may run into a few obstacles, especially if your personal artistry, taste, or values is out of synch with those of society. You may also feel a little lazy about working to achieve your aims, and need to get clear about the fact that you are not always motivated to get out into the world and face all its challenges. Exposing your talents to the world may leave you feeling entirely too vulnerable some of the time, and for this reason you feel more powerful when you have good allies standing next to you.

Venus trine MC: You attract fortunate opportunities to rise to positions of prominence with Venus in trine aspect to your Midheaven, but you may not always cultivate those opportunities. The choice is yours. Whether you're developing your artistry as a means of making your place in the world or in business, you can be quite successful, but feel most powerful when you put effort behind your opportunities. You can also be influential in aiding others along their paths, and may feel better about opening doors for someone else than running headlong into the spotlight yourself.

Venus quincunx MC: The energy of Venus in quincunx to your Midheaven has its plus and minus sides. On the plus side, you may be drawn to pursue accomplishments in areas that allow you to use your talents, artistry, and value judgments. On the minus side, you may not feel particularly motivated! If your self-esteem is strong, you'll be more focused on achieving your ambitions, and by working to strengthen your sense of self-worth, you can open many doors for yourself.

Venus opposition MC: With Venus in opposition to your Midheaven, you feel most comfortable at home, out of the spotlight, doing the things you do best. Exposing your talents or artistry to the world can seem threatening, or you may simply not feel very motivated to reach out into the world. If you're afraid, there may be other factors at work that you need to address. You can actually accomplish a great deal, and may even do your best work behind the scenes. First, however, you have to establish a powerful base of self-esteem, and that means incorporating things into your life that are truly meaningful to you as a person and allowing yourself to feel good about your choices.

Mars conjunct MC: Mars' energy conjunct your Midheaven activates your sense of ambition and can play a strong role in your need to establish power and autonomy through your life work. You'll be most attracted to career circumstances that provide breakthrough opportunities and allow you to utilize your leadership. Your need for crisis and competition in your career are strong, so finding a career that incorporates crises or positive outlets for competition will be necessary if you are to avoid hostility. Pay attention to the way you handle power plays in your profession, since your desire to achieve your aims can blind you to the needs or sensibilities of others.

Mars semisextile MC: Through the semisextile of Mars to your Midheaven you have an intensified drive to achieve the realization of your personal ambitions. You handle competition very well, and you need to choose a career path that provides a sense of challenge. You probably work better in situations that allow you to be in charge since you're not always happy following orders unless they will get you somewhere.

Mars semisquare MC: You may be impatient with your career development with Mars in semisquare aspect to your Midheaven. Ambition accompanies your aims, and you are not likely to stop until you've achieved the success you desire. But sometimes your own frustration or inability to handle power is troublesome. You need excellent outlets for diffusing your anger if you are to be successful in the world. Staying physically active can help, and choosing life work that challenges you to use your courage and strength can be a perfect match for your energy.

Mars sextile MC: When you are focused on your ambitions you are capable of carrying through until you reach your goals. Mars in sextile aspect to your Midheaven adds a strong drive to your abilities to achieve success in the world. You enjoy work that has plenty of challenges, but you can also be successful in areas that simply allow you to stay active.

Mars square MC: Your drive to accomplish your ambitions can be especially powerful with Mars in square aspect to your Midheaven. Sometimes all you can see is the goal, and you can engender hostile responses or create hurt feelings from others if you fail to recognize the effects of your climb to the top. You're probably most stimulated by opportunities that are challenging, but you need to watch a tendency to try to achieve success at any price.

Mars trine MC: You don't mind working hard to accomplish your goals. The energy of Mars in trine aspect to your Midheaven confers a strong measure of courage and confidence where career matters are concerned, and blazing trails may be second nature for you. You can handle competition, and may even perform better when you rise to meet challenges.

Mars quincunx MC: With Mars in quincunx aspect to your Midheaven, you probably feel quite ambitious about achieving your goals, but may not have an easy road getting there. Those bumps and twists and turns in your life path may not always be the result of your own efforts, but you do create a few, particularly when you lose patience and break away before you've accomplished your aims. Learning to cooperate with others is important, since sometimes your methods may be difficult for others to understand or accept. Once you've made a few adjustments in your attitude, you can rise to the challenge at hand. Just try to get clear about your motivations before you pull out all the stops.

Mars opposition MC: You seem to attract a great deal of confrontation or challenge in pursuit of your aims. With Mars in opposition to your Midheaven, you are strongly driven to realize your ambitions, but your methods may need careful evaluation if you are to get there without destructive results.

Jupiter conjunct MC: Reaching for the stars is only the beginning with Jupiter conjunct your Midheaven. You have great expectations for your accomplishments in the world, and your confidence and optimism can go a long way in helping you get there, but sometimes you can present more hot air than substance, especially if you've run headlong into a situation that is foreign to your expertise. Generally, however, your enthusiasm works to your benefit, and your comfort when you're in the public eye can be a great asset.

Jupiter semisextile MC: Your tendency to push the limits in regard to achieving your ambitions is stimulated by Jupiter's energy in semisextile to your Midheaven. Working in fields that place you in the public eye can be an asset to your success, but you may not always feel confident when you're in circumstances that are new or unusual. Once you've gotten your feet wet, you're okay, and then your plans for the future keep you moving ahead.

Jupiter semisquare MC: You're likely to jump right into situations, even if they're a little over your head, with Jupiter's energy in semisquare to your Midheaven, but if you find yourself treading water, you won't like the feeling of not getting anywhere. You like to feel forward motion toward achieving your ambitions, and those times that require you to slow down can be a little frustrating. Continually evaluating your goals will help you maintain a sense of personal power within your profession or in your efforts within your community.

Jupiter sextile MC: Jupiter's energy in sextile aspect to your Midheaven affords excellent opportunities to get ahead in the world. When you've set your sights on your ambitions, your confidence and optimism help you realize them. Once you begin to put your efforts into achieving your goals, you experience amazing results and find that your own success inspires the respect and admiration of others. When in positions of influence, you can also be instrumental in aiding others in the achievement of their goals and ambitions.

Jupiter square MC: Sometimes your expectations concerning your ambitions or profession are unrealistic. Jupiter's energy in square aspect to your Midheaven stimulates you to push the limits, and sometimes you simply go too far too quickly. Setting a pace within a reasonable frame of reference is not really your style, but it can help if you've run into some problems along the way toward achieving your ambitions. The gift of this aspect is a continual feeling of optimism, even when times are hard. It is that very optimism that may help you get there while you work through all the rough places along the way.

Jupiter trine MC: With Jupiter in trine aspect to your Midheaven, the doors to achieving your ambitions are likely to open rather easily. You have excellent connections, but your confidence in your skills and abilities is what draws the attention of the people who are there to use their influence to support your aims. From positions of influence, you can also be generous and helpful to others. Sometimes you can be a little lazy about reaching your goals, especially if you feel you deserve to be there already, but once you put your efforts into something, there's no stopping you.

Jupiter quincunx MC: Aligning your expectations with your ambitions is not always easy with Jupiter in quincunx aspect to your Midheaven. Sometimes you go too far. Other times, your aim seems too short. You have the most trouble when you're shooting from the hip instead of taking careful aim toward your ambitions. By making adequate preparations, which may include the right educational background, and concentrating your efforts toward realistic goals, you can accomplish success. You just have to adjust your sights.

Jupiter opposition MC: Through Jupiter's opposition to your Midheaven you expect a lot from life. The problem is that you don't always like to put forth the effort to attain it. Although believing that you deserve good things is part of getting them, using your energy to accomplish your aims is also necessary. Developing a strong sense of gratitude for the gifts you receive and extending your generosity to others can be a good foundation. Applied effort is the mechanism that will assure a real sense of personal power.

Saturn conjunct MC: Saturn's energy conjunct your Midheaven focuses your ambition. You can be quite successful in a professional career path, particularly if you are following a calling that suits your individual needs. Clarifying your motivations will help you determine if you're working toward achievements that will be personally satisfying, but you will probably discover that you simply cannot put a lot of energy into something that does not fit you. Teaching, training, and guiding others is an excellent direction for your need to utilize your power, as long as you allow others to grow at their own rates. You may also prefer to work in executive positions or to run your own business. The key to your success is knowing how to use your power effectively.

Saturn semisextile MC: Saturn's energy in semisextile aspect to your Midheaven strengthens your resolve toward achieving your aims and ambitions. You may run into a few obstacles along your path to success, but can generally use them as stepping stones once you take the time to deal with them. Although you can work reasonably well within structured circumstances, you may be most effective when you have the chance to direct yourself or be your own boss.

Saturn semisquare MC: Saturn's energy in semisquare aspect to your Midheaven provides some definite boulders in your path toward success. You may experience some delays in your opportunities to rise to the top, and will probably find that you will get there only by focused, disciplined effort. If you become resentful toward others whose success seems easier than your own, you will work against yourself. Instead, learning what you need to know and concentrating on the tasks before you will smooth your path. Your inner work involves learning to believe in yourself and developing a desire to be responsible for yourself. From this point of view you can create aims that will provide a real sense of accomplishment and self-empowerment.

Saturn sextile MC: With Saturn's energy in sextile aspect to your Midheaven, you use your sense of personal responsibility and self-discipline to help you manifest your goals. Your desire to achieve success in the world is strong, and you will gain recognition for your efforts among your peers and those who can appreciate the quality of your work. You will want to establish yourself in a career, and can be influential in aiding others who seek your counsel or guidance in their own career paths.

Saturn square MC: Saturn's energy in square aspect to your Midheaven provides a powerful challenge in regard to achieving your ambitions. You may actually perform best when you're under pressure, and you rarely choose goals that are easy to achieve. But if you are well-prepared and have the confidence in yourself required to rise to the occasion, you can accomplish a great deal. The problem you may run into is in your motivation. It is crucial that you explore the underlying reasons for your goals, since if you are trying to satisfy someone else and gain little satisfaction for yourself, you will feel that you have failed—even if you reach the summit of achievement. The obstacles in your path are usually quite apparent, but sometimes it is not so easy to figure out what to do about them.

Saturn trine MC: Saturn's energy in trine aspect to your Midheaven helps you focus your aims and choose ambitions that provide a real sense of personal accomplishment. You may be very well-suited for a professional career, and do not mind working to achieve your goals. A structured approach to success, such as a well-defined educational path, may be easier for you, and you are likely to appreciate the guidance and support of an excellent mentor or teacher. You may also feel empowered when you have the opportunity to teach or guide others.

Saturn quincunx MC: Saturn's energy in quincunx to your Midheaven indicates a series of frustrations and difficulties along the pathway to success. You feel uncertain of your abilities, or may not put enough effort into developing the skills you need to assure your success. This happens most often when you feel pressured by circumstances that undermine your self-confidence, and the work you must do involves re-evaluating your goals and starting again. If you've experienced an interruption in your education or have been unable to complete the requirements necessary to accomplish your aims, you may lose your resolve. If you really want to change your life circumstances, you can apply yourself to the task at hand. Take a careful look at your limitations, but also find ways to capitalize on your strengths.

Your own inertia can be your worst enemy: just tell yourself to keep moving, and stay focused on your aims.

Saturn opposition MC: You may not trust your ambitions, or may feel that you don't really deserve to realize them with Saturn in opposition to your Midheaven. This can be especially true if you've not experienced the type of support you needed from your family. Even if your parents seemed to be supportive, were their aims for you centered on what you needed or what they expected? Sometimes necessity just gets in the way, and that's understandable. If you are afraid of failure, you may never get what you want from life. You must establish a strong foundation, and from that foundation you can accomplish anything. The foundation may be educational; it may revolve around establishing a home. Whatever it is, when you concentrate on building it, you will realize the value of standing on solid ground while you reach for success.

Uranus conjunct MC: The electric energy of Uranus at your Midheaven draws you into the public eye. You are driven to follow a path that is unlike the "norm." You want to accomplish something unique, and will accept success only when it reflects your talents, personal genius, and individual abilities. You also need a great deal of independence in your profession. As a result, you forge pathways into areas that are not easily understood by everyone (like your parents). If you listen to your inner voice and pay attention to your needs within the world, you can create an amazing series of accomplishments that will ultimately speak for themselves. But in the process, you may gain a bit of notoriety. After all, it's not really your way to stay with something that does not work (including relationships), or to get stuck in a career that hides your talents. You'll probably have your fifteen minutes of fame (at least). What you do with it is up to you.

Uranus semisextile MC: The energy of Uranus in semisextile aspect to your Midheaven stimulates your desire to work independently and in a field that illustrates your unique talents. Your efforts in your career can be ground-breaking, but you may not always have long-term success from them. That's usually okay, since you may make more than one career change over your lifetime. The self-fulfillment you seek arises mostly from giving yourself the room you need to experiment with your ambitions.

Uranus semisquare MC: The disruptive energy of Uranus in semisquare aspect to your Midheaven can get in your way of experiencing the satisfaction you desire from your career, especially if you fail to focus your energy on aims that suit your individuality. You always feel a little restless concerning your life path, and function best in careers that rely upon your ingenuity and independence. Sometimes you may not be very reliable, and learning to discipline yourself is not always easy.

Uranus sextile MC: The influence of Uranus in sextile aspect to your Midheaven brings an intense need to exercise autonomy and independence in your career. You are most satisfied with ambitions that support your individuality, and can be quite successful in fields of endeavor that require you to employ your intuitive insights. Since you can have sudden bursts of energy, you need room in your life for change and will be most fulfilled when your life path takes interesting twists and turns.

Uranus square MC: Your rebellious nature can get in the way of achieving your aims. The energy of Uranus in square aspect to your Midheaven stimulates your need for independence, and sometimes the changes you create or experience can turn your life upside down. You will probably not enjoy a regular 9:00 to 5:00 job, and if given the chance to be more flexible, you may perform better. In order to achieve the satisfaction you desire from a career or profession, you need to feel that your efforts stand out from the crowd. It takes some maturity to figure out how to do that without appearing purely disruptive, but you can accomplish it if you desire. You probably don't care about fitting into a mold anyway, and when you learn to use your uniqueness to your advantage, you'll be amazed at the results.

Uranus trine MC: Your special talents are an extreme asset to achieving success in the world. With the energy of Uranus in trine aspect to your Midheaven, you can use your individuality to your best advantage most of the time. You're here to create some new pathways, and forging ahead into innovative or unusual areas of endeavor can assure success on many levels. You feel most powerful when you achieve a sense of independence through your ambitions.

Uranus quincunx MC: For you, the road to success is definitely bumpy. Uranus is in quincunx aspect to your Midheaven, indicating a series of unexpected disruptions in your path to self-fulfillment. Some of these will be of your own choosing (unconscious motivations included), but others seem to come from nowhere. You do not like to feel that you are restricted to a singular identity, and your career path will reflect that. Innovative, technological, and unusual fields of endeavor will be more satisfying pathways, and you may create your own career identity by developing your special talents and skills. Your greatest obstacle is overcoming your need for sensational excitement all the time. Sometimes, you may have to be satisfied with a regular day.

Uranus opposition MC: With Uranus in opposition to your Midheaven, you feel strongly about creating a life path that allows you to experience independence on as many levels as possible. Alternative lifestyles, unusual career options, innovative approaches to success all describe the ultimate possibilities. Your own rebellion can disrupt your opportunities, especially if your actions or attitudes fly in the face of convention to such an extent that you seem to be a threat. Building a bridge between your viewpoints and those of the more traditional thinkers may give you a little latitude.

Neptune conjunct MC: The energy of Neptune in conjunction to your Midheaven adds a sense of uncertainty to your life path. It's hard to know if you've made the right choice because you are a bit impressionable in this area. The only way you can know is to connect to your inner self and listen to the promptings of your spiritual voice. This is different from following an illusion, though! Even when you accomplish success, you may not feel that you've gotten there unless your consciousness is centered. Your spiritual aims play an important role in your sense of self-fulfillment, and you may discover that you have to sacrifice your selfish aims in order to achieve a true sense of satisfaction in your life path. The power you seek from your life path arises from your need to connect to The Source, and your choices about the way you get there can be wide-ranging. Reaching out to others through your spiritual quest may be your most empowering option.

Neptune semisextile MC: Neptune's influence through the semisextile aspect to your Midheaven adds a need to experience fulfillment through serving the needs of others. Success for its own sake will probably not appeal to you, but if your success allows you to make a difference in the quality of life, you will happily utilize it in that capacity. You're not necessarily driven to achieve the kind of power that feels like control, but are, rather, prompted by the need to feel the power of connection that arises from your spirituality.

Neptune semisquare MC: It's difficult for you to see where you need to go with your life path under the influence of Neptune in semisquare to your Midheaven. You can be easily influenced by the desires and demands of others, and may circumvent your own needs in order to satisfy someone else. You may gladly give of yourself when there is a real need, but will resent yourself if you've fallen victim to deception. You may be most fulfilled in careers that reach out to the needs of others in some manner, or that allow you to develop your spirituality more fully.

Neptune sextile MC: Neptune's energy in sextile aspect to your Midheaven stimulates your desire to use your career in service to the needs of humanity and the fulfillment of your spiritual ideals. You may also be drawn to a career in the arts, and if you achieve success in this area, you may turn your energy and influence toward empowering others in some manner.

Neptune square MC: Neptune's energy in square aspect to your Midheaven can be confusing in regard to finding the right path to personal fulfillment. If you have difficulty setting your personal boundaries, your life may be so deeply influenced by the desires of others that you seem to have no direction of your own. You do need an outlet for your compassion, but you have to maintain your sense of inner strength and awareness in order to perform in such a way that will really make a difference. Losing your path is also possible, particularly if you give up on your dreams or ambitions.

Neptune trine MC: The energy of Neptune in supportive trine aspect to your Midheaven suggests that many of the accomplishments you're making for yourself can pave the way for others. Work that has a spiritual basis, or that allows you to reach into the psyche and soul of others, can be personally empowering. You are capable of surrendering your will to the will of a Higher Power in order to achieve your aims. This aspect also underlines the importance of your role in making your dreams happen in harmony with your Highest Needs. However, you can also be unmotivated, and may even be lazy, living in a dream instead of making it real. The difference is applied effort.

Neptune quincunx MC: You may have to re-evaluate your dreams from time to time with Neptune in quincunx aspect to your Midheaven. You can become disenchanted, particularly if you're following a path that seems to waste your talents and abilities. But you may also feel that your drive to accomplish success in the world vacillates. Listening to your inner voice in this regard can help, and knowing when you need to pull back can help you keep your energy strong. Work that makes a difference to the world in some way will be more fulfilling than just putting money in some guy's pockets. Your dreams of a better life can be distracting, especially if you always think that the grass is greener on the other side of that proverbial fence.

Neptune opposition MC: With Neptune in opposition to your Midheaven, you may not have strong ambitions for success in the world. You may be prompted to withdraw, and may not feel that you have a clear direction anyway. The only way you can find direction is to get outside yourself in a positive sense. Although meditation and contemplation can be helpful tools, they are helpful only if they offer some objectivity. Reaching out to others will help you see yourself more clearly, but you do have to keep you your personal boundaries intact! It's a very tricky balance.

Pluto conjunct MC: Your passion about your life work can be immense with Pluto in conjunction to your Midheaven. You need to work in a field that allows you to influence change and bring rejuvenation. Learning how to trust your own power is important, so that you are not tempted to use your success in the world to wield your power over others without regard to their needs or desires or the effects of your actions.

Pluto semisextile MC: Establishing an impressive position in the world is important for you, and with Pluto in semisextile aspect to your Midheaven, it's crucial that you adopt a clear sense of values when following your career path. You will seek out a path that allows you to create change or accomplish healing in some manner, and you need to learn how to deal with those who might use their own power for selfish interests. You'll probably expose a few people with hidden agendas, so it's important that you are honest about whether or not you have your own if you are to escape the same fate.

Pluto semisquare MC: Moving beyond your limitations is important with Pluto in semisquare to your Midheaven. Your own personal traumas may actually be the springboard to your success, particularly if you make the effort to rise above them and deal with the challenge of fulfilling your hopes. This success may not be measured in career alone, but in the strides you make in your personal growth. But if you allow your defeats to stand in the way, you will experience continual vulnerability. It seems as though you have no choice, but you do. You can continue to suffer, or you can experience the true nature of healing by focusing on a life path that allows you to experience and create true personal power.

Pluto sextile MC: You are likely to rise to positions of prominence with Pluto in sextile aspect to your Midheaven. This is particularly true if you dedicate your life to bringing about positive transformation. Whether you accomplish this through the healing arts, performing arts, through raising a family, or doing something else that accomplishes renovation—you need to know the satisfaction that comes from utilizing your personal power.

Pluto square MC: You may learn about power the hard way. With Pluto in square aspect to your Midheaven, you've probably experienced some disappointments in your lifetime that are the results of some type of abuse. Whether this abuse was physical or psychological, whether it was from the hands of someone you trusted or a system that failed you, you feel that you can use your personal trauma as an excuse for lack of accomplishment. You may decide to set your targets on destruction, and you have the power to be quite destructive, but in the process, you destroy yourself. Amazingly, you also have the capacity to use your pain to heal yourself, and can experience a renewal of power that is unequaled. Then your influence and use of power can have a very different effect: that of clearing the way for healing in the world around you.

Pluto trine MC: Pluto's energy trines your Midheaven, fortifying your needs to accomplish personal fulfillment through your life path. You feel most empowered when your work allows you to effect changes. Your options for career span the spectrum of possibilities, but you can be especially drawn to the healing arts, psychology, political reform, urban renewal, or work that gives you a chance to help others establish their own sense of power. You can be very effective in positions of influence, and can become a formidable force when challenged by those who abuse their own power.

Pluto quincunx MC: Although you may feel driven to achieve a pre-eminent position in the world, you may find that the experience of getting there is not easy. Pluto's energy in quincunx aspect to your Midheaven encourages you to forge ahead in developing your life path, but your aims will have to be adjusted before you can effectively accomplish them. In the process of getting there, you may discover strengths or talents you did not know you have, and you may also find that some of the areas you felt were important are not as fulfilling. As long as you're willing to be somewhat flexible in dealing with changes, you'll accomplish what you set out to do, and more. But if you resist change or feel resentful when you have to alter your path, you may hold yourself back.

Pluto opposition MC: Confronting your needs to own and express your power is necessary with Pluto in opposition to your Midheaven. You may have dealt with power struggles all your life, or you may still have abandonment issues from your childhood. As a result, your own sense of mistrust can actually undermine your ability to achieve your aims. The manner in which you deal with authority figures is crucial to your success, since if you continually feel a need to undermine the power of authority, you may be missing the point. You need to determine when authority is used to your benefit and learn to resist when it is used in a counterproductive manner. This is not easy because you don't like being controlled in the least, but finding the core of your own power requires that you own up to the fact that you have some fascination with the process. This struggle for control can prompt you to do things that are somewhat destructive until you determine that you have a choice! You can actually use this same force to expose corruption, investigate what lies beneath the surface, or rejuvenate what once appeared useless.

Money, Self-Worth, and Personal Power: The 2nd House

Someone once said that money makes the world go around, and from all evidence, it certainly seems to be a powerful force. Money, in fact, symbolizes a kind of power. With money, you can have what you want. With more money, you can have more of what you want. Without money, you may want what you cannot have. Your relationship with money is an extremely intimate and seductive force. The way you use your resources— money, time, energy—says a lot about how you perceive your own power and personal worth. This facet of yourself is expressed through the 2nd House. Here, you express your value systems. The important special link between finances and self-esteem cannot be understated, and is especially important for you as a woman. In order to extract the real value of your talents and services from others in the world (such as what you are paid for your job), you must first value yourself.

The Sign on the 2nd House: Your Worth

Aries on the 2nd: The qualities of Aries influencing your 2nd House add impulsiveness and spontaneity to the manner in which you use your resources. You also realize that you have to put energy into your life in order to get anything out of it, but you may not be consistent in your approach to doing this! Your downfall is impulsive spending, so it's probably a good idea to keep your credit cards on ice unless you really need to use them. You can quickly exhaust your resources if you're not careful. With Mars ruling this house, you are willing to work and expend energy to build your resources, and prefer to be in charge of your own finances. Your self-esteem grows when you assert your courage and when you feel you have freedom to create your life on your own terms.

Taurus on the 2nd: Through the influence of Taurus on your 2nd House you recognize the importance of building a solid financial base. When your finances are in good shape, you feel free and alive, but when you're overly concerned about financial security, you become rather tightfisted and have difficulty sharing your resources. Learning to trust your own ability to generate the material security you need is one of your primary lessons, and in order to accomplish this task, you must begin by stabilizing your sense of self-esteem. Reminding yourself that you deserve to have your needs fulfilled, and that you are attracting abundance enough to share, helps to build your base. With Venus ruling this house, you have the ability to attract the resources you need, and feel better about yourself when you can also give your time, money, and energy to those you love. Learning about money and finances may be of interest to you, and once you have a grasp of the basics, you may actually become an accomplished financial manager.

Gemini on the 2nd: The qualities of Gemini on your 2nd House cusp radiate a need to understand the nature of your own value systems. Your approach to handling your personal resources can be somewhat scattered and variable. Developing some consistency about spending can be extremely helpful, and will also fortify your self-confidence. It's clear that money and material matters take up some of your thinking, and you have some good ideas when it comes to utilizing your resources. Maintaining some objectivity about your finances, and applying flexibility to the manner in which you generate and utilize your time, money, and energy, will be personally empowering. With Mercury's energy influencing your sense of self-worth, your personal esteem can be strengthened when you make the effort to develop your mind.

Cancer on the 2nd: The qualities of Cancer radiate through your 2nd House, indicating that you take a protective approach to handling your finances and personal resources. Your emotional attitude about material things plays an important role in your values, and you may find that you hang on to some things simply out of sentimentality—including your deeply ingrained attitudes about money. If you've been taught that money is the root of all evil, you find it quite difficult to abandon that attitude and allow yourself to feel good about financial success. When you stop to evaluate your own need for material security, you'll find that establishing a solid financial base is an important step toward strengthening your worth on many levels. The energy of your Moon plays a major role in your approach to finances, and you need to recognize the cyclical nature of the economy if you are to deal with it effectively. You may even work well in a profession that is cyclical in its production and demand, or you can be successful in areas that rely on time-honored resources, like real estate, antiques, or the food industry. Since you feel drawn to use your resources, including time, money, and energy, to assist others, it makes sense that you'll be more effective when you know how to attract, develop, and positively maintain your own.

Leo on the 2nd: Leo's qualities radiate through your 2nd House, adding a need to be in control of your own finances, time, and resources. You have an uncanny ability to draw on resources, even when you think you've reached the bottom of the barrel. In essence, when you are feeling strongly about yourself and are willing to put forth the effort to meet your needs, there's very little that can stop you from achieving those aims! Even if you are married and share your resources, you prefer to be in charge of the finances, or at least have control over some of your own money. Someone else telling you what to do with your time, money, or energy engenders a sense of resentment, since having power in this area of your life is a matter of personal pride. Your self-worth is strengthened by maintaining an awareness of your personal needs and allowing yourself to feel good about enjoying their fulfillment. Since your Sun's energy plays a major role in the way you develop your self-esteem, you'll discover that you feel good about yourself when you've gained the recognition you need for your efforts. You can be a little selfish with your finances, and may not like the idea of giving up something you want for someone else. Sometimes this can get in your way, and achieving a balance between giving and receiving is one of your greatest challenges.

Virgo on the 2nd: The qualities of Virgo radiate through your 2nd House, adding discrimination to the manner in which you use your resources. Whether you're expending time, money, or energy, you like to know where it's going and what effect it will have. You are adept at handling money, and are not likely to waste your resources on something of poor quality or questionable value. You're the woman who'll take the time to read about your purchases or to investigate the feasibility of a projected budget. Mercury's energy influences this house, stimulating your need to gain an understanding of the best ways to handle your finances. You are also learning about the power of your mind in attracting the kind of resources you need. Your self-esteem is strengthened by maintaining a keen awareness of the manner in which you use your available resources. Getting the best use out of what you have makes a lot of sense to you.

Libra on the 2nd: The qualities of Libra radiate through your 2nd House, and you frequently feel that you are the woman who has champagne tastes and a beer budget. Learning how to manage your finances is very important. You have excellent taste, and are drawn to the most expensive things in life—you know quality when you see it. Before you give up on your ability to have all those things, take a look in the mirror. Now, there's quality staring right back at you, and by developing your own gifts you can generate amazing resources. The problem is that little lazy side of you that sort of wishes someone else would do it for you. Although you can make excellent use of your partner's resources, your personal esteem is much stronger when you know how to generate your own! With Venus ruling this house, your sense of self-worth is crucial to your financial success, and vice versa. You are tempted to spend money you don't have when you're feeling low, and that only adds to the problem and diminishes your self-worth. Developing financial objectivity is crucial to your sense of personal power.

Scorpio on the 2nd: Scorpio's qualities radiate through your 2nd House, intensifying your need to make the best use of your personal resources. You have a lot invested in establishing financial strength, and are very possessive when it comes to your finances. For this reason, you may not like the idea of anyone else controlling your money, although you might appreciate advice or support that increases the value of your resources. Sometimes it's not easy for you to share, especially when you're feeling vulnerable, and you can even be a little stingy with your time if you don't like the person asking for it! That's perfectly okay, as long as you're clear about your motivations. You may even withhold favors when you've been emotionally wounded, and in the process of protecting your vulnerability can keep yourself from having something you want. If someone insults your personal worth, you completely shut them out, feeling that you don't want to waste your time with anyone who cannot see your value. Just be sure you're clear about this before you torch that bridge! Learning to get the most for your time, money, and investments extends to your desire to learn a bit about economics. With Pluto's energy influencing this house, you are focused on avoiding waste. For this reason, recycling makes a lot of sense to you, and you can stretch your resources much further when you apply this to everything you own—including your time and energy!

Sagittarius on the 2nd: The qualities of Sagittarius radiate through your 2nd House, adding a sense of confidence and optimism to the manner in which you use your resources. You can be very generous, and enjoy having enough resources to share with those you love, but you also feel tempted to overspend, and need to be particularly careful when it comes to accumulating debt, since you don't like the feeling you have when your money is controlling you! Setting limits is crucial, and you'll be much happier when you're operating within a reasonable budget—as long as that budget leaves some room for flexible, spontaneous expenditures. Having to count every penny makes you crazy! Jupiter's energy influencing this house adds good fortune in finances, especially if you take a responsible attitude toward the way you spend money. Your self-worth is strengthened when you know you're using your resources to create opportunities for yourself or others.

Capricorn on the 2nd: The qualities of Capricorn radiate through your 2nd House, adding a sense of responsibility and a need for control in the realm of finances. Although you think of yourself as generous, you can actually be a bit stingy, especially if you're caught up in your fears about money. You may also be reluctant to share your time or other resources unless your expenditure of energy gets you something in return. At a pure level, this can be okay, but it's not easy to stay at that level. You must maintain an awareness of your sense of personal worth, because when your self-esteem is low, you show too much restraint when it comes to expending your resources. With Saturn's energy influencing this house, you'll learn that responsible uses of your personal resources helps you feel more stable and complete. Whenever you take the irresponsible route, your guilt feelings can be extremely tough on your sense of self-worth.

Aquarius on the 2nd: The qualities of Aquarius radiate through your 2nd House, adding a need to use your personal resources to accomplish change in the world around you. You may have difficulty sustaining a steady source of income, but will ultimately learn how to create an approach to using your time, money, and energy in a more efficient manner. This arises from developing an understanding of the real nature of material resources and the power that accompanies a sound financial base. With Uranus ruling this house, you may experience sudden changes in your finances, and the way you respond to those changes will determine how you feel about yourself. Since your self-esteem is tied to your need for freedom, learning to manage your time and money provides the basis you require to manifest your dreams. You cannot afford to be selfish with your energy, and need to work toward achieving a balance between spending and saving what you have.

Pisces on the 2nd: The qualities of Pisces radiate through your 2nd House, indicating that you need to learn the spiritual significance of your material resources. You feel better about yourself when you're sharing what you have, but may not always know when to draw the line between your personal needs and the needs of those around you. This is true on the material plane through your finances and in the realm of your personal energy, which is another resource. Neptune's influence in this house adds a need for caution where finances are concerned since you can miss important details that could be costly in the long run if you're looking only on the surface. You may also have difficulty keeping track of your resources, and need to devise some type of system that helps you maintain a connection between what you have and what you can afford to spend. Giving up control of your finances to someone else may seem to be the easy way out, but if you do so, you still need to know what's happening or you may wake up one day to discover that you have no idea how to deal with this part of your life.

Planets in the 2nd House

Sun in the 2nd: The energy of your Sun in the 2nd House adds emphasis to your need to maintain a conscious awareness of your sense of self-worth. This does not mean that you have to be selfish, but rather that you need to know your values and honor them through the way you utilize your personal resources. You're probably a very resourceful woman, and by generating opportunities for creative self-expression will not only improve your self-esteem, but can attract material rewards. You are empowered when your finances and material worth are strong and stable, and your desire to be financially stable will prompt you to make career choices that offer reasonable financial rewards. To feel truly accomplished, strengthen your self-esteem by opening your heart and taking actions that uphold your most profound values.

Moon in the 2nd: The energy of your Moon in the 2nd House stimulates vacillating financial conditions, and material security has a strong effect on your emotional stability. You need to accept the cyclical nature of your finances, because there will be times when your financial outlook changes very rapidly and other times when the changes are more gradual. You may experience financial rewards in fields that relate to the domestic front, the food industry, or women's needs. Since your attitude toward money is changeable, it's a good idea to operate from a budget for your usual expenses, and to make sure these expenditures are always covered. You are adept in financial matters, and have a good sense of the connection between your money and your self-worth. That still may not stop you from overspending when you're feeling low, so be aware of the link between your emotional neediness and the manner in which you spend your money!

Mercury in the 2nd: Mercury's energy in your 2nd House indicates that the way you think has a dramatic effect on your sense of self-worth. You benefit from learning ways to use your mental energy to change your attitude about money and finances. You also experience financial gain through communications, writing, public relations work, sales, secretarial work, or the computer industry. You, of all women, can turn your ability to talk into gold.

Venus in the 2nd: Through the energy of Venus in your 2nd House you attract resources and material stability quite readily. You are very aware of the relationship between your self-esteem and your finances, and learned early that when you're feeling good about yourself, it's easier to get what you want. Although you're not likely to be extremely greedy with your finances, you can be self-indulgent. You love the best of everything and feel empowered when your life involves at least a few of the pleasures you enjoy. Occupations involving the arts or that cater to things women love—fashion, jewelry, cosmetics, hair dressing—can bring rewards.

Mars in the 2nd: Mars energy in your 2nd House is a driving force when it comes to your finances. You'll discover that you don't mind working when it pays off. But you also spend your resources very quickly and need to learn to curb impulsive spending if you are to enjoy real financial success. Credit cards can be a bad idea unless you know how to use them. Otherwise, you can have your resources so scattered and spread so thin that you simply can't keep up. You may find that the recreation or fitness industry offers excellent opportunities for you to make money, but you will enjoy almost any area that allows you to be somewhat active. If you learn to use your resources wisely, your self-worth will remain intact. Otherwise, you actually wound yourself by wasting your time, energy, and material resources.

Jupiter in the 2nd: With Jupiter in your 2nd House, you have a great deal of confidence in your ability to attract and use your money, time, and energy. Your optimism is contagious, and when you've found something that makes you feel good, you want to share what you've learned with others. For this reason, you're a natural in sales, teaching, advertising, or investing. Since you like to travel, you may use your resources toward traveling or find that work involving travel is rewarding. The downfall of this placement is your tendency toward extravagance, since setting limits is difficult.

Saturn in the 2nd: With Saturn's energy in your 2nd House, you worry about whether or not you have enough time, money, or energy to have everything you need. Although this energy can be helpful in dealing with the necessities of life, you must watch a tendency to block your own prosperity through excessive self-limitation. Self-discipline when it comes to spending helps you feel more stable. You'll see the best results when you develop a budget or plan for your finances, especially if that plan allows you to feel comfortable now while creating a nest egg for your future.

Uranus in the 2nd: The influence of Uranus in your 2nd House brings unexpected changes in your finances. This can be on either side of the spectrum, and financial windfalls are just as probable as financial losses. You prefer work that links your efforts with your rewards more directly, so something like sales, running your own business, or a profit-sharing situation will be much more to your liking than a fixed income. It's not a good idea for you to waste your resources on speculation unless you can afford the risk, although you are rather inventive when it comes to making money. Your self-worth is strongest when you are utilizing your special talents, and it is through these abilities that you generate the greatest rewards.

Neptune in the 2nd: Since Neptune's energy operates best on the spiritual plane, it does not always have the best effect when residing in a material house like the 2nd House. Your financial judgment may not be very good because you don't pay much attention to the details involved. Keeping track of your finances is simply not a high priority, but it is a necessary one. If you're in the dark concerning your finances, your self-esteem ultimately suffers because you're only fooling yourself by running away from your need to stay connected to where your resources are being used. You become more financially stabilized when you learn to trust the right people to help you manage your money, time, and resources. You'll make connections to those individuals more easily when you make the effort to see others realistically. You experience your greatest rewards when doing things for others and when you're allowing your compassion to flow freely and completely through your creativity. Music, the arts, and nonprofit agencies are good career options.

Pluto in the 2nd: Pluto's energy in your 2nd House brings control issues to the realm of personal finances. It is here that you experience great challenges, and you have some extreme experiences learning about the real nature of money and materiality. You attract resources through working in fields that involve transformation, healing, and renovation, and revitalize your own worth by allowing your needs to be in charge of your own money. You can share, but may not want to share everything. That's okay, as long as you're honest about it!

Shared Resources, Sex, and Attachments: The 8th House

Resources you share with others are reflected in the 8th House. Whether you're considering joint property and finances, inheritance, debts, insurance settlements, or tax obligations—this area is not as free and easy as the 2nd House, which is more about what you want for yourself alone. Another layer of this part of your life deals with your sexuality, and the manner in which you open intimately to others. The link between sexual sharing, emotional content, and finances becomes apparent in intimate partnerships: sexual blackmail occurs all the time in unhealthy relationships. I frequently advise couples who seek my counsel to explore their deeper feelings about trust and emotional safety when there are money problems, and also encourage couples to look at the connection between their finances and their sex life! These are 8th House issues.

This is a very personal space, and it is probably one of the most guarded aspects of any woman's psyche. It is here that much wounding has taken place over many centuries, and it is here that the mask of propriety has to be removed in order to openly accept and integrate the fact that you are a person who needs wholeness and healing, and who yearns to bond at the most alchemical level with life itself.

Here you also find your compulsions. It's no wonder that you don't display this part of yourself to just anybody. You have to feel safe to open this facet of yourself, and you realize that this vulnerability can be used against you in power plays. What you may not always remember is that this is also where you have the power! In true tantric traditions, it is through the vessel of a woman's sexual energy that a couple can ride the wave of sexual ecstasy. This also extends to other power aspects of any relationship. If your transformational and magical qualities are blocked, the whole of the relationship will suffer.

The Sign on 8th House: What You Want (The Hidden Agenda Version)

Aries on the 8th: Aries' impulsiveness drives your approach to sexuality, and you are fascinated by the raw power of sexual energy. When you're attracted to someone, you don't mind being the assertive partner, although sometimes you jump into situations you're not really ready for emotionally. Learning to distinguish the difference between your desires and needs can be problematic, especially in your youth. Although you may be experimental in your approach to exploring your sexuality, if you're not emotionally ready for the bond created by sexual sharing, you may discover that you feel trapped. Power struggles arise in your sexual life, but are more likely to be experienced in the realm of joint finances. Responsible use of joint resources is different from impulsive spending that creates debt, and if you and your partner have different attitudes about money, you may discover that these attitudes are the source of your greatest conflicts. If you're not in sync in your needs for intimacy, the money issue may flare up when you're really angry about the intimacy aspect of the relationship. It may be up to you to take the first step in resolving this problem, and although just cutting away from the relationship may seem like the easiest way out, if you've failed to address your deeper needs and issues about intimacy, you'll repeat the same impulsive patterns with the next man.

Taurus on the 8th: Your approach to the bond of power created in your sexual relationships is intense with Taurus influencing your 8th House. You need to feel deep love for a man before you are comfortable with the vulnerability that accompanies sexual sharing. When you express this aspect of yourself, your sensuality guides you into the realm of desire and fulfillment, and you'll be much more satisfied with a relationship that delights all your senses. You can become very attached to your partner, and your possessiveness can lead to jealousy if you feel threatened. For that reason, it is important that you understand the real feelings you have for each other, and it's equally important to realize that the changes you experience over time may alter those feelings in some way. You may not like that fact, since you don't like the idea of letting go of your attachments, but unless you can allow room for the creative qualities of love to change you, you'll never experience the real alchemy of bonding with your partner.

Although you may take an apparently passive approach in dealing with joint finances, you probably have your eye on what's going on, and if you discover problems, deception, or difficulties here, you will lose trust in your partner. Money issues within your relationship can be handled amicably as long as there is trust and you feel that you have a say in what's going on. If a relationship ends, you'll discover that your attachment to the things you've accumulated is a major issue. If you attempt to maintain harmony with your ex by giving him everything, you'll only resent yourself. But if you don't know where to draw the line, you'll hurt yourself. Maybe you should consider a pre-nuptial agreement before you marry, even if you don't have many resources. It might solve a number of potential problems later on.

Gemini on the 8th: Gemini's influence in your 8th House adds an exceptional curiosity concerning sexuality. You need variety in your sex life, and although that can be accomplished with one partner, you'll probably experiment a bit (even if only in your mind) to compare the differences and similarities. Learning what brings you pleasure is part of your sexuality, but learning how to communicate sexually is at the core of your need for intimacy. Once you're involved in a close relationship, you'll share special signals with your partner that only he understands. These signals are part of your bond. You may also find that you develop a powerful psychic and intuitive link with your partner that allows you to communicate in a very unique manner. In joint financial areas, you can benefit when you understand as much as possible about the finances in a marriage or partnership, and your need to know may ultimately result in very valuable insights on your part. All contracts need very specific definition concerning roles and responsibilities. If a relationship ends, you'll feel better if you specify a well-defined property settlement, even though you may vacillate about what you want or need.

Cancer on the 8th: Cancer's influence in your 8th House adds a need for emotional bonding with your sexual partner. Once you open up to a partner sexually, you find that you share your deepest feelings and desires more readily. It is important that you understand the multiple levels of sexual relationship and realize the type of bond that is created when you share yourself on this level. Once you experience the path of energy that is created when you open a doorway to another soul, you feel both vulnerable and ecstatic. Even when you're not together, you discover that you have emotional responses to what's happening with your mate. When all is well, the energy continues to flow, but if there are problems, you'll sense something like a dam in the flow of energy. If your relationship ends, you may still feel this connection. For this reason, it's crucial that you release your emotional attachment when a relationship ends or you may find that you are drained from the loss of energy that occurs when your ex turns his energy toward someone else! In matters of joint finances, you experience positive rewards from establishing strong financial security, and need a partner who can plan for the future, in addition to handling the present financial requirements of your relationship. If you end a partnership, the most difficult thing will be transforming or eliminating the home you've built together.

Leo on the 8th: The influence of Leo on your 8th House adds strong creative needs to your sexuality. Your experience of sexual sharing can be one of the keys to opening to a full experience of loving, although you may be more concentrated on your own satisfaction than that of your partner. Now, that's not to say that you don't enjoy providing satisfaction to your partner, but you may find it difficult unless you're satisfied, too. On a deeper level, you need an intimate relationship that will strengthen you spiritually and emotionally, and will not feel that you can open up completely unless you have the respect of your partner. From this point, you share yourself fully and completely. Your loyalty to the relationship can be very strong, and you expect that same deep commitment from your mate. In matters of the resources you share and create together, you want to have an influence in these matters. Even if you're not managing the finances of your relationship, you need to know what's going on. Your controlling nature emerges when you feel that you're not appreciated, but it's equally important that you show your appreciation for and to your partner.

Virgo on the 8th: Your approach to sexual intimacy can be rather methodical with Virgo influencing your 8th House. But you do have your sensual side, and enjoy the experience of sharing with another on this intimate level. You are a very good technician sexually, and enjoy learning all sorts of things about sexuality; but you can't really experience the depths of intimacy from this mental level alone. You're probably pretty picky about your sexual partners, and may not feel particularly comfortable allowing true intimacy. Intimacy that involves sharing on multiple levels can be a real test for you, and the key to getting there may be openly talking about your needs with your partner. In matters of joint finances, the resources you create together are well-defined, and you may make some effort to spend your money with knowledge and insight. You'll be happiest when you reach a real consensus with your partner over joint expenditures since you don't really like to compromise, especially where quality is concerned. Finding a partner you can trust in financial matters may be a gift from the heavens for you since you may not always be confident in your own financial awareness.

Libra on the 8th: For you to experience the depths of intimacy, you need to feel that you have balance in your relationship. Libra's influence over your 8th House brings a need for harmony to your sexual relationships and stimulates your desire for an experience of sharing and equality in this regard. The alchemy you experience when you bond with your sexual partner creates an inner harmony and becomes the basis for your harmonious interaction on other levels. You're most comfortable when your values are compatible with your partner, and you need a relationship with a man you can truly appreciate. Finances work best when they're shared, and even if you each have control over certain monies individually, your joint finances will always be best managed when you work them out together. If you end an intimate relationship, you may try to maintain the good feelings you have for one another, although this can be a lot to ask, especially if fair treatment means that you get the short end of the stick. So before you agree to anything, be sure you're being fair to yourself, too!

Scorpio on the 8th: Scorpio's influence in your 8th House adds a need for intensity to your sexually intimate relationships. The more intense, the better. Although you like spontaneity, you relish those private moments when all barriers drop away and you expose your soul to your partner. Even though this may be your approach, you may not always find a partner whose experience is the same as your own. So, it's a good idea to establish a sense of trust before you jump into the deep end of the pool of intimacy. You're seeking a partner whose needs and desires act as the catalyst for true alchemy when matched with your own intensity. In matters of finance, you may not be as trusting, and you tend to attract partners who are just as protective of their own resources. Joint finances require full disclosure if they are to operate smoothly, but that does not mean you have to give up all control. In fact, you will not feel good about giving away your power in this area. Before you make a marriage commitment, it is important that you talk about your ideas concerning money, and that you understand the financial situation of your partner, and vice versa. If you fail to address these matters, they can become problematic issues later on.

Sagittarius on the 8th: Sagittarian qualities drive your approach to the 8th House side of yourself. You expect truth and honesty from yourself and will never be comfortable if you shy away from the exploration of your power base. Joint resources are a source of support and reward, but they need to be handled with honesty if you are to gain the most from them. Your need for an adventurous sexual relationship are strong, and you'll be most open in a relationship that allows a wide range of exploration. You might enjoy exploring sexuality through Tantra, which allows you to experience a broader range of connections to your partner. Deception in a relationship will never work for you, and you'll feel most open to the alchemy that creates a bond with your partner when you share compatible ideals and beliefs. Be aware of a tendency to jump into intimacy too quickly in your relationships. If you discover you're not really compatible on multiple levels, you will not be able to maintain your emotional bond.

Capricorn on the 8th: Your approach to sexual intimacy is quite cautious due to the influence of Capricorn on your 8th House. Although you enjoy the games of love, when it comes to intimacy, you're not entirely footloose and fancy free. Before you achieve real intimacy, you need to establish trust and mutual respect. Otherwise you may never fully open your heart and soul to the relationship. You can be quite sensual, and will find it easier to experience the levels of sexuality that transport you into ecstasy when you indulge your sensual side. Once you've made an emotional commitment in a relationship, you may not relinquish it easily, so it's very important that you make choices for reasons that fit your deepest needs. You need to be careful of your tendency to be attracted to someone for the things or financial security he can provide, since if this is your basis for getting together, you may ultimately feel trapped by the relationship.

Aquarius on the 8th: You enjoy an unusual approach to achieving real intimacy. The influence of Aquarius on your 8th House stimulates a desire to experience unconditional acceptance through exploring the intimate side of your relationship, which includes your sexuality. Allowing room for experimentation, creating an opportunity for honest and open communication, and acknowledging and supporting your mutual emotional and physical needs strengthens the bond you have with your partner. You can be aloof in this area, particularly if you are afraid of the effects of allowing another person to become this close. Just going through the motions will never give you what you need—which is to be transported into another realm through the alchemy of love. The resources you create with a partner may grow best when you have a vision of what you want to create together. This shared vision can deepen your bond, and if you're involved in doing things for others, you may discover that you somehow grow closer to one another.

Pisces on the 8th: The influence of Pisces on your 8th House adds a need for drama and romance as key ingredients in your intimate relationships. You think this is the way everyone approaches intimacy, but it's not true! To unlock your deeper yearnings, you might enjoy role playing or sharing your fantasies. You may also be very drawn to a partner who shares similar spiritual aspirations. It's important to learn the difference between spiritual bonding and fanciful romance, and it may take some time before you've clarified them. Within the union you desire, both partners surrender to the experience of love and allow the flow of love itself to change them. You may be attracted to men who are wounded in some way, and may feel that loving can heal them. This may be true, but if you sacrifice yourself in the process, you'll be left with feelings of disappointment. The same is true in matters of joint finances because you can go too far trusting your partner financially. Even if he manages the money, you need to sit down on a regular basis to discuss where you are so you are not shocked into disbelief if problems arise. But you need to avoid making your partner the scapegoat for your financial problems.

Planets in the 8th House: Deep Motivators

Sun in the 8th: With the Sun in your 8th House, you need to experience power as a positive transformational experience. If you have experienced the loss or death of someone dear to you, especially a father or male partner, or if you've suffered abusive relationships, you may feel that you have been diminished in some manner. This is particularly true if you've placed your identity too firmly in your relationship. Unless you grow to understand the real nature of the spiritual and emotional connections in your life, you may be stuck in these old wounds and in your pain of loss. Until, that is, you decide that you want to be whole again. Your lifetime is oriented toward experiencing a complete rebirth, and you may choose careers in the healing arts, psychology, metaphysics, the sciences, or related fields as a means to explore these deeper questions. What you need to know is the way to regain your sense of self on another level once you've left it behind. This is the experience of the medicine woman, the wounded healer, the awakened shaman. It is your path to power.

Moon in the 8th: Your Moon's energy in the 8th House signifies the experience of soul-level transformation as part of the process of establishing a real awareness of your power as a woman. This may arise through childbirth, the loss of a dear friend, illness or death of your mother, severe illness of your own, or working in a field that encourages and supports transformation and healing. You need to confront the nature of total regeneration on an emotional and spiritual level in order to feel powerful, whole, and complete. These are not easy tasks, and may result in deep wounds, feelings of inadequacy, or fears of loss or abandonment. Although any of these may be justified, staying stuck in the wound is not your ultimate goal. Learning to extract yourself and to experience rebirth allows your soul to evolve, and that's why you're here.

Mercury in the 8th: Mercury's energy in your 8th House draws your attention to the power of the mind. Learning to focus your mental energy in the areas of life's mysteries satisfies a certain level of curiosity, but you also feel the need to share a deep level of communication with your mate. Although your intimate relationship provides a level of understanding with the man you love, it also provides a key to understanding your own inner nature. The things you articulate with your partner may very well be the secrets of your soul you've been hiding from yourself—so listen carefully! Even though you may be drawn into relationships that involve a transformation of consciousness, you need to be very careful about allowing your partner to shape your ideas or you will lose your ability to clarify things for yourself. You can also be just as guilty in trying to force your ideas, especially during power struggles. Your mind can be healer or slayer on many levels, including intimacy.

Venus in the 8th: With the energy of Venus in your 8th House, you experience an emotional intensity that rivals the power of the seas. It's easy to become overly attached to your partner, and you may also find that it is difficult to let go of old love wounds. If you've been hurt, it can be difficult for you to open your heart again. You may feel that your partner is more worthy than you, but deep within yourself, you know that is not true. It's just an excuse you use to keep yourself from experiencing the love you really desire. Your fear of losing ultimate love can actually work against your ability to attain it. If you've compromised for something that seems "safe," a partner you could afford to lose, then you may never know the fullness of love. This approach cannot only undermine your power, but can result in your abandonment of your quest for ultimate love. Once you agree to allow yourself to approach intimacy and loving by risking your heart, you finally experience what you so desperately seek. Even if it does not last forever, you will have known it, and the love itself can heal you. You need to experience transformation through love, and that is the key to your real sense of personal prosperity!

Mars in the 8th: With Mars in your 8th House, you feel driven to explore your sexuality as fully as possible. This can be positively regenerating if your relationships are healthy; but you can also run into major power struggles if you've not established your own sense of strength. Sometimes it's difficult for you to draw the line between pain and pleasure, and although you push your limits, you sometimes exhaust your own energy if you go too far. You may also experience cruelty, abuse, or emotional pain through your intimate relationships, particularly if you jump into situations before you've explored their true nature. Although this energy can ultimately bring healing into your life, you need to clarify for yourself why you attract abuse in the first place if you are to avoid falling into the same traps in the future.

Jupiter in the 8th: Jupiter's energy in your 8th House stimulates a strong sexual appetite. In your quest for the ultimate orgasm, you jump into sexual relationships that become emotionally entrenching before you're ready. This can create a bit of internal conflict, particularly since you like to feel free in your relationships. If you've thought to yourself that you're more spiritual than this, you may be ignoring a very important part of your psyche. You can be spiritual and sexual at the same time; it's all a matter of your focus! You can also discover the price of sexual irresponsibility if you do get into intimacy too quickly. On the financial side of things,

Jupiter's energy here can attract inheritance, and if you are to use these resources to their ultimate benefit, you need to eliminate any guilt you have about them.

Saturn in the 8th: With Saturn in your 8th House, you need to carefully explore your attitude toward your own sexuality. Your fears can be extremely inhibiting, and if you are too judgmental about your own sexual needs, you may ultimately become so entrenched in guilt that you cannot enjoy a truly intimate relationship. You may not want to give up your power to your partner, sexually or financially, but your desire for financial power may prompt you to commit to a relationship that seems secure. There is a difference between security and stagnation, and if you are to experience the real power that arises from a trusting, committed relationship, it must be focused on growth in order to move toward the positive end of the spectrum. There can be a lot of control issues in your intimate relationships, and you may be the one who creates them through your own fears. If you are to experience a free flow of energy that leads to true power, you must learn to let go of your attachments and rebuild your security base on principles that provide stability without guilt and resentment.

Uranus in the 8th: You may need to gain a deeper insight into your sexuality and emotional attachments with Uranus in your 8th House. You can be rather impulsive in your sexual attraction, and can become addicted to the part of your sexual relationships that is exciting and all-consuming. You know the feeling: it's when you've lost your mind and tingle all over when you think about that man. This chemistry is enticing, but it is only one key to opening a much more satisfying door. The problem you run into is remaining focused throughout the different stages of a relationship and allowing yourself to rekindle this passion. You need intimate relationships that allow a lot of room for experimentation and ample opportunities to keep your options open. This can be difficult if you're looking for a traditional marriage, so drop the traditional part and create your own approach to experiencing an abiding love. You will never enjoy a relationship that takes away your independence, and if you are in a situation that is stultifying, your first response will be to rebel against it. This is the way you regain your power. Maybe the best step is to avoid giving it up in the first place!

Neptune in the 8th: You really do not have to sacrifice yourself in order to have the intimacy you desire, but with Neptune's energy in your 8th House, you may be tempted to give up your own desires to those of your partner. You're better off playing fantasy games, role playing, and using your sexual dramas to keep your interest in one another strong and passionate. Although the fairy tales may lead you to believe that Prince Charming will come along, wake you from your long sleep, and carry you off to his castle, that is rarely the case! Your dream of an all-consuming love can work against you since allowing your needs to be consumed by anyone can be dangerous, but allowing your selfish desires to drown in the sea of passion from time to time can be another story. You also need to be very careful in dealings with joint finances because your tendency is to trust without qualification, and that can suck up your power right away. You may be very psychic about your partner and his abilities, but you still need to know what's happening with your resources!

Pluto in the 8th: Pluto's energy in your 8th House does not necessarily attract excessive power struggles with your partner, but you certainly will be alert to that possibility! You have a very keen sense concerning your own sexuality, and exploring the depths of your sexual needs allows your power to emerge more fully. In financial matters, whether or not there are problems depends largely on your ability to be honest with yourself and your partner about what you need and expect in this area. You can be an excellent money manager, and with a partner whose vision and values support your own, you can create a strong power base. If you feel threatened by your partner or the way he uses his resources, you're probably better off completely extracting your resources from his until you are clear about your mutual goals.

Your Drive to Make it Happen: Mars

Mars energy is about getting what you want by going after it. Mars is drive. Mars is courage. Mars is desire. Mars is unabashed sexuality. Mars is the fuel for personal power. Men do Mars quite effectively, right down to fighting and war, but you also have a warrior spirit, an Amazon Self. This is your Mars. If you fail to own and utilize your own Martian force, you lose power. This is your passion, and identifying and utilizing it will confer a positive mantel of power to your personality.

Mars Signs: Passion Defined

Mars in Aries: With Mars in Aries, your passions run hot. Your power emerges from your sense of courage and enthusiasm, and when you're really turned on to something or someone, you are quite assertive. You lose power if you jump into anything too quickly, and undermine your influence when you are too aggressive.

Learning how to handle anger is important, too, since you may be a bit short-tempered, but once you've expressed your anger, you usually go right on. You enjoy taking the lead in sexual exchange, and become frustrated if you run into rejection or denial. Sharing sex with a partner who enjoys the playful elements of sexuality allows you to experience the more profound levels of energy. You're most attracted to men who are independent and strong-willed, but are capable of standing up to them when you need to. Staying physically active helps you maintain your power on many levels, and if you've fallen into a sedentary life, you will find that regaining your physical vitality by increasing your activity level empowers you.

Mars in Taurus: With Mars in Taurus, you may not feel comfortable in hot pursuit. You prefer to draw your lover into your nest where you can then take charge. You do like sex; in fact, you are extremely sensual and can be a very patient lover with a strong sexual appetite. You can also be extremely possessive, which can be your downfall. If you are feeling insecure, feelings of jealousy and possessiveness emerge and undermine your sense of personal worth, and if there is trouble in a relationship, you can also become resentful, an emotion that drains your vitality. Once you've established a sense of personal security, these negative manifestations are diminished, and you feel that you can build a more stable power base. But this requires trust in yourself and a desire to share your energy, time, and resources.

Mars in Gemini: With Mars in Gemini, you are empowered when you learn to focus your energy. It's all too easy for you to scatter your life force, and when this happens, you run out of steam. Your sharp and alert mentality and wit are the juices that keep you going, and may be the qualities you use to entice the men you find attractive, but you may also attract men who just do not want to grow up. You know them—the "Peter Pan" types. If you take the time to look inside, you may find that you are the one who would prefer to remain as free as you felt when you were a young girl, and relationships that allow your little girl self to play will always be more interesting than those that require you to feel grown up. In sexual relationships, you devote a great deal of energy to communicating what you do and do not enjoy, and can use sex as a means of communication in and of itself! (You know the story: "What do you mean you don't know how I feel? Weren't you in this bed last night?!") When you're angry, you lash out with words, and can use very wounding words indeed if you've been hurt. To maintain your personal power, you need to learn to say "no" more easily since some commitments simply serve as draining distractions. On a physical level, nourish your nervous system. When your nerves are frazzled, you feel out of control and unmotivated.

Mars in Cancer: Your sensitivity can undermine your power with Mars in Cancer. When you're fearful or uncertain, you may not feel confident about taking assertive action and can miss opportunities to get what you want from life. This leads to feelings of insecurity that weaken your sense of personal power. Your desires run deep, but your ability to stand up for yourself is not very strong. You love a steamy sexual relationship, but may not feel comfortable requesting what you want from your partner. Sometimes you just have to take the risk and show him what to do, and then all sorts of amazing things can happen! You'll enjoy a relationship with a sensitive man, but may not like overly sensitive men who need to be mothered all the time—mothering is okay in some instances, but there are places you'd like to drop it. You can strengthen your power and vitality by working on your solar plexus. Yoga breathing exercises may help, or you might benefit from practicing tai chi.

Mars in Leo: You possess strong reserves of energy with Mars in Leo, and can definitely assert domination and control when necessary. You adore positions of power and can be quite effective when operating as a leader or director of others, but if you feel threatened, you can quickly undermine your own power through feelings of jealousy or excessive pride. In either case, you may not back down once you've drawn battle lines, simply because your pride won't let you. You attract men with the same attitudes, and if you are in a heated disagreement, can carry it to very destructive ends unless you know when to let go. Sexually, you are dramatic and demonstrative, and enjoy sexual sharing that is playful and passionate. You need a man who knows his own power, and will be most open when you know you have mutual respect and admiration for one another.

Mars in Virgo: With Mars in Virgo, you direct your personal power toward work. You feel good at the end of the day when you've produced something, and are empowered when your accomplishments are appreciated for their attention to detail and fine quality. You undermine your effectiveness when you fuss over nonessential details, and lose energy when you become caught in your own insecurities, which arise from your feelings of imperfection. So what if your hips are not perfect! Who defines those things, anyway? You are most attracted to men who are healthy, well groomed, and kind-natured, and will probably not give a boorish lout the time of day. In the bedroom, you enjoy sensual sharing to the ultimate, and may be quite knowledgeable about sexuality—to the surprise of anyone who thinks you are a bit prudish. Well, they've not been alone with you in an intimate setting! But sometimes you can think too much about what you're doing and forget to let go and enjoy the passion of the moment. And watch those feelings of regret that occur after the fact when you're wondering if you were okay. Yes, you were. And you are.

Mars in Libra: Although you have definite ideas about what is and is not proper in relationships between men and women, you throw caution to the wind when you're strongly attracted to a man. With Mars in Libra, you spend a lot of time thinking about the right partner, and if you think you've found him, you may not have a lot of patience when he hems and haws trying to decide whether or not to ask you out. Go ahead. Take the lead. At least you'll know, and you can do things that still give him a chance to salvage his pride. You probably know all the techniques from long years of practice. Your power is strengthened through your charm and grace, but is undermined when you're lazy or too dependent. Just because you think having the right man will make life easier, don't count on it. Your relationships are your proving ground, where you learn that you must stand up for yourself and ask for what you need. They also provide your opportunity to become considerate of the needs of your partner. In the bedroom, you love all that romantic stuff—the pretty design, soft pillows, sweet fragrance, the right lighting, wonderful music—and when you've got the ambiance just right, you let your passions loose. Sexual sharing that allows for a real exchange of energy, exemplified by tantric teachings, may be just what you need. That old approach of two minutes and you're done just does not satisfy your need to feel the bond you want with your partner. It may not be him who's resisting.

Mars in Scorpio: With Mars in Scorpio, you can be relentless about pursuing what you want. You are also quite sexual and need high levels of intensity to feel fully satisfied sexually. That means you can't just approach a sexual encounter passively, waiting for sex to be over, and then sigh a little sigh. You are driven to participate, fully and completely, to reach the plateaus you are capable of achieving. The real alchemy that arises when you've allowed your sexual energy to be released full force is like a magical elixir for you. Exploring your sexual needs and understanding their importance in your life is primary to experiencing the wholeness you need as a woman. When you are not sexually active, you can consciously direct this same force into your creative efforts. You are adept at developing the connection to your own kundalini force, which you can use in any capacity in your life. You also possess an everlasting charisma that adds to your personal power. Although you may not be especially temperamental in an open way, when you do become angry, you can be destructive and forceful. Your tendency to repress feelings of anger can be harmful. It might be a good idea to do some anger therapy if you feel that your Mars energy is blocked or repressed. Your power also grows when you surrender your energy to true healing. You can heal with a look, your words, your touch, and your thoughts. Harnessing this energy by directing it through your Higher Self will entirely transform your life.

Mars in Sagittarius: Your confidence and enthusiasm are your power sources with Mars in Sagittarius. When you have your aim set on something, your self-assurance helps you achieve it. Staying physically active helps you maintain your power, and you'll appreciate a man whose love of adventure and travel are equal to your own. You lose power when you feel too hemmed in, whether by the expectations of others or by situations that limit your options. You can undermine your own strength by running away before you've had a chance to explore the fullest possibilities of your current situation! You are quite sensual, and enjoy a sexual relationship that leaves ample room for playful exploration of the many frontiers you and your partner possess. Your downfall in sexual relationships arises when you jump in before you've had a chance to think about what you're doing. Learning to consider the effects of your actions will be highly empowering!

Mars in Capricorn: An earthy sensuality radiates through your Mars in Capricorn. Even though you think you have yourself under control, you have an amazing sensual appetite. That's okay, because when you indulge those needs within a safe and trusting relationship, you actually feel better about yourself. It's when you try to repress your needs that you get into trouble. Playful sexual activity may not be easy for you, especially if you're worried about whether or not you're doing everything in the proper way. Well, that's a matter of what you need at the moment, not some test of your abilities. You may actually find that sexual play involving some type of restraints is quite appealing for you, whether you're the restrainer or restrainee! You strengthen your sense of power in the world by working hard to achieve your goals, and you are strongly self-reliant. You'll probably resist outside restraints, and will always perform better when you can do things your way. Establishing the difference between self-control and excessive controlling behavior and attitudes are among your primary lessons in life.

Mars in Aquarius: With Mars in Aquarius, you feel most powerful when you're free and unfettered. You may interpret that to mean that you really do not need anyone else, but you know that you enjoy the support and company of others. What you do not need is their negative criticism or doubts of your abilities. You attract unusual men; you also have an affinity for men who are better friends than lovers. Your own independence can be stultifying to a man who wants to control you, and your open assertiveness will catch a few guys off guard. Well, you probably like that . . . . Sexually, you are experimental and want to try many of the theories you've been testing in your mind, but before you can have the sexual relationship you want, you first have to develop trust, understanding, and communication with your partner.

Mars in Pisces: Your personal power arises first within your artistic sensibilities with Mars in Pisces. When your energy is flowing through your creativity, you are whole and complete. This spiritual force can also be experienced by adopting a more introspective approach to life and surrendering to your higher needs to support and guide you. Your power is directly linked to that of the Source, from whose heart you feel true compassion. Sexually, you love romance, role-playing, and lovemaking that involves the stuff dreams are made of. The right setting is important, and you can really open to your lover when you feel secluded from intrusions from the outside world. You may dream of the perfect lover, but attract needy men or men whose dreams are totally unrealistic. If that's the case, take a look at your own need to rescue—if you are sending out those rescue beams, you'll get plenty of willing, wounded men in need of repair. You may be the one sending out the wounded victim vibes, so be careful. If you seem to be too needy, you'll find men who want to control and direct your life. That is definitely not power. This vacillation between addiction and co-dependency can be your pattern until you turn inside and discover the real power that resides deep within yourself. You have unlimited power to create life on your own terms, but it must be focused in order to manifest.

Discipline and Focus: Saturn and Power

Saturn plays the role of the big controller in your life. Sometimes that control seems to come from outside. You know—all the rules and regulations, the authority figures, the intimidating people who tell you what to do—this is the Saturn of the outside world. You have the same traffic cop in the back of your own mind telling you what is right and wrong, chiding you when you make a mistake, holding you back when you're about to do something stupid. Saturn control can be a good thing. This is your energy for self-discipline, clarity, and focus. You need Saturn, but you need Saturn in its most productive sense. You do not need the guilt, intimidation, and self-limitation that keep you from having what you require from life.

Saturn in the Signs: Your Method of Control

Saturn in Aries: Your power is confirmed when you have joined your needs for freedom with personal responsibility for your actions. With Saturn in Aries, you resist taking control of your own life, even though that's what you want most of all. Your resistance stems from a fear of growing up. After all, life is much easier when somebody else takes the fall for you, and that may be why you're subconsciously looking for a man to take on a father role. You may just be afraid of stepping out into the world on your own, even though there are no real reasons for your fear. When you are not taking responsibility for yourself, you run headlong into situations that inhibit your freedom and squelch your power. Learning to be more conscious of your own life force and allowing that energy to spontaneously flow through you brings exceptional power. Self-centered immaturity and a lack of trust quickly diminish the stability and power you need.

Saturn in Taurus: Your endurance levels are amazing with Saturn in Taurus, and it is endurance that is the source of your personal power. You lose power when you feel insecure and when you allow jealousy, resentment, or possessiveness to overtake you. Although you may think that holding onto the people and things you love will add to your power, sometimes you simply have to let go and allow change to work its own magic in your life. When you look at your inner drives, you may discover that you are driven by a fear of loss or abandonment. Even if this has not been confirmed by life experiences, it can play a huge role in your approach to your relationships and career endeavors, and it affects your self-esteem. Learning to concentrate on fostering growth and dealing with your emotional attachments by allowing some change to infiltrate your life will be very empowering in the long run.

Saturn in Gemini: Through Saturn in Gemini you experience power when you're learning and sharing what you know. Whether you're in the role of student or teacher, the growth you feel when you're enhancing your understanding provides strength, stability, and confidence. Your power is diminished when you become distracted from your focus; staying on task is not always easy. After all, there are so many options out there! Your personal power can be wasted on worry and negative thinking. Once you accomplish the task of positive thinking, you have the power to create a life filled with opportunity and abundance.

Saturn in Cancer: When you are safe and secure at home, you feel powerful. When your parents show their approval, you are especially confirmed. This is okay; there's nothing to be guilty about, but why is it that if you veer away from the path set by those who have gone before that you get nervous? As long as you use your sense of self-control to maintain the stability and serenity you need in your own life, you're in a pretty good space, but try to avoid falling into the same ruts over and over again, and remember that you cannot take care of everybody else by telling them what to do or keeping them protected from the world forever. Sometimes those little birdies just have to fly on their own. So do you!

Saturn in Leo: You may believe that power equals control. Although sometimes being in control confers power, at others it just means you've gotten into a lot of trouble by taking on responsibilities that do not belong to you. Your pride can drain your vitality, and sometimes just admitting that you do not know something can be a great release. Your greatest obstacle to establishing personal power is a true sense of self-love. This is very different from selfishness or self-absorption, which arise when you feel insecure or uncertain. Learning to love begins with the way you feel about yourself, and your own worthiness for love may be accomplished by simply telling yourself that you deserve love. Showing loving kindness to others is also part of the equation, and once this energy is flowing in your life, you will know how to use, maintain, and grow your power in the most positive sense.

Saturn in Virgo: It's hard to say whether you actually like hard work or if you just attract it with Saturn in Virgo. Applying your energy and efforts toward the task of accomplishing something enhances your sense of power. You may not know how to ask for the support of others, and may feel that you are somehow inadequate, imperfect, or undeserving. It is these feelings that block your empowerment. When you do gain recognition, the manner in which you handle it will tell you if you're over that hump or not. If you can say, "Thank you, " and know inside that you deserve it, you've arrived! Learning to positively critique others and create a method of offering support and guidance that empowers others is the other part of your equation for power.

Saturn in Libra: You are most empowered by your ability to maintain balance and objectivity in your life. With Saturn in Libra, you have an excellent sense of justice and a need to learn about the true nature of cooperation and mutual support. Your greatest lessons concerning personal power arise within your personal relationships, which illustrate just how far you've come in your tasks of cooperation, understanding, and acceptance. If you are extremely judgmental and apply rules to others that you do not apply to yourself, you'll discover that you lose self-respect and consequently lose power. Your power is also undermined when you give greater acceptance and respect to others than you give to yourself.

Saturn in Scorpio: You are learning about the power of ultimate life experiences through Saturn in Scorpio. Although you can be very controlling, you may also attract people who test your self-control and whose emotional impact in your life tests the line between love and hate. You can be an extremist, and if you allow your energy to swing too far in one direction, the output of energy required to bring everything back into balance can drain your power. You need to experience what it's like to exercise power over your own life, and may fight bitterly with anyone who tries to get in the way of decisions that involve your personal sanctity—decisions over such things as reproduction, medical care, choices about death. Before you can deal with these things effectively, you have to know how you feel and what drives you in these matters. Just giving in to your fears, guilt, or shame in these areas will quickly drain your vital force and leave you open to the control of others. You are faced with learning the difference between destructive uses of power and healing transformation.

Saturn in Sagittarius: Your sense of personal power is strong when your life is a reflection of your deeply held beliefs and ideals. You have to walk the talk in order to be totally free and alive. Because you feel a strong need to share your thoughts and ideals with others, you may always be teaching (or preaching!), but the kind of teacher you become will be determined by whether or not you make room for real diversity. If you are caught in self-righteous idealism, you ultimately lose power because you move away from the Source of Truth.

Saturn in Capricorn: When you're climbing toward the realization of your ambitions, you feel your power as a stabilizing force. You have a strong desire to be in control and will perform at your peak when you have a chance to take charge, but there is a difference between being in control and browbeating others into submission! The way you use your power determines whether or not you really own it. You also need to take a careful look at your attitude toward the responsibilities in your life. To truly take responsibility for yourself, you need an attitude that allows you to grow, change, and accept things as they are. From this standpoint, you can assert your own energy and manifest a reality that creates true stability. In your relationships, you have to learn to allow others to make their own mistakes. It's too easy to do things yourself since you don't really like having to clean up the mess others make. Learn to say "No" for the right reasons! The illusion of power conferred by social standing and prestigious positions is meaningless unless you've really earned those positions and use them to create opportunity and support in the world around you.

Saturn in Aquarius: Your power base with Saturn in Aquarius reflects a need to blend freedom with responsibility. Your idealistic concept of a society centered on humanitarian principles begins with your embrace of the true diversity of humankind. On a personal level, you are faced with the quest of blending your personality consciousness with that of your Higher Self. When you are directing your life from this viewpoint, decisions concerning career, family, and personal security are empowering. You can be an extremist if Saturn's energy is frustrated by difficult aspects, and you lose power if your opinionated nature adds a coldness to your spirit. Learning to evaluate your life circumstances through the lens of objectivity may not be easy for you, but you'll feel much more in control of your own destiny when you surrender your ego-based opinions to a higher ideal. Associating with others whose aims are destructive can diminish your power, so choose your friends and allies wisely.

Saturn in Pisces: It may not be easy for you develop your own set of ideals, since Saturn's energy in Pisces is very impressionable in this regard. Your sense of security depends on the people around you, or you may surrender control of your life to someone else too easily. Setting personal boundaries increases your power in a positive way because you learn to distinguish between your needs and the demands of others. You feel that you have to rescue the world in order to have a worthwhile life, and that's a pretty tall order. They say charity begins at home, and for you, that's a very good place to start. Meditation and spiritual practice are an excellent platform for your personal stability as long as you are not using these practices solely as an escape mechanism. Your total self is empowered when you learn to distinguish between the teacher and the teachings to which you are devoted. Surrendering to your Higher Self as your ultimate teacher may be the most empowering of all your life experiences.

Saturn Aspects: Limits of Power

Sun conjunct Saturn: With your Sun and Saturn in conjunction, you have a lot invested in controlling your own life. You take yourself too seriously, and it's possible that your fears of losing control can actually be inhibiting to a true sense of personal power. If you're hanging on to the past with great tenacity, you'll serve yourself well when you decide to let go and focus on the things you can actually do something about. It's crucial that you are aware of your underlying motivations for your life since you can be tempted to live your life trying to please everyone but yourself. If you must be validated from the outside to feel powerful, your arrival at the summit may be a bittersweet victory.

Sun semisquare Saturn: The semisquare connection between your Sun and Saturn adds a sense of anxiety to your personal identity. You continually wonder if you've met your mark, and even when you succeed, focus more on your mistakes than your accomplishments. It's not easy to allow joy into your life when all you think about are your limitations, but you'll be able to open that window a bit when you train your focus on your strengths, too.

Sun sextile Saturn: You handle power and control easily. The supportive sextile between your Sun and Saturn indicates the ability to carry your responsibilities with confidence. You'll feel most empowered when you have a specific direction, and operate best within a reasonable structure.

Sun square Saturn: Your struggle to gain control in your life is frustrating with your Sun in square aspect to Saturn. You feel that control equals power, and may attempt to control everyone and everything around you just to stay safe, or, you may get caught in situations where you've lost control and have fallen under restraints imposed by others. Self-control, self-discipline, and focus contrast sharply to totalitarianism. It's easy to fall victim to your own negativity or cynicism, which can undermine your personal strength. Reality and negativity can be quite different, but sometimes your view of reality focuses first upon what's wrong before you ever get to what's right. Sometimes the battle to prove yourself can, in itself, be empowering. The true test of your strength arises when you still feel respect for yourself even though you feel you've fallen short of the mark. It's putting forth the effort and continuing on with forgiveness in your heart that are the important parts. You've chosen a life of challenge, and may have many obstacles in your path. Learning how to handle your responsibilities is the key to your power, and setting your priorities marks the structure that will be your security platform. Ultimately, you will reach the summit, and if you've done it by exerting your strength, using your best abilities, and with a focus on your real priorities, the victory can be sweet indeed.

Sun trine Saturn: You are confident about yourself and your ability to achieve what you want from life. With your Sun and Saturn in trine aspect, you use responsibility, self-discipline, and structure to your advantage in building your security base. It is this base that strengthens your power as an individual. As you've matured, you've discovered the importance of focus, and are most successful when you have well-defined objectives. You use your achievements as stepping stones, and will be most satisfied with your life when your choices reflect a clear sense of yourself as a whole woman.

Sun quincunx Saturn: You feel uncertain about your abilities with your Sun in quincunx to Saturn, and that lack of confidence weakens your sense of personal power. Setting goals is not particularly easy for you since you tend to be dissatisfied when you attain them. Part of that dissatisfaction arises from your tendency to always be looking on the other side of the fence and feeling that you would have been better off if you had made different decisions. Accepting where you are is actually the beginning of establishing a sense of personal power because, until you are operating from the "be here now" perspective, you will never have the foundation you need to build solid security in your life. You benefit from programs that are designed to create self-improvement. Deciding what you want from life is step one. Step two is allowing enough flexibility to alter your objectives or the manner in which you get there without undermining your security.

Sun opposition Saturn: Your fears are the enemy of your need for personal strength, power, and stability. When you cannot confront your fears, you have difficulty handling your responsibilities. With your Sun in opposition to Saturn, you grow in power by creating a solid foundation that is based on responsible attitudes. This involves making a realistic assessment of your needs and determining the best ways to meet those needs through your own efforts. Learning to deal with difficult people confronts you with the awareness of cause and effect in your life. You will grow through developing tolerance, understanding, and self-awareness.

Moon conjunct Saturn: Your deep sense of personal power is based on taking responsibility for your feelings, needs, and thoughts. With your Moon in conjunction with Saturn, it's easy to fall into depression and it may be difficult to create joy. Becoming self-empowered is a direct result of learning how to overcome emotional obstacles, and if fear or anxiety is your obstacle, the best medicine is creating and growing true joy in your life. Your power is there, but it is difficult to harness when you're depressed. From a depressed state, you are filled with inertia. When you are inhibiting the flow of emotional energy in your life, you lose power. Begin by embracing the power that arises from your feminine force, and by accepting being a woman as a positive experience. Determine that you will celebrate your victories fully and completely, and remember that laughter can be very empowering!

Moon semisquare Saturn: With your Moon in semisquare aspect to Saturn, you can diminish your personal power by trying too hard to control your emotions. Negative thoughts, feelings, and attitudes seem easier to cultivate than positive, optimistic qualities, but you have a way out. When faced with challenges, you actually use your awareness of your feelings, even if those feelings involve fear or anxiety, as a springboard to get you moving. Your grasp of the need to be responsible for yourself does not have to be depressing, but can instead prompt you to do things that strengthen your sense of security and help you build a solid foundation for your long-term growth. In your relationships, watch a tendency to cling or to function from a level of neediness. When you're too needy, you deny your own power.

Moon sextile Saturn: With your Moon in sextile aspect to Saturn, you are capable of building solid emotional networks in your life, and those connections support and strengthen your power as a woman. Your common sense is one of your most empowering qualities! You are confident about your ability to meet and fulfill your own needs.

Moon square Saturn: The square aspect between your Moon and Saturn stimulates negative attitudes toward yourself and your needs, and may even add a feeling of resentment toward yourself for being a woman. If society, relationships, or your conditioning have illustrated that being a woman is a liability, you have two choices. By accepting this condition, your power as a whole person is inhibited. By deciding to overcome the obstacles in your path, your power grows, but you must guard against a tendency to develop harsh emotions, since when you are cold or unfeeling, you're denying a part of yourself. Taking responsibility for your feelings is very different from inhibiting your needs or repressing your nurturing qualities. You can be powerful and be a woman, too.

Moon trine Saturn: Life can be a positive learning experience for you with your Moon in trine aspect to Saturn. Your sense of emotional strength is empowering, and your ability to take responsibility for meeting your needs allows you to trust the world and her people. Relationships with other women, including your mother, may be a source of strength and support in your life. Building a network with other women based on trust, friendship, and mutual understanding is empowering for all involved.

Moon quincunx Saturn: Worrying about whether or not your answers are right, or your data is sufficient, can slow you down. Mercury is frustrated by Saturn's energy in your chart, indicating that you tend to compare what you know to what you think someone else knows. That's a good way to never have the chance to say what's on your mind. Do your research, study for your exams, and then go for it!

Moon opposition Saturn: Your are empowered when you've established strong emotional stability. With your Moon in opposition to Saturn, you are willing to work toward that end, but may be afraid that you'll never get there. You have to overcome your fear of not having what you need from life, and will feel empowered when you confront your fears and anxieties. Self-acceptance is the first, and most important, step in this process.

Mercury conjunct Saturn: There is a difference between realistic thinking and depressive cynicism, and sometimes you have to struggle between those two places with Mercury in conjunction to Saturn. You're probably a very good student, with a self-disciplined mind and good sense of judgment. This is empowering, but when you sink into negative thinking, you lose strength.

Mercury semisquare Saturn: With Mercury in semisquare aspect to Saturn, you have to safeguard against allowing negative mental attitudes to undermine your optimism and confidence. Learning to let go of worry and to avoid fretting over things you cannot do anything about will be very empowering to you.

Mercury sextile Saturn: Your realistic attitudes provide a strong foundation for your personal success with Mercury in sextile aspect to Saturn. Since you are a superb planner, you'll find that you feel confident because you're prepared. Your intellectual development is a strong source of power in your life.

Mercury square Saturn: It's easy to allow negative thinking to sap your power with Mercury square Saturn. Your attitudes about work and education are important parts of your life foundation, and if you fail to form the mental discipline necessary to accomplish your aims, you will be disappointed in the results.

Mercury trine Saturn: Your mental attitudes are centered on responsible thinking with Mercury in trine aspect to Saturn. You'll find that when you are guiding or teaching others, or sharing what you've learned from life experiences, you are rewarded with a sense of inner confidence. You know the power of your mind and have the capability of changing your life through techniques like affirmation and positive thinking.

Mercury quincunx Saturn: When you're caught in a difficult situation, you can usually figure out what to do. With Mercury in quincunx to Saturn, you sometimes get caught because you failed to plan for contingencies. This can leave you feeling very exposed and frustrated, diminishing your sense of personal worth and power. Sometimes changing this is as simple as studying for an exam, taking the time to balance your checkbook, or putting a map in the car before you head out for a trip.

Mercury opposition Saturn: You know that you can alter the course of your life by developing your mind and adopting positive mental attitudes. With Mercury in opposition to Saturn, you have to prove it to yourself, though. When you're stuck in negative thinking, your own inertia may keep you from accomplishing what you want to do, but you can fulfill your aims when you apply yourself, and the results are very empowering!

Venus conjunct Saturn: It is imperative that you develop a solid sense of self-worth with the energy of Venus conjunct Saturn. When you doubt your value as a woman, your power sinks and your creative drive disappears, but when you open yourself to the simple beauty of life and work to cultivate an attitude of giving, the tide turns. Selfish attitudes weaken your power base, and when you feel that you cannot afford to give of yourself, you actually diminish your capacity to experience the love you need. Although you may not be able to wake up tomorrow and feel that life offers abundance and opportunity, you can make the achievement of that feeling a very realistic personal goal. Abundance begins in your heart and extends to the decisions that reflect your real values.

Venus semisquare Saturn: You may be plagued with low self-esteem through the influence of Venus in semisquare aspect to Saturn. When you're feeling low, it's tempting to withdraw and limit yourself. This is definitely not a power statement! You can become empowered by sharing yourself, your talents, your resources with the world. Selfish attitudes, hanging on to resentment, irresponsible spending, and greediness are symptoms that your power base needs to be re-evaluated.

Venus sextile Saturn: Developing your ability to love is a source of great power in your life. With Venus in sextile aspect to Saturn, you experience the reward of enduring love that stems from a true appreciation of yourself and others. You know that through love you can accomplish anything, and it is this force that carries you through when everything else around you fails. Your ability to use good judgment in money matters is a direct result of your discrimination and strong self-worth. This strengthens your power base on multiple levels.

Venus square Saturn: Your disappointments seem to override your self-confidence. The energy of Venus in square aspect to Saturn tests your ability to maintain faith in the nature of love itself, and also tests your sense of self-worth. If you base your worth entirely upon others and their responses and reactions, something as trivial as a curt remark can wound your self-esteem, and then your power flies out the window! You may also be stuck in old emotional wounds, like a lost love, allowing your pain and regret to block your ability to let love heal you. You are empowered when you keep your heart open, sharing yourself with the world around you, and embracing yourself fully and completely. Concentrating on strengthening your self-worth is necessary if you are to experience a real sense of personal power. Learning how to manage your material resources is part of this experience, and if you can apply reasonable discipline to your spending and avoid the temptation of buying things when you don't really have the resources (watch those credit cards!), you'll be happier in the long run—and more powerful, too!

Venus trine Saturn: Sustaining your self-worth seems natural with Venus in trine aspect to Saturn. You know that you build solid foundations when you develop your talents, share what you have, and teach what you know. Love is the key to your power, and sometimes being there for someone else in times of trouble strengthens you, too. You also have a good ability to manage your finances, which forms an excellent base for power on many levels.

Venus quincunx Saturn: You feel that you always seem to want the wrong things with Venus in quincunx to Saturn. This undermines your trust in your own judgment and weakens your self-worth, which, in turn, diminishes your sense of personal power. You learn from your life experiences that sometimes what you want is not what you need, and by adjusting your wants to include things that have real and practical value, you will build a sturdier platform. Otherwise, you will continue to waste your resources, time, and energy on people, situations, and things that don't meet your needs.

Venus opposition Saturn: If you feel you're not worthy, you're very likely to attract men and others who will illustrate that very point. With Venus in opposition to Saturn, your life works like a reflecting pool when it comes to your self-worth. If you're trying to base your personal worth on the way everyone else feels about you instead of building a strong sense of self-esteem, you'll never experience the fulfillment you seek. To become an empowered woman, you need to look in the mirror and see the reflection of all that you want and need to be. Even if you're not quite there yet, when you feel that drive deep in your heart, you're capable of making that realization happen. Your attitude toward money also reflects your self-worth, so think about that before you go on a spending jag just because your sweetheart forgot your birthday.

Mars conjunct Saturn: The energies of Mars and Saturn in conjunction indicate strong self-control as a means of getting what you want from life. When you are focused on something, there's little that can deter you from achieving your aims; that is, except for your own fears and insecurities! You really can have patience when you need it, even though you might prefer immediate gratification. You are strongly attracted to men who own their own power, and feel best in relationships with men who are in control of their own lives without trying to control yours. As a result, you may have a few power struggles from time to time. Maybe you need one of those cars they use in driver's education, with two sets of controls!

Mars semisquare Saturn: With Mars and Saturn in semisquare aspect, you struggle with issues of control and domination, in your relationships and with life itself. You do not trust your own power and can attract others who test your ability to take control of your life by offering you their own set of directions and limitations. When you determine your priorities, you may feel somewhat reluctant to put them into action, but once you've set upon your path, you can be quite effective at directing and controlling your own life. Pay attention to your tendency to try to control the outcome of everything, though, and learn to accept responsibility for your own mistakes. This is not power talking, it's fear. Sometimes you gain power by knowing when to stop and let the traffic move right past you.

Mars sextile Saturn: The cooperative sextile aspect between Saturn and Mars indicates that you are effective in controlling your own life. Your ability to respect the limitations of others and to honor your own is part of this self-direction, but so is your ability to take charge when necessary. You probably like being in positions of power, and can be a very effective leader or executive. Dealing with authorities is reasonably easy for you, too, although you still may have your qualms about whether or not some people in power really deserve to be there!

Mars square Saturn: Sometimes you just do not handle restraint very well, especially when it feels defeating. With Mars in square aspect to Saturn, you are struggling with the lessons of right use of power, and you have to deal with this experience through your own actions and those of others. Developing positive self-restraint—not total inhibition—is the key to working with this energy properly. If you've experienced limitations that seem to be beyond your control, you always have control over at least one factor: your response! Learning to use the blocks, frustrations, and limitations in your life as stabilizing forces can make a huge difference in your sense of personal power. If you're continually bumping into the same old barriers, or if you're stuck in the same fear of your own desires, you will never know the power you so deeply crave. You are the perfect candidate for passive-aggressive behavior in that you project your own frustrations and insecurities onto others, or blame others for your mistakes. Taking charge of yourself is your major responsibility; trying to control others can be an exercise in futility.

Mars trine Saturn: Since you have Mars in trine aspect to Saturn, your deliberate focus of energy can work to your advantage. You resist outside controls because you are quite capable of directing and controlling your own energy. When you need to be cooperative, you can, and when you are in situations that require you to take direction, you can be graceful about it. You don't like giving away your power by taking on useless power struggles.

Mars quincunx Saturn: You do not always respond well to restraint and limitation with Mars in quincunx aspect to Saturn. If you can see the reason for particular restrictions, you are capable of making the necessary adjustments and moving on. Through this approach, your power base remains strong, but if you keep bumping into the same old walls and never figure out why, you will ultimately lose energy and become exhausted from your frustration. Be alert to your tendency to adopt passive-aggressive behaviors when you're feeling insecure.

Mars opposition Saturn: You can be overly controlling with your Mars in opposition to Saturn. Not only can you hold yourself back, but you can try to inhibit the actions and energy of others. Although you may not necessarily look for opportunities to get in somebody's way, when you're in a negative frame of mind, feeling threatened or insecure, your own fears work like a wall of resistance. Watch for your first response to new situations. If you feel a big "No" welling up inside you, stop for a moment and look at your fears. Caution is one thing. Excessive fear drains your power. You also need to learn about the difference between directing your anger and stuffing it. When you repress angry feelings, they ultimately come out in destructive ways, and may be directed toward the wrong target!

Jupiter conjunct Saturn: You are learning the lessons of manifesting true abundance in harmony with your needs with Jupiter in conjunction to Saturn. Your life can be a full, self-affirming, and empowering experience only when you apply yourself and use your talents to reach beyond your current circumstances. It's tempting to rest on your laurels with this energy, and there are times when it's nice to drift with the currents of life, but if you feel a little uninspired, it could be the result of too little effort on your part.

Jupiter semisquare Saturn: Learning to make the best use of your assets is a key lesson with Jupiter's energy in semisquare aspect to Saturn. This includes both your financial resources and your talents. Asserting the discipline necessary to strengthen your talents and abilities is not high on your priority list, but when you do put effort into refining your skills, your opportunities to use them increase. Taking the time to learn about money, or at least putting reasonable effort into managing your resources, can make a big difference in your ability to use your assets. These efforts build your sense of personal worth, thereby expanding your power.

Jupiter sextile Saturn: Your reasonable judgment and practical approach to the job at hand are supported by Jupiter in sextile aspect to Saturn. By setting your sights on goals that are meaningful to your growth, you achieve success, and this is the core of power that lasts throughout your lifetime. You're willing to put forth the necessary effort and discipline to make your dreams come true.

Jupiter square Saturn: You spend a lot of energy trying to get out of responsibilities with Jupiter in square aspect to Saturn. If you were to apply the same amount of energy toward those responsibilities, you would feel self-confirmed and accomplish more in the long run! The easy way out is not the path of greatest reward for you, and waiting for somebody to come along and rescue you will result in disappointment and lack of self-trust. You may not trust your own abilities, but how will you know whether or not you're capable unless you try? If you refuse to try because you're not an expert, well, you already know the answer to that one. Genius is created, it doesn't just "happen."

Jupiter trine Saturn: You can be a little lazy with Jupiter in trine aspect to Saturn. Things seem to come easily, and it's good to know that you have a little cosmic insurance policy, but if you are to know true abundance that sustains and supports you and that arises from the core of your own power, you have to put some effort into creating your life on your own terms. If anyone can learn to manifest abundance, it is you. You know how to make the right connections, but what do you do with them? Your awareness and knowledge inspires others who may not be as fortunate, but who have the desire to change their lives.

Jupiter quincunx Saturn: Sometimes you test the good graces of the Universe with Jupiter in quincunx aspect to Saturn. You push your resources to the limit, and then, just in the nick of time, pull everything together. You tend to over-obligate yourself—almost. If you continue to do this, you deplete your reserve with a resulting lack of faith that undermines your self-confidence. Knowing when to put your efforts into something and when to pull back takes a little experience, and once you get into the rhythm, you'll do okay. Every now and then, the music changes. Just be sure you're listening.

Jupiter opposition Saturn: Developing a true understanding of the link between freedom and responsibility is important with the energy of Jupiter in opposition to Saturn. You can vacillate between the desire to create your life on your own terms and the desire to have someone else take on the responsibilities. When you forge a real partnership between yourself and those who share your life, re-evaluating your roles and responsibilities over the course of time, you can have truly workable relationships that support your sense of personal power. These relationships extend to the world through your connection to employer and employee, teacher and student, etc., but if you go to extremes, the lack of balance in your life will undermine your power and you can be stuck with responsibilities that do not belong to you.

Saturn conjunct Uranus: With Saturn and Uranus in conjunction, you rebel against restraints in your life as a means of accomplishing a sense of control and power. The manner in which you stage your rebellion makes all the difference between whether or not it is empowering or defeating. You cannot afford to be stuck doing things the way they've always been done. You're here to stimulate progress, new alternatives, and reasonable innovation. But you must do this in a responsible manner or the effectiveness of your efforts will be undermined.

Saturn semisquare Uranus: Dealing with authority is not always easy for you with Saturn in semisquare aspect to Uranus. You are uncomfortable in traditional roles and are most empowered when you bring innovation and change into your life by exercising your talents and individuality. You may have to do this within the existing structure, which means you'll have to be a little more patient and much more aware of the limitations around you. If you resist the emergence of your own individuality out of fear or guilt-ridden responsibilities, your power will dwindle away and you'll end up with a life filled with dissatisfaction.

Saturn sextile Uranus: You are an innovator with Saturn in sextile aspect to Uranus. Using your energy, efforts, and influence to bring about changes in the world around you is invigorating and empowering, and is part of the reason you were born in the first place! You can be an exceptional teacher, illustrating how to use the lessons of the past to build bridges to a more promising future. Whatever your field of endeavor, you act as a responsible agent of change, enhancing the evolutionary process. You are effective working independently, owning your own business, or creating avenues that have never been tried before.

Saturn square Uranus: Sometimes your rebellious attitudes get you into trouble with Saturn in square aspect to Uranus. You can feel your own power dwindling away when you stay stuck in a tired, outworn situation for too long, and if you fail to act, you'll become more frustrated with each and every passing day. When you learn to identify the restrictions, expectations, and problems inherent in any situation before you make a commitment, you can deal with them better. Sometimes you simply have no choice but to take on burdens you don't want to carry; but you can alter your attitudes and carry them your own way. Embracing your need to change and grow is part of the equation. Once you've satisfied your responsibilities, you have more freedom. If you ignore them, shirk them, or palm them off onto some willing man, it may be that man who gets the chance to move ahead while you're stuck in the kitchen washing dishes. Once you learn to blend independent and innovative action with personal responsibility, there is no end to what you can accomplish. Now that's empowering!

Saturn trine Uranus: You have a knack for using your ingenuity to your benefit with Saturn in trine aspect to Uranus. You are blessed with many talents, but until you apply the discipline, effort, and energy to them that are necessary to develop them to their fullest, you may only accomplish mediocre success. It is tempting to live vicariously through your talented children, although if you put your energy into supporting and guiding them to do what they need to do for themselves, you'll learn something about yourself in the process! To become totally free to be yourself, use your respect for the traditions of the past and then alter them to support and reflect your unique self-expression. You're the woman who will start family traditions of your own, and you can extend that same energy into the social system through your efforts in your career.

Saturn quincunx Uranus: Even when you try, you're probably not comfortable in traditional roles. The influence of Saturn in quincunx aspect to Uranus will probably result in your experience of circumstances that are not really what you planned for yourself, but which you are required to fulfill. The attitude you adopt in meeting your responsibilities makes all the difference in whether or not you stay stuck in circumstances that inhibit your growth. Stubborn rebellion alone is ineffective, but revolutionary efforts that open avenues for your self-expression result in options that surprise even you. If you are to be fully empowered, you must adopt a viewpoint that allows you to create change within existing structures.

Saturn opposition Uranus: You have to take a very careful look at your internal battle between your need to be free and your feelings of inhibition. With Saturn in opposition to Uranus, you attract strongly inhibiting life circumstances if you carry your rebellion too far, or, if you are afraid to exercise your independence, you can be stuck in situations that are simply repressing. You need to feel safe, which is normal, but you also need to know what it's like to feel your wings unfurl and fly free. That yearning for freedom can be more than a dream when you put the discipline and focus into your life required to cultivate your special talents and abilities. To empower yourself, you think that you have to suffer first. Think again. Taking responsibility is a far cry from suffering! Just suffering through something because you're afraid to do anything about it is no assurance that the situation will change, or that you will be rewarded! If you're uncertain, obtain objectivity by seeking helpful advice or instruction before you proceed. Just remember that you do not have to obtain approval to be yourself.

Saturn conjunct Neptune: Your views of reality are colored by your dreams and imagination with Saturn conjunct Neptune. These energies are empowering when used with techniques such as creative visualization followed by applied action, but you can lose your way if you spend your time and energy dreaming. You're the woman who needs to build an anchor for your castles in the air. Passive attitudes will undermine your power base, leaving you with a feeling of distrust of yourself and disappointment in life. Honesty with yourself and with others is crucial if you are to have what you need. Any time you project a dishonest attitude, it will cost you dearly. This includes honesty about your beliefs and ideals, which must be based on fulfilling your higher needs. Giving responsibility for your soul to an imaginary power will never work. Finding the real power of the Source, however, brings amazing results.

Saturn semisquare Neptune: You can become stuck in your illusions with Saturn in semisquare aspect to Neptune. Illusions that are fear-based create massive anxiety, which can be a major power drain. If you feel unsupported, misunderstood, or lost, look within yourself to determine if you've been expecting more of the world than it can offer. You must begin by finding the core of your own power inside yourself, and then find a way to link your compassion, hopes, and dreams to the world around you. Exercising active spirituality is the key to knowing true spiritual power. Prayers alone will never accomplish what prayers and action together can do.

Saturn sextile Neptune: Your ability to blend your spirituality with your everyday reality is empowering at a very deep level in your life. With Saturn in sextile aspect to Neptune, you are prompted to discover the compassion that flows from the heart of divine love and understanding, and to send that compassion into the world through your creativity. You are a goddess, creating your life by listening to your inner voice.

Saturn square Neptune: Saturn's square to Neptune can have a real dampening effect on your dreams, yet it can also provide a good contrast between illusion and possibility. By developing your link to your spiritual self and integrating that spirituality into your everyday life, much of the frustration of this aspect will dissipate. Just believing in something because that's what you were taught can actually drain your spiritual power. You need to find that link between your beliefs and the reality of your life. You may always be a little skeptical, but you don't have to let it ruin your life. Go ahead, get on the haunted house ride at the fair. You might have a wonderful time!

Saturn trine Neptune: You feel a deep sense of faith and trust in the experience of life with Saturn in trine aspect to Neptune. Your spirituality plays an important role in your sense of power as a whole woman, and you find that your spiritual focus gives you strength when the mundane world falls short. Listening to your inner voice is just as important as learning the factual evidence presented by data, and you can blend your inner understanding with the external "facts" to create a wonderful manifestation of your dreams and hopes. Your faith in yourself and your ability to trust your own judgment is a strong part of your power base. This is the power of surrender to higher law.

Saturn quincunx Neptune: Sometimes it's difficult to know exactly where to aim your ambitions with Saturn in quincunx aspect to Neptune. In different periods of your life, you've found that you've needed to surrender your selfish desires to something more powerful or to the pressing needs of others, but you've also discovered that there are times when you must believe fervently in your own dreams and do whatever you can to make them reality. This vacillation is part of your natural rhythm, and although these rhythms are not as predictable as the change of seasons, they are very much determined by changes prompted by your inner needs for growth. You are most empowered when you adjust your priorities based on your honest spiritual revelations and centered within your awareness of the highest possible principles.

Saturn opposition Neptune: You are empowered when you build a bridge between your spirituality and the material plane. With Saturn in opposition to Neptune, you are tempted to go to extremes—selfish desire versus sacrifice, greedy materialism versus absolute escape. The balance point resides within you, and you must learn to blend your spirituality into your everyday life experience if you are to feel fully empowered. You can't be spiritual part of the time. Life must become your meditation.

Saturn conjunct Pluto: With Saturn conjunct Pluto, it's tempting to destroy what you cannot control. If you're feeling frustrated with the path you've chosen, or if it seems to have been thrust upon you, destructive actions will only result in a feeling of groundless insecurity. You possess the power of transformational focus, and can bring healing and change into your life by eliminating the things you do not really need. If your insecurities are driving you, you may attract a man who seems safe and protective, only to discover that you've become the victim of an overly controlling person. If your power base is threatened, you can become rather plutocratic yourself, with this type of attitude working to undermine the respect you desperately desire to achieve. You must be aware of the need to take responsibility for your actions, or they will surely work against you.

Saturn semisquare Pluto: Saturn's energy in semisquare to Pluto brings the need to learn how to deal with power struggles in a constructive manner. If you continually bend your will to the will of others, you become resentful and bitter, and this attitude assures that your power will dwindle. If you try to force others to bend to your will, the same is true. By adopting the practice of honesty within your relationships at home and at work, you'll make headway. Avoiding corruption, maintaining a strong focus of becoming personally responsible for your actions and attitudes, and looking beneath the surface can be empowering. Undermining behaviors, vengeful attitudes, and jealousy serve only to diminish or destroy your personal worth.

Saturn sextile Pluto: You are an agent of positive, healing change in the world with Saturn's energy in sextile aspect to Pluto. You understand the power of releasing what you no longer need, and respect the need to make room for the transitions life requires of you. Those life stages can be periods of self-confirmation, and your actions and attitudes when faced with change support and inspire others.

Saturn square Pluto: You may be afraid of changes that are the result of actions that seem to be beyond your control with Saturn in square aspect to Pluto. It is crucial that you are aware of the root of these fears since you may actually be responding fearfully to something just because the fear is so deeply ingrained you feel you have no choice in the matter. If you've suffered loss, been abandoned, abused, or neglected, these fears will act like a shield to keep you from experiencing the security, stability, and inner strength you need. If you desire to break out of this prison, you can confront and address your fears and use them as stepping stones to your ultimate escape. Learning how to deal with others who try to overwhelm you with guilt or raw power is another key to finding your own strength. If you are not secure, you may also adopt attitudes that are difficult for those around you, serving to further wall you in. Inner exploration through psychotherapy and supportive counseling can help you get to the root of these issues so that you are dealing with them once and for all. If you do nothing, you may feel stuck forever.

Saturn trine Pluto: You are capable of using your power and influence in positive ways with Saturn's energy in trine aspect to Pluto. Taking responsibility for your need to bring about transformative change prompts you to pursue careers that involve healing in some way. You have a deep faith in the process of higher law, and can be a very effective innovator, researcher, teacher, physician, or artist— using your expression in the world to illustrate your awareness of the power of the human spirit.

Saturn quincunx Pluto: You feel frustrated in situations that fall short of your expectations, and are sometimes disappointed when you arrive at the summit of your goals. The influence of Saturn in quincunx to Pluto brings an energy of continual drive to push into different areas of manifestation, so that when you reach one summit, you find it leads somewhere else. You can either be disenchanted with yourself through this process, or realize that your deep need to experience life from its many different levels is important to you. If you go about this process in a healthy manner, you will be able to peel through the layers of yourself without causing destruction and discover amazing power at the core of your being. If you resist your own growth or force power issues on others all of the time, you can be wounded, which may make it more difficult to get to your core power.

Saturn opposition Pluto: You are faced with the need to understand power at its very core. Saturn's energy in opposition to Pluto brings a confrontation with your own fear of power. This can manifest through a fear of death, an insecurity with personal life-changing choices, or self-destructive behaviors. The range of possibilities is actually quite broad, but the current of energy is that which takes you to the ultimate awareness that you have to surrender your limited, selfish awareness to the power that flows from the Source. Whether you accomplish this through creative or artistic means, through restoring furniture, tearing down old barns, or working with the psyche in some way, is not important. You need to experience what happens when you build a bridge between your life and the power of healing. Your life is about transformation. It's not an easy path, but it is your path.

Pluto: Power from the Source

Plutonian control is sometimes difficult to grasp, but it's definitely there. When you feel this control from outside yourself, it is undermining and extremely intimidating. The force of Pluto is buried deep within your psyche. It is unleashed and grows like the process of mitosis in a fertilized cell, which is altered, splits off, combines with other cells, and ultimately becomes an organism. Through Pluto, you experience the power of life, birth, healing, and the ultimate change of death. If you are trapped in a mire of shame, guilt, and self-destructiveness, you may have undergone a Plutonian transformation as a result of trauma earlier in your life. It is this same force that plants the seeds of change, which eventually lead to the creation of a new self.

Pluto in the Houses: Where You're Compulsive

Pluto in the 1st: Pluto in your 1st House was interpreted earlier in this chapter.

Pluto in the 2nd: Pluto in your 2nd House was interpreted earlier in this chapter.

Pluto in the 3rd: The power of your thoughts determines your experience of life. Pluto's energy in your 3rd House prompts you to transform your thinking. You must learn to trust your own intelligence and to develop your mind in such a way that allows you to experience an understanding of life at core levels. You ask questions, although many are never verbalized. They just drive you, like a relentless taskmaster, to look beneath the surface. You can be overcome by compulsive thought patterns, and when you do, you find it difficult to release yourself from them. These compulsions are a power drain, especially if they reach the obsessive level. Take the time to listen to your own thoughts. Do they offer self-confirming messages or destructive mutterings? Once you find a way to use your mind to heal your life, you will know the power you've been seeking.

Pluto in the 4th: You learned about power from your parents and may have felt that one parent had a very strong hold on your life (they still may), but all the while, you found yourself resisting their control or trying to undermine it. You tested limits. You knew just how far to push without getting the rug pulled from beneath your feet. Or did you? Now that you are a woman, you may have difficulty feeling that your foundation is ever firm or stable enough. You know deep within yourself that you need to destroy the unfitting or unfair images you have of your family, their traditions, or their false identities. You may also feel some guilt that you cannot fully identify. This is the guilt your soul recalls. It may not be entirely your own. It may be something you felt as early as the time you spent in your mother's womb. It might be something from another lifetime that you remember at a cellular level, a feeling that haunts you when you are alone. Let it go. Find yourself. Step into your power and allow yourself to be healed. Then, and only then, will you finally feel that you've found home.

Pluto in the 5th: Your creative efforts are an important element in your life. Pluto's energy in your 5th House drives you to reach into your soul and find your creative spirit. You must trust yourself enough to exercise this creativity. It heals you. It is the key to creating life on your own terms. You may also discover that your approach to children is a key factor in your own self-respect. When you look at a child and see the wonder, feel the hope, and desire to be a catalyst for his or her own creativity without trying to shape him or her into the image you want them to be, you're allowing this force to work positively. If you see your children as little pieces of clay you can mold however you wish, you may be sorely disappointed if they destroy your creation when they reach adolescence or adulthood. Perhaps this struggle results from your own childhood experience. You've heard about the inner child? Well, your little girl has always been powerful, but she may not know what to do with that power. It's up to you to show her.

Pluto in the 6th: Pluto's energy in your 6th House prompts you to unlock your power to alter and transform your own life through self-improvement. The quality of your life depends on the way you handle experiences that may seem to be beyond your control, like your genetic heritage, or an illness, or the society within which you live. Taking care of your health by finding the root of real healing power in your life is one of the most crucial factors you face. Completely surrendering control of your life to the will and direction of others will leave you feeling disconnected to yourself. You can find the right healers, helpers, and supporters, but you must first acknowledge the part you play in these processes.

Pluto in the 7th: Pluto's energy in your 7th House brings direct power struggles within cooperative relationships and partnerships. You may resist the idea of a functional partnership because you do not want to give up control, or you may attract a partner who overwhelms you with his power when you do not trust your own ability to direct your life. You cannot escape power issues. One way or another, you must realize that you really do have the power to direct your own life and to reflect your power in a positive sense. Until you finally exercise that power, you are caught in an endless game of transforming yourself to fit your partner's needs, or finding that you are never what you want to be. Try looking in the mirror. The woman looking back at you is important.

Pluto in the 8th: Pluto in your 8th House was interpreted earlier in this chapter.

Pluto in the 9th: You learn about power through your spiritual and religious teaching with Pluto in the 9th House. Your need to connect to the Power of the Universal Mind is behind many of your deepest aspirations. You will be dissatisfied if you give your spiritual power to another human being. It belongs to you and to the direction of the teacher within your higher consciousness. It's tempting to hold on to religious ideals with a fervent dedication that is almost impossible to release. By separating your emotional attachment to your beliefs from the truth of your spiritual awareness, you will become empowered at the highest level.

Pluto in the 10th: With Pluto in your 10th House, achieving a sense of power is definitely among your ambitions. This is a highly creative position for Pluto, since exercising your ability to bring about transformational change and healing through your career path can be quite a challenge. If you decide not to follow a career path, you are a powerful force in your family, and may even play an influential matriarchal role as you mature. However, you're likely to run into power issues with others, too, since as you become more adept at moving through the chain of command, your presence and strength attracts power struggles with others. This is not the only option—you may find that you enjoy rubbing shoulders with the movers and shakers—after all, that's where you belong. Before you can achieve the levels of success you deeply desire, you may have to address buried resentments, guilt, or shame that have their origins in your past. In essence, you can become a vessel for regeneration and healing, and your own wounds may be the keys to your power to influence change in the lives of others.

Pluto in the 11th: With Pluto in your 11th House, you may meet many of your power issues within the social sphere, particularly around special interest groups or when dealing with political processes. You're not the women who enjoys sitting on the sidelines if you're part of a group, especially if something could be done more effectively. If you have not developed a strong sense of your own ideals and beliefs, you can fall under the influence of others who would usurp your power in order to boost their own. Once you've awakened to your own ideals, drives, and directives, you can be a highly influential leader and instigator of social change. The extent of your efforts depends on you and the choices you make for yourself.

Pluto in the 12th: With Pluto in your 12th House, you may be tempted to repress your emotions, particularly those that have to do with the deep needs that spring from the shadowy side of yourself. You may even have problems with depression or addictive behaviors, which create a kind of emotional trap, until you learn to delve into the depths of your being and clean out the ghosts and dragons from your past that still haunt your dreams. Old resentments act like a potion that poisons your imagination and undermines your ability to trust your inner self. Once you've conquered your own demons, you may feel driven to help others confront their own, and you can become an extremely effective healer.

Pluto Aspects: Wounding, Resentment, and Power Drives

Any energy activated by an aspect to Pluto gains increased intensity. In different chapters and sections of text, Pluto's connections to other planets has been defined. In the context of power, Mars-Pluto and Uranus-Pluto contacts are especially significant and are interpreted below. Saturn-Pluto contacts have already been carefully explored in this chapter (see the "Saturn" section).

However, where Sun, Moon, Mercury, or Venus are involved with Pluto, there are also power drives present that frequently operate in the modes of hidden agenda. If the aspects are flowing (the semisextile, sextile, and trine), the need for power becomes less driving and more easily used. When the conjunction between the personal planets (Sun, Moon, Mercury, and Venus) and Pluto occurs, there is a compulsive nature associated with the expression of these energies. In fact, these compulsions can show up in relationships, career, and personal growth arenas, and can be difficult to control unless you're using clear objectivity to understand your drives.

With the harsher aspects (semi-square, square, quincunx, and opposition) from the personal planets to Pluto, there is almost always a deep sense of guilt or resentment associated with expressing the energy of the Sun, Moon, Mercury, or Venus. These wounds need careful attention throughout life and require a woman to be open with herself about the hurts that have led to feelings of loss, guilt, disappointment, or resentment. These aspects are good targets for psychotherapeutic exploration, since they indicate issues that are hidden beneath the surface that can rob you of your power. If Pluto is in a difficult aspect to the Sun, the power issue is centered around the power of life itself. There may be an issue about surviving that colors your psyche, and there are usually issues concerning your relationship with your father. If Pluto is in a difficult aspect to the Moon, the question of nurturing support arises (and power issues concerning the mother or your own femininity emerge). When Pluto is in a frustrating aspect to Mercury, power issues arise through learning, communication, educational pursuits, and sometimes even through learning abilities or physical problems centered in the nervous system. Difficult aspects between Pluto and Venus speak directly to self-worth and financial issues, and were explored in the chapter "Opening Your Heart."

The real power-supply aspects between Mars or Saturn and Pluto will be apparent in your life. You may see some of the issues you experience from a generational level with Uranus and Pluto contacts. These are explained below.

Mars-Pluto Contacts: Power, Pain, and Healing

Mars conjunct Pluto: With the energies of Mars and Pluto joined, your sexual drive and need to express power are extremely important. Trying to ignore them will only complicate your life. Learning where your power, and that of another, begins and ends is a crucial lesson, especially if you're driven to reach the top at all costs. You may also find that you're easily intimidated by others who negatively use or abuse power until you learn to assert your own strength of will. These energies together intensify your passion, and when you want something, your passionate desires can be unstoppable until you are satisfied. Sexual fulfillment ranks high on your priority list, as it should, since you not only understand the nature of desire but have the ability to achieve a powerful bonding with your lover and partner. In situations that require strength or control, you can harm or heal, depending on the focus you choose for your drive and energy. You must begin with yourself by accepting the regenerative power you hold and utilize throughout your life. You can be much like the High Priestess, and by focusing on this archetype, you will find pathways that allow you to become a truly powerful and influential woman.

Mars semisextile Pluto: With Mars and Pluto in semisextile aspect, there can be an easy flow of energy in situations that need to change. You may also find that you're especially attracted to circumstances that allow you to utilize your healing energies—whether through your creativity, within your family, or in specialized fields like medicine. Allowing yourself to become a vessel for regenerative change keeps your life on track and helps to maintain the natural flow of energy you need to accomplish the realization of your desires. A positive attitude toward your sexuality is important—you may truly understand the concept of sexual healing. Learning about the spiritual nature of your sexuality is a crucial element, and you'll benefit from exploring a broad variety of ways to achieve true sexual ecstasy.

Mars semisquare Pluto: Mars and Pluto in semisquare aspect create an undercurrent of dissatisfaction with yourself and the men in your life. This does not mean that you can't have good relationships or that your sex life will be forever frustrating, but if you're having trouble, look at your own feelings of guilt or inhibition in these areas. To embrace and fulfill your sexual needs, you may have to go beyond a simple understanding and experience of your sexuality into a heightened awareness of the true nature of sexual energy. Additionally, to achieve the realization of your deeply held desires in any area of your life, you must uncover hidden issues that could sabotage your success. Pinpoint your resentments. If they are the result of bad experiences from the past, it's up to you to find a way to heal and move beyond the old trauma into the light of the present moment. Once you've learned to let go of old resentments and guilt, you may find that you are a wonderful vessel for healing in the lives of others. This is an aspect of shamanism and requires honest confrontation with your deeper needs and desires.

Mars sextile Pluto: Mars and Pluto in sextile aspect is like a special potion of strength and power—but you have to learn to tap into this power if it's going to do you any good! You have the capability to understand and the experience levels of personal strength and control that set you apart from the ordinary. You also enjoy the pure ecstasy of your own sexuality and appreciate a partner whose desires can be as unfettered as your own. Although there may be other blocks from frustrating energies elsewhere in your chart, this is the quality that allows you to transform difficulties and overcome adversity.

Mars square Pluto: With Mars and Pluto in square aspect, there are definite power issues present in your life. Whether you suffer from personal loss or pain residing in your past, or are in current abusive circumstances that feel like you've lost your power, at some point in your life you may have to deal with abuse of power. Sometimes this aspect indicates deeply buried resentment or guilt that hides in the abyss of your past. Without addressing these old issues, you may always feel that you are somehow undermined, no matter what you do. The beauty of this aspect is that you are continually prompted to find out what's hidden deep in your psyche around issues like sex, death, and power. If you hold resentment toward men, find out why. Deciding that they're all dogs will not do you much good—it only builds more negativity. The way you use your own sexuality says a lot about how you feel concerning power and yourself. Exploring your sexual needs in many different contexts may provide the answers you seek. Ignoring your sexual needs only leads to greater frustration and more resentment toward yourself. This is an aspect of choice—the choice to direct your energy toward regeneration and healing, or the choice to live a self-destructive life. That's a lot of personal power!

Mars trine Pluto: With Mars and Pluto in a trine aspect, you have an excellent ability to bring about transformational change by directing your personal dominion in positive ways. This is an aspect of magical strength and power, but works only if you consciously work to develop it. Your sexuality can be a gift, and the way you use your personal magnetism dictates the difference between success and failure in every area of your life. You need a place to exercise your magnetism in creative ways.

Mars quincunx Pluto: The energies of Mars and Pluto in quincunx aspect can be frustrating, especially if you're repressing desires. If you wonder why you're so drawn to people and situations that test your idea of power and control, this is the magnet that attracts those things! Learning where the boundaries are drawn is important, since you need to exercise your own power and must learn to allow others to use their own. Your sexual energies wax and wane according to the pressures you're feeling in your life, and making the necessary adjustments that will allow you to experience the satisfaction you yearn to achieve can make a big difference in the way you feel about yourself.

Mars opposition Pluto: Mars and Pluto in opposition to one another is a constant test. You're always faced with people who are controllers. Do you think that could be because you like to be in control yourself? Well, you'd better answer that in the affirmative, since you love the idea of power and are hungry to experience it. The way you use it is crucial, and the way you allow others to assert their power over you is also extremely important. You can be either abusive or abused, depending on what you hold in your deep desires. You may think it can't be that easy, but in your heart of hearts, you know it's true. You're fascinated by all the things everybody considers taboo, and you need to at least look into those fascinations in healthy ways or you're likely to undo yourself—not a pretty picture. You can be the ultimate temptress, so why not learn how to use that energy in its best sense and let the Goddess residing within work through you? Uncovering your hidden power by developing your inner self will allow you to become completely transformed and alter your life accordingly, especially if your motives are pure.

Uranus-Pluto Contacts and Power

Uranus conjunct Pluto: You were born when Uranus and Pluto were in conjunction. This aspect occurs only rarely (about once a century) and influences an entire generation. If you were born in the 1960's, you're among a generation of women whose impact on social change can be very strong if you are united in your focus. As an individual, you relish change for its own sake, and if you are to use the power of these energies to their highest benefits, you need to develop an awareness of the impact of the changes you are about to create. You may be challenged by the task of setting new trends for the uses of technology and the power of the mind, but may also become a voice for true social conscience and join together with others to champion the value of human rights and positive social transformation. However, you must also learn to develop fulfilling outlets for your individual self-expression if you are to know the true power these energies can bring into your life.

Uranus semisextile Pluto: You were born with Uranus and Pluto in semisextile aspect, which occurs only rarely (usually about once or twice in a century), and which has a generational influence. Alongside others in society, you may have exceptional opportunities to bring new ideologies and unusual social changes into operation during your lifetime, but you may also take steps on your own to alter the status quo.

Uranus semisquare Pluto: You were born when Uranus and Pluto were in semisquare aspect, an influence that impacts a generation. You may or may not feel that as an individual you need to use this energy to break through barriers in social conscience, science, and technology, but you will likely experience radical changes that alter the quality of your life. The way you respond to changes that appear to be beyond your control will determine whether or not you feel reborn in the face of transformation.

Uranus sextile Pluto: You were born at a time when Uranus and Pluto were in sextile aspect, an influence that impacts a generation and occurs only rarely. You are one of a generation of women who can bring about positive alterations in the fabric of society by making room for changes that require the honest use of power. This aspect indicates an amazing ability to maintain your focus on the ideals that have deep meaning for you, and if you target true healing or restoration, you can see it through to its conclusion and rebirth.

Uranus square Pluto: You were born at a time when Uranus and Pluto were in square aspect, a cycle that occurs rarely and influences an entire generation. These energies in square aspect bring great turbulence and unrest, and indicate that those born under its influence face the task of dealing with unpredictable change that may not be under their control. If you are channeling this energy into your personal life, you may face power issues in their most negative and intense manifestations, but can also experience the true nature of release and rebirth of the spirit. Attempting to take control over things you cannot control can have a negative influence in your life.

Uranus trine Pluto: You were born when Uranus and Pluto were in trine aspect, a cycle that influences an entire generation and indicates a strong period of social and political change. Your efforts as an individual working in concert with others focused on the same cause or ideal can have (and has probably already had) significant influence in your sense of personal identity. You are a woman who can rebuild in the face of destruction, who sees hope and healing in the face of crisis.

Uranus quincunx Pluto: You were born when Uranus and Pluto were in trine aspect, a cycle that influences an entire generation. This influence shows a kind of breakdown in the fabric of society and signifies that you were born during a period of unrest and upheaval. The adjustments necessary for dealing with these changes require you to find and utilize the best and brightest aspects of yourself.

Uranus opposition Pluto: You were born long ago when Uranus and Pluto were in opposition to one another, an aspect that influences an entire generation and illustrates a drive by the women of your generation to challenge the status of power for its own sake.

~

Bibliography

Beattie, Melody. *Codependent No More*. San Francisco: Harper and Row, 1987.

Bolen, Jean Shinoda. *Goddesses in Everywoman*. San Francisco: Harper and Row, 1984.

Burt, Kathleen. *Archetypes of the Zodiac*. St. Paul: Llewellyn Publications, 1988.

Cohen, Alan. *The Dragon Doesn't Live Here Anymore*. South Kortright: Eden Company, 1981.

Cunningham, Donna. *Healing Pluto Problems*. York Beach: Samuel Weiser, Inc., 1986.

Dreyer, Ronnie Gale. *Venus: The Evolution of the Goddess and Her Planet*. London: The Aquarian Press, 1994.

Greene, Liz and Sasportas, Howard. *Dynamics of the Unconscious*. York Beach: Samuel Weiser, Inc., 1988.

————. *The Inner Planets*. York Beach: Samuel Weiser, Inc., 1993.

————. *The Luminaries*. York Beach: Samuel Weiser, Inc., 1992.

Haddon, Genia Pauli. *Body Metaphors*. New York: Crossroad, 1988.

Hamaker-Zondag, Karen. *Astro-Psychology*. Wellingborough: The Aquarian Press, 1980.

Hebel, Doris. *Celestial Psychology*. New York: Aurora Press, 1985.

Hickey, Isabel. *Astrology: A Cosmic Science*. Bridgeport: Altieri Press, 1974.

Leonard, Linda Schierese. *The Wounded Woman*. Boston: Shambhala, 1983.

Lunsted, Betty. *Astrological Insights into Personality*. San Diego: ACS Publishing, 1980.

Oken, Alan. *Astrology, Evolution and Revolution*. New York: Bantam, 1976.

Person, Ethel S. *Dreams of Love and Fateful Encounters*. New York: Penguin Books, 1988.

Rudhyar, Dane. *The Lunation Cycle*. Berkeley: Shambhala, 1971.

Spiller, Jan. *Astrology for the Soul*. New York: Bantam, 1997.

Star, Gloria. *Astrology for Women: Roles and Relationships*. St. Paul: Llewellyn, 1997.

Steinem, Gloria. *Revolution from Within*. Boston: Little, Brown and Company, 1992.

Stone, Merlin. *When God Was a Woman*. New York: Harvest HBJ, 1976.

Tyl, Noel. *The Horoscope as Identity*. St. Paul: Llewellyn Publications, 1974.

Wolfe, Amber. *Personal Alchemy*. St. Paul: Llewellyn Publications, 1993.

Zweig, Connie. *To Be a Woman*. Los Angeles: Jeremy Tarcher, 1990.

Index

☽ REACH FOR THE MOON

Llewellyn publishes hundreds of books on your favorite subjects! To get these exciting books, including the ones on the following pages, check your local bookstore or order them directly from Llewellyn.

ORDER BY PHONE

- Call toll-free within the U.S. and Canada, 1-800-THE MOON
- In Minnesota, call (651) 291–1970
- We accept VISA, MasterCard, and American Express

ORDER BY MAIL

- Send the full price of your order (MN residents add 7% sales tax) in U.S. funds, plus postage & handling to:

  Llewellyn Worldwide
  P.O. Box 64383, Dept. K686–6
  St. Paul, MN 55164–0383, U.S.A.

POSTAGE & HANDLING

(For the U.S., Canada, and Mexico)

- $4.00 for orders $15.00 and under
- $5.00 for orders over $15.00
- No charge for orders over $100.00

We ship UPS in the continental United States. We ship standard mail to P.O. boxes. Orders shipped to Alaska, Hawaii, The Virgin Islands, and Puerto Rico are sent first-class mail. Orders shipped to Canada and Mexico are sent surface mail.

International orders: Airmail—add freight equal to price of each book to the total price of order, plus $5.00 for each non-book item (audio tapes, etc.).

Surface mail—Add $1.00 per item.

Allow 2 weeks for delivery on all orders.
Postage and handling rates subject to change.

DISCOUNTS

We offer a 20% discount to group leaders or agents. You must order a minimum of 5 copies of the same book to get our special quantity price.

FREE CATALOG

Get a free copy of our color catalog, *New Worlds of Mind and Spirit*. Subscribe for just $10.00 in the United States and Canada ($30.00 overseas, airmail). Many bookstores carry *New Worlds*—ask for it!

Visit our web site at www.llewellyn.com for more information.

Astrology for Women
Roles & Relationships

Gloria Star, editor

Despite the far-reaching alterations women have experienced collectively, individual women are still faced with the challenge of becoming themselves. In today's world, a woman's role is not defined so much by society's expectations as by the woman herself. This book is a first look at some of the tasks each woman must embrace or overcome.

Ten female astrologers explore the many facets of the soulful process of becoming a whole person:

- Jan Spiller—The Total Woman
- Demetra George—Women's Evolving Needs: The Moon and the Blood Mysteries
- M. Kelley Hunter—The Mother-Daughter Bond
- Carol Garlick—Daughter's and Fathers: The Father's Role in the Development of the Whole Woman
- Barbara Schermer—Psyche's Task: A Path of Initiation for Women
- Gloria G. Star—Creating Healthy Relationships
- Madalyn Hillis-Dineen—On Singleness: Choosing to Be Me
- Ronnie Gale Dreyer—The Impact of Self-Esteem
- Kim Rogers-Gallagher—Who Should I Be When I Grow Up?
- Roxana Muise—The Sacred Sisterhood

1–56718–860–5, 5³⁄₁₆ x 8, 416 pp., charts, softcover

$9.95

To order, call 1–800–THE–MOON
Prices subject to change without notice

THE LLEWELLYN ANNUALS

Llewellyn's **MOON SIGN BOOK** and Gardening Almanac: Approximately 450 pages of valuable information on gardening, fishing, weather, stock market forecasts, personal horoscopes, good planting dates, and general instructions for finding the best date to do just about anything! Articles by prominent forecasters and writers in the fields of gardening, astrology, economics and cycles. This special almanac, different from any other, has been published annually since 1906. It's fun, informative and has been a great help to millions in their daily planning. 5¼ x 8 format. State year **$6.95**

Llewellyn's **SUN SIGN BOOK:** Horoscopes for Everyone!: Your personal horoscope for the entire year! All 12 signs are included in one handy book. Also included are forecasts, special feature articles, and an action guide for each sign. Monthly horoscopes are written by Gloria Star, author of *Astrology for Women*, and *Astrology: Woman to Woman*, for your personal sun sign and there are articles on a variety of subjects written by well-known astrologers from around the country. Much more than just a horoscope guide! Entertaining and fun the year around. 5¼ x 8 format. State year **$6.95**

DAILY PLANETARY GUIDE: Llewellyn's Astrology Datebook: Includes all of the major daily aspects plus their exact times in Eastern and Pacific time zones, lunar phases, signs and voids plus their times, planetary motion, a monthly ephemeris, sunrise and sunset tables, special articles on the planets, signs, aspects, planetary hours, rulerships, and much more. Large 5¼ x 8 format for more writing space, spiral bound to lie flat, address and phone listings, time-zone conversion chart and blank horoscope chart. State year **$9.95**

Llewellyn's Astrological Pocket Planner: Daily Ephemeris & Aspectarian: Designed to slide easily into a purse or briefcase, this planner is jam-packed with those dates and planetary information astrologers need when forecasting future events. Comes with a regular calendar section, a smaller section for projecting dates into the year ahead, a 3-year ephemeris, a listing of planetary aspects, a planetary associations chart, a time-zone chart and retrograde table. 4¼ x 6 format. State year **$7.95**

Llewellyn's **ASTROLOGICAL CALENDAR** with horoscopes for everyone: Large wall calendar of 48 pages is our top seller. Beautiful full-color paintings. Includes special feature articles by famous astrologers, and complete introductory information on astrology. It also contains a lunar gardening guide, celestial phenomena, a blank horoscope chart, and monthly date pages which include aspects, Moon phases, signs and voids, planetary motion, an ephemeris, personal forecasts, lucky dates, planting and fishing dates, and more. 10 x 13 size. Set in Eastern time, with conversion table for other time zones worldwide. State year **$12.95**